DISEASES OF GREENHOUSE PLANTS

DISEASES OF GREENHOUSE PLANTS

J T FLETCHER

Regional Plant Pathologist
Agricultural Development and Advisory Service
Wye, Kent

LONGMAN London and New York

Longman Group Limited
Longman House, Burnt Mill, Harlow
Essex CM20 2JE, England
Associated companies throughout the world

*Published in the United States of America
by Longman Inc., New York*

© Longman Group Limited 1984

First published 1984

British Library Cataloguing in Publication Data
Fletcher, J. T.
    Diseases of greenhouse plants.
    1. Greenhouse gardening   2. Plants – Diseases
    I. Title
    635'.049   SB415

    ISBN 0-582-44263-X

Library of Congress Cataloging in Publication Data
Fletcher, J. T., 1933–
    Diseases of greenhouse plants.

    Includes bibliographies and index.
    1. Greenhouse plants – Diseases and pests.
2. Greenhouse management. I. Title.
SB608.G82F56 1984   635'.0444   83-18703
ISBN 0-582-44263-X

Printed in Singapore by
Kyodo Shing Loong Printing Industries Pte Ltd

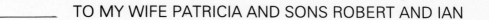 TO MY WIFE PATRICIA AND SONS ROBERT AND IAN

CONTENTS

PREFACE

There has not been a book entirely devoted to the diseases which affect greenhouse grown plants since 1923 when W. F. Bewley's *Diseases of Glasshouse Crops* was published. Since then many new discoveries have been made. Almost all our knowledge of virus diseases has been gained and there have been many advances in the studies of other diseases. In addition, systems of crop culture have also changed considerably.

Traditionally, crops were grown in glasshouses, but within the past fifteen years polythene and other sheet plastics have become extensively used. Now, with heat conservation in mind, consideration is being given to rigid plastics, often double layered to minimise heat loss. Because of the widespread use of plastic, it is no longer appropriate to talk about glasshouse crops and for this reason greenhouse has been chosen in this book to refer to both glass and plastic covered structures. In addition, mushrooms are included in the book, partly because the mushroom crop was often grown in glasshouses as a catch crop and many mushroom farms have evolved this way, and also because many of the factors which govern disease control apply equally well to mushrooms and greenhouse crops.

Disease control in the greenhouse and mushroom house is vital to successful crop production. Because of the enclosed environment, conditions favourable for disease development are sometimes maintained for considerable periods leading to epidemic disease development. Growers often complain of the 'overnight' appearance of disease development. Disease leads to crop loss either by reduced total yield or by poor quality of the product.

The first step in successful disease control is the recognition of disease. When identified at a very early stage in its development the chances of successful disease control are greatly increased. Too often diseases reach epidemic levels before action is taken and then it is often too late. It is essential to look critically and often in order to spot the very first symptoms of disease. Once recognised it is important to identify the cause so that the most appropriate control measures can be applied.

The aim of this book is to help with the identification of diseases and their control. With this in mind, the emphasis is placed on the kinds of symptoms and where these occur on the plant. Much information on the cause of the disease can be gained from the symptoms and their distribution. In order that the reader may understand the events which precede symptom production, some basic information is given on the causes of disease, the development of epidemics, sources of pathogens and their mechanisms of spread. Individual diseases are described in detail under the heading of the crop. A very brief description of the culture of each crop is included to outline the 'normal' procedure for the production of a healthy crop including the crop duration, the temperature used, carbon dioxide enrichment of the atmosphere and any other relevant features of environmental control. When investigating a disease outbreak it is often helpful to know how the affected crop has been produced and how growing conditions have deviated from the accepted standards.

At the beginning of most of the crop chapters, all the diseases are listed and grouped according to the part of the plant they affect. Some diseases affect several parts of the plant, i.e. leaves, stems and flowers, and these are repeated under each plant part. These lists are included to help with the identification of the disease on the basis of the location of the symptoms. For instance, if the symptoms are seen on the stem of a particular plant the list of stem diseases can be consulted and the reader can then study the symptom descriptions for the individual diseases to find which agrees most closely with those observed.

In addition to the symptoms some details of the behaviour of the pathogen and conditions which favour epidemics are included as well as an account of the current control measures. Fungicide recommendations are continually changing and new materials and methods of application are added to the list. It is always advisable to consult the manufacturer's literature when using a fungicide to ensure it is used precisely as recommended. Where there is no information available, as is often the case, particularly for pot plants, it is wise to try the fungicide on a few plants first before spraying the whole batch. Fungicides without label recommendations must never be used on edible crops.

Much of the information in this book has been gathered during the 25 years of my association with the glasshouse and mushroom industries. I have learned much from growers, advisers and research workers and, in particular, I would like to thank the growers and advisers I worked with in the Lea Valley, Yorkshire, Lancashire, Northumberland, Cumbria, Kent and Sussex.

In the preparation of this manuscript I have been greatly encouraged and helped by Dr Colin H. Dickinson of the University of Newcastle, and to him I express my warmest thanks. I also wish to express my most sincere thanks to Patricia Manchee who not only typed my script but also helped to correct errors.

Many of the photographs in the book have been kindly provided for my use and I thank the following for their help: Mr P. T. Atkey, Professor G. L. Barron, Dr J. P. Blakeman, Mr John Bloom, Mr G. Culpan, Miss Marion Ebben, Mr P. J. Fiske, Dr M. J. Griffin, Mr C. E. Hart, Mr R. A. Lelliott, Professor B. H. MacNeill, Dr P. G. Markham, Dr M. W. Miller, Miss K. Plaskitt, Dr A. Presly, Mrs E. M. Renshaw, Mr D. G. Soper, Dr Pauline M. Smith, Dr A. M. Skidmore, Mr N. K. Sylvester, Dr J. A. Tomlinson and Dr W. C. Wong.

This book has been written independently of the Ministry of Agriculture, Fisheries and Food, and the views expressed here do not necessarily reflect those of the Ministry or of the Agricultural, Development and Advisory Service.

Finally I wish to pay a special tribute to the late Mr Harold R. Jones who was for many years senior biology teacher at Lydney Grammar School. His encouragement, skill and enthusiasm enabled me and many of his former pupils to continue to enjoy the subject he so ably taught.

INTRODUCTION

The production of crops in a glasshouse, a polythene tunnel or a mushroom house involves intensive systems of cropping in which it is often difficult to apply many of the aspects of good husbandry used in the field. Mono-cropping is common practice and, at best, a few crops are rotated but generally at such frequent intervals that the rest period for the soil is of little benefit. Rotation of the soil is almost impossible, the only exception being the use of mobile greenhouses or the very expensive process of changing the soil, which is only possible on a small scale. Such systems of intensive cropping inevitably lead to the build-up of pathogens, particularly in the soil, and it is these that are responsible for some of the most important diseases of protected crops. Growers have overcome the problems of soil-borne pathogens by the use of soil treatments. Soil sterilisation by heat or chemicals must be repeated at regular intervals in order that healthy crops are continuously produced. Soil treatment is expensive, particularly if heat is used, and chemical sterilants have biological limitations in that they create problems with chemical residues which may delay crop planting or result in unacceptably high residue levels in the produce. For these reasons, growers of some crops have turned to soil-less systems of crop culture such as the use of peat in polythene bags, the use of a circulated nutrient solution (NFT), or the use of a synthetic medium such as rock wool. In addition, plant breeders have made a valuable contribution to the control of soil-borne pathogens, particularly of the tomato crop, and it is now possible to obtain tomato cultivars resistant to a number of diseases.

The greenhouse offers the grower a unique opportunity to control the aerial environment. The advent of computer control adds further to the degree of control which can be achieved. With modern equipment, it is possible for the grower to control the temperature, humidity and carbon dioxide concentration of the atmosphere, as well as the quantity of water and nutrients applied to the plants. With supplementary lighting the grower can also control the day length, as well as increase the light intensity. This degree of environmental control could enable air-borne pathogens to be totally suppressed without the use of fungicides, providing enough were known about the basic biology for the correct adjustments of the environment to be made. Such disease control can be achieved with a number of pathogens, particularly those that depend upon a high relative humidity for epidemic development. However, environmental control is expensive because it requires expensive fuel and equipment, and it is often more economic to combine some adjustment of the environment with fungicidal control.

Looking to the future, there is much that can be done to reduce the cost of disease control of protected crops. So far, biological control has not been exploited to any extent, and the protected environment is perhaps the one in which such methods could be most successfully used both for the control of soil-borne and air-borne pathogens. There are already highly successful systems of biological control to suppress pests such as red spider mites, whiteflies and aphids. In addition, there is scope for the further development of resistant cultivars of all the major crops, and even the methodical testing of existing cultivars would provide valuable and much needed information on their susceptibilities to common diseases.

New systems of crop culture have introduced a new dimension into the field of fungicide usage, and there are still very few fungicides that are available for growers to use in a nutrient solution. Advances are being made in the more traditional methods of fungicide application and the ingenuity of growers is constantly apparent. Low or very low volume systems, fogs and dusts are all less costly to apply, because of the lower labour content. Research is needed to ensure that such systems are biologically as effective as the traditional high volume methods.

The protected cropping industry is in a very critical period of its history, but the continuous innovation of growers, which has seen the industry through difficult times in the past, will undoubtedly play a large part in ensuring its success in the future.

CHAPTER 1

PLANT DISEASE

Most plants are diseased if we accept a strict definition which includes any significant harmful deviation from the normal physiological processes of the plant. Abnormalities at the cellular level are not always readily recognisable but, when the physiological disturbance is large the affected plant shows characteristic signs or symptoms, it is said to be diseased. The scope of this text is to cover diseases which result in symptoms production. Some of these are less obvious than others, as for example when disease is recognised by its effect on quantitative or qualitative aspects of crop yield. It is important to realise that different causes of disease may result in similar symptoms, hence symptoms alone may not always allow the cause of the disease to be positively identified. Also, plants may be affected by more than one disease at the same time and this will further confuse the symptom picture. There are exceptional diseases (for instance, mixed virus streak in tomatoes) where characteristic symptoms result from the combined effects of two separate agents, in this case two viruses, and the resultant symptoms are more severe than those induced by each separately. Such an interaction is known as synergism. Symptoms are the expression of disease and they are often modified by the environment, the nutrition or the developmental stage of the plant.

CAUSES OF DISEASE

Diseases are caused by agents acting singly or in combination. The study of the cause of disease is termed aetiology, and that of the factors affecting outbreaks and the spread of disease within the crop as epidemiology. Rapid spread of disease results in an epidemic. Organisms which cause disease are parasites and are known as pathogens. Those pathogens totally dependent on the plant they parasitise (host) as a food source are known as obligate parasites whilst others are able to survive equally well on dead, organic material, as saprophytes, and these are known as facultative parasites. The rusts and powdery mildews are obligate parasites whereas grey mould (*Botrytis cinerea*) and most other fungal pathogens are facultative parasites. Forms of some pathogens may be more aggressive (*virulent*; opposite *avirulent*) than others. A specialised form of a pathogen may be referred to as a strain, race or *forma speciales*.

Diseases may be caused by pathogens or by non-pathogenic agents. Fungi are the commonest pathogens and account for a large proportion of the diseases of greenhouse crops. Other important agents are viruses, viroids, mycoplasmas and bacteria. There are also disorders caused by pests such as insects, mites and nematodes and some larger animals such as slugs, snails, wireworms, moles and mice. Non-pathogenic agents include a number of physical and chemical factors, such as mineral deficiencies and toxicities, chemical pollutants, pesticides administered accidentally, and various environmental factors such as temperature extremes or problems arising from too much or too little water. Diseases which result from non-pathogenic causes are often termed 'physiological disorders'.

Microbial plant pathogens

Fungi

The vegetative form of most fungi is a thread-like hypha and collectively, these hyphae form the mycelium. Hyphae may or may not be divided internally by cell walls into cells and are said to be respectively septate or non-septate. Fungal mycelium may vary in texture, being fluffy or adpressed, and hyphae may sometimes be aggregated into mycelial strands or rhizomorphs. The diameter of the hypha and its growth rate varies with the species of fungus and the environment. Many greenhouse plant pathogens have an optimum temperature for growth between 15–25 °C. The colour of a fungus colony, whether it is growing parasitically or saprophytically, often reflects the colour of the spores it produces. Spores are a means of reproduction and dissemination of the fungus and may result from an asexual or a sexual process. Spores produced from the vegetative mycelium as a result of simple cell division will be identical genetically to the parent but, because they are often produced in very large numbers, there may be a very small proportion that are mutants, i.e. genetically different from the parent hyphae. Such mutants may be important in adapting the pathogen to a new environment, e.g. the presence of a fungicide or disease-resistant host. New characters may also be expressed as a result of sexual recombination of the genetic material from two parents.

The structures which produce asexual and sexual spores as well as the spores themselves often characteristic of the species and, together with the vegetative characteristics of the mycelium, are the main basis of fungal classification. Generally, asexual spores are the most important causes of plant disease epidemics although sexual spores are often concerned in the long-term survival of many pathogens. The fungi are divided into four major groups, and although it would be inappropriate to give a detailed account of fungal classification here it is relevant to know some of the main characteristics of these groups (Table 1.1).

In addition to the sexual and asexual spores, some fungi produce other structures which aid in their dispersal or their ability to withstand adverse conditions. Individual hyphal cells may take on this function by developing a thickened wall to become spore-like. Such cells are known as chlamydospores except when they are formed terminally when they are called aleuriospores (Fig. 1.1). Mycelial structures may also become very resistant to adverse environmental conditions by developing a tightly packed aggregate bounded by a dark coloured rind. These are known as sclerotia (Fig. 1.1b) and after a long period of dormancy may 'germinate' to produce hyphae or

TABLE 1.1 Classes of fungi with genera associated with greenhouse plants

Division and Sub-division	Class	Genera
Myxomycota	Ascrasiomycetes	
	Hydromyxomycetes	
	Myxomycetes (slime moulds)	Fuligo
	Plasmodiophoromycetes	Plasmodiophora
		Spongospora
Eumycota		
Mastigomycotina	Chytridiomycetes	Olpidium
	Hyphochytridiomycetes	
	Oomycetes (downy mildews and some damping-off fungi)	Bremia
		Peronospora
		Phytophthora
(Phycomycetes)		Plasmopara
		Pythium
Zygomycotina	Zygomycetes (bread moulds)	
	Trichomycetes	
Ascomycotina (Ascomycetes)	Hemiascomycetes	Erysiphe
	Plectomycetes (powdery mildews and false truffle)	Leveillula
		Microsphaera
		Sphaerotheca
		Diehliomyces
	Pyrenomycetes	Chaetomium
		Giberella
		Nectria
		Penicillium
	Discomycetes	Peziza
		Sclerotinia
		Diplocarpon
	Laboulbeniomycetes	Didymella
	Loculoascomycetes	Mycosphaerella
		Pleospora
Basidiomycotina (Basidiomycetes)	Hemibasidiomycetes (rusts, smuts)	Puccinia
		Uromyces
		Ustilago
	Hymenomycetes	Agaricus
		Armillaria
		Coprinus
		Corticium (Rhizoctonia)
		Exobasidium
	Gasteromycetes	
Deuteromycotina (Fungi Imperfecti)	Blastomycetes	Itersonilia
	Coleomycetes (leaf spots, stem and root rots)	Ascochyta
		Colletotrichum
		Gloeosporium
		Heteropatella
		Macrophoma
		Marssonina
		Pestalotiopsis
		Phoma
		Phomopsis
		Phyllosticta
		Septoria

Division and Sub-division	Class	Genera
	Hyphomycetes (leaf spots, vascular wilts, mushroom pathogens and weed moulds)	*Alternaria* *Botrytis* *Cephalosporium* *Cercospora* *Cladosporium* *Chrysosporium* *Corynespora* *Cylindrocarpon* *Cylindrocladium* *Dactylium* *Doratomyces* *Fulvia* *Fusarium* *Heterosporium* *Mycogone* *Myceliophora* *Myrothecium* *Papulospora* *Phialophora* *Ramularia* *Scopulariopsis* *Sepedonium* *Stemphylium* *Thielaviopsis* *Trichoderma* *Ulocladium* *Verticillium* *Zygophiala*
	Agonomycetes (Mycelia Sterilia)	*Sclerotium*

sometimes the sexual spores as in *Sclerotinia sclerotiorum* or asexual spores as in *Botrytis cinerea*.

Mastigomycotina. These are fungi with non-septate mycelium which branches at acute angles. Both asexual and sexual spores are produced and many have a motile spore form. Examples of pathogens in this group are the downy mildews (*Bremia lactucae*, *Peronospora parasitica*), the damping-off fungi (*Pythium* and *Phytophthora*), potato blight (*Phytophthora infestans*) and *Olpidium brassicae*. The asexual spores are called sporangiospores and are borne in sporangia (Fig. 1.2). Sporangia germinate in water, where they produce zoospores which swim and infect a suitable host plant. In the absence of free water but at high relative humidities, sporangia germinate by producing a germ-tube; direct germination of this type is almost equally effective in plant infection. The sexual spores of the Mastigomycotina are usually thick-walled, able to withstand adverse environmental conditions and remain viable in plant debris or in the soil for long periods (Fig. 1.3). They eventually germinate when environmental conditions are suitable. Germination is triggered by the presence of exudates from a susceptible host.

Sometimes included in this group, but now more frequently separated into a further group (the Plasmodiophorales of the Myxomycota), are some fungi which do not produce mycelium but exist as simple, single-celled organisms

FIG. 1.1 (a) Aleuriospores of *Mycogone perniciosa*, the terminal cell is thick walled and remains viable for long periods.
(b) Sclerotia of *Botrytis cinerea* are also able to withstand adverse environmental conditions.

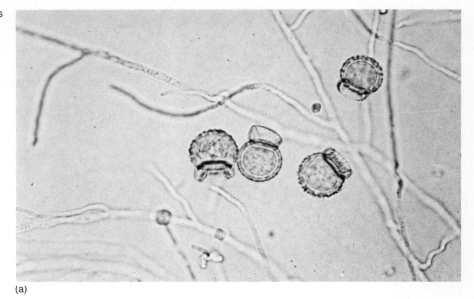

(a)

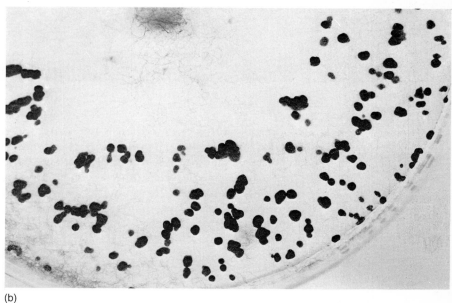

(b)

totally dependent upon a motile zoospore stage for both asexual and sexual reproduction. Important pathogens of this type are *Spongospora* spp. and *Plasmodiophora* spp.

Ascomycotina. This large group of fungi includes the yeasts which, unlike other members of the group, do not produce mycelium. The majority produce septate mycelium which often branches at a wide angle, sometimes at right angles. There are many important pathogens, such as the powdery mildew fungi. e.g. *Sphaerotheca fuliginea*, also *Sclerotinia sclerotiorum* and *Didymella* spp., which cause stem rots of various plants. The most charac-

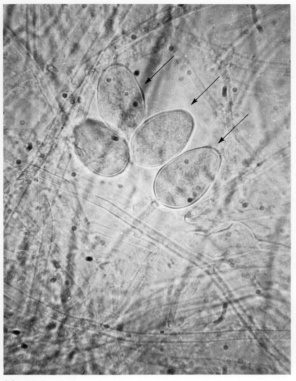

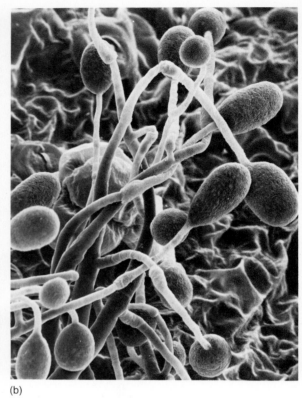

(a)   (b)

FIG. 1.2 Sporangia of
(a) *Phytophthora
erythroseptica*.
(b) *Phytophthora
infestans*. Copyright (b)
ICI Plant Protection
Division.

teristic spore form of the group is the sexual spore which is produced in a
sack-like structure known as an ascus. There are generally eight ascospores
in each ascus, and the asci are formed within structures known as ascocarps.
These may be spherical cleistothecia with no obvious exit pore (*Pleospora* spp.
and powdery mildews), chianti bottle-shaped perithecia (*Mycosphaerella* spp.)
and disc-shaped flat, open apothecia (*Sclerotinia* spp.) (Fig. 1.4). Ascospores
are often propelled from the ascus and this can be an important factor in the

FIG. 1.3 Resting spores
of
(a) *Olpidium brassicae*
and
(b) *Bremia lactucae*.
Photograph
(b) reproduced by kind
permission of Professor
G. L. Barron.

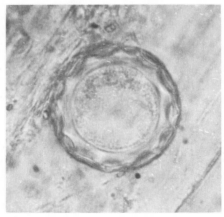

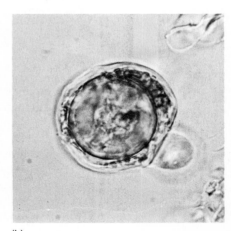

(a)   (b)

FIG. 1.4 (a) Perithecium of *Didymella bryoniae*. (b) Two apothecia from a germinating sclerotium of *Sclerotinia sclerotiorum*. (c) Apothecia of a species of *Peziza*.

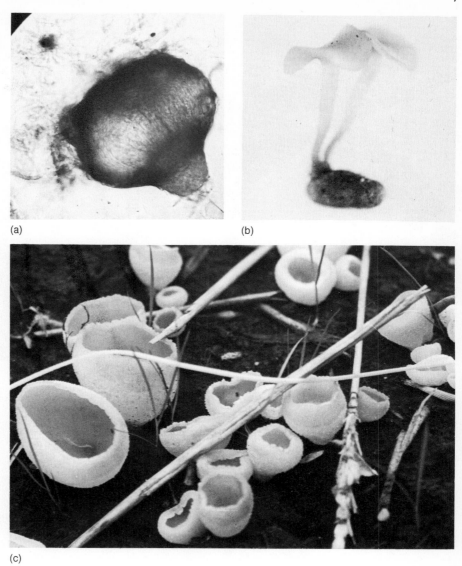

(a)

(b)

(c)

development of an epidemic. The sexual and asexual spores germinate without a motile stage and produce germ-tubes which, in suitable circumstances, infect the host plant. The asexual spores, which are a variety of shapes and sizes, are known as conidia, and the stalks they are produced on – conidiophores (Fig. 1.5). They may also be formed in characteristic structures which are similar to those of the Deuteromycotina.

Basidiomycotina.   It is usually considered that this group contains the most evolutionarily advanced fungi although it is a very diverse collection of genera. The mycelium is septate, often with right-angled branches. The mycelium may be aggregated in some members of the group to form strands or rhizomorphs. Sexual reproduction is similar in all members of the group and involves the formation of a basidium. This is a fertile cell which produces

(a)

(b)

FIG. 1.5   Conidiophore (i)
with conidia (ii) of:
(a) *Botrytis cinerea*
(b) *Verticillium albo-atrum.*
(c) *Sphaerotheca
fuliginea* Photograph (a)
reproduced by kind
permission of A. H.
Presly. Photograph (c)
Copyright ICI Plant
Protection Division.

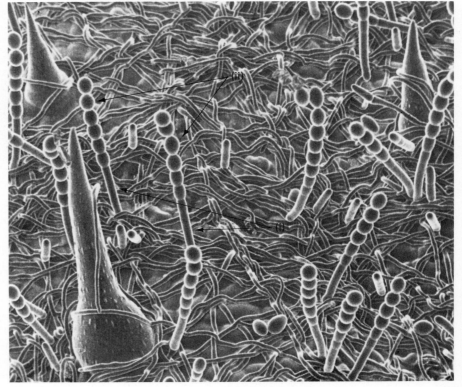

(c)

two or four spores (basidiospores) each borne on a short stalk (sterigmata), and when ripe they are often propelled from these. Pathogens in this group include the honey fungus, *Armillaria mellea* and *Rhizoctonia (Corticium) solani*, and the rust and the smut fungi. Asexual spores are not commonly produced.

Deuteromycotina. This is a large and variable group with many plant pathogens, generally without a regularly produced sexual spore stage. It is likely that most are Ascomycotina. The mycelium is generally septate, often branching at a wide angle. Asexual conidia are produced in a variety of structures. One of the most commonly formed by pathogenic members of the group is the pycnidium which is usually brown or black and flask-shaped. Large numbers of conidiospores or pycniospores ooze from the pycnidia when water is present (Fig. 1.6). Two of the main classes of this group, the Coleomycetes and Hyphomycetes contain many genera of fungi which are pathogens of greenhouse plants.

Other structures producing conidia are acervuli, which are cushion-like masses of hyphae producing large numbers of conidia; sporodochia, and synnema which are masses of conidiophores tightly packed together (Fig. 1.7). Important pathogens in this group belong to the genera, *Phoma*, *Phomopsis*, *Ascochyta*, *Septoria*, *Gloeosporium*, *Mycogone*, *Verticillium*, *Fusarium*, *Cladosporium* and *Alternaria*. Some of the sporing structures described occur commonly in the Ascomycotina.

FIG. 1.6 A pycnidium (a) of *Didymella chrysanthemi* with a chain of pycniospores (b) oozing from it. Photographs reproduced by kind permission of Dr J. P. Blakeman.

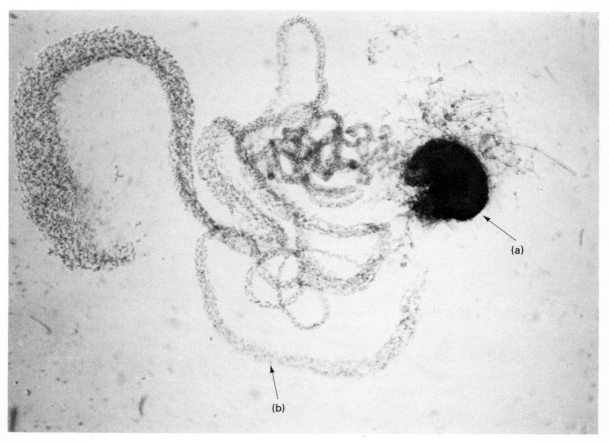

FIG. 1.7 Sporodochium of *Diplocarpon rosae* (a) and in close-up (b). Copyright ICI Plant Protection Division.

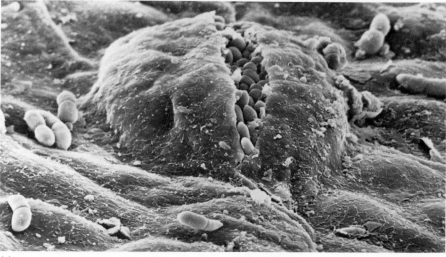

(a)

Bacteria

Most plant pathogenic bacteria are small (1–4 μm long), single-celled, generally rod-shaped organisms. Bacterial cells are bounded by a wall but they lack an organised nucleus, although they contain both deoxyribonucleic acid (DNA) and ribonucleic acid (RNA). Their growth rates can be very rapid and they multiply by simple division of the cell into two daughter cells (binary fission) (Fig. 1.8). Many bacterial species move in liquid media by means of flagella, which may be at one end of the cell (polar) or distributed all around each cell (peritrichous) (Fig. 1.9). One group of plant pathogenic bacteria, the Streptomycetes, produce a mycelium and spore chains and resemble fungi. Another group resemble the rickettsias which are obligate parasites. Although some bacteria produce spores most plant pathogenic species do not, and for this reason are unlikely to survive in adverse conditions for very long periods although some can survive for more than a year in dried plant tissue and exudate. Bacteria are classified according to their shape, their staining reaction in Gram's staining procedure (Gram positive or Gram negative), and by a series of biochemical tests designed to elicit their ability to utilise such substrates as sugars (by fermentation, oxidation or hydrolysis), complex carbohydrates (pectins, cellulose) and proteins. Most plant pathogenic bacteria are Gram negative, require oxygen (aerobic) or are capable of growth in low levels of oxygen (facultatively anaerobic). Gram negative pathogenic genera include *Agrobacterium*, *Erwinia*, *Pseudomonas* and *Xanthomonas*. Gram positive pathogenic bacteria are in the genus *Corynebacterium*.

Bacteria are readily disseminated in irrigation, soil or drainage water, by raindrops or irrigation splash and even in an aerosol of water created by vigorous watering or spraying of crops. Other means of transmission are by seed infection, vegetative propagation of infected plants and soil debris. Bacteria may also be carried from crop to crop by vectors including insects (particularly flies), man (on clothes and tools) and on the surface of air-borne fungal spores.

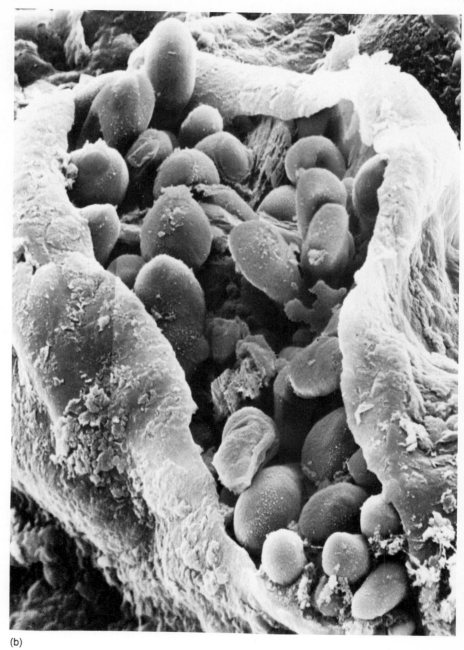

(b)

Bacteria often require higher temperatures than fungi for optimum growth and it may be for this reason that bacterial diseases of plants are most serious in the warm temperate, subtropical and tropical regions. There are some notable exceptions to this generalisation and such diseases as Bacterial Canker of tomatoes (*Corynebacterium michiganense*), Wilt of carnations (*Pseudomonas caryophyllii*) and the Leafy Gall and Crown Gall diseases (*Corynebacterium fascians* and *Agrobacterium tumefaciens*) can result in considerable losses in

FIG. 1.8 Bacterial cells of *Corynebacterium michiganense* dividing into two by the formation of a dividing cell wall. This form of reproduction is known as binary fission. Copyright ICI Plant Protection Division.

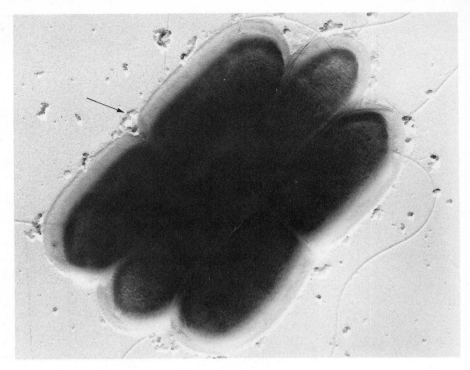

temperate climates. Despite the high temperatures which characterise the greenhouse environment, there are relatively few bacterial pathogens of greenhouse crops.

Viruses

In comparison with fungi and bacteria, viruses have extremely small particles which can only be seen with an electron microscope. They do not have a cellular structure but consist of a protein coat which surrounds a core of nucleic acid. The nucleic acid governs the behaviour of the virus and determines its host range, its virulence as a pathogen and the symptoms it induces. Viruses reproduce within the plant cell and are capable of utilising the plant's metabolites to produce more virus particles instead of plant nucleoprotein. The question of whether viruses are living organisms has long been debated. They are certainly well adapted to the environment in which they reproduce, but most of them are unable to remain viable for very long once they are removed from living plant cells.

Virus particles vary in shape and size; some are rigid rods, e.g. Tomato Mosaic Virus particles are approximately 300 nm (1 nanometre = 1 millionth of a millimetre) by 18 nm wide; some are flexuous rods, e.g. Lettuce Mosaic Virus, which is approximately 750 nm × 13 nm, some are spherical or isometric in shape (actually 20-sided icosahedrons), e.g. Arabis Mosaic Virus, which is 30 nm in diameter; and recently some viruses have been described that are bullet-shaped, e.g. Lettuce Necrotic Yellows Virus with particles 227 × 66 nm (Fig. 1.10). Naked nucleic acids known as viroids are known to induce some diseases, e.g. Chrysanthemum Stunt.

FIG. 1.9 Arrangement of
flagella on bacterial cells.
(a) Polar.
(b) Peritrichous. Copyright
ICI Plant Protection
Division.

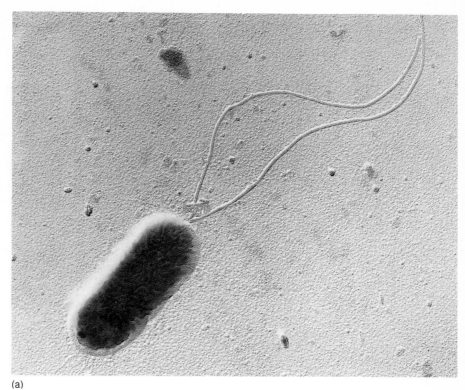

(a)

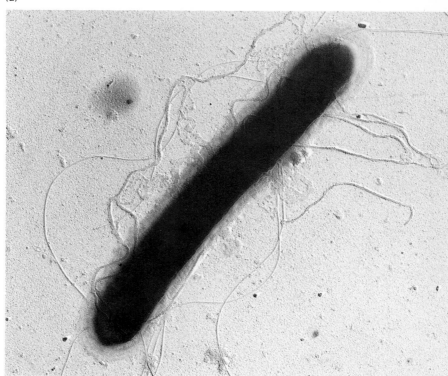

(b)

FIG. 1.10 Shapes of virus particles:
(a) straight rods of Tomato Mosaic Virus (TMV).
(b) Flexuous filaments of Carnation Vein Mottle Virus.
(c) Spherical or polyhedral particles of Arabis Mosaic Virus.
(d) Bullet-shaped particles of Lettuce Necrotic Yellows Virus (LNYV) and a single straight rod particle of TMV. Copyright for photographs (a), (b), (c), Glasshouse Crops Research Institute, and (d) National Vegetable Research Station and reproduced by kind permission of P. J. Atkey and Dr J. A. Tomlinson respectively.

(a)

(b)

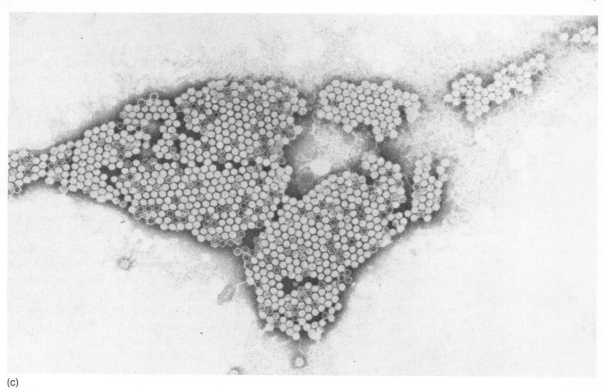

(c)

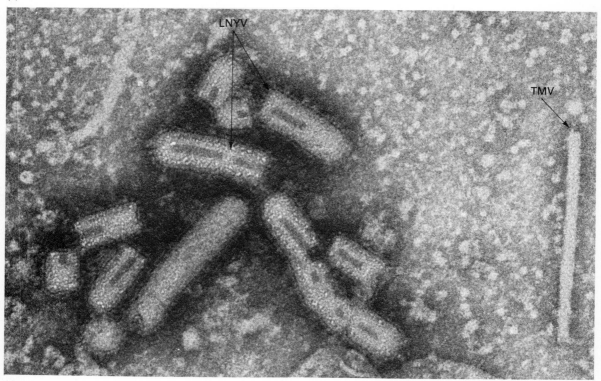

(d)

Viruses may be transmitted from plant to plant in many different ways although the mechanism is generally specific for each virus. Thus, Tomato Mosaic Virus is mechanically transmitted and, merely by touching or brushing an affected plant, sufficient particles of the virus are picked up from broken leaf hairs to transmit the virus to the next plant that is touched. Tomato Mosaic Virus, although the most infectious of plant viruses, is not naturally transmitted in any other way, not even by sucking insects, in spite of their intimate contact with the infected plant cell. Cucumber Mosaic Virus is transmitted by various aphids. Virus particles are picked up on the mouth parts of the aphid, the stylets, and carried to the next plant to be inserted into the cell by the stylets. In this relationship, the virus is acquired by the aphid after a short feeding period and transmitted almost immediately without any interval being necessary between acquisition and transmission. The ability to transmit is equally rapidly lost. Such viruses are said to be stylet-borne or non-persistent. Another kind of relationship also exists and is typified by Beet Western Yellows Virus which affects lettuce. Here the virus is only acquired after a prolonged period of feeding and is not transmitted immediately but after a so-called latent period which may be up to 24 hours. These are known as persistent viruses and they can usually be found within the aphids and are not confined to its mouth parts. Persistent viruses are sometimes referred to as circulative viruses or propagative viruses where, in this latter case, the virus concentration actually increases within the aphid vector. There is no evidence that propagative viruses cause diseases of aphids. In all cases, persistent viruses, once acquired, are transmitted for the rest of the life of the aphid. Aphids are by far the most common vectors of viruses and some species, for instance *Myzus persicae*, the peach potato aphid, transmits many different viruses. Some aphids transmit only one virus and conversely some viruses are transmitted by many different species of aphid. Only a few viruses have specific aphid vectors. Cucumber Mosaic Virus has more hosts and more aphid vectors than any other virus. Other insects, such as leaf hoppers, thrips and some beetles, can transmit some viruses and mites are also virus vectors.

Viruses may also be transmitted by other organisms. Arabis Mosaic Virus and Strawberry Latent Ring Spot Virus, both of which affect roses, are transmitted by dagger nematodes. Fungi such as *Olpidium brassicae* can transmit Lettuce Big Vein, which is thought to be a virus disease, and Cucumber Necrosis Virus is transmitted by a related species, *O. cucumerinum*. The potato and tomato powdery scab fungus, *Spongospora subterranea*, can transmit Potato Mop Top Virus.

One simple way of transmitting viruses from one crop to another is by vegetative propagation. Until recently many of the vegetatively propagated greenhouse crops were infected by virus diseases, some of them with complexes of many viruses. The technique of heat treatment and culturing excised meristematic stem apices has enabled clones of chrysanthemums and carnations to be freed of many viruses, and stocks now exist that are free from all known virus diseases of these crops. Fortunately, viruses do not often colonise the meristematic tissue of plants and for this reason the apical meristem in chrysanthemums and carnations is often virus-free when the rest of the plant is not. The frequency of such virus-free meristems is greatly increased by growing plants for 3 weeks at 37 °C before removing the meristem. A combination of heat treatment and meristem culture enables a high proportion of virus-free meristems to be obtained and by careful culture, stock plants for propagation can be grown from these. It is essential to check cuttings produced in this way in order to eliminate any that are still infected, particularly to ensure that heat-tolerant strains of viruses do not become widespread. Similarly, seeds are often virus-free when the rest of the plant is diseased so in some crops healthy seeds can be obtained from otherwise virus-diseased plants. This is so with Cucumber Mosaic Virus but not with Lettuce Mosaic Virus, where a small proportion of the seeds from affected plants are infected internally.

There is still much to be learned about virus diseases. Recently it has been shown that some virus disease symptoms are only fully expressed by a combination of particles of the same virus which are usually similar, but not always, in particle morphology but which contain different kinds of RNA. Some aphid-transmitted viruses are only capable of transmission in the presence of particles of another virus known as the helper virus. The exact mechanism of the assistance given by the helper virus is not fully understood.

Mycoplasmas

It is only comparatively recently that mycoplasmas have been recognised as causes of plant diseases, although they have long been known to cause diseases of animals. In many ways they resemble bacteria in that they lack a nucleus. They have a triple layered non-rigid outer membrane but they have no cell wall and are therefore highly pleomorphic, varying from short rods to filaments (Fig. 1.11). Some have been cultured on artificial media. They are larger than virus particles, being similar in size and, to some extent, in structure to some bacteria. Mycoplasmas may be mechanically transmitted but are more often transmitted by leaf hoppers. Their relationship with the leaf hopper vector is of the persistent type. Many diseases produced by mycoplasmas were formerly thought to have been caused by viruses and are characterised by such symptoms as yellowing of the foliage (yellows), production of many small shoots (witches brooms) and the production of leaf-like structures in place of the flower parts (phyllody or green petal).

Pests

Insects, mites, nematodes, woodlice and mammals which feed on plants are usually referred to as pests. It is not intended to cover pests in this text, but it must be recognised that they are an important cause of loss in greenhouse crops, sometimes producing symptoms similar to those of pathogens. Aphids, whiteflies and mites are probably the most important pests damaging a wide variety of crops. In addition, they can also act as vectors for some viruses. Beetles and caterpillars damage plants by feeding, or mining, on leaves, stem, roots and sometimes flowers. Some soil-borne insect larvae, such as the cutworms and wireworms, and adult springtails and symphilids, may be a problem, particularly on a new site or where soil treatment is not regularly practised.

Damage resulting from pests can often be recognised because of the obvious biting, chewing, mining or rasping by the pest involved. Generally,

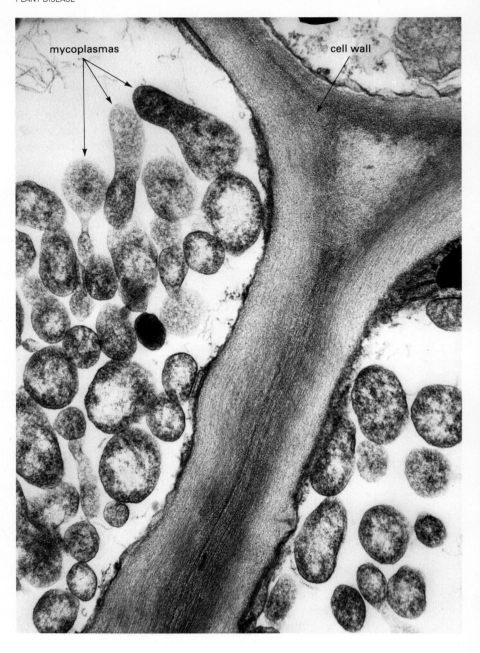

those insects which feed by sucking, e.g. aphids, mites and bugs, or by rasping, e.g. thrips, produce physical damage which shows as yellowing or silvering of the foliage, often with growth distortion, and others damage the foliage by mining (Fig. 1.12). When symptoms are severe these insects are often present in such large numbers that it is not difficult to identify them as the cause of the symptom.

Nematodes have long been a problem in greenhouse crops, particularly the potato cyst nematode which affects tomatoes and the root knot nematode

FIG. 1.12 (a) Red spider mite damage on a cucumber leaf; (b) aphid damage on tomato fruits; (c) leaf miner damage on chrysanthemum leaves.

(a)

(b)

(c)

which induces characteristic galls on the roots of both tomatoes and cucumbers (Fig. 1.13). Nematodes are slender, round worms, 0.1–2 mm in length, that feed saprophytically or parasitically. Most soils have a large population of saprophytic nematodes, often referred to as free-living nematodes. Certain species are often found in the root zone of plants. Parasitic nematodes feed on plant roots inducing symptoms of root decay (potato cyst nematode) or large swellings (root knot nematode) or small galls (dagger nematodes). The last group are also capable of virus transmission and in this respect can be very important inhabitants of soil, particularly in rose nurseries. The parasitic stem and leaf nematodes live on the surface of the aerial parts of plants

FIG. 1.13 Root knot
nematode galls on tomato
roots.

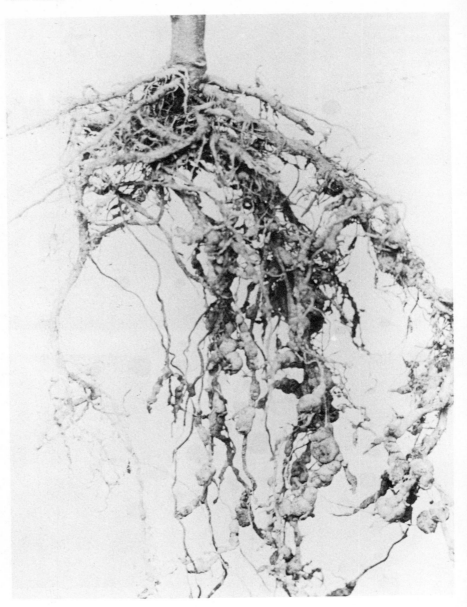

causing distortion of stems, leaves and flowers (Fig. 1.14). Damage caused
by nematodes is often similar to that caused by fungal pathogens e.g. leaf
chlorosis, stunting, wilting or growth distortion.

Non-pathogenic disorders

Non-pathogenic diseases or disorders (sometimes called physiological disorders) are diseases where a pathogen is not the primary cause of the symptoms.
Often micro-organisms colonise the damaged tissue, increasing the extent of
the disorder. Such secondary organisms may be facultative parasites, such as
Botrytis cinerea. The most common causes of non-pathogenic diseases are

FIG. 1.14 Distortion of chrysanthemum leaves and flowers caused by stem and leaf feeding nematodes.

nutritional imbalances, environmental abnormalities, such as excessively high or low temperatures, disturbed water relations, atmospheric pollution, wind, lightning and bruising, overdoses of pesticides, unsuitable pesticides and genetical abnormalities.

Nutritional disorders

Deficiencies of the major elements required for plant growth frequently result in the production of symptoms in greenhouse crops. Nitrogen deficiency is perhaps the most common, showing as a reduction in growth rate, accompanied by mild yellowing (chlorosis) of the youngest leaves. Potash deficiency, although less common, is distinguished by the yellowing and, in acute cases, the necrosis of the leaf margins. Phosphate deficiency sometimes occurs during the propagation of such plants as tomatoes, producing a purple pigment which is very conspicuous on the undersides of the leaves. Magnesium deficiency symptoms are frequently seen in tomato and cucumber crops, appearing as chlorosis between the veins on the oldest leaves, whilst manganese deficiency tends to result in yellowing along the veins, giving a network pattern which is particularly obvious in the youngest leaves. Iron deficiency may sometimes occur on highly alkaline soils and occasionally in peat culture when it is truly deficient. The characteristic symptom is the total chlorosis of the youngest parts of the plant – particularly obvious in tomatoes and hydrangeas (Fig. 1.15).

Minor element deficiencies are uncommon but can occur, usually resulting

FIG. 1.15 Interveinal chlorosis in hydrangeas resulting from iron deficiency, note the green veins (a) and the interveinal yellow areas (b).

in symptoms of chlorosis or necrosis accompanied by a reduction in growth. Boron deficiency in carnations affects the stem apex resulting in the development of many lateral buds (Fig. 1.16). Calcium deficiency in tomatoes is thought to be one of the main causes of blossom-end rot of the fruit.

Toxicities of plant nutrients can also cause disease symptoms. Frequently during propagation, an excess of soluble salts in the compost gives rise to a very high osmotic concentration in the soil water and the plant is unable to obtain sufficient water for normal growth. Such affected plants generally show symptoms of water shortage although they rarely wilt. Similar effects from high soluble salt concentrations in the soil can occur at any stage in crop

FIG. 1.16 Boron deficiency in carnations where the apical bud of the main stem stops growing (a) and lateral shoots develop (b).

development and are characterised by darkening of the foliage, and a reduction in growth rate accompanied by stunting and temporary wilting.

Some soils have a high natural manganese content which can become more soluble and available to the plant after soil treatment with heat. Tomato and cucumber plants show marked symptoms of manganese toxicity on such soils. Similarly, toxic levels of nitrate and ammonium ions are released in many soils following treatment by heat or methyl bromide. These ions are very toxic and they prevent root growth or even result in root death in extreme cases.

Environmental effects

The temperature of a greenhouse affects not only the growth rate of the crop but also the relative humidity of the air and, both directly and indirectly, by its effect on growth, the amount of water available in the soil. In extreme cases freezing or very high temperatures result in plant death but occasionally other symptoms are caused by short periods of low or high temperatures. Many greenhouse crops are unable to withstand prolonged periods of low temperature, and even short periods well below the normal growth optimum, but above freezing, can result in damage. For instance, the yellow and necrotic ring spots which occur on saintpaulia leaves can be reproduced by resting a cold coin on the leaf surface for a few hours. Similarly, a broken pane of glass in a cucumber house which allows a cold draught of air to blow onto cucumbers produces a corky surface on the fruit (Fig. 1.17). Temperatures near to freezing cause the lower epidermis of lettuce leaves to separate from the rest of the tissue giving a silvery appearance which is generally accompanied by bubbling of the surface.

High temperatures can also be damaging, producing scorch symptoms on leaves, fruit and flowers. Sun scald is a recognised disorder of tomatoes occurring when ripening fruit is subjected to very high temperatures (Fig. 1.18). Temperature fluctuations induce very uneven growth which produces split calyces in carnations – a well known disorder of this crop.

Periods of low temperature increase the relative humidity (the amount of water held in the air is directly related to the air temperature; the relative humidity is the degree of saturation of the air at a given temperature and is not a measure of the quantity of water held in the air). Plants lose most water by transpiration through the stomata on the leaves and stems. Guttation through the leaf margins can also result in the loss of further small quantities of water (Fig. 1.19). When the relative humidity is high, water loss slows down, because transpiration is controlled by the difference between the inside relative humidity of the leaf and that of the external atmosphere, particularly if reduced transpiration is accompanied by active water uptake by the roots. An accumulation of water in the leaves, especially at the leaf margins, induces the symptom known as glassiness in lettuce. A similar accumulation of water occurs in the leaves of many other greenhouse-grown plants, often producing blister-like outgrowths. This symptom is referred to as oedema. When the relative humidity is low excessive water loss can occur, and if leaf dehydration results the affected cells will die, becoming necrotic. This often happens in lettuces, giving the Tipburn symptom.

Too little soil water can also produce disease symptoms. Plants wilt when

FIG. 1.17 Low temperature damage to cucumber fruits showing as corky light brown lines on the skin surface.

FIG. 1.18 High temperature scald on tomato fruit causing bleaching of the affected areas.

FIG. 1.19 Droplets of
guttation water (a) from
the margins of cucumber
leaves.

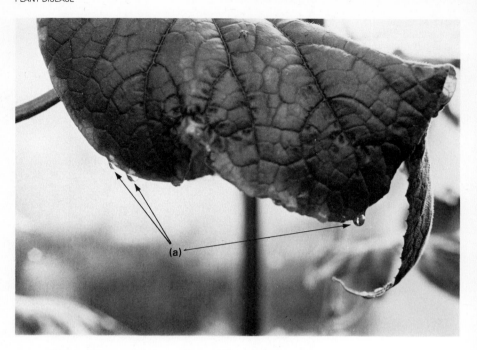

short of water, with the youngest foliage showing the symptoms first. Sometimes a temporary shortage of water results in flower abortion in greenhouse
grown vegetables and is responsible for, at least in part, symptoms of
blossom-end rot in tomatoes and peppers. Excessive water may cause wilting
symptoms but a prolonged lack of air in the soil leads to root decay and plant
death. Waterlogged roots are often black in colour and cylindrical sections
of the outer root cortex are easily detached.

Atmospheric pollution

The most common source of pollution on most nurseries is the boiler. Boiler
fumes containing sulphur dioxide can be very damaging. Even at low
concentrations the gas, which is very water soluble, can damage flowers and
prevent fruit set, and in extreme cases can cause leaf scorch symptoms. Other
forms of atmospheric pollution are infrequently the causes of damage to
greenhouse crops. Pollutants produced as a by-product of carbon dioxide
production used by many growers to increase crop yields and chemicals used
or stored within the greenhouse may sometimes give rise to symptoms.
Chemicals such as nitrous oxide, ethylene and ozone are all known to cause
damage characterised by necrosis of the leaves or in the case of ethylene, by
distortion of growth. Weather conditions which prevent the normal air
exchange rate of the greenhouse (generally reckoned to be about three
complete air change per hour) will increase the chance of damage occurring.
Inversion conditions on frosty nights and fogs are probably the worst.

Physical damage

Damage from wind, lightning, machinery and operators does not occur very frequently in greenhouse crops, although all of these agents can produce symptoms. The damage is generally recognised by the physical effect, such as leaf tearing and scorching or bruising of the affected plant. Very little air movement is needed to damage well developed chrysanthemum blooms, and many mushroom strains show scaly symptoms on the cap surface if air movement is excessive.

Toxic chemicals

Many pesticides are used on greenhouse crops and some plants are more sensitive to certain products than to others. For example, chrysanthemum cultivars show a considerable range of sensitivity and whereas one cultivar may be safely sprayed with a chemical another will show marked symptoms (phytotoxicity). The fungicide dinocap, produces mosaic-like symptoms on some chrysanthemum cultivars and the use of DDT on cucumbers is another example where the crop can become acutely chlorotic if sprayed by this chemical. More frequently crop damage occurs because the pesticide is applied at too high a concentration or at the wrong stage of the development of the crop. Symptoms vary from the death of the growing point, to chlorosis or necrosis and distortion of the leaves. Herbicides are perhaps the most common chemical cause of disease symptoms. Damage may result from inadvertent applications with contaminated spraying machinery or as a result of spray drift entering the greenhouse through the ventilators or doorways. Occasionally, herbicides applied outside will affect the crop if they enter the greenhouse through drainage channels.

Herbicides of the growth regulator type, the hormone weedkillers, such as 2,4-D, 2,4,5-T, TBA and MCPA cause apparent wilting (epinasty) within a day of application and sub-lethal doses result in considerable leaf distortion, with the veins of the leaves of dicotyledons becoming parallel and the lamina tissue being reduced to small, green, blister-like islands. Affected leaves often become cup-shaped or hooded (Fig. 1.20). As the plant recovers the symptoms become less pronounced, but even slightly affected plants show leaf distortion – often most evident at the tip of the leaf which is drawn out to a very fine point (Fig. 1.21). Tomato fruits on such affected plants are generally elongated, plum-shaped and seed-less (Fig. 1.22). Lettuce, cucumbers, tomatoes and peppers are among the most sensitive plants but carnations and chrysanthemums appear to be far less sensitive to these chemicals.

Sodium chlorate is one of the more poisonous herbicides and is often used to kill off all vegetation, especially around greenhouses and on roadways. Few plants recover from the damage it causes. Occasionally, the chemical enters the greenhouse as a contaminant of soil, water, pots or boxes. Typical symptoms of sodium chlorate damage are chlorosis along the veins of the leaves which become necrotic after a short time and the plant then dies. The chlorosis along the veins is particularly apparent in the youngest leaves. Similarly, paraquat and some of the aminotriazole herbicides can produce disease symptoms. Paraquat splash produces circular, brown spots on affected leaves and, in exceptional circumstances, the herbicide can be taken up from the soil, resulting in brown streak symptoms on the stems of affected plants. Aminotriazole herbicides contaminating the soil, cause plants to produce chlorophyll-free (bleached) new leaves. Chrysanthemums affected by this

(a)

(b)

FIG. 1.20   Distortion of
tomato leaves caused by
2,3,6-TBA:
(a) 'hooded' distortion of
leaflets;
(b) parallel venation and
distortion. Reproduced by
permission of Blackwell
Scientific Publications Ltd.

Picloram   T.B.A.

FIG. 1.21   The effect of
picloram and 2,3,6-TBA on
the serration of tomato
leaflets. Reproduced by
permission of Blackwell
Scientific Publications Ltd.

FIG. 1.22 Distortion of tomato fruits caused by sub-lethal doses of the herbicide MCPA.

FIG. 1.23 Gill formation on the surface of a mushroom (Rose Comb) resulting from contamination of the casing by a mineral oil.

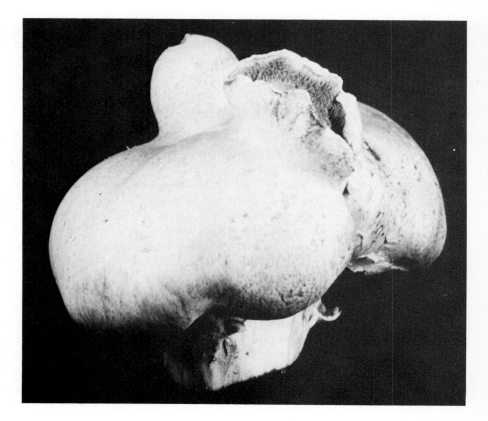

herbicide show spectacular loss of green colour in the youngest growth. An unusual symptom of chemical contamination is seen in the mushroom crop where the presence of some chemicals, especially mineral oils, and phenols at the time of sporophore development, results in the production of gill tissue on the top of the cap as well as in the normal position. This symptom is described as Rose-comb (Fig. 1.23).

Genetical abnormalities

Symptoms resulting from genetical abnormalities may often be confused with virus diseases. In the tomato crop silvering of the foliage is of common occurrence. During propagation small silver spots, usually angular in shape, may appear on the leaves, particularly if the plants have been exposed to low temperatures. Such affected plants generally grow quite normally when planted out. When tomatoes are planted very early in the season, silvering may affect the whole of the plant apex, the leaves are silver-grey, are often rolled and the plant fails to set fruit. Such silvering is genetically determined and if it affects mature plants it can result in considerable crop loss.

Mutants (random genetical changes) are frequently seen in carnation and chrysanthemum crops where some of the petals or even a half of the flower may be a different colour from the rest. Angular, yellow, mosaic-like patches occur on the leaves of some plants, and although these may be considered a disorder in lettuce they are commercially exploited in pot plants such as ivies.

A streak symptom on stems and leaves, eventually resulting in the collapse and death of the plant, has been found in some tomato cultivars, in particular Syston Cross. This disease has been called autogenous necrosis and is known to be due to a genetical abnormality.

FURTHER READING

Anon. (1973) *A Guide to the Use of Terms in Plant Pathology*. Commonwealth Mycological Institute, Kew, England.

Ainsworth, G. C. (1971) *Ainsworth and Bisby's Dictionary of the Fungi*. Commonwealth Mycological Institute, Kew, England.

Buchanan, R. E. and Gibbons, N. E. (1974) *Bergey's Manual of Determinative Bacteriology*. The Williams and Wilkins Company, Baltimore, MD.

Dickinson, C. H. and Lucas, J. A. (1982) *Plant Pathology and Plant Pathogens*. 2nd edition. Blackwell Scientific Publications, London.

Gibbs, A. and Harrison, B. (1976) *Plant Virology, The Principles*. Edward Arnold, London.

Horsfall, J. G. and Cowling, E. B. (1977) *Plant Disease: Vol. IV – How pathogens induce disease*. Academic Press, London.

Matthews, R. E. F. (1981) *Plant Virology*. Academic Press, London.

Webster, J. (1970) *Introduction to Fungi*. Cambridge University Press, Cambridge.

CHAPTER 2

DISEASE DIAGNOSIS – ASSEMBLING AND INTERPRETING THE FACTS

Accurate diagnosis of a disease is usually the first step towards its successful control. When the disease has been identified and its cause is known the necessary steps can be taken for its control. To make a diagnosis it is necessary to examine various factors in order to obtain information from which conclusions can be drawn. Some of the factors which are taken into account include the nature of the symptoms on the plant parts, the distribution of affected plants in the crop, when the symptoms first occurred and the pattern of spread, if any, since the outbreak of the disease. All the relevant agronomic details, such as cultivar, pre-planting soil treatment, nutrition and the use of pesticides, also need to be considered (Fig. 2.1). Of all these, the nature and the distribution of the symptoms are the most important and are dealt with in more detail.

The first stage in the investigation of the disease outbreak is an examination of the crop and the distribution of affected plants.

FIG. 2.1 Collecting information for disease diagnosis.

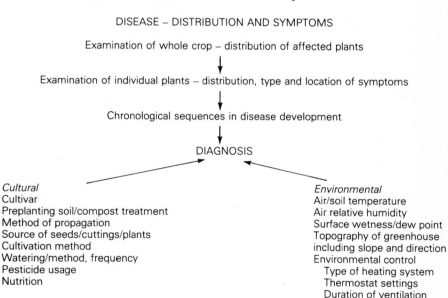

DISEASE – DISTRIBUTION AND SYMPTOMS

Examination of whole crop – distribution of affected plants

↓

Examination of individual plants – distribution, type and location of symptoms

↓

Chronological sequences in disease development

↓

DIAGNOSIS

Cultural
Cultivar
Preplanting soil/compost treatment
Method of propagation
Source of seeds/cuttings/plants
Cultivation method
Watering/method, frequency
Pesticide usage
Nutrition

Environmental
Air/soil temperature
Air relative humidity
Surface wetness/dew point
Topography of greenhouse
including slope and direction
Environmental control
Type of heating system
Thermostat settings
Duration of ventilation

THE DISTRIBUTION OF AFFECTED PLANTS

Distributions are either random or non-random, depending upon various factors including the disease, the crop, its planting pattern and the mechanism of spread of the pathogen. Generally the larger the area of plants the more straightforward the interpretation of the distribution. For instance, two plants showing symptoms in a crop of ten or so may mean very little, whereas small patches in a crop of several thousands can give a useful indication of the cause. Plants grown in pots or boxes may also show characteristic patterns of disease symptoms. What are the factors affecting the distribution pattern? There are many, but some of the most commonly encountered will be discussed.

Individual plants

The position of a single affected plant, even in a large greenhouse can provide valuable information. For instance, if the plant is near a point in the greenhouse frequently visited by the grower, for example the tap, telephone or record sheet, it is possible that the pathogen is readily transmissible and is being spread by the grower. According to the crop, the actual disease can often be identified from this together with other information. Single affected plants near a doorway may have resulted from the introduction of the pathogen through the open door. Aphid attacks begin in this way and as they are frequently virus vectors the first symptom of diseases caused by aphid-borne viruses may appear in such positions. Single diseased plants with a random distribution throughout the crop occur if the pathogen is seed-borne, e.g. Lettuce Mosaic Virus in lettuce crops, or when the pathogen is cutting-borne, e.g. Fusarium Wilt in carnations. With both of these diseases the number of affected plants usually represents a small proportion of the total population but the few that are present are randomly distributed. With other diseases a much higher proportion of the crop may be affected; for instance, if soil has been poorly sterilised, root diseases may occur at random throughout the cropping area.

   Very low levels of disease showing a random pattern of affected plants may also result from genetical abnormalities, for example when silvering occurs in tomatoes.

Large groups of plants

Groups of diseased plants are very common in greenhouses, often with all or many of the plants in a section of the greenhouse showing symptoms. These groups may have a random pattern or they may have a regular distribution. Large groups of plants are often affected when the environment in the greenhouse is markedly uneven. The topography of the site can influence the environment in this way if the greenhouse slopes in an easterly direction, or even in both easterly and southerly directions along and across the house, respectively. This results in high areas and low areas within the greenhouse and heat rises to the highest points. There is then a temperature differential along the length and sometimes also across the greenhouse. Temperature has a direct effect on the moisture-holding capacity of the air and on the relative humidity, which varies with temperature. Many fungal pathogens are dependent upon wetness of the leaf surface or on long periods of very high humidities for spore germination and infection, and for this reason parts of the greenhouse may be much more favourable for disease development than others. It is often possible to see disease distributions affected by such environmental factors; and even the soil environment is influenced by the air temperature. Grey Mould (*Botrytis cinerea*) is often most common in the coldest part of the greenhouse because in this position the humidity is highest for longer periods of time and water persists on the leaf surface. By contrast powdery mildew may be more common in the warmest parts as powdery mildew spores germinate at high humidities, but not in water. High temperatures are often followed by long periods of high humidity which occur when the temperature drops at night thereby providing ideal conditions for powdery mildew development.

Soil temperature can affect disease distribution and rows of affected plants along all the outside edges of the greenhouse often indicate favourable soil temperatures in these areas for particular pathogens. Such areas, because of the nearness of outside land are often wetter and more difficult to sterilise. Phytophthora root rots of tomato commonly occur in such positions.

Small randomly distributed groups

Soil-borne diseases may occur in a random fashion although they often do not show a characteristic pattern in greenhouse crops because of the extensive use of soil sterilants. But because some pathogens are difficult to control, particularly those fungi which cause vascular wilts, such diseases as Fusarium and Phialophora Wilt of carnations often reoccur in apparently randomly distributed patches but in exactly the same areas in the same greenhouse in every crop (Fig. 2.2). Also, apparently random patches are occasionally clearly associated with the planting pattern or a particular planter. Such a distribution of wilt can indicate a high proportion of affected cuttings within a bundle of plants all of them planted by one person (Fig. 2.3).

FIG. 2.2 A random distribution pattern of Phialophora Wilt (*Phialophora cinerescens*) in carnation beds.

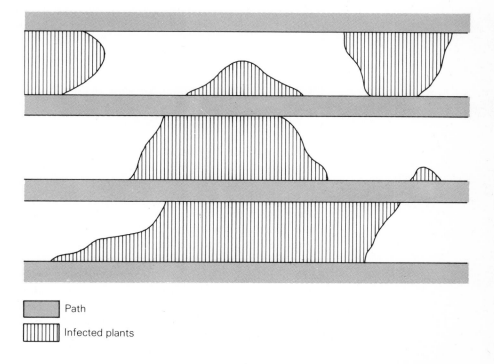

Path

Infected plants

FIG. 2.3 Distribution of Fusarium Wilt (*F. oxysporum* f.sp. *dianthi*) of carnations indicating an association of the disease with particular bundles of cuttings.

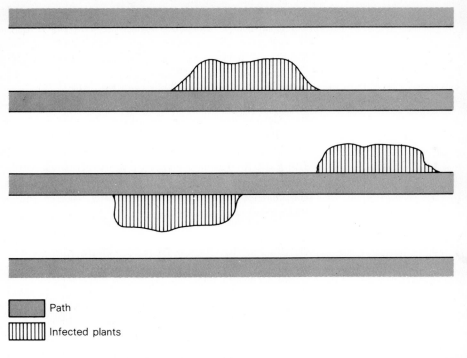

☐ Path

▥ Infected plants

As well as disease symptom distribution patterns in greenhouses, characteristic random distributions can occur in boxes of bedding plants. Generally, overall effects are attributable to physical or chemical problems such as acute water shortage, too much fertiliser or toxic levels of chemicals, but random patches of affected plants are more likely to result from pathogenic causes. Seed-borne diseases usually appear as small patches of affected plants usually confined to one or two areas in a few boxes, e.g. Leaf Spot of lobelia caused by *Alternaria alternata*. Damping-off diseases on the other hand may affect a large porportion of seedlings although initially starting from small patches. They are caused by soil-borne fungi and if the compost is contaminated all the plants raised in it may eventually damp-off.

Small non-randomly or regularly distributed groups

Patches of affected plants under gutters or under ventilators usually indicate disease associated with wetness, toxic metals in water dripping from the roof, or air-borne pathogens. Leaky gutters give wet patches of soil affecting the efficiency of soil sterilisation and the availability of nutrients. Where the gutters are metal, toxic levels of metal ions sometimes accumulate, or even cause scorch of the plants if the contaminated water drips directly onto the foliage. Such symptoms are seen in lettuce crops especially when condensation water runs down the metal structure before dripping onto the plants. In the centre of the greenhouse the ventilators present similar problems both of toxic drip from the oil used to lubricate the system or from toxic air-borne pesticides. Greenhouses in areas of intensive cereal production are always liable to the risk of herbicide spray damage, especially as most agricultural spraying is done in May and June, often when temperatures are high and the greenhouse ventilators are open. The worst affected plants occur in groups under the ventilators as these receive the highest dose of the spray drift. Aphids may enter the greenhouse in a similar way and aphid-borne viruses may show a similar disease distribution pattern. Often the plants under the ventilators are wetted by rain and these conditions are suitable for the development of some fungus diseases especially rust and leaf spots. In carnation crops, carnation rust often starts in the beds under the ventilators, particularly in older greenhouses where the ventilators leak, even when they are closed.

Lines of affected plants in a row usually occur if a contagious disease is transmitted during cultural operations. Such patterns are obvious in tomato crops affected by Didymella Stem Rot when the fungus pathogen is transmitted on contaminated knives or hands. Once contaminated by cutting a stem lesion, the knife blade can remain contaminated for as many as 30 subsequent cuts. Often the operator works in the same direction along a row of plants every time he works in the crop so the affected area extends down the row even though the adjacent row may be disease-free (Fig. 2.4). Similarly, Tomato Mosaic Virus is readily spread on the hands of the grower and a very clear pattern of distribution of Tomato Mosaic develops according to the direction of working through the crops (Fig. 2.5).

Directional patterns of disease distribution can also occur for environmental, physical or chemical reasons. The sunny side of the greenhouse at midday may become extremely hot and fruits and flowers are damaged as a result. Conversely on the coldest side, damage may occur to young growth and tender fruit as the temperature on that side is a few degrees below the safe limit. The application of unsuitable pesticides, unsuitable spraying conditions, mixtures which are not compatible, or at too high a concentration, may produce damage to foliage and fruit. Such damage reveals uneven distribution of the pesticide when the damage is confined to the side of the plant or part of the plant which was sprayed. Cucumber fruits are very prone to damage by any of these causes reacting by producing brown dry corky tissue which inhibits fruit expansion and results in distorted and cracked fruit.

Chemical contamination of the wood used to make bedding boxes can

FIG. 2.4 Distribution of Didymella Stem Rot (*Didymella lycopersici*) in a tomato crop indicating the spread of the pathogen on hands and/or knives.

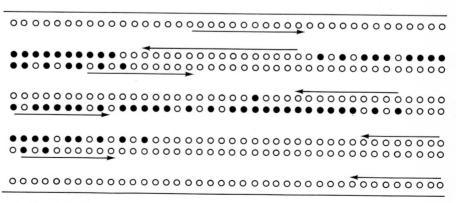

○ Healthy plant
● Didymella infected plant
→ directions of working crop

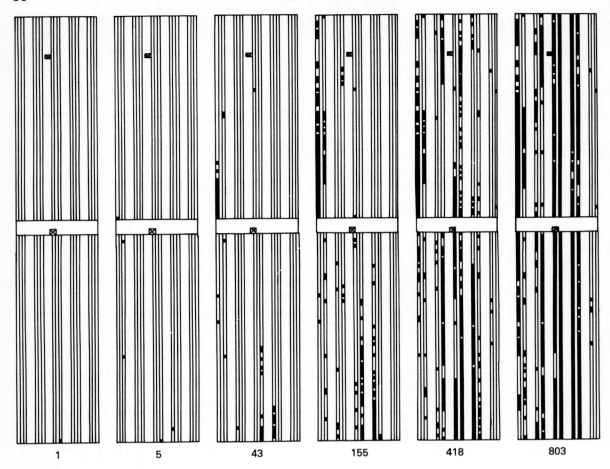

1   5   43   155   418   803

⊠ – Standpipe   ▪ – Plants with T.M.V. symptoms

FIG. 2.5 Distribution of TMV in tomatoes showing spread according to the direction of working the crop. Crown Copyright.

result in half boxes being affected, particularly if one of the base boards is contaminated by a highly toxic herbicide such as sodium chlorate.

THE DISTRIBUTION OF SYMPTOMS ON AFFECTED PLANTS

The distribution of the symptoms on an affected plant must be considered next. It is sometimes possible to distinguish between symptoms caused by fungal, bacterial or virus pathogens and to differentiate between these and symptoms caused by physical or chemical damage and nutritional disorders merely by observing the distribution and characteristics of the symptoms on the affected plants.

Symptoms may occur on all the leaves, on either the youngest or oldest, on one or other side of the plant. Some are confined to one or both leaf surfaces, or the leaf margins or on the lamina, between the veins or independently of the vein pattern. Such variation in the distribution of symptoms is well illustrated by the nutrient deficiency and toxicity symptoms of tomatoes, which are summarised in Tables 2.1 and 2.2. Much can be learned from the distribution of symptoms on leaves but less about the cause of the disease from the distribution of symptoms on stems and roots.

Symptoms on the older leaves

Leaf blotches, spots and discoloration confined to one or two of the oldest leaves of a plant usually indicate a nutritional disorder. Symptoms of magnesium deficiency occur most commonly on the older leaves especially on tomatoes, cucumbers, peppers and chrysanthemums. Physical damage such as scorch, with a distribution on the leaf which is independent of vein pattern and of varying shape and size, may be confined to the lower leaves especially when associated with the application of a pesticide drench or a fertiliser.

Wilting of the older leaves only is often indicative of the presence of a fungal or bacterial vascular pathogen. The wilt is generally progressive until the whole plant is affected.

Symptoms mainly on the older leaves but with a decreasing incidence towards the younger

Nutritional deficiency symptoms show this distribution with the leaves developing characteristic interveinal chlorosis or chlorosis along the veins. When soil magnesium levels are very low, up to half of the leaves on the plant may be affected. Similarly manganese toxicity symptoms, which sometimes occur after steam treatment of the soil, and marginal leaf scorch resulting from potassium deficiency, are usually most prominent on the older leaves.

Many fungal and bacterial leaf spots develop in greatest intensity on the oldest leaves. Such spots and blotches can usually be distinguished from those caused by other agents because:
1. They are often approximately the same size and shape on all the oldest affected leaves and are consistent in colour and texture.
2. There is a gradation of lesion size from the oldest to the younger leaves, the smallest lesions appearing on the youngest leaves with an increase in lesion size towards the base of the plant.
3. Most frequently the youngest leaves are either not affected or have only very small pin-point chlorotic or necrotic specks.
4. The spots and blotches may be surrounded by a different coloured margin.
5. The margins of the spots and blotches are often diffuse or at least not sharply delimited from the healthy tissue.

Symptoms mainly on the younger leaves

This symptom distribution of spots and blotches occurs with nutritional disorders, virus diseases, some fungal and bacterial diseases and physical or chemical scorches. Symptoms of mineral deficiencies confined to the top part of the plant include those of calcium and manganese. Calcium deficiencies affect the growing apex and the leaves become pale green in colour or completely chlorotic when it is severe. Manganese deficiency shows as a pattern of chlorosis alongside the veins on the upper leaves which causes the vein pattern to stand out. Virus disease symptoms are often apparent in the youngest fully-expanded leaf. They may also decrease in intensity in the older leaves, which with some diseases, e.g. Cucumber Green Mottle Mosaic, are symptomless. The yellow or green mosaic, ring spot or yellow spot patterns, resulting from virus infection are generally independent of leaf vein pattern.

When spots and blotches are caused by some fungal and bacterial pathogens the upper leaves are most severely affected especially when the pathogens are introduced through the ventilators or when spread results from overhead irrigation, e.g. with Potato Blight and Bacterial Leaf Scorch on tomatoes.

Spots, blotches and blemishes, caused by physical or chemical factors can occur anywhere on the plant but most frequently are found on the youngest and medium aged leaves. This may be explained by the fact that these leaves are generally the most sensitive and the upper part of the plant is frequently the portion most exposed. The distribution and appearance of physical and chemically induced spots and blotches have some characteristic features:

(a) The distribution is frequently directional occurring on one side of the upper part of the plant.

(b) The damage often results from a single event and is then confined to one or two leaves.

(c) Because the symptoms result from the single event there is no obvious progression of symptom development.

Spots which result from chemical damage are frequently circular or show an obvious pattern according to the flow of the damaging liquid; they are uniform and generally brown in colour, and they have a very sharply defined edge. They are of various sizes on a plant or even on a single leaf in spite of their otherwise identical appearance. There is no obvious progression of development of the spots.

Wilting of the youngest leaves and growing tips only results from malfunctioning of the roots which may be temporary because of a shortage of water, waterlogging of the soil or a high soluble salt level in the soil, or perhaps permanent due to a loss of roots by physical, chemical, pest or pathogen injury. Excessive water loss, the result of either very low relative humidity or virus infection. can induce wilting in the very youngest leaves.

Symptoms confined to very young leaves

Growth regulator herbicide damage, caused by such herbicides as 2,4-D, or MCPA appear first in the youngest leaves, affecting their shape and development. Plants growing in soil with a high soluble salt level, frequently show a deepening in green colour in the youngest leaves, whilst the other leaves appear normal. Such plants often have a decreased rate of growth.

Symptoms mainly confined to the upper leaf surface

The powdery mildew pathogens occur most commonly on the upper surfaces. Colonisation of the lower leaf surface may occur but is both less frequent and less severe. Symptoms of pest damage, especially if caused by red spider mites and thrips, are more conspicuous on the upper leaf surface.

TABLE 2.1 Nutrient deficiency symptoms and their distribution on tomato plants

Nutrient deficiency	Symptoms	Distribution
Nitrogen	Overall pale green colour of leaves and spindly growth	Whole plant but beginning on the older leaves
Phosphorus	Leaves dark green with purple discoloration on the undersides. Yellowing and purpling of the older leaves, plants stunted	Whole plant
Potassium	Marginal leaf scorch, interveinal chlorosis	Whole plant but beginning on the older leaves
Magnesium	Interveinal chlorosis; leaves becoming entirely yellow	Older leaves
Calcium	Leaves pale green at their tips and along their margins eventually becoming chlorotic and necrotic	Younger leaves
Sulphur	Interveinal chlorosis, purpling of the veins with purple spots and necrotic patches developing between the veins	Whole plant
Manganese	Pale green interveinal chlorosis often confined to the tissue alongside the veins	Younger and medium aged leaves
Iron	Pale, interveinal chlorosis, rapidly becoming yellow to white but with the veins remaining green. No necrosis	Younger leaves
Boron	Distal portions of leaflets chlorotic with the veins slightly necrotic. When acute the main growing point dies and lateral shoots develop	Older and medium aged leaves but also the apex, when acute
Zinc	Necrotic spotting of the leaves and downward curling of the petiole	Mainly the younger leaves
Copper	Upward curling of the leaflets into tubes; petioles curl downwards	Mainly the younger leaves
Molybdenum	Pale interveinal chlorosis	Older leaves

TABLE 2.2 Nutrient toxicity symptoms and their distribution on tomato plants

Nutrient toxicity	Symptoms	Distribution
Nitrogen	Growth stunted and slow, plants dark green, leaves small	Younger leaves
Phosphorus	Induces manganese and iron deficiencies – see Table 2.1	
Potassium	Growth stunted and slow, plants dark green	Whole plant but in particular the younger leaves
Magnesium	None	
Calcium	Induces iron and manganese deficiencies – see Table 2.1	
Sulphur	None	
Manganese	Necrotic spots between the veins on the older leaves with brown streaks on the petioles and stem. Interveinal chlorosis and reduced leaf size of the younger leaves	Younger and older leaves affected but show different symptoms
Iron	None	
Boron	Marginal necrosis and curling of the leaflets with interveinal necrotic spots Affected leaves are dry and papery	Older leaves
Zinc	Stunted plants with thin stems, leaves reduced in size. The younger leaves show interveinal chlorosis with purpling of the undersides; older leaves are less affected but may curl downwards	Whole plant but particularly the younger leaves
Copper	Similar to zinc toxicity	Whole plant
Chloride	Similar to nitrogen and potassium toxicities	Whole plant

Symptoms mainly confined to the lower leaf surface

The downy mildew and rust pathogens sporulate on the under surface of the leaves. However, both groups generally induce mild symptoms, such as chlorosis, on the upper leaf surface directly above the sporulating lesions.

Symptoms associated with the stomata of the leaf are most commonly found on the under surface where the stomata occur in greater numbers. Oedema is a common example of such a symptom. Corkiness of the leaf or small water soaked blisters, develop on the leaves of many different species of plants when environmental conditions prevent transpiration.

Symptoms mainly confined to the leaf margin

Some nutrient deficiencies such as those of potassium, result in chlorosis or necrosis of leaf margins. Toxic levels of systemic pesticides also cause chlorosis at the leaf margins often with a non-continuous distribution of the chlorotic tissue. Similarly, excessive water loss through hydathodes can lead to dehydration of tissue of the leaf edge resulting in necrosis, which is referred to as tipburn in lettuce. Some bacterial vascular pathogens that produce toxins e.g. *Corynebacterium michiganense* characteristically produce marginal wilting of leaves followed by marginal necrosis.

Symptoms confined to the lamina

Leaf spots and blotches occur most frequently on the lamina and away from the leaf margin. Sometimes the symptom is confined to the centre of the leaf, particularly the main vein or perhaps to a lesser extent the secondary veins. Initially, only the veins are affected when the plant is poisoned by sodium chlorate but when contamination is severe the whole leaf and eventually the whole plant dies. Symptoms which are entirely and regularly interveinal generally indicate a mineral deficiency or toxicity (Fig. 1.15). Those totally independent of vein pattern are more likely to be induced by a pathogen.

Symptoms confined to one side of a plant or part of one side

This distribution is typical of symptoms resulting from physical or chemical damage and frequently all plants within the crop are affected. Such a distribution occurs following the accidental application of herbicide with a contaminated sprayer, but the intensity of the symptom may decrease with distance away from the point where spraying began. Temperature or chemical damage often affects one side of the plant because of the plant's position in relation to broken glass or exposure to the sun or the source of the chemical.

Wilting of a part of a plant occurs when a stem is damaged, often by a fungal lesion, either at the junction of the main stem and a lateral or somewhere along the lateral stem. The leaves at the distal end of the stem then show wilt symptoms. Some vascular wilt pathogens e.g. *Fusarium oxysporum* f.sp. *lycopersici* invade part of the vascular tissue and result in one-sided wilting of the affected plant.

Wilt-like symptoms on all leaves

Such symptoms may occur following exposure to a growth regulator herbicide and generally appear within 24 hours of the event. Although the plant appears to have wilted the leaves are found to be turgid. Such a plant reaction is known as epinasty. A similar symptom occurs in tomato plants during the early stages of Fusarium Wilt development. Wilt of the whole plant also occurs during the advanced stages of vascular wilt and root rot diseases, as well as with prolonged periods of drought.

SYMPTOM DISTRIBUTION ON STEMS

The most common stem symptom is a canker or decayed area forming a stem lesion. Such lesions occur at any point on the stem from soil level to the stem apex. At soil level they usually indicate attack by a soil-borne pathogen. Those confined to the nodes or damaged areas of the stem may result from pathogenic colonisation of senescent plant tissue or by the transfer of the pathogen during cultural operations. Stripes and streaks occur on the medium aged and youngest stem tissue particularly following attack by a virus pathogen but yellow streaks to the base of the stem and confined to one side are indicative of Fusarium Wilt especially in tomatoes and cucumbers. Vascular staining of the xylem tissue is diagnostic of vascular wilt diseases and can be differentiated from vascular staining resulting from root decay because it extends well above soil level and is not confined to the basal 10 or 20 cm of the stem. The development of adventitious roots at the base of the stem indicates the presence of a stem lesion at or below soil level.

SYMPTOM DISTRIBUTION ON ROOTS

Root rot is the most common symptom. Pathogenic root decay generally begins with the development of small lesions which extend and may eventually affect the whole root system. Rapid overall root rot is more likely to result from adverse soil conditions such as waterlogging or chemical toxicity. The uneven distribution of root rot may occur if soil sterilisation has been done poorly either during propagation or in the greenhouse. Tomato plants grown in a pathogen-free propagation compost but planted into a contaminated greenhouse will develop symptoms of root decay on the new roots as they grow into the greenhouse soil, while those in the propagation compost will remain in a healthy condition at least initially. The converse can also occur if the propagation compost is contaminated and the greenhouse soil pathogen free.

COMPLETING THE COLLECTION OF INFORMATION

Additional information which may help in the diagnosis of the disease can be obtained from the details of the production of the crop from seeds or cuttings to the point when the symptoms were first seen. Some of the most relevant are:

Seeds.   Details of the source and storage before sowing can be imported, as poor storage conditions, and even the use of toxic ink on the packets, can affect seed performance. Sometimes particular stocks of some cultivars are known to be infected by a pathogen.

Cuttings.   The source and conditions in which the cuttings have been produced, their subsequent storage after rooting, and condition on arrival, can give some indication of their suitability to produce a disease-free crop.

Cold stored cuttings are often slow to establish and some pathogens are encouraged by low temperatures during storage, e.g. *Alternaria dianthi* on carnations.

Compost or soil treatment before sowing or planting.   The method of sterilisation and the details of the process may indicate weaknesses in the system and suggest possible causes of diseases, especially if the cropping history of the greenhouse is known. It is important to know the time interval between sterilisation of the soil and planting as toxic levels of chemicals can occur (see below: Chemicals, peat or manure added to the soil).

Water source.   Mains water is usually pathogen-free but dyke and pond water can be a potent source of pathogens or chemical pollutants.

Boxes and pots.   Contamination of containers with pathogens or chemicals can result in the early appearance of diseases.

Stakes, ties and irrigation lines.   Contamination can again result in the reintroduction of pathogens at an early stage even though the soil has been very carefully sterilised.

Chemicals, peat or manure added to the soil.   The addition of materials to the soil or compost before sterilisation may lead to trouble. Heat treatment following the addition of organic sources of nitrogen, for example, farmyard manure, organic fertilisers, may result in toxic levels of some chemicals, e.g. ammonium ions. The time interval and storage conditions following heat treatment, are very important as a 3-week period is usually the time when toxic levels of nitrite or ammonium ions are at a maximum, although this period varies with the compost and is lengthened with low temperature storage. Under normal conditions 6 weeks storage is usually sufficient for the safe use of heat-treated soil or compost.

FURTHER READING

Agrios, G. N. (1978) *Plant Pathology*. Academic Press, New York.
Anon. (1981) *Diagnosis of herbicide damage to crops*. Ref. book 221, HMSO, London.
Butler, E. J. and Jones, S. G. (1949) *Plant Pathology*. Macmillan, London.
Horsfall, J. G. and Cowling, E. B. (1977) *Plant Disease: Vol. I – How disease is managed*. Academic Press, London.
Kingham, H. G. (1973) *The U.K. Tomato Manual*. Grower Books, London.
Streets, R. B. (1969) *The Diagnosis of Plant Diseases*. Cooperative extension Service and Agricultural Experimental Station, University of Arizona Press, Tucson, Arizona.
Wallace, T. (1951) *The Diagnosis of Mineral Deficiencies in Plants by Visual Symptoms. A Colour Atlas and Guide*. HMSO, London.
Wheeler, B. E. J. (1969) *An Introduction to Plant Diseases*. John Wiley and Sons, New York.

CHAPTER 3

SYMPTOMS AND PLANT FUNCTION

A symptom may be characteristic of a particular disease or may be common to various diseases. A combination of symptoms diagnostic of one disease is known as a disease syndrome. Symptoms may occur on the roots, stems, leaves, flowers and seeds, and it is important to observe all the symptoms when investigating a disease. A casual examination of a diseased plant can often be misleading for, whereas a wilting plant may indicate the presence of a vascular wilt pathogen, the symptom may also result from attack by other pathogens, various physical or chemical factors, or be a direct result of adverse environmental conditions. Close examination of the plant will often enable some, if not most, of the irrelevant factors to be eliminated. A consideration of the function of the various parts of the plant will often help in the understanding of the effects of the disease and in this way may suggest where the examination may be concentrated in order to determine the cause (Fig. 3.1).

Roots

Roots have three primary functions, uptake of water and nutrients, transport of these materials and plant anchorage. The uptake of water and nutrients is most active in the root hair zone, which is located very near to the growing tip. Transport is through the central vascular core or stele and the surrounding cortical tissue often functions as a food storage area. The central vascular core also gives the root its strength and the extent of the root system determines its effectiveness as a means of anchorage. Symptoms of disease on roots usually appear as rots, cankers, galls, proliferation of the root system, general discoloration and, in exceptional cases, a loss of the normal tropism. Root decay first affects the outer tissues of the root including the cortical cells which show symptoms of discoloration, brown in most cases but occasionally red as with Phoma Root Rot of chrysanthemums. Cortical decay can be quite extensive and yet plant growth may not be seriously affected, e.g. Brown and Corky Root Rot of tomatoes. This is almost certainly because the vascular tissue is still functioning and the plant is producing a sufficient quantity of new roots to enable the root hairs to take up water and nutrients. Conversely *Phomopsis sclerotioides*, which causes Black Root Rot of cucumbers, sometimes colonises roots in a very short time decaying all tissues. When this happens the root system ceases to function, wilting occurs and deficiency symptoms appear in the leaves. Root decay may also be slow although eventually complete and it is quite usual for chrysan-themums to be in flower before the full effects of Phoma Root Rot become

FIG. 3.1   Disease
symptoms.

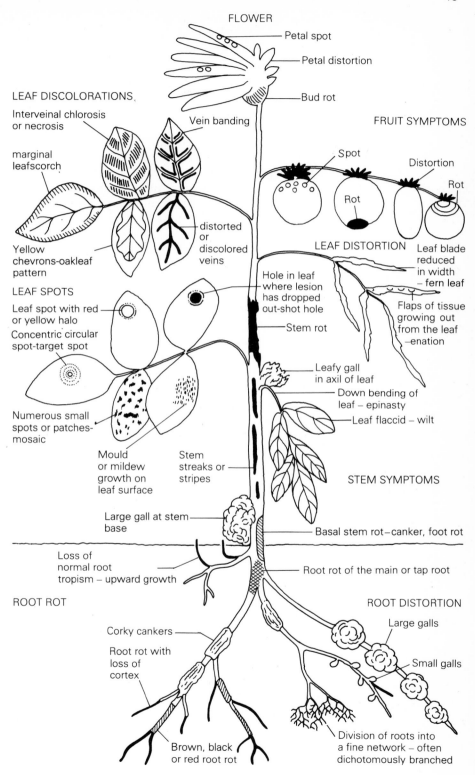

FLOWER
— Petal spot
— Petal distortion
— Bud rot

LEAF DISCOLORATIONS,
Interveinal chlorosis
or necrosis

Vein banding

FRUIT SYMPTOMS

marginal
leafscorch

Spot
Distortion
Rot

Rot

Yellow
chevrons-oakleaf
pattern

distorted
or
discolored
veins

LEAF DISTORTION

Leaf blade
reduced
in width
– fern leaf

LEAF SPOTS

Hole in leaf
where lesion
has dropped
out-shot hole

Leaf spot with red
or yellow halo
Concentric circular
spot-target spot

— Stem rot

Flaps of tissue
growing out
from the leaf
–enation

Leafy gall
in axil of leaf
— Down bending of
leaf – epinasty
— Leaf flaccid – wilt

Numerous small
spots or patches-
mosaic

Mould
or mildew
growth on
leaf surface

Stem
streaks or
stripes

STEM SYMPTOMS

Large gall at stem
base

— Basal stem rot–canker, foot rot

Loss of
normal root
tropism – upward growth

— Root rot of the main or tap root

ROOT ROT

ROOT DISTORTION

Large galls

Corky cankers

Root rot with
loss of
cortex

Small galls

Brown, black
or red root rot

Division of roots into
a fine network – often
dichotomously branched

obvious. Root rot also adversely affects the anchorage of the plant but as many greenhouse plants are supported by string or stakes it is uncommon for the loss of anchorage to be apparent. However, occasionally it is dramatically illustrated by cucumber plants growing in straw bale beds. As the straw decomposes the beds sink and as the plants are tied to a supporting wire, a considerable tension develops. Healthy roots, under such tension, may be as tight as 'bow strings', but if root decay occurs the affected plants are pulled out of the bed.

Pathogens may sometimes stimulate cell division in the root tissue, and galls or small tumorous outgrowths are formed. These are generally corky or roughened on their surface and vary in size with the pathogen and the host. For instance, the crown gall bacterium, *Agrobacterium tumefaciens*, can induce very large galls at the base of the stem and on the main roots of many woody hosts, such as roses. Root knot nematodes stimulate gall formation on the roots of tomatoes and cucumbers. These may be so extensive that they hang like strings of beads when the root system is excavated. The dagger nematodes produce small galls (2–3 mm) on rose roots which are not immediately apparent. If the cells of the roots respond by increasing in size rather than dividing, the roots may swell and crack to form a canker-like lesion on the surface. This results when tomatoes are affected by *Pyrenochaeta lycopersici* although the corky cankerous symptom is confined to the thicker roots, and the thin roots show a brown rot. Unless galls or corky cankers are extremely extensive they do not seriously affect plant growth. Generally such diseases gradually increase in intensity with successive crops and the presence of some plants with symptoms indicates the need for control measures to be applied in order to prevent loss of yield in future crops.

An unusual symptom resulting from the activities of the bacterium *Agrobacterium rhizogenes* is the growth of cucumber roots in an upward direction (negatively geotropic) so that they emerge and grow vertically from the soil surface.

Damage to the growing tips of the roots has a marked effect on plant growth as it seriously interferes with water and nutrient uptake. Affected plants show extensive branching of the roots, frequently with dichotomous divisions. As a result of this root damage the plants are stunted and the leaves show mineral deficiency symptoms in spite of having an apparently extensive root system.

Vascular wilt pathogens enter the plants through the roots but the infected roots remain symptomless until the plant reaches an advanced state of wilting and then they decay.

Stems

The major functions of the stem are support for the plant and transport of nutrients and water. Stem symptoms include cankerous lesions, streaks or stripes, galls, and distortions. The support function of many greenhouse plants is taken over by strings or stakes but even then plants may collapse if the stem decays. Such stem collapse is common when tomato plants are affected by aggressive pathogens like *Didymella lycopersici*. In contrast *Botrytis cinerea* may produce numerous localised lesions which do not penetrate far into the stem and the plant grows normally. Stem lesions can affect the transport function of the stem and cause wilting. The vascular wilt pathogens also have this effect by causing blockages in the vascular tissue. Some of them also produce toxins.

Stem distortions are not commonly induced by pathogens although the leafy gall bacterium (*Corynebacterium fascians*) causes a proliferation of the growing apex of buds which produce a tight bunch of leafy outgrowths commonly known as a leafy gall. This symptom is sometimes seen in bedding plants and also in some pot plants and is disfiguring without adversely affecting plant growth. Similarly, damage to the stem apex can result in fasciation, where the growing point becomes multiple but the resultant stems do not separate completely and remain fused side by side to produce a large flat stem. Fasciation is common in cucumbers although its exact cause is not known.

Leaves

For green plants the leaves and to a lesser extent the stems, are the main carbohydrate manufacturing areas. In the process of photosynthesis, carbon dioxide and water are converted, in the presence of light and chlorophyll, into carbohydrates. This involves the exchange of gases through the leaf surface. Water is also lost through the leaves mainly via the stomata by transpiration but also by guttation, through hydathodes situated at the leaf margins. Diseases which affect the photosynthetic area of the plant or interfere with the normal water relations will also influence plant growth. Leaf symptoms may develop on the whole or a part of the leaf surface and the effect on plant growth is sometimes proportional to the leaf area affected. Symptoms on leaves show considerable variation in both shape and colour. They may be chlorotic or necrotic and regular or irregular in shape, delimited by the veins, surrounded by a halo which may be yellow or red, or holed in the centre to give a so-called shot-hole symptom. Leaf symptoms caused by pathogens may show no obvious pathogen, with little or no surface growth of fungal mycelium or sporing structures, e.g. Downy Mildew on roses, or they may have obvious fungal mycelium and sometimes sporing structures, e.g. Lettuce Downy Mildew and Grey Mould on all crops; or they may have sporing structures such as acervuli, pycnidia, pustules or sporodochia but with no obvious mycelial growth, e.g. Carnation Rust and Rose Blackspot.

Pathogens, physical or chemical damage, adverse environmental or nutritional conditions, often interfere with the function of chlorophyll and the affected leaves may become pale in colour, show marked chlorosis and eventually necrosis, or severe chlorosis and necrosis accompanied by premature defoliation. Such symptoms are non-specific although when the distribution is taken into account there may be some indication of their cause.

Changes in the hormonal balance of the plant can affect the development of the leaves and result in a modification of their shape. A reduction of the lamina to tendril-like strands of tissue occurs in tomatoes infected by Cucumber Mosaic Virus and also by some strains of Tomato Mosaic Virus. Bubbling of cucumber leaf tissue is a symptom caused by Cucumber Green Mottle Mosaic Virus, and of low temperature damage in lettuce. Outgrowth of the leaf surface to form small flaps on the underside of the leaves (known as enations) occurs in tomatoes affected by certain strains of Tomato Mosaic Virus.

Leaves play a vital role in the regulation of the plant's water relations. The rapid loss of water from the leaves by transpiration has a direct effect on the uptake of water and nutrients through the roots. When transpiration is reduced the plant may show a reduction in growth rate and in extreme circumstances, leaf damage occurs. Excessive water loss results in wilting and although this symptom is most frequently associated with high temperatures, low humidity and insufficient water uptake through the roots, it can also result from pathogenic attack which increases the rate of transpiration, e.g. during the early stages of development of Fusarium Wilt and Tomato Mosaic in tomatoes. By shading the crops and by frequent damping, the relative humidity can be raised, transpiration reduced and wilting prevented.

Excessive water loss through the hydathodes at the leaf margin may lead to permanent cell damage and leaves then show localised marginal necrosis. The tips of leaves are also often most severely affected although with lettuce, tomatoes and cucumbers the entire leaf margin may be necrotic. Conversely a reduction in water loss may lead to the leaf tissue around the stomata becoming saturated with water. In the winter, lettuces frequently show this symptom, usually referred to as glassiness. If the condition is recognised at an early stage and water loss encouraged by reducing the relative humidity of the air, permanent damage to the affected tissue can be avoided.

Good plant growth and successful cropping always involves a balance between water uptake by the roots and water loss through the leaves. The main effects of leaf disease are therefore not only to reduce the photosynthetic area but also to interfere with the plant's water relations, both of which are vitally important functions.

Flowers, fruits and seeds

Seeds are produced as a result of fertilisation which occurs in the flower. The main biological function of the flower is the perpetuation of the species. Pollination and fertilisation are vital processes for the successful production of a tomato crop but this is not so with cucumbers where unfertilised female flowers swell to form seedless fruits. Many flowers of greenhouse plants are sterile and they are grown because of their aesthetic beauty. Diseases of these affect the quality of the end product.

Flowers may show symptoms of loss in colour as seen in chrysanthemums affected by Tomato Aspermy Virus, loss in size as with Chrysanthemum Stunt Viroid, spotting of petals, commonly seen in many plants such as cyclamen affected by *Botrytis cinerea* or complete collapse of the flower as when the capitulum of chrysanthemums decays as a result of attack by *Didymella chrysanthemi*, the cause of Ray Blight.

The quality of fruits may be similarly affected. Ghost Spot of tomatoes and the non-pathogenic Cold Mark disorder of cucumbers disfigures the surface and reduces quality. Some fruits are decayed by pathogens, for instance both *Didymella bryoniae* and *Cladosporium cucumerinum* rot cucumber fruits. Internal discoloration of tomato fruits sometimes develops when the plant becomes infected by Tomato Mosaic Virus although decay does not occur. The seeds in such fruits may be blackened and shrivelled and their germination impaired. Similar discoloration and damage to seeds occurs in tomatoes and sweet pepper fruits affected by Blossom End Rot.

There are a number of seed-borne diseases of bedding plants, but generally these do not affect the appearance of the seed. The pathogen attacks the seedling after germination.

DISEASE AND CROP LOSS

It has already been seen how disease influences the essential functions of plant organs and in this way may reduce plant growth and yield. In addition disease symptoms on flowers and fruits often have a direct effect on quality (Fig. 3.2). Yield is sometimes, but not always, related to the quantity of disease present. For instance there may be a direct relationship between the extent of root decay or the leaf area affected and yield reduction. The interpretation of disease levels and yield losses is, however, complicated by a number of factors such as the pathogen–host interaction, the rate of colonisation and spread of the pathogen, the time of disease development in relation to crop maturity, compensation made by healthy plants in the crop and various environmental and cultural factors which affect the development of an epidemic. Some examples of diseases and their effects on yield are considered in more detail.

Pathogen–host interaction

At the extreme, some pathogens are capable of killing their hosts within a short time of infection. This may happen at any growth stage with some pathogen–host combinations but with others the effect of the pathogen is more dependent upon the developmental stage of the plant. For instance, vascular wilt pathogens such as *Phialophora cinerescens* or *Fusarium oxysporum* f.sp. *dianthi*, both of which affect carnations, kill plants within weeks of initial infection. Crop loss with these pathogens is directly related to the number of plants diseased. If a carnation bed 1.25 m wide with a total area of 19 m² is first spanned by a Phialophora patch in the tenth month after planting, the estimated crop loss from such a single patch is approximately 11 per cent of the flower production. Similar losses occur with Fusarium Wilt. It is unusual for wilt disease outbreaks to be confined to single patches and sometimes

FIG. 3.2 Disease and yield loss.

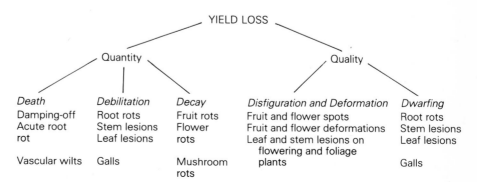

whole beds are lost during a 24 month period of cropping, with much greater losses in yield.

Pathogens which cause stem lesions can have equally devastating effects although there is considerable variation between them. Both *Phytophthora nicotianae* and *Rhizoctonia solani* attack the stem base of newly planted tomatoes and a single lesion may result in plant death. However, tomato plants are most likely to be affected by these diseases within the first 6 weeks after planting out and it is unusual for plants to be killed by these pathogens after this time.

Tomato stem lesions caused by *Didymella lycopersici* and *Botrytis cinerea*, although superficially similar in appearance, do not have the same effect on the plant, for whereas it is usual for Didymella lesions to ring the stem and kill plants, Botrytis infrequently does so. Indeed it is often difficult to detect any yield reduction resulting from Botrytis stem lesions (see Table 3.1).

TABLE 3.1 *Botrytis cinerea* stem lesions per tomato plant in relation to yield

Number of stem lesions/plant	2	4	5	16
Yield/plant in kg	3.15	3.06	3.1	3.3

From Fletcher and Scholefield (1976) *Annals of Applied Biology*, **82**, 529–36

Fungal pathogens of mushrooms attack the sporophores making them unmarketable. For instance, with Wet Bubble disease caused by *Mycogone perniciosa*, a yield reduction of over 12 per cent has been recorded (Fig. 3.3). Similarly, chrysanthemum flowers with Petal Blight or Grey Mould are also unmarketable. In contrast Botrytis-induced ghost spots on tomato fruits do not make the fruits unmarketable but can seriously affect their quality.

Pathogen colonisation and spread

Pathogens which rapidly colonise tissue and have an effective means of spread are more likely to cause large yield losses than those that develop more slowly. It has already been shown that the vascular wilt pathogens can cause a considerable loss in yield but their mechanism of spread from plant to plant is often slow and confined to root contact. A very rapid development of

FIG. 3.3 Relationship between the number of mushrooms affected by *Mycogone perniciosa* and the yield. (From Fletcher, Drakes and Talent (1974) *Annals of Applied Biology*, **79**, 1–7.

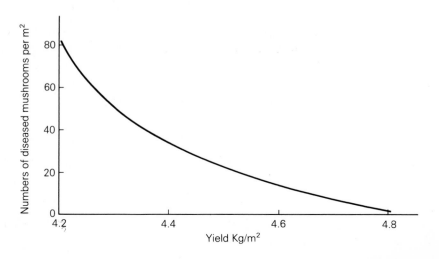

disease is seen with Tomato Mosaic Virus and Cucumber Green Mottle Mosaic Virus both of which are highly infectious. These viruses can cause up to 25 per cent reduction in yield if all the plants become infected at a very early growth stage. This is, of course, an extreme situation and it is more usual for spread to occur over 2 or 3 months until eventually all the plants are diseased. Overall yield may then be reduced by 10 or 12 per cent.

Root rotting pathogens generally have a gradual debilitating effect on the plant although rarely killing it. Some pathogens are very slow to recolonise treated soil while others move quickly and this can result in large differences in their effects on yield. *Pyrenochaeta lycopersici*, causes a brown root rot and corky lesions on tomato roots and is generally first apparent about 10 weeks after planting. It is a slow growing pathogen but progressively rots the roots so that the longer the crop duration the greater the extent of root decay. For instance, in one experiment 8 weeks after planting in untreated soil, about 8 per cent of the root area showed symptoms, after 16 weeks the decayed area had increased to 40 per cent and at 23 weeks to 50 per cent. Such an attack would be expected to reduce the yield by about 20 per cent. It has been demonstrated that the amount of root rot 16 weeks after planting is correlated with the final yield reduction (Fig. 3.4).

When there are differences in the initial inoculum level, Brown Root Rot

FIG. 3.4   The relationship between tomato root rot and yield. (From Ebben (1971) *Proceedings of 6th British Insecticide and Fungicide Conference*, 243–250.

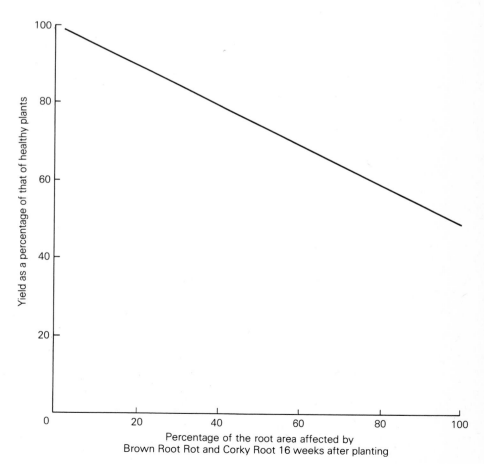

develops at different rates and if the crop is of long duration, it is common for root rot eventually to progress to fairly high levels by the end of the season even though the initial inoculum level was low. In such a crop, there will not be a clear relationship between the final level of root decay and yield. The most effective soil treatments result in clear differences in root rot maintained throughout the crop (see Table 3.2). Even then it is often very difficult to relate the amount of Brown Root Rot at the end of the season to the yield obtained from these plants.

TABLE 3.2   Brown Root Rot and Corky Root of tomatoes in relation to soil treatment and yield

Soil treatment	Percentage Brown Root Rot at the end of the crop	Yield (kg/plant)
Nil	70	1.5
Formalin	72	2.3
Chloropicrin	10	3.2
Steam	2	3.6

From Last and Ebben (1963) *N.A.A.S. Quarterly Review* No. 62, 68–75

Phomopsis sclerotioides, which causes Black Root Rot of cucumbers, may rapidly decay the roots of plants even after soil treatment because the pathogen is a quick recoloniser of treated soil. In an experiment in which cucumber beds were made with a pathogen-free medium but placed on soil which had a high inoculum level and compared with beds made up with infested soil, differences in yield were recorded as soon as harvesting began although, by the end of the season, the extent of root decay was similar in both treatments (Table 3.3).

TABLE 3.3   Numbers of cucumbers per plant, at 30, 60 and 90 days after planting into *Phomopsis sclerotioides* infested and uninfested soil

Days after planting	Number of cucumbers per plant	
	Infested beds	Uninfested beds
30	1.5	1.75
60	5	15
90	9	22

From Wiggell and Simpson (1969) *Plant Pathology*, **18**, 71–7

Disease development in relation to crop maturity

This point has already been made with Tomato Mosaic, Cucumber Green Mottle and tomato and cucumber root rots where the greatest reduction in yield occurs when the disease develops early in the life of the crop. A similar relationship exists with some foliar diseases and it has been shown that Leaf Mould of tomatoes caused by *Fulvia fulva*, has little effect on yield until it has been present and colonising at least 50 per cent of the plant's leaf area for about 6 weeks. This has important implications for tomato growers because disease development late in the season may not be worth the cost of controlling. But there are other considerations, such as the possible carry-over of the pathogen to subsequent crops if it is allowed to build up, and in the case of Tomato Leaf Mould, the possible allergic effect of a high spore concentration on the workforce. For these reasons, disease control is sometimes practised even though it is known that the yield will not be increased.

Environmental and cultural factors and crop loss

There are a number of environmental and cultural factors which have a direct or indirect effect on disease development and can thereby influence the extent of crop loss caused by disease. Pre-planting soil treatment, choice of cultivar, crop nutrition and of course the use of fungicides can all influence disease development and these are dealt with in Ch. 5.

FURTHER READING

Agrios, G. N. (1978) *Plant Pathology*. Academic Press, New York.

Dickinson, C. H. and Lucas, J. A. (1982) *Plant Pathology and Plant Pathogens*. 2nd edition. Blackwell Scientific Publications, London.

Fletcher, J. T. (1973) *Glasshouse Crops Disease Control – Current Developments and Future Prospects*. Proceedings 7th British Insecticides and Fungicides Conference, 857–64.

Horsfall, J. G. and Cowling, E. B. (1977). *Plant Disease: Vol. III – How plants suffer from disease*. Academic Press, London.

James, W. C. (1974) Assessment of plant disease and losses, *Annual Review of Phytopathology*, **12**, 27–48.

Ordish, G. (1951) *Untaken Harvest*. Constable, London.

CHAPTER 4

EPIDEMIC DEVELOPMENT

The effects of some diseases on crop yield have been described in Ch. 3. Generally, economic losses occur following the development of a disease epidemic. Such epidemics result when the disease develops rapidly and the majority of plants are acutely affected.

All epidemics start with the initial introduction of the pathogen. The source of the pathogen may be within the crop or very near it, or it may be introduced from a considerable distance. With the majority of diseases of greenhouse crops the sources of pathogens are frequently local, often originating within the crop itself. There are a great many potential sources and any one can be important if conditions favour infection, spread and epidemic development. When considering sources it is important to understand the mechanisms of survival of the pathogens.

SURVIVAL OF PATHOGENS

Pathogens survive between periods of active parasitic growth in a variety of ways, depending on the type of organism involved (Fig. 4.1). Some fungal pathogens produce propagules which can exist for long periods in a dormant state. Such propagules include resting spores, thick walled mycelial cells (chlamydospores or aleuriospores) and sclerotia. Other fungal pathogens are in an active state for much of the time on either their regular hosts, or on alternative hosts, which may be weeds growing near the greenhouse or the same host in a nearby greenhouse or field. Some pathogens are able to grow well as saprophytes, colonising and using any inorganic food source available to them.

Viruses are generally unable to persist for any length of time outside the living plant, but there are exceptions. Tomato Mosaic Virus is the most notable as this virus remains viable for a very long time (up to 50 years has been recorded) particularly in dry plant debris. Some viruses infect other hosts including weeds although they most commonly have a restricted host range. Cucumber Mosaic Virus is an exception as it has the largest host range of all known plant viruses and can infect many crop plants and a number of common weeds, including chickweed (*Stellaria media*), annual nettle (*Urtica urens*) and red dead nettle (*Lamium purpureum*).

Bacterial pathogens often survive in a dormant state in dry conditions in debris or in the soil.

FIG. 4.1 Mechanisms of
survival of pathogens.

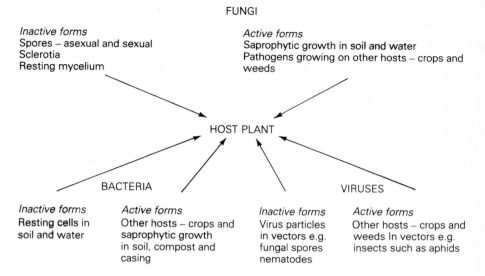

FUNGI

Inactive forms
Spores – asexual and sexual
Sclerotia
Resting mycelium

Active forms
Saprophytic growth in soil and water
Pathogens growing on other hosts – crops and
weeds

HOST PLANT

BACTERIA

VIRUSES

Inactive forms
Resting cells in
soil and water

Active forms
Other hosts – crops and
saprophytic growth
in soil, compost and
casing

Inactive forms
Virus particles
in vectors e.g.
fungal spores
nematodes

Active forms
Other hosts – crops and
weeds In vectors e.g.
insects such as aphids

SOURCES OF PATHOGENS

The interval between greenhouse crops is short so that spores which are
capable of short-term survival may live long enough to infect the succeeding
crop. For instance, lettuces, mushrooms, pot plants and chrysanthemums
may be grown in succession with an interval of a few days between crops
or there may be an overlap of crops in the same greenhouse. Pathogens
affecting these crops may easily survive from one crop to the next. Rotation
is not commonly practised in greenhouses although, by using mobile greenhouses, it is possible to reduce the incidence of some soil-borne diseases
(Fig. 4.2). Frequently the first crops grown on a nursery or mushroom farm
are relatively free from disease and, although this may appear to be the luck
of the beginner, the usual and more logical explanation is that the pathogen
is either not present, or is present at too low a level to affect the crop early
enough in its development to produce an epidemic. This situation generally
changes very quickly with successive cropping and most growers all too soon
gain experience of the effects of the main diseases of the crops they are
growing.

Probably the single most important source of some of the most important
pathogens is the soil and to a lesser extent the compost used for propagation.
This source has long been recognised by growers who have attempted to
overcome it by expensive heat, chemical or physical treatments. Where roots
are affected by pathogens the distribution of the pathogen in the soil will
closely follow that of the root system. Thus on a 'deep' soil it may be
necessary to treat the top 60 cm in order to eliminate the soil-borne source
of a root rotting or vascular wilt pathogen.

Debris, whether in the soil or elsewhere, also provides an important source
of pathogens and, although a crop may be removed from the green-house
as efficiently as possible, there is always some debris left behind. Debris heaps
on the nursery provide a continuous source of pathogens especially if the

debris is transported on boots, tools or machinery to the cropping houses. Other important local sources include surfaces where air-borne spores may have been deposited, e.g. the greenhouse roof structure, benching, stakes and wires. Other potential sources of contaminated debris and spores include containers such as pots and boxes, and the water supply, especially if it is local pond water fed by drainage from nearby land or the roof of the greenhouse. Even mains water when stored in uncovered tanks can become contaminated.

Pathogens may also originate from sources some distance from the crop. Many fungal spores are readily wind disseminated and a few spores can be carried many miles and may enter a crop through the open ventilators or doorway. Similarly, some pathogens are carried by insects and other animal vectors including man, and by these means travel long distances.

For many greenhouse crops, especially those propagated vegetatively, diseased young plants or unrooted cuttings, can be very important initial sources. Chrysanthemums and carnations and many pot plants are grown from cuttings, often by specialist propagators, and there is an extensive business in the sale of young plants. In this way diseased plants can be distributed even on an international scale (see p. 98). Pathogens may also be seed-borne and this source is very important for a few viruses and bacteria and also some fungal pathogens notably of bedding plants.

FIG. 4.2 Mobile greenhouse moved on a system of rails and rollers (a) to any one of three sites allowing rotation of the land.

DISPERSAL OF PATHOGENS

Some pathogens are very specialised and can only grow successfully on a limited range of host plants, or even on only one host species. For these it is imperative for their survival that they have an efficient means of dispersal. Efficient dispersal also allows those with wider host ranges to build up to epidemic levels more rapidly. The rapid dispersal of spore-producing pathogens may lead to an increase in disease from low intensity to high intensity in a very short time. Indeed, to the casual observer the disease appears to have developed overnight! Pathogens of this type include those with air-borne fungal spores such as *Fulvia fulva, Botrytis cinerea*, and the powdery or downy mildew pathogens, where most plants in a crop can show symptoms of disease in a very short time. Such pathogens produce large numbers of spores and successive generations occur rapidly.

Initial dispersal may take place from a single source or from multiple sources. Following initial spread, patches of diseased plants develop and these are often referred to as primary foci. Once established in the crop such primary foci provide more propagules of the pathogen for secondary spread. Spread through the soil is generally less rapid and, unless there is a multiple source of the pathogen in the crop, epidemic levels are less likely to occur. Tomato Mosaic Virus is an exception for, from small initial levels, an epidemic results in a short time, largely because of the highly infectious nature of the virus (Fig. 4.3) and subsequent rapid spread by workers who handle the infected plants. Epidemic levels of Fusarium wilt in carnations may also occur if the disease develops shortly after planting giving a very long period for spread.

Fungi, bacteria and virus pathogens have various mechanisms of dispersal

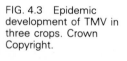

FIG. 4.3 Epidemic development of TMV in three crops. Crown Copyright.

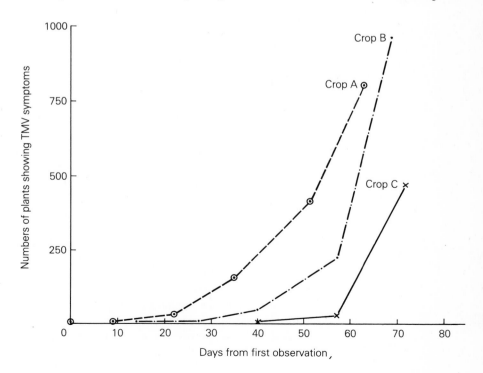

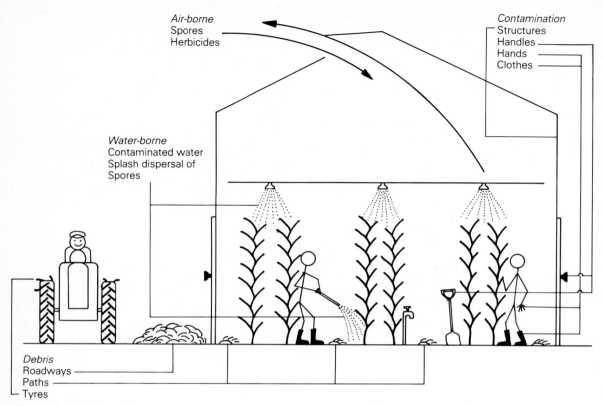

Air-borne
Spores
Herbicides

Contamination
Structures
Handles
Hands
Clothes

Water-borne
Contaminated water
Splash dispersal of
Spores

Debris
Roadways
Paths
Tyres

FIG. 4.4 Mechanisms of dispersal of plant pathogens.

and some of the most relevant for those of greenhouse crops are described and illustrated in Fig. 4.4

Dispersal of fungi

The most generally effective means of dispersal of fungal pathogens are air-borne spores. Many pathogens produce very large numbers of asexual spores and each of these is capable of initiating disease. Spores are liberated in various environments although some require fairly specific conditions for maximum spore release. Thus, although the downy mildew pathogens produce spores at high relative humidities, the spores are most readily released at low relative humidity when the sporangiophores dry and twist. A similar situation occurs with *Botrytis cinerea* although it is likely that the movement of the affected plants by workers or wind results in spore release. Powdery mildew spores are produced in long chains and only slight air movement is necessary to launch these into the air. The sexual spores of some fungi may also be air-borne and may be actively shot into the air. The sclerotia of *Sclerotinia sclerotiorum*, for instance, lie dormant in soil but after an interval, during which they have been subjected to low temperatures, they produce apothecia and the ascospores are ejected from the asci. Similarly, basidiospores of various agaric fungi are propelled from the basidium and become air-borne. Once air-borne, spores can travel long distances, but most land within a few metres of their source and certainly within the greenhouse. They may fall on either a host plant, on the structure, or on the soil. Some, however, may leave the greenhouse through gaps in the glass or through ventilators or doorways and then be carried longer distances. Once outside the greenhouse the chance of any one spore reaching a suitable host is very small but as they are produced in such large numbers there is always this possibility.

Water is one of the most important means of dispersal of fungal spores of pathogens of greenhouse crops. Water droplets landing on lesions splash and smaller droplets of water are dispersed each carrying a spore load. In addition, water moving over the soil surface carries spores with it. Water splash and movement of water on the surface of a mushroom bed is perhaps the most important means of dispersing the fungal pathogens of this crop. Both *Mycogone perniciosa* and *Verticillium fungicola* are dispersed in this way, splash causing local spread on the bed around the source of the pathogen and excess water running-off the bed resulting in spread to other beds. Water splash can also transport soil-borne pathogens to susceptible host tissue as happens with *Phytophthora nicotianae*, the fungus which causes Buckeye Rot of tomatoes. This disease develops when contaminated soil is splashed onto the fruit of the lower trusses.

Some fungal pathogens spread through the soil, either by mycelial growth or by growing along or in the roots of host plants. Pathogens which grow along roots can spread from one host to another at points where roots come into contact. The gradual extension of vascular wilt diseases along a row of tomato or cucumber plants, or more dramatically along a bed of carnations, are examples of this mechanism of spread of soil-borne pathogens. Such spread may also result from both root contact, and the movement of spores and contaminated debris on the soil surface. The root rot pathogens of tomato and cucumber illustrate different rates of mycelial growth and root colonisation by the two fungi involved. Whereas *Phomopsis sclerotioides*, which causes Black Root Rot of cucumbers, rapidly recolonises sterilised soil so that the whole cucumber root system may become affected in a relatively short time, *Pyrenochaeta lycopersici*, the cause of Brown and Corky Root Rot of tomatoes, has a much slower rate of growth and may severely affect only half of the root system and not progress to the other half even by the end of the crop.

Growth through the soil by rhizomorphs of *Armillaria mellea* sometimes leads to patches of roses being affected. An old tree stump left from a hedgerow frequently serves as a food source from which the rhizomorphs radiate out.

Although vectors are probably most important as disseminators of virus diseases, they do have a role in the dispersal of some fungal pathogens. Man is an important vector for diseases such as Didymella Stem Rot of tomatoes and Black Stem Rot of cucumbers. Both of these diseases are caused by pathogens which produce large numbers of pycnidia and if affected tissue is handled the spores are picked up on hands and knives. It has been shown that spores can be spread for up to 30 cuts after using a contaminated knife. Similarly, once the hands become contaminated with the spores of *Verticillium fungicola*, the cause of Dry Bubble disease of mushrooms, the pathogen may be transmitted to anything that is touched, including healthy mushrooms (Fig. 4.5).

Insects, by carrying spores, are agents of spread of fungal pathogens. The spores of *Verticillium fungicola* readily stick to the legs of mushroom flies

FIG. 4.5 Transfer of spores of *Verticillium fungicola* following contamination of a thumb:
(a) First print onto agar after contamination;
(b) 80th print;
(c) print obtained after washing hands twice in soap and water after (b).

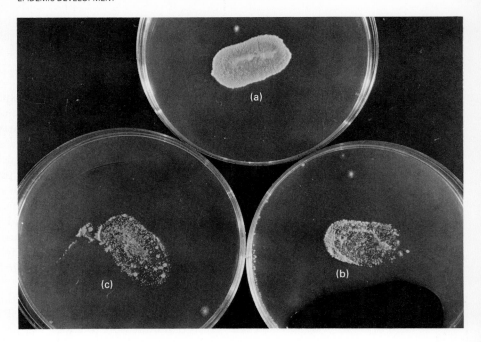

and are carried from crop to crop on the farm and possibly from farm to farm.

Very long distance dispersal of fungal spores can occur if the pathogen is transported on seeds or on plants. Seed-borne pathogens may be contaminants of the seed surface, usually as spores, mycelial fragments or contaminated debris, or the pathogen may be internal either as mycelium or as spore producing structures. A number of diseases of bedding plants are seed-borne, in particular those caused by *Alternaria* species (e.g. *A. alternata* on lobelia and *A. zinnaea* on zinnias). With all seed-borne diseases primary foci occur as a result of the pathogen spreading from the seed and subsequently spread is by one or other of the means of dispersal already described.

As many greenhouse crops are vegetatively propagated there is always the danger of dispersal of pathogens on infected cuttings, young plants or on stock plants. Very long distance spread may occur and diseases become internationally important when plants are produced in parts of the world where the natural conditions of temperature and light intensity favour both rapid crop growth and some pathogens. The increase in Fusarium Wilt of carnations during the past decade is almost certainly attributable to the dissemination of infected cuttings produced in a warm temperate climate. Such conditions are particularly favourable for the pathogen *Fusarium oxysporum* f.sp. *dianthi*. On a more local scale *Verticilium dahliae* has frequently been distributed in chrysanthemum cuttings which remain symptomless until flower buds are initiated, some weeks after planting. Foliage plants are now very frequently transported around the world and it is not surprising to find alien pathogens occurring on these. A recent example of such international dispersal has been the occurrence in England of *Sclerotinia rolfsii* on *Syngonium podophyllum*.

Dispersal of bacteria

Bacterial pathogens are dispersed in most of the ways already described for fungi. Man, insect vectors, water (both water splash and as an aerosol) and plant material are the main means of dispersal. *Pseudomonas tolaasii*, the cause of bacterial blotch of mushrooms is known to be spread by water, flies and pickers. Water splash spreads *Ps. tomato*, which causes speck of tomatoes and is also a likely means of dispersal of the tomato bacterial canker pathogen (*Corynebacterium michiganense*). This latter pathogen is also seed-borne and this is known to result in long distance spread. The bacterial wilt pathogen of carnations (*Ps. caryophyllii*), is spread in infected cuttings, as is wilt of pelargoniums caused by *Xanthomonas pelargonii*. Bacterial wilts are now far less common since the development of national schemes to produce pathogen-free stock plants.

Dispersal of viruses

Viruses are not dispersed as particles in the air but carried by vectors, in debris or in living plant material. Vectors play a vital role in the spread of many viruses which affect greenhouse crops and some are totally dependent upon one vector as their sole means of dispersal, e.g. Tomato Spotted Wilt Virus which is spread by thrips (*Thrips tabaci*). The efficiency and rate of dispersal of a virus is dependent upon its infectivity, the number of susceptible host plants and for some viruses the frequency of occurrence of vectors. One of the most striking dispersal rates occurs with Tomato Mosaic Virus (TMV) which is highly infectious and very readily spread by man on his clothing and hands. It is perhaps surprising that a virus as infectious as TMV is not spread by insects for, although aphids, whiteflies and other insects are frequently found on greenhouse tomatoes, they play no role in its dissemination. Few viruses are as infectious as TMV and because most growers have a rigid control programme for insect vectors, many of which are also pests of the crops, epidemic spread of other viruses is infrequent. Cucumber Mosaic Virus is sometimes an exception when infestations of the aphid vector *Myzus persicae* occur in the crop. Nematode vectors of viruses are rather less important in greenhouse crops than in field grown crops, largely because of the frequency of heat or chemical sterilisation of the soil and the relatively short time period over which most crops grow to maturity. Occasionally in roses, nematode-transmitted viruses do occur, although symptoms do not develop until the second year of cropping.

Patches of affected bushes appear as the viruliferous nematodes move with water through the soil feeding on the roots and if the greenhouse is situated on a slope, a down slope spread of the disease may become apparent.

Some fungi are known to be virus vectors, e.g. *Olpidium cucurbitacearum*, which transmits Cucumber Necrosis Virus in greenhouse-grown cucumbers in Canada.

Both nematode and fungal transmission of viruses can result in the long distance spread of virus pathogens in contaminated soil used for the propagation of plants. Such dispersal probably accounts for the rapid spread of Big Vein, a virus-like disease of lettuce, which is known to be transmitted by the fungus *Olpidium brassicae*. This disease has caused considerable crop loss in the nutrient film method of lettuce production as a result of the use of affected plants from lettuce plant propagators. Once established the vector produces motile zoospores which are capable of reinfecting each new crop as it is planted. The circulation of the nutrient medium ensures the easy dispersal of viruliferous spores throughout the crop.

Like fungi, viruses can be dispersed both in seeds and in vegetatively propagated young plants. Although many viruses are not seed-borne some important ones are, e.g. Cucumber Green Mottle Mosaic Virus, Lettuce Mosaic Virus and TMV. Primary foci of disease start from such seed sources. Many of the vegetatively propagated ornamentals, for example, carnations, chrysanthemums and pelargoniums have for many years been distributed as cuttings often affected by virus diseases. Such dispersal is international. Nuclear stock schemes for propagation of virus-free plants are now in operation in various countries and have gone a long way towards reducing the spread of virus and other pathogens in cuttings.

FURTHER READING

Dickinson, C. H. and Preece, T. F. (1976) *Microbiology of Aerial Plant Surfaces.* Academic Press, London.

Horsfall, J. G. and Cowling, E. B. (1977) *Plant Disease: Volume II – How disease develops in populations.* Academic Press, London.

van der Plank, J. E. (1963) *Plant Diseases: Epidemics and Control.* Academic Press, London.

Scott, P. R. and Bainbridge, A. (1978) *Plant Disease Epidemiology,* Blackwell Scientific Publications, London.

Thresh, J. M. (1974) Temporal patterns of virus spread, *Annual Review of Phytopathology,* **12**, 111–28.

CHAPTER 5

STRATEGIES FOR DISEASE CONTROL

It is essential for crops to be profitable for the commercial grower, and for him, disease control must always be considered with this in mind. Other plant producers, for instance the research worker and the amateur, may have other objectives and be striving to achieve a level of disease control which the commercial grower would find economically unacceptable. In many circumstances the commercial grower is prepared to tolerate low or even moderate levels of disease providing profitability is not affected.

The two basic approaches to disease control are prevention or disease avoidance (applied before disease occurrence), and treatment after disease symptoms are seen (Table 5.1). Control by prevention can be costly because it entails an economic outlay irrespective of whether the disease occurs. For various reasons including costs, fungicide residues and pathogen resistance, it is advisable to follow the principle of minimum fungicide use wherever possible. But there are circumstances where routine applications of fungicides can be justified and these include: the control of diseases where methods or fungicides are not available to give effective control once the disease has appeared; where the pathogen is so infectious that even the lowest levels of disease cannot be tolerated; where nursery management is such that regular crop inspection and disease monitoring is not feasible.

For many diseases control measures of any sort need only be applied when the disease reaches a critical level. Below this level the disease has little or no effect on yield but once the level is reached it is important to start applying control measures. Unfortunately, the biological information on critical disease levels has not been determined for many diseases of protected crops

TABLE 5.1 Strategies for disease control		
Control by prevention		Use of clean seeds and planting material
		Resistant cultivars and rootstocks
		Soil treatment with heat or chemicals
		Soil-less systems of culture and isolated beds
		Environmental control – to prevent disease developing
		Hygiene – elimination of pathogen sources
		Statutory methods – legislation to prevent the introduction of pathogens
		Fungicides as protectants
Control by treatment after disease appearance		Hygiene – the prevention of pathogen dispersal
		Environmental control – to prevent spread and epidemic development
		Fungicides to eradicate and protect
		Biological control

but there are some guidelines for a number of common diseases. For example with Tomato Leaf Mould (*Fulvia fulva*), it is known that severe levels must be present for 6 weeks before yield is affected. The same is likely to be true for powdery mildew diseases and even Grey Mould on such crops as cucumbers and tomatoes.

When considering disease control the grower must take into account various factors including:

a. the likelihood of the disease occurring;
b. the potential for yield and quality loss if or when the disease occurs;
c. the cost of disease control in relation to the likely return.

Complete disease control is rarely achieved and in many cases should not be attempted. There are many strategies available to the grower and these are discussed in detail in this chapter; the use of fungicides is treated separately in Ch. 6.

DISEASE-FREE SEEDS AND PLANTS

Most growers are entirely dependent upon their seed merchants for supplies of seeds. The incidence of seed-borne diseases of greenhouse plants is generally low. Seeds are an important source of some virus diseases, for instance Lettuce Mosaic. Lettuce seed crops are usually grown in areas of low aphid activity to produce virus-free seeds. Some bedding plant diseases are seed-borne but these can generally be controlled by seed treatment. Where there is a potential risk of seed-borne disease, seed treatment is frequently used. Seed treatments may be either physical or chemical (Table 5.2). Cucumber Green Mottle Mosaic Virus on cucumber seeds can be easily controlled if dry seed is heated at 70 °C for 3 days. This treatment does not impair germination

TABLE 5.2 Physical and chemical treatment of seeds for the control of seed-borne pathogens

Method	Host	Pathogen
Isolation of seed crops	Lettuce	Lettuce Mosaic Virus
Hot-air treatment of seeds, 70 °C for 3 days	Cucumber	Cucumber Green Mottle Mosaic Virus
Hot-water treatment of seeds, 50 °C for 25 minutes	*Phlox drummondi*	*Septoria drummondi*
Steam-air treatment of seeds, 40 °C for 10 minutes	Various bedding plant species	*Alternaria* spp.
Fungicide dust treatment iprodione	Lobelia	*Alternaria alternata*
captan/thiram	Various bedding plant species	*Pythium* spp.
Fungicidal seed soak, 30 °C for 12 hours with thiram	Lobelia	*Alternaria alternata*
Seed extraction by fermentation	Tomato	Tomato Mosaic Virus
Seed treatment with hydrochloric acid		
Seed treatment with trisodium orthophosphate		

providing the seed is dry and dormant at the time of the treatment. Fungicide treatments both as dusts and as soaks have been successfully used. A thiram suspension (0.2 per cent a.i.) at 30 °C used as a seed soak for 12 hours considerably reduces the level of *Alternaria alternata* on lobelia seed. Iprodione dust is also effective against this pathogen and also other *Alternaria* species which cause seed-borne diseases of some other bedding species.

Cuttings are always potential sources of pathogens. Virus diseases have been minimised or even eliminated from many vegetatively propagated crops such as carnations, chrysanthemums and pelargoniums by raising stocks of virus-free plants. Many of the older cultivars of the vegetatively propagated crops have been freed from the viruses which most of them contained. Great use has been made of the uneven distribution of the virus particles in affected plants in the preparation of these stocks. The meristematic tissue of some plant species may be free from viruses even though the rest of the plant is infected. If the growing tip including the meristem is excised and carefully cultured, usually on an agar medium, a virus-free plant can be obtained. The meristem is usually 0.1–0.5 mm long and must include one leaf primordium. Heat treatment of the parent plant at 35–54 °C for times varying from minutes to days can inactivate some viruses, and used with meristem culturing can increase the chance of producing virus-free plants. Stocks of plants raised in this way have formed the nucleus of nuclear stock programmes. Such plant material has the added advantage in that it is also free from vascular wilts, many of which are cutting-borne. Because of the attention to hygiene and great care used when nuclear stock plant material is produced, the plants are frequently also free from most other pathogens.

RESISTANT CULTIVARS AND ROOTSTOCKS

The use of disease resistant cultivars is, in theory, the easiest and most convenient way of achieving disease control. Ideally cultivars should be resistant to all the diseases of the crop. There are, however, very few crops where even a small proportion of the cultivars are resistant to more than a small number of diseases. The tomato is one of these. Over 70 diseases are known to occur on the tomato and there are some cultivars resistant to four of them, Tomato Mosaic, Leaf Mould, Verticillium Wilt and Fusarium Wilt. Unfortunately, many pathogens exist as strains, each with different virulence genes, so that a cultivar may be resistant or tolerant to some but not all strains of the pathogen. Of the currently available tomato cultivars, Nemato combines resistance to more races or strains of individual pathogens than any other. It is resistant to five race groups of *Fulvia fulva* (A, B, C, D and E) to race 1 of *Fusarium oxysporum* f.sp. *lycopersici*, to *Verticillium albo-atrum* and *V. dahliae* (races unknown) and to four strains of TMV (strains 0, 1, 1:2 and 2). This cultivar is exceptional, most of the others are resistant to only one disease at best and perhaps only to some strains or races of a pathogen. In some circumstances even this can be enough. One of the outstanding demonstrations of disease resistance is shown by the cucumber cultivar Butchers Disease Resister (BDR). This cultivar was introduced into the Lea Valley in 1903 and is resistant to *Cercospora melonis*, a fungus which devastated English cucumber crops from 1896–1907. BDR was selected by a local grower from a badly affected crop because of its immunity to the disease and was developed commercially. Since its introduction, *Cercospora melonis* has become a very uncommon pathogen. Most of the modern cucumber cultivars are resistant to Cercospora, many of them containing the original BDR resistance genes.

All too frequently resistant cultivars remain disease-free for only a short time, either because more new strains of the pathogen evolve, or because the pathogen population is a mixture of many different strains with one or more predominating at a time. The balance of strains of the pathogen often responds quickly to changes in the host population. It is difficult, if not impossible to determine whether a pathogen population is a mixture of different strains with some present in extremely low proportions or whether the pathogen produces virulent mutants at infrequent intervals (perhaps one in every million or more spores or virus particles) which are normally lost from the population unless there is a suitable resistant host present on which they can grow. Often such mutants, although able to grow on resistant cultivars are not as able to compete with other strains and do not survive because they are less fit. But for various reasons some newly introduced resistant cultivars rapidly lose their resistance.

The earliest tomato cultivars resistant to TMV remained resistant in commerce for only one season. Before their introduction, when only cultivars susceptible to all strains of TMV were grown, TMV strain 0 was predominant, if not the only strain infecting plants. Cultivars with the *Tm*-1 gene should therefore have been resistant to the virus population. The planting of *Tm*-1 resistant cultivars resulted in a large change in the pathogen population with TMV strain 1 predominating within a very short time. The incidence of strain 1 increased in proportion to the frequency with which *Tm*-1 cultivars were grown. Whether it is considered that the *Tm*-1 host caused the change in the TMV population, i.e. induced a mutation to occur, or whether it was acting merely as a filter and bulking up minimal components of the virus population, it is clear that cultivars with only the *Tm*-1 gene are of little value to the grower. The policy of plant breeders has often been to introduce a new cultivar at frequent intervals containing another gene for resistance and prepare yet another before the pathogen population has changed to overcome the existing ones. This policy, which exploits single gene resistance (or major gene resistance as it is often called), requires continuous work on the part of the plant breeder and on the part of the grower who has to make a rapid evaluation and be prepared to change to the new cultivars as required. Neither of these changes are always possible in a short time or even desirable, particularly if there is only a limited number of genes available. When all the genes have been used, the total resistance resource has been fully exploited. A more logical approach, but one which is more difficult and considerably more time consuming, is to combine as many genes as possible into each cultivar. Resistance of this type will only break down if the pathogen produces a complex race capable of overcoming all the resistance genes at once (Fig. 5.1). Some plant breeders have followed this approach by combining all the known sources of TMV resistance into tomato cultivars so some cultivars contain genes *Tm*-1, *Tm*-2 and the allele of gene *Tm*-2, *Tm*-2^2. These cultivars, for example Pagham Cross and Kirdford Cross, have been grown commercially for a number of years and so far no TMV strain

FIG. 5.1 Tomato Mosaic Virus – resistant genes and virus strains.

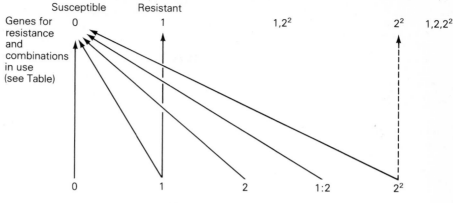

Known strains – Tomato Mosaic Virus

Resistance genes	TMV strains						
	0	1	2	(2^2)	1:2	$(1:2^2)$	$(1:2:2^2)$
0	+	+	+	+	+	+	+
Tm-1	−	+	−	−	+	+	+
Tm-2	−	−	+	−	+	−	+
Tm-2^2	−	−	−	+	−	+	+
Tm-1; Tm-2	−	−	−	−	+	−	+
Tm-1; Tm-2^2	−	−	−	−	−	+	+
Tm-1; Tm-2, Tm-2^2	−	−	−	−	−	−	+

↑ & + = Susceptible
− = resistant
(   ) TMV strains not yet found except for TMV strain 2^2 which has occurred very infrequently.

capable of overcoming their resistance has been found (if found it would be called TMV strain 1, 2, 2^2). However, most tomato crops now grown are of cultivars with only the resistance gene Tm-2^2 and, although these have been grown for 4 years, there have only been a few instances where TMV strain 2^2 has been found. Even then, the isolates have been poorly fitted and the disease has been easily controlled by the removal of affected plants, a procedure which never worked when susceptible cultivars were grown and when strain 0 predominated (see Fig. 5.2). This indicates that single gene cultivars are not always at a disadvantage even when the pathogen is as variable as TMV. A single gene which confers resistance like that shown by the Tm-2^2 cultivars is said to be durable and the cultivar shows durable resistance. Durable resistance is not, however, always governed by single genes. The mechanism of resistance conferred by the genes is probably a major factor accounting for differences in durability.

The lettuce crop provides examples of cultivars where the use of multiple resistance (R) genes has not been successful for the control of Downy Mildew (*Bremia lactucae*). Some of the cultivars which contain up to three R genes have succumbed to downy mildew as quickly as those with only single or even no R genes. Eleven R genes have been identified and ten are known to

FIG. 5.2 (a) The occurrence of Tomato Mosaic, the influence of resistant cultivars and the commercial use of cross protection on the incidence of TMV strains 0 and 1;
(b) incidence of TMV strains 0 and 1 from 1966–1975 in the UK.

pre 1966	TMV susceptible cultivars only. TMV strain O present in all crops. Tomato Mosaic widespread and severe
1966	Resistant cultivars with gene *Tm*-1 introduced. TMV strain O dominant. Tomato Mosaic widespread and severe
1967–8	TMV resistant (*Tm*-1) cultivars Supercross and Virocross grown to a limited extent. TMV strain 1 found in 4.5% of crops in 1967. and 24% of crop in 1968. Tomato Mosaic widespread and severe.
1970	TMV multigene resistant cultivars introduced. TMV strain 0 and 1 present in other crops. Tomato Mosaic widespread and severe.
1972–5	Cross protection with avirulent TMV strain MII-16 (strain 1) introduced. Strain 1 dominant in inoculated crops. Tomato Mosaic common but not severe.
1975	TMV resistant cultivars with *Tm*-22 gene used in approximately 50% of all tomato crops. Strain 1 dominant in susceptible cultivars. Tomato Mosaic not common or severe.
1980	TMV resistant cultivars with *Tm*-2^2 gene dominant. TMV uncommon.

(a)

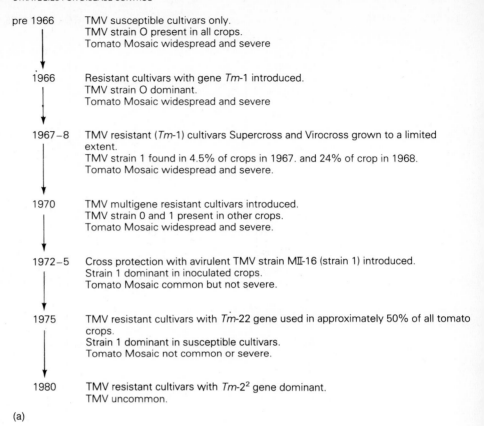

(b)

occur commonly in populations of the pathogen in Europe. The eleventh is less common but so has been the use of the corresponding R gene. If this R gene is more widely used it seems likely that the appropriate virulence gene will soon become more common. At present there does not appear to be an easy way of solving the problem of breeding lettuce cultivars resistant to downy mildew as the pathogen is capable of meeting every new challenge with a new multivirulent race, although in the USA some lettuce cultivars have remained resistant for some years.

A somewhat intermediate situation exists with tomato cultivars resistant to Tomato Leaf Mould. The pathogen, *Fulvia fulva*, is known to exist as a number of races, each capable of overcoming one or more of the resistance genes of the host. For convenience, in Europe the races of the pathogen have been grouped into five groups known as A, B, C, D and E with each group comprising a number of strains. Tomato cultivars are available with R genes for one or more of the groups, and Abunda, Bellina, Duranto, Else, Goldstar, Marathon, Nemato, Sonatine, Shirley Resistase and others are thought to be resistant to all of them (Table 7.2). Most of the other cultivars are resistant to two or three groups – usually A, A and B, or A, B and C – and although they have often become infected the extent of the damage is not as great as when a fully-susceptible cultivar is attacked. Although virulence genes capable of overcoming all known R genes are known to exist, some of the strains with complex combinations of virulence genes may be somewhat less fit. In such cases combining resistance with chemical control is more likely to be successful than relying on each method of control in isolation.

In addition to cultivars which have been bred for resistance to certain diseases, naturally-occurring resistance is known in cultivars of some crops, e.g. chrysanthemum cultivars to Verticillium Wilt. Much of this resistance has not been exploited in breeding programmes and there is still considerable scope for its use (Fig. 5.3).

Resistant rootstocks

Breeding resistance into commercially-acceptable cultivars takes a long time, and when resistance to more than one disease is required the procedure can be very lengthy. One way of providing a temporary solution for the control of root-infecting pathogens is the use of resistant rootstocks. Some closely related species, known to be disease resistant have been successfully used as rootstocks e.g. *Cucurbita ficifolia* which is resistant to cucumber Fusarium Wilt. It would involve a long and complex breeding programme to breed this resistance into a commercially acceptable cultivar and the use of the species

FIG. 5.3 Disease resistance in greenhouse crops.

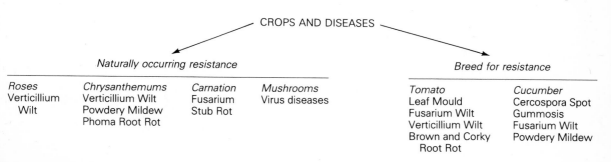

as a rootstock provides an acceptable level of resistance. Disease-resistant rootstocks have been used for a number of greenhouse crops, including tomatoes, cucumbers, carnations and roses. With roses, grafting is done for reasons of vigour and longevity of the crop in addition to disease resistance (Table 5.3).

TABLE 5.3 Disease resistant rootstocks for greenhouse crops

Crop	Rootstock	Disease controlled
Tomato (*Lycopersicon esculentum*)	Hybrids between *Lycopersicon hirsutum* and *L. esculentum* e.g. KVF, KNVF, KNVF2 KNVF/TMV Identistock KVF, Hires (Signaal) (KNVF/TMV)	Fusarium (F) and Verticillium (V) Wilt, Brown and Corky Root Rot (K), Root Knot Nematode (N), Tomato Mosaic Virus (TMV)
Cucumber (*Cucumis sativa*)	*Cucurbita ficifolia*	Fusarium Wilt *Phomopsis sclerotioides*
Carnation (*Dianthus caryophyllus*)	*Dianthus* spp.	Phialophora and Fusarium Wilts
Roses (*Rosa* spp.)	*Rosa chinensis indica major* *Rosa canina* selections *Rosa manettii*	Powdery Mildew Verticillium Wilt

NB Fusarium resistance (F) is to race 1 (sometimes referred to as race 0) except for KNVF2 which is resistant to races 1 and 2 (0 and 1).

The most successful and widespread use of grafting has been with tomatoes where a number of different rootstocks are available. Generally, grafting is a useful way of controlling soil-borne diseases of tomatoes particularly where soil sterilisation has either been done poorly or not at all. Control of Tomato Brown and Corky Root Rot caused by *Pyrenochaeta lycopersici*, and of the wilt pathogens, is possible by choosing the correct rootstock.

The main problems with grafting are the high labour requirement and the incomplete resistance of the rootstocks which may allow less common diseases to increase in importance e.g. Phytophthora Root Rot and Calyptella Root Rot of tomatoes. Also, it is important to use a TMV-resistant rootstock for a TMV-resistant cultivar otherwise TMV infection of the rootstock can result in severe necrosis of the fruit of the TMV resistant scion.

Methods of grafting tomatoes

The most common method involves a system of arching (Figs. 5.4a–g). It is easy to graft young plants removed from the soil and repotted immediately after grafting. With care, a very high success rate is often achieved.

Grafted plants, when planted into soil which has been chemically or steam sterilised, often grow very vigorously and this can be a disadvantage unless it is recognised at an early stage. By correct nutrition, the vigour can be used to produce greater yields.

If the main reason for grafting is to control vascular wilt pathogens, e.g. Fusarium and Verticillium Wilts, it is essential to sever the susceptible rootstock before planting. This is best done by, gradually, cutting through the stem of the scion below the graft union after the graft has taken. If the scion stem is cut through in one operation, especially before the graft union is complete, there is a danger that the whole plant will wilt and die. It is not necessary to remove the scion root if a root rot disease is to be controlled.

PATHOGEN-FREE SOIL

Some of the most devastating diseases of protected crops are caused by soil-borne pathogens. The fungi causing vascular wilts, root rotting fungi, fungal pathogens of mushrooms (if the casing is considered analogous to the soil), all have major effects on yield. It is therefore of considerable importance that soil-borne disease control is effective. The factors to be considered are:

1. The distribution of the pathogen in the soil and the nature of the survival structures.
2. The growth rate of the pathogen through the soil.
3. The type of disease caused, i.e. a localised rot or a systemic invasion.
4. The duration of the crop.
5. Nursery management and rotation.

Distribution of pathogens in the soil

In most soils the number of fungi per unit weight of soil decreases with soil depth so that populations at 40 cm are far less than at 20 cm. If the subsoil is relatively infertile, possibly unweathered boulder clay, then fungal populations decline very sharply. The top 20 cm of soil is likely to have the highest fungal and bacterial population of both saprophytes and parasites. Many root pathogens show distributions very closely associated with the distribution of the host root system; hence, if the soil is deep and the roots penetrate to depths of 1 metre or more it is likely that root pathogens will also be present at these depths. In general the highest concentration of fungal and bacterial pathogens occurs in the top 20 cm of soil and it is this layer which must be effectively treated (Fig. 5.5). The various survival structures have been described in Ch. 1 and those pathogens which produce resting spores or sclerotia are more difficult to kill than those which exist in the soil as mycelium or thin walled spores.

Growth of pathogens in soil

Some fungal pathogens are capable of saprophytic growth through the soil, e.g. *Rhizoctonia solani*, *Phytophthora spp.* and *Pythium spp.*, *Phomopsis sclerotioides* and *Pyrenochaeta lycopersici* but the rate of growth varies with the pathogen, the soil type, particularly whether it is organic or mineral, and conditions such as the temperature and moisture content.

Rhizoctonia solani causes severe disease on light soils especially when they are slightly dry and such conditions are thought to favour its growth through the soil. Conversely, Pythium and Phytophthora are known to flourish in wet soils partly because they depend upon a motile zoospore stage. In fact with such pathogens, spread may not be by active fungal growth but by the distribution of zoospores in the soil water, by drainage or by surface water movement from excessive watering. Some pathogens, e.g. *Rhizoctonia solani*

FIG. 5.4 Methods of grafting tomatoes. (a)–(c) Lifted plants; (d)–(g) plants in the pot. Reproduced by permission of Grower Publications H. G. Kingham (ed.) (1973) *UK Tomato Manual*. Grower Books, London.

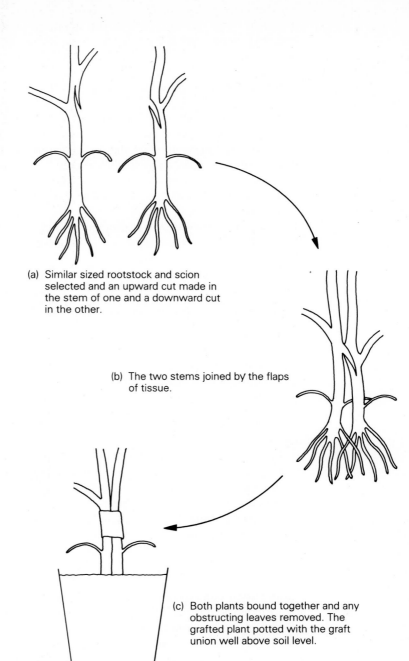

(a) Similar sized rootstock and scion selected and an upward cut made in the stem of one and a downward cut in the other.

(b) The two stems joined by the flaps of tissue.

(c) Both plants bound together and any obstructing leaves removed. The grafted plant potted with the graft union well above soil level.

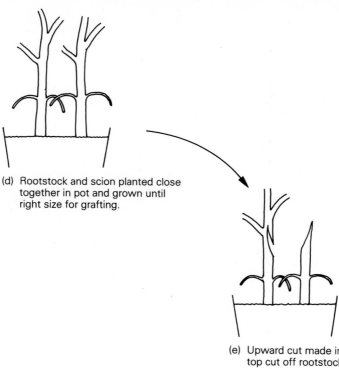

(d) Rootstock and scion planted close together in pot and grown until right size for grafting.

(e) Upward cut made in scion and top cut off rootstock with a diagonal cut.

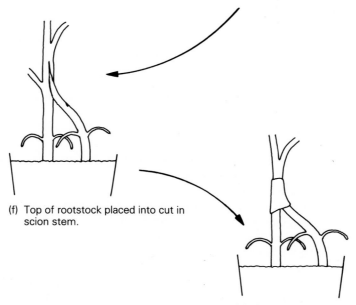

(f) Top of rootstock placed into cut in scion stem.

(g) Obstructing leaves removed and the two plants bound together.

FIG. 5.5 Distribution of pathogens in the soil in relation to root growth.

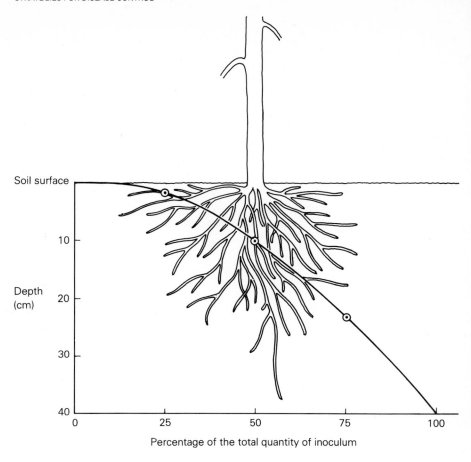

and *Phomopsis sclerotioides*, grow particularly well in partially sterilised soils because of the elimination of some, or all, of the antagonistic organisms.

Types of disease caused

Soil-borne pathogens cause two main types of disease, a localised decay of the root or stem base, or following entry through the root, systemic colonisation of the whole plant. Root rotting pathogens, e.g. *Pyrenochaeta lycopersici* affect tomato roots causing brown lesions at the point of entry and when large roots are affected, the lesions may be swollen and corky in appearance. The pathogen slowly colonises the roots but at high inoculum levels multiple infections result in severe root rot. Experimentally it has been shown that if inoculum is placed on one side of the root system, only that side is affected even though the tomato plant may grow in the same soil for many weeks. Even more dramatic is the appearance of the root system of tomato plants propagated in 'clean soil' and planted out into infested soil. In both cases the symptoms are confined to the area where the pathogen was originally situated. Conversely, vascular wilt pathogens of tomatoes affect the whole plant from a single point of infection below soil level. This difference is important when considering the efficiency of soil treatment as it is more essential for treatments to be effective when attempting the control of soil-borne vascular wilt pathogens than root rotting pathogens. Whereas 75 per cent reduction of the inoculum concentration in the soil may be satisfactory for root rot control, it could result in damaging levels of Fusarium or Verticillium Wilt.

Duration of the crop

The length of time the crop is expected to be in the soil is particularly important in relation to the growth rate and virulence of the pathogen. For instance, with Tomato Brown Root Rot and Phoma Root Rot of chrysanthemums, short duration crops are less likely to suffer severe losses even when grown in untreated soils with a relatively high inoculum concentration. Longer term crops of carnations, roses and cucumbers are likely to become severely affected if pre-planting soil treatment is not thorough.

Nursery management and soil rotation

On nurseries where the soil is monocropped it is very important to treat the soil routinely. Possible exceptions are all-year-round chrysanthemums where treatment for summer crops is less necessary. Nurseries where crops are rotated, e.g. tomatoes followed by one or two crops of lettuce or by cucumbers, and lettuce or cucumbers, and tomatoes in alternate years, are also likely to be affected by soil-borne diseases because the interval between the same crop is not long enough to allow more than a slight decrease in pathogen populations. The cropping sequence most likely to result in low disease levels is the tomato-lettuce-lettuce rotation where soil-borne diseases of lettuce can be controlled with fungicides and the short term tomato crop can be successfully grown with less than perfect soil treatment.

In any sequence of cropping it is necessary to have a minimum changeover period between crops so that the greenhouse is utilised for a maximum time during the year. This limits the type of soil treatment to one which can be done quickly and which will allow planting to take place within a short time of completion of the treatment. Any treatment which requires a long period for the dispersal of toxic chemicals will not fit into a close rotation. For this reason, treatment of soil with steam or methyl bromide is particularly acceptable for many growers as treated soil can be planted within a few days of the completion of the soil treatment.

SOIL TREATMENT

Heat and chemicals are used to treat soil in order to eliminate soil-borne pathogens. This process is known as soil sterilisation but strictly speaking this is not correct as even the most effective treatment does not eliminate all living organisms and the soil is not sterile after treatment. Partial sterilisation or pasteurisation are perhaps more accurate terms as they are usually used to describe the selective or partial elimination of micro-organisms from a medium. The aim of soil treatment is to kill all the disease-causing organisms, the pests and the weed seeds, at the same time leaving the beneficial organisms, especially the nitrifying bacteria and the antagonistic micro-organisms.

Because the process is most commonly referred to as soil sterilisation, this term is used in this text.

The efficiency of soil treatment with a sterilant, whether steam or chemical, depends upon a variety of factors including the soil type, and pre-treatment preparation, efficiency of application of the steam or chemical, the soil temperature and the moisture content at the time of treatment, drainage, types of pathogen or pest to be controlled, inoculum concentration, speed of recolonisation of the soil by the pathogen, and the duration of the crop in the treated soil. When the pathogen is deeply embedded in plant debris, for example in woody tomato roots, it is unlikely that all of it will be killed unless the exposure time of the debris to the sterilant is abnormally long. Pre-planting preparation of the soil increases efficiency if the large fragments of plant debris are removed. Similarly, in soils where root penetration may be as much as a metre, it is unlikely that steam or chemical sterilants will penetrate far enough to eliminate all the inoculum. Inevitably the roots of the new crop will eventually reach the lower zones and become infected. Inoculum concentration at depth is unlikely to be high so disease incidence may be insignificant unless the pathogen causes a vascular wilt disease. When done thoroughly, soil sterilisation should reduce the inoculum to a level which will allow crops to be grown economically. Although the effectiveness of the treatment is largely dependent upon the method used, quite often the results are influenced to a great extent by the operators. Treatment done poorly, whether with steam or chemicals, leads to unsatisfactory results.

Sterilisation by heat

Until recently heat, usually as steam, was the most commonly used to sterilise soil. In 1977 it was estimated that approximately half of the tomato growers in the UK used a pre-planting steam treatment. Before this, the proportion was higher but now fewer growers use heat and more use chemicals largely because of the increasing price of fuel. Steam sterilisation of the soil is the most effective way of controlling soil-borne pests and pathogens. Few organisms can withstand a moist soil temperature of 65 °C maintained for 10 minutes. Earthworms, insects, nematodes, weed seeds, most fungi, and bacteria are killed at this or lower temperatures. Generally the temperature must exceed 50 °C before there is any measurable effect and treatment at 60 °C and above is increasingly effective. An exceptionally difficult pathogen to eliminate is TMV, which when present in plant debris, especially thick roots, can withstand 10 minutes treatment at 90 °C. Clearly it is impossible for growers to attempt to achieve 90 °C or above throughout the total volume of soil the plants will grow in.

It is very unusual for the soil to be heated evenly. Inevitably there are cold areas and, in addition, steam rarely penetrates below the depth of cultivation. Generally, the most economic treatment is obtained by raising the soil temperature to 75 °C in the top 20 cm which usually ensures that the colder areas reach the thermal death point of most of the pests, pathogens and weed seeds. If soil is heated to temperatures in excess of 82 °C, toxic levels of ammonium, nitrite and manganese ions may result particularly in soils with a high organic matter content or a high natural manganese level and low pH

FIG.5.6 The effects of
heat treatment on the
nitrogen cycle in soil.

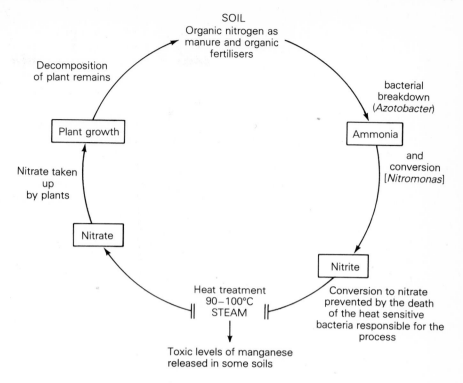

(Fig. 5.6). Toxicity problems can usually be avoided by allowing 6 weeks to elapse between treatment and planting (see Steam-air mixtures, page 81).

Methods of steam sterilisation

Methods of steaming soil have changed during the past 50 years and nowadays treatment from the surface downwards is by far the most common. This method is known as sheet steaming and is attractive because it is less expensive than other forms because of its lower labour requirement. Earlier methods usually involved the use of some form of buried pipes. The Hoddesdon pipe method is probably still the most effective of all the methods of soil sterilisation.

Hoddesdon pipes.   Steel pipes between 2 metres and 4 metres long are used and are L-shaped but with a relatively short vertical section (0.5 metres or less). Small holes (3 mm) are positioned in the horizontal section 12–13 cm apart on either side of the lower portion of the tube and the tube is closed at the far end. The soil is first cultivated to a fine tilth and should be fairly dry. A trench is dug 30 cm deep, the pipes inserted side by side, about 25 cm apart and all are connected to the steam source. It is important to introduce the steam slowly to avoid 'blowing out'. As the steam escapes through the smaller holes it condenses on the soil particles heating them as it does so. The soil becomes heated as the steam penetrates further from the pipe moving in an upward and sideways direction. Some slight movement may take place downwards although this is generally not more than 2.5–3 cm. Eventually the steam reaches the soil surface which is covered by a canvas sheet, sacking or a plastic sheet. Very little steam should escape before the soil is heated evenly to the surface and following a further 10 minutes treatment the whole volume of soil should be satisfactorily treated. Treatment times of 20–30 minutes are usual. The area treated at any one time is dependent upon the quantity of steam available but is generally not more than 5 or 6 m².

Inefficient soil treatment can result with this method if the movement of the steam through the soil is uneven and some areas become very wet whilst others are insufficiently treated. The surface is the last to be heated and is therefore the area most likely to be undertreated. This is unfortunate as the highest inoculum concentrations usually occurs in the surface layers. There may also be difficulty in ensuring that the long pipes are inserted horizontally because, if they are not, there will be variation in the depth of the soil treated. The large labour requirement and the very heavy manual work involved with the Hoddesdon pipe method is also a major drawback. The labour problem has been partly overcome by the use of spiked pipes.

Spiked pipes.   These consist of pipes similar in shape and size to Hoddesdon pipes but instead of small holes on the underside, short lengths of narrower pipe with pointed sealed ends and known as spikes, are fixed at 22–30 cm intervals. The spikes have a number of small holes 2 cm from their ends. The soil is prepared in the same way as for the Hoddesdon pipe method and the spikes are then pressed into the soil. Steam is slowly passed through the pipes into the spikes and through the holes into the soil.

The advantage of this method is the elimination of much of the high labour requirement and the hard work of the Hoddesdon pipe method but, because the holes in the spikes frequently become blocked, areas of soil are often missed. Such blockage is due either to soil or condensed water accumulating at the base of the spikes. Another disadvantage is the tendency for steam to follow the pathway of least resistance through the soil which is up the sides of the spikes, resulting in excessive steam condensation in those areas eventually leading to very wet soil and poor treatment.

Both Hoddesdon pipes and spiked grids may be joined into units known as 'grids' or 'comb grids' (Fig. 5.7). Such grids are usually shorter than the individual pipes but are useful for special purposes such as the treatment of isolated beds where they can be constructed to fit the bed size. Similar grids may be used in containers to treat propagating compost.

A further attempt to minimise the labour content of the Hoddesdon pipe method was the development of the steam plough.

Steam ploughs.   The depth of soil to be treated must be loosely cultivated in order to pull the metal pipes through the soil. These pipes are joined together to form a grid which is so designed that when it is winched through the soil it travels in a straight line and maintains a constant depth. By regulating the steam flow and the speed of movement of the grid (usually about 6–7 m/hour), it is possible to treat soil satisfactorily to a depth of 30 cm or sometimes slightly more. This requires a greenhouse free from obstructions and also very good anchorage points at each end of the run. It is also essential to have an automatic braking device to prevent disasters if the

FIG. 5.7 A comb grid with a metal cover used to steam treat soil.

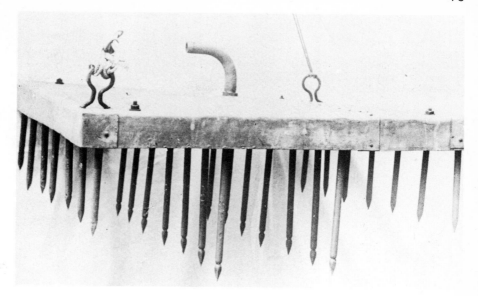

plough wanders off its set course. The labour involvement is less than with Hoddesdon pipes although a considerable amount of work is necessary at each end of the house.

Steaming from the surface downwards. This method of steaming is the most widely practised. Although generally not as efficient as the Hoddesdon pipe or steam plough methods it is often very satisfactory and has the added advantage that it requires far less manual labour. There are various methods used which have evolved from modifications of earlier systems. For example, some spiked grids are covered by a metal sheet or pan which traps steam on the soil surface. The first attempts to steam from the surface downwards without the use of modified grids was with metal hoods. These semicircular structures, of about 3 × 0.5 metres in size and trough shaped, were laid side by side and the steam introduced from one end. Because of their weight, a pressure was built up (approximately 9.8 kg/m^2 or 2 lb/ft^2) underneath these hoods. This pressure ensured a high surface temperature and pushed the steam down into the soil, which if loosely cultivated was effectively sterilised as far down as the soil was loose. The treatment time with hoods was usually short (about 30–45 min) and small areas (about 6–7 m^2) were treated at any one time. The labour requirement is moderately high but there is less heavy work. A disadvantage of the system is the need to walk over the treated area to move the hoods to the next position.

At present plastic sheets (polyvinyl chloride) are universally used to treat large areas (30 × 3 m) (Fig. 5.8). The steam is trapped under the sheet and, providing the soil is roughly cultivated, it will penetrate to approximately two-thirds of the depth of cultivation. As the steam moves into the soil it displaces air which must be able to move either sideways or downwards. Some of the most effective sheet steaming has been achieved on very open and well drained soils. The steam is generally introduced at one end of the sheet with a hose pipe blowing the steam into a bucket or box. The box used in the Humberside area of the UK is long and narrow and the method has

FIG. 5.8 Use of a plastic sheet to trap steam on the soil surface enabling the soil to be heat treated. Copyright Glasshouse Crops Research Institute.

become known locally as the 'coffin method' of steaming. Generally a heavy gauge PVC sheet (0.25 mm thick) is used and is anchored at its sides by weights (chains or sausage-shaped sacks filled with sand) or dug into the soil. The steam inflates the sheet in 1–1.5 hours, depending on the area treated, and once the sheet is inflated it is maintained in this position for up to a further 8 hours. The steam pressure under the sheet is very low (0.5 kg/m²) but this can be increased slightly by covering the sheet with netting or heavy cloth. The area which can be successfully treated with the steam available can be calculated from the steam output of the boiler. A boiler capable of producing 1000 lb of steam per hour will treat approximately 500 ft² as the steam requirement is approximately 2 lb/ft²/hour (lb × 250 = Kcal). Also as a general guide, steam penetrates the soil at the rate of 3–4 cm/hour.

Results with sheet steaming are sometimes poor. When first introduced, the technique was looked upon as a cheap and quick method of soil treatment and became known as 'flash steaming'. Treatment periods of as little as 2–3 hours resulted in 6–10 cm of soil being effectively treated which was usually far from adequate to give satisfactory disease control for long term crops. The efficiency of the method is influenced by:

1. *Soil type*: The more open the soil the better the results achieved. Soil with a high clay fraction cultivated to give moderate to large clods allows very good steam penetration and is effectively treated, providing the exposure time is long enough to allow the heat to penetrate the clods. Sandy soils, which run together, are difficult to treat as are those with a high peat fraction and high water content.

2. *Cultivation*: The aim should be to achieve roughly cultivated soil and not a fine tilth. Manual or machine digging is the most suitable preparation; rotavation is generally unsatisfactory unless the soil has a high clay fraction.

   The soil should be cultivated to a depth of approximately a third more than the depth required for the steam to penetrate.

3. *Drainage*: Any factors which impede drainage also affect the efficiency of steaming. A soil pan, high water table or a high moisture content of the soil, all reduce the ability of the steam to move through the soil and displace the air. Generally the drier the soil the more condensed steam it can absorb and the more effective the steam treatment.

4. *Sheet anchorage*: If the sheet is poorly anchored or has holes in it, the steam is lost either by the sheet lifting and the steam blowing out, or through the holes. This decreases the efficiency of the process. Sometimes growers allow air to be sucked in with the steam when the sheet is being inflated and, although this speeds up inflation, it usually results in poor soil heating. This is thought to be due to the air settling on the soil surface and forming an insulating layer, which prevents the soil from heating up quickly.

Permanent underground pipes. Other attempts have been made to achieve the efficiency of the buried pipe method by utilising permanently buried underground pipes or drain tiles. Steam is blown through these and if they are initially put in with steam treatment in mind (covered by coarse gravel or ash) they can be used satisfactorily. As they are usually buried deeply to be below the depth of normal cultivation (50–55 cm), the surface soil is often the least well treated. By securing a PVC sheet over the area and trapping all the escaping steam, it is possible to improve the treatment of the surface soil. Blockage of the holes in the buried pipes results in a serious loss of efficiency.

The distribution of steam with the main methods of soil treatment are shown in Fig. 5.9.

Steam air mixtures.   When some soils are heated to 100 °C, toxic levels of chemicals especially manganese, ammonia and nitrites, can occur. Soils high in manganese can present particular problems for growers of tomatoes and cucumbers as both of these crops are sensitive and show toxicity symptoms. Soils with a high organic matter content or where organic fertilisers have been added are liable to have toxic levels of ammonia and nitrite shortly after being heated to temperatures at or near 100 °C. This is because the bacteria in the soil which are capable of converting ammonia and nitrite to nitrate are killed by this temperature, whereas those which convert ammonia to nitrite are not. For this reason nitrite accumulates and peak concentrations are reached approximately 3 weeks after heat treatment (Fig. 5.6). Generally by 6 weeks or longer if the soil temperature is low, the concentration has declined to safe levels. The problems of manganese, ammonia and nitrite toxicities can be largely overcome if the soil is not heated above 82 °C (180 °F). Above this temperature the valuable bacteria which convert nitrite to nitrate are killed. A maximum temperature of about 82 °C is achieved with a steam and air mixture in the proportion of 1 part steam to 1.5 parts of air. If the proportion of air is increased, the temperature of the mixture is further decreased. The steam–air mixture can be used in the same way as steam. Only on some soils have steam–air mixtures been found to have sufficient advantage to justify the extra expense of producing the mixture and are infrequently used.

Other forms of heat treatment of soil.   Sterilisation by electrical heating, baking and heating the soil with paraffin burning machines have all been used

FIG. 5.9 Patterns of effectiveness of various methods of steam treatment of soil.
(a) Hoddesdon pipes;
(b) spiked pipes;
(c) sheet;
(d) sheet and buried pipes.

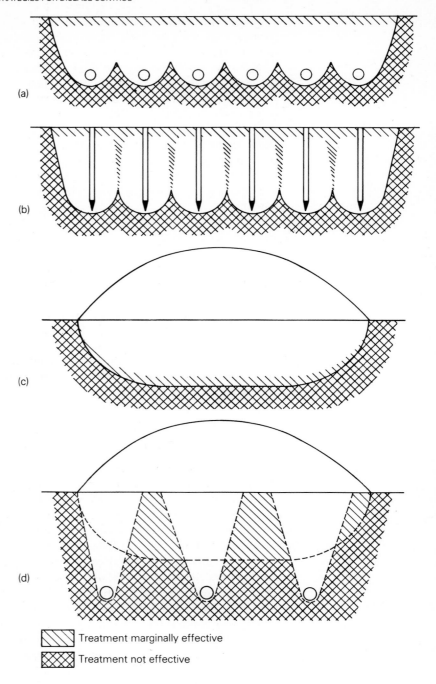

but these methods are generally confined to the treatment of loam for propagating compost.

Sterilisation with chemicals

The ideal chemical soil sterilant should eradicate all pests and pathogens but not the beneficial organisms such as the nitrifying bacteria and the antag-onists. It should be very effective in the vapour phase in order to distribute evenly in the soil, and to penetrate deeply. A sterilant should be effective at autumn and winter greenhouse soil temperatures (8–10 °C), and should be able to kill pathogens without an excessively long treatment time (preferably 1–2 days or less). The chemical should be readily dispersed from the soil or break down to non-toxic products at the end of the treatment period. Any residues left behind should be non-toxic to plants and operators. The ideal chemical should be safe for the operator to use and not unpleasant to handle. Economic criteria can be added to this list. Few chemicals come even close to meeting all these requirements.

Best results can be achieved with chemical soil sterilants if the soil is well prepared and the correct chemical chosen for the pest or disease to be controlled. The method of application may vary and the chemical chosen may be formulated as a gas, a liquid consisting of the active ingredient dissolved in an organic solvent used undiluted or diluted in water, or as a dust or granule.

Before treatment the soil should be cultivated to a depth of 30–35 cm, have a fine tilth and be level. The moisture content should be approximately 60–70 per cent of the field capacity, which is about the normal optimum for propa-gating compost and greenhouse soil at planting. A soil is at field capacity when it has been saturated and the excess water has drained away. When a diluted chemical is applied in large volumes of water it is essential that the soil should drain well and evenly to avoid the sterilant collecting in the poorly drained areas. Peat or well decomposed organic manure should be added to the soil before soil treatment. It is inadvisable to add undecomposed organic manure as this is often very difficult to treat and may release toxic ions. Organic nitrogen sources in the soil may break down to ammonium and nitrite ions, as already described for steam sterilisation, although generally to a lesser extent with chemical soil treatment. This factor should, however, be taken into consideration when planning the planting programme.

Choice of chemical soil sterilant

The choice of the sterilant used is often determined by the requirements of the grower. If he wants to replant the greenhouse with a minimum time interval between crops, he has to choose a chemical which is quickly effective and is rapidly lost from the soil after treatment. At present his choice is limited to methyl bromide. If he is able to allow a longer interval, perhaps as much as 10 weeks between treatment and planting, other sterilants can be used such as those which have methyl isothiocyanate as their active ingre-dient. Various products are registered for use as soil sterilants but regulations vary from country to country and local lists must be consulted before choosing a material. The main chemical sterilants in use in Europe include methyl bromide, various products based on methyl isothiocyanate, formal-dehyde, chloropicrin and dichloropropane-dichloropropene (Table 5.4).

Methyl bromide. This chemical is very poisonous to all living organisms and in many countries, including the UK, it can only be applied to the soil, mushroom compost, or within buildings by registered contractors. Methyl

	Verticillium and Fusarium Wilts	Damping-off and Basal Stem Rots	Root Rots	Potato Cyst and Root Knot Nematodes	Insect Adults and Larvae	Weed Seeds and Seedlings
Methyl bromide	★★★	★★★★	★★★★	★★★★	★★★★	★★★★
Methyl isothiocyanate	★★	★★★★	★★★	★★★★	★★★	★★★
Chloropicrin	★★★★	★★★★	★★★	★★★★	★	★★★
Formaldehyde	★	★★★	★★★	★	★★★	★★

★★★★ Very effective – ★ poor.

TABLE 5.4 A guide to the effectiveness of chemical soil sterilants

bromide liquid boils at 3.6 °C so at greenhouse temperatures it is a gas. The gas is heavier than air, tends to move down a slope and has very good powers of penetration moving freely in the pore spaces in the soil. Its movement can sometimes pose problems if it enters the greenhouse drainage system and finds its way into neighbouring houses. The gas is odourless at fumigant concentrations but most formulations contain a small proportion of chloropicrin, a tear gas, in order to give warning if leaks occur.

The contractor applies methyl bromide either from a centrally placed gas cylinder or from small canisters. In some countries, field application is done using tractor-mounted soil injection equipment. After preparing the soil, which must be moist but without waterlogged patches, the area to be treated is covered with a gas-tight polythene sheet. Generally 150 gauge is used and as this gauge sheet is slightly permeable to the gas, thinner gauge sheeting is not recommended. The gas is most frequently introduced from a centrally situated cylinder via a heating coil which vaporises the liquid. It is then distributed throughout the sheeted area through plastic tubing. If canisters are used they must be spaced on the soil surface before the sheeting is in position. The cans are subsequently pierced to release the gas. Even distribution of the gas is achieved if the air and soil temperatures are above 10 °C and preferably at 15 °C. The sheet should be slightly elevated above the soil surface when the canister method of application is used, but when introduced through tubing the sheet is left on the soil surface.

The sheet is left in position for 4 days, during which time the gas concentration in the top 20–30 cm of soil should be sufficient to kill pathogens and pests. The lethal dose of methyl bromide varies with the organism. A high concentration of gas for short duration, may be as effective as a lower concentration for a longer period, although it is likely that to be lethal, the gas concentration must reach a critical level for at least a short period, the actual level depending upon the organism and its state of dormancy. The effective concentration is therefore the product of the concentration and the time of exposure which is usually stated as the CTP (concentration time product). CTP values between 1000 and 5000 are often achieved in greenhouse soils with methyl bromide (Fig. 5.10).

After removing the sheet and ventilating the greenhouse the area is usually tested by the contractor to ensure that there is no methyl bromide gas present. When the safe point is reached the grower is able to rotavate the land and prepare it for planting which can take place almost immediately. It is thus possible to have an interval of no more than one week between crops, enabling a very rapid change over and maximum use of the greenhouse.

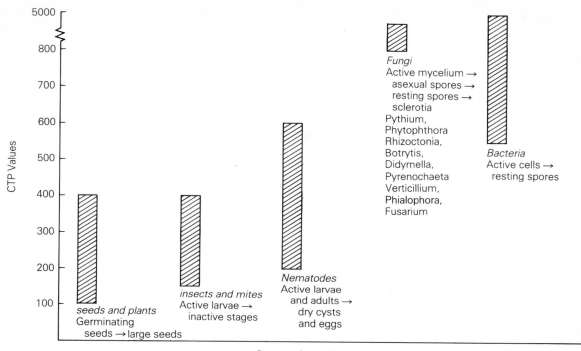

CTP Values

5000
800
700
600
500
400
300
200
100

Fungi
Active mycelium →
   asexual spores →
   resting spores →
   sclerotia
Pythium,
Phytophthora
Rhizoctonia,
Botrytis,
Didymella,
Pyrenochaeta
Verticillium,
Phialophora,
Fusarium

Bacteria
Active cells →
   resting spores

Nematodes
Active larvae
and adults →
dry cysts
and eggs

insects and mites
Active larvae →
inactive stages

seeds and plants
Germinating
seeds → large seeds

Groups of organisms

FIG. 5.10   The
sensitivities of the major
groups of organisms to
methyl bromide in order of
sensitivity within each
group.

Methyl isothiocyanate (MIT). There are a number of soil sterilants which depend on methyl isothiocyanate for their activity. Although the mammalian toxicity of MIT is not as high as that of methyl bromide, the chemical is still unpleasant to use especially in a confined space. MIT is effective against many pathogens and pests, although in practice results are often disappointing. This is almost certainly because of the uneven distribution of the sterilant in the soil. Various attempts have been made to improve the efficiency of application and the distribution of the material by formulating the chemical in different ways. A concentrate in xylol has been used to inject into the soil and a metham sodium formulation is diluted in water and used as a drench. The granular or prill formulations, known as dazomet, are generally rotavated into the soil. Mixtures with other sterilants such as chloropicrin or dichloropropane-dichloropropene have also been used to try and increase the spectrum of activity and general efficiency.

Most effective results are achieved when the soil is finely cultivated to a depth slightly deeper than that required to be treated. It should be moist (approximately 70 per cent field capacity), or dry if the soil is to be drenched, and the temperature should be not less than 7 °C at 15 cm. If the temperature is low, or falls shortly after application, it becomes increasingly difficult to free the soil of all toxic residues. Generally, the lower the soil temperature the greater the interval between treatment and planting. Some soil types are more effectively treated than others. Sandy light soils are most suitable; those with high organic matter content (in excess of 5 per cent) are generally less successfully treated. When drenched, the higher the volume of diluted sterilant used the more effective the penetration, and therefore the treatment (27 litres/m² is often recommended).

Following application by injection, drenching or rotavation, the surface of the soil is sealed either by rolling, surface watering or by covering with a polythene sheet. A time interval of at least 4 weeks is usually allowed to elapse before the greenhouse is well ventilated and the soil rotavated. If the soil temperature is low it may be necessary to wait for a very much longer period. When soil treatment is done after the end of October, low soil temperatures are common and it is then vital to wait the full time of 10–12 weeks before planting.

A simple test can be made for the presence of MIT in the soil. The soil is sampled at 10–20 cm depth making sure the sample is representative of the treated area. It is then placed in a container (for example a screw top jar) and some cress seeds sprinkled on the soil surface. A similar jar of untreated soil must be set up which is as near identical as possible to the treated soil. The two jars are sealed and placed in a warm (20 °C) position. If there is no MIT left in the soil the seeds in both jars will germinate in the same time, generally within 3–4 days. Any delay in germination in the treated soil indicates the presence of MIT and the soil should not be planted. The test can be repeated at 3–4 day intervals until there is no detectable inhibition of germination and it is then safe to plant the soil.

MIT is probably most effective for the control of damping-off, stem base and root rot pathogens, nematodes, soil inhabiting insect pests and weed seeds. In commerce it is least effective against vascular wilt pathogens or against any pathogens where the inoculum concentration is extremely high. Its main advantage over other chemicals is its relatively low cost, but this is often outweighed by the disadvantage of the time interval between application and planting and, because of the difficulty of the distribution and penetration of the sterilant throughout the soil, results can often be erratic.

Formaldehyde.   Once widely used as a soil sterilant, it has now been superseded by other more effective chemicals. The commercial 38 per cent solution, known as formalin, is diluted to give a 2–5 per cent solution, the soil is drenched with the solution and generally the higher the volume used the more effective the treatment. As much as 50 litres/m² have been used, but at such high volumes the soil must be well drained otherwise the time interval between application and planting becomes excessive. Generally the higher the soil temperature the shorter this interval. A gap of 6 weeks is allowed to elapse between treatment and planting especially when the soil is treated during the winter months.

Formaldehyde is also used to clean benches, boxes, pots and structures and is probably the most effective material for this purpose.

Chloropicrin.   Chloropicrin is a tear gas, is extremely unpleasant to use and should be only applied by trained operators. In the UK it is no longer approved for use in greenhouses. Previously it was injected into the soil and was most effective against fungal pathogens. The soil is covered after injection and in 4 to 6 weeks replanting can take place providing the greenhouse had been ventilated and the soil well cultivated.

Dichloropropane–dichloropropene (DD).   Once extensively used for the control of nematodes, especially the Potato Cyst and Root Knot Nematodes, this mixture is now rarely used alone and most frequently in mixtures with MIT. It is injected into the soil, using a hand operated injector gun, at 30 cm centres to a depth of 20 cm. The injection holes are sealed and the soil cultivated 6 weeks after treatment and again before planting.

Use of soil-less systems and barriers

An alternative way of controlling soil-borne diseases is to use a rooting medium other than soil, which is known to be free from pathogens and pests (Fig. 5.11). Various systems of culture have been devised using a variety of rotting media including gravel, straw, peat, fibre-glass wool, and liquid nutrients. The early attempts, often referred to as hydroponic culture, in which nutrient solutions were pumped through gravel in concrete beds, were not entirely satisfactory mainly because of the frequent occurrence of nutritional problems. The use of straw bales as a rooting medium for cucumbers has been widely adopted, partly because of the benefits of disease control but also because of other advantages with this system. For instance, the microbiological decomposition of the straw provides a warm rooting medium and also results in carbon dioxide enrichment of the atmosphere within the greenhouse. Attempts to isolate the bales from the greenhouse soil by standing them on a barrier such as sheets of polythene, have generally been unsuccessful because of the increased difficulty of adjusting the plants' nutritional and water requirements. Peat dug from depth and used in polythene bags, is free from pathogens, and peat bag culture has been very successful for some crops. The bags are often stood on polythene sheets which completely cover the greenhouse soil. Tomatoes, carnations and lettuce have all been successfully grown in this way. Very good crops of tomatoes and lettuce are achieved with the nutrient film technique (NFT), in which a complete nutrient solution is allowed to flow through a thin plastic gutter and the plants are stood in the solution which just covers their roots. The solution is continuously circulated around the system and the nutrient level, pH and conductivity regularly monitored and adjusted when necessary. Plants growing in such a system would appear to be likely to be very prone to diseases but this has not been the case in practice. The water-borne pathogens, such as *Pythium* and *Phytophthora* are generally easy to control and only epidemic levels of Big Vein and Powdery Scab, as a result of infection by the water-borne fungi *Olpidium brassicae* and *Spongospora subterranea*, have occurred. *Olpidium brassicae* is the vector of Lettuce Big Vein, and has proved to be an extremely difficult organism to eliminate from NFT lettuce systems. *Spongospora subterranea* causes Powdery Scab on the roots of tomatoes as well as on potatoes but is also a vector of Potato Mop Top Virus. This virus has not yet been found in NFT grown tomatoes.

Cucumber culture in NFT has not been very successful but good crops have been grown in synthetic fibre blocks known as rock wool. The plants are propagated in this medium and stood on rock wool pads which are kept moist and supplied with nutrients by means of an irrigation system.

NFT and rock wool are satisfactory means of avoiding soil-borne diseases but it is essential to maintain high standards of hygiene with such systems in order to prevent pathogen introduction and risk epidemic losses. Both systems involve a considerable amount of expertise on the part of the grower

(a)

(b)

FIG. 5.11 Alternative ways of growing crops using soil-free media.
(a) Peat in pots;
(b) peat in bags;
(c) cucumbers in rock wool blocks standing on rock wool pads;
(d) tomato roots in a nutrient film system.

(c)

(d)

who has to ensure adequate water and nutrient supplies at all times. Each system is liable to disasters if, for any reason, the nutrient/water system fails or overdoses of fertilisers are given. Control of these and other aspects of the crop environment can now be achieved by the use of computers. Some fungicides are safe to use in NFT systems, and details of these are discussed in Ch. 6.

Another approach to the control of soil-borne pathogens is the use of isolated beds. Peat or soil is used as the rooting medium and the bed, which is usually a trough and constructed of concrete, is isolated from the greenhouse soil (Fig. 5.12). Cheap isolated beds have been made by using polythene, but it is difficult to cultivate and sterilise the peat or soil between crops without puncturing the polythene.

Isolated beds were once extensively used for the cultivation of carnations particularly on nurseries where vascular wilts (both *Phialophora cinerescens* and *Fusarium oxysporum* f.sp. *dianthi*) were problems. The advantage of the isolated bed is mainly one of confining the roots to the rooting medium in the bed. Metal grids constructed to fit the bed ensure effective steam treatment at the end of each crop although good results have also been achieved with a modified sheet steaming technique. Isolated beds have not been extensively used for tomato or cucumber culture and the development of the peat bag method has largely superseded this technique for these crops.

FIG. 5.12 An isolated or raised bed used for the culture of carnations.

CONTROLLING THE ENVIRONMENT

The greenhouse grower has the unique ability to exert some control over the environmental conditions in which his crops are growing. The main environmental factors which affect crop growth and disease development are temperature of both air and soil, relative humidity, soil water content, and light, both as day length and light intensity. All of these can be controlled to a greater or lesser extent depending upon the sophistication of the equipment available (Fig. 5.13). Control of disease by environmental manipulation is generally not cheap if it involves the use of fuel but it has the advantage that there are no chemical residues or phytotoxicity problems. It can be used in conjunction with fungicides and results in minimal fungicide usage. Although the various facets of the environment interact, for instance temperature affects humidity, each is considered separately to illustrate some of the effects of each factor on disease development and control.

Pathogens often have fairly clearly defined temperature optima for infection, colonisation and disease development, although the optimum temperature may vary with different pathogens and also for each of the stages leading to symptom expression. Frequently the most favourable temperature for a pathogen is around the temperature optimum for the crop and little can be done to control disease by temperature manipulation unless a short spell of sub-optimal conditions for the crop will result in a dramatic decrease in disease development. This occurs with Verticillium Wilt of tomatoes caused by *Verticillium albo-atrum* where temperatures in excess of 25 °C prevent its further development. A spell of about 3 days at these temperatures arrests the development of the pathogen and, on return to more normal temperatures, the disease has considerably declined. Similarly, false truffle (*Diehliomyces microsporus*), a competitive fungus in mushroom production, is favoured by high compost temperatures and becomes a problem when the compost

FIG. 5.13 Equipment used in the greenhouse to assist in environmental control.
(a) An aspirated screen containing thermostats and recording equipment;
(b) a propane burner used to produce carbon dioxide.

is at 21 °C or above. By keeping the compost temperature at 15 °C for the initial period of crop development, the effects of this competitor can be diminished if not eliminated.

Often the temperature which inhibits development of the pathogen is also damaging to the crop. Temperatures of about 30 °C almost completely inhibit growth and sporulation of *Botrytis cinerea* but this temperature is not used to control diseases caused by this pathogen because most crops would be damaged by such a high temperature. A possible exception is the cucumber crop where in very low greenhouses temperatures may reach 45 °C for short periods in sunny weather. *Botrytis cinerea* is uncommon in these crops.

Temperature has a direct effect on symptom expression and symptoms can be reduced in intensity by manipulating the temperature. Carnations infected by the wilt fungus *Fusarium oxysporum* f.sp. *dianthi* show no symptoms at 10 °C but a change of temperature to 20 °C results in rapid symptom expression. Similarly, tomato plants infected with a distorting strain of Tomato Mosaic Virus develop severe distortion symptoms at 10 °C but not at 20 °C. With a yellow mosaic strain of TMV, the yellow coloration is much more marked at higher temperatures. Pelargoniums grown at low temperatures show very marked symptoms of Pelargonium Leaf Curl and Ring Spot Viruses, but at high temperatures (often summer temperatures are high enough) the distortion and yellow ring spot symptoms disappear. Pelargonium plants may sometimes be cured by a period of warm summer temperatures. The effect of high temperatures on virus distribution in the plant is utilised in the heat treatment and meristem cutting technique which has been successfully used to free cultivars of carnations, chrysanthemums and pelargoniums from virus diseases.

Temperature has a direct effect on relative humidity (RH) and this is probably the single most important factor in the development of foliar pathogens of greenhouse crops. The amount of water held in the air is dependent upon the air temperature and, by altering the temperature, it is possible to vary its capacity. For instance at 10 °C the air may be fully saturated, i.e. near to or at 100 per cent RH, but by raising the air temperature 1 or 2 °C the quantity of water held at 10 °C is only enough to produce a relative humidity of 97 and 93 per cent respectively. Similarly, by dropping the temperature to 9 °C, the air can no longer hold all its water and surface condensation occurs, i.e. dew point is reached. The situation is, of course, dynamic, so that raising the temperature may only reduce the humidity for a short time as more water can be taken up by the warmer air and, if the greenhouse is kept closed, the atmosphere will return to saturation. By warming the air and by ventilating so that there is a continuous, if only very slow, movement of air throughout the crop, it is possible to maintain a constant state of water loss both from the plant and all other surfaces of the crop. These conditions are are likely to be less favourable for infection and sporulation. Such diseases as Potato Blight, Downy Mildew of lettuce and cucumbers, rust diseases and Bacterial Blotch of mushrooms are all dependent upon deposition of water on the plant surface, i.e. conditions of dew point within the crop. Dew point is most frequently reached in greenhouses in the spring or early summer when, during the day, the greenhouse temperature is high, perhaps up to 25 °C and as the sun goes down the temperature falls to 18 °C. A temperature drop of 7 °C may take place over a period of 5 or 6 hours and if the greenhouse is closed throughout this period dew point will be reached at 22 °C (assuming 85 per cent at 25 °C and a constant water content of the air throughout this period) and water will condense on the plant surface and continue to do so for a considerable time. This can only be avoided by ventilation and heating even though the air temperature may be above the desired temperature for the crop.

Recently computers have been used to monitor environmental conditions and to adjust heating and ventilating to control both temperature and relative humidity. The control of relative humidity with a computer is likely to be less expensive in terms of fuel consumption than control by conventional means because minute adjustments can be continuously made and the excessive use of heat and ventilation avoided. Computers can be programmed to control the relative humidity at 85 per cent or below or they may be programmed to keep a constant water vapour pressure so that at a temperature maximum of, say 22 °C, the relative humidity is 85 per cent but as the temperature falls the control of the vapour pressure does not result in an increase in the relative humidity. Which ever method is used, it is advisable to attempt to control the relative humidity at 85 per cent maximum because, at the leaf surface, it is likely to be about 10 per cent higher and most fungal spores can germinate well at relative humidities above 95 per cent.

Powdery mildew diseases are different in their requirement as spore germination is inhibited by the presence of water but encouraged by very high humidities, i.e. 95 per cent RH and above.

To minimise foliar diseases it is necessary to ensure that water is lost from the crop by the normal physiological processes and evaporation is occurring from all other surfaces of the greenhouse. Although this is easily achieved by simultaneously heating and ventilating, the cost of this procedure is considerable. Ventilation alone will help to minimise the risk of epidemic spread of fungal pathogens and everything possible should be done to allow air movement throughout the crop. Fans can sometimes help although there is little point in circulating saturated air and such air movement may disperse spores of pathogens making the situation worse. Heat saving techniques, such as thermal screens, can result in long periods of high relative humidity and may increase the disease risk.

The amount of water reaching the soil is under the control of the grower, although on deep peaty and clay soils there is often a large water reserve which is sufficient for plant growth even if the crop is not watered. The wetness of the soil can affect the development of some diseases, especially those which are spread by pathogens with a motile zoospore stage, e.g. species of *Olpidium, Pythium* and *Phytophthora.* Epidemic spread of Pythium Stem Rot of chrysanthemums (Iceberg disease) occurs after the soil has been flooded. Damping-off diseases caused by *Pythium* can be similarly encouraged. The effects of root rots of most crops are accentuated when the soil is wet because the healthy roots do not function well. In all these instances control of the water supply can help to reduce the incidence of the disease.

The amount of water has an indirect effect on disease incidence because it affects the availability of nutrients. Generally, wet soils have lower levels of soluble salts and in these conditions growth can be rank. Tomatoes or cucumbers grown in this way are more likely to be susceptible to stem rotting diseases, in particular those caused by *Botrytis cinerea.* Similarly, such tomato plants appear to be more susceptible to bacterial Pith Necrosis (*Pseudomonas corrugata*).

Day length and light intensity are not factors that have a marked direct effect on disease development and therefore control. Day length adjustments are made in the production of chrysanthemums, and day length and light intensity controlled in the propagation of plants such as lettuces, tomatoes and cucumbers. Often, the use of additional light, particularly early in the year, results in plant growth which appears to be less disease prone. Although light is known to have an effect on the germination of spores of some pathogens, this factor has not yet been utilised for the control of diseases of greenhouse crops. Shading is often practised by growers when crops are wilting, but this is probably because of the effect it has on the temperature in the greenhouse rather than its effect on light intensity.

HYGIENE

Most people have a clear concept of hygiene and all that it entails, particularly when they consider themselves and their homes. Its value is never doubted; there are many clear examples of illness and even death attributable to lapses in hygiene. What is involved in hygiene in the culture of greenhouse crops is sometimes less clear, although the principles are very much the same as those applied in the home. The grower must aim to minimise the chance of crop diseases occurring by ensuring that he has done all that is possible to eliminate sources of the pathogens. The argument is further compounded by introducing an economic dimension; what is economically worthwhile? It is very difficult to evaluate the benefits gained by spending a lot of time on hygiene but it is true to say that, in general, where simple rules of hygiene are strictly adhered to there are fewer disease epidemics than where only a token gesture, or no attempt at all, is made. Generally, attention to the detail of hygiene is accompanied by tidiness and efficiency and the work environment is correspondingly more pleasant than that where dirt, debris and chaos predominate. In the context of greenhouse crops, hygiene can be defined as, 'the reduction or elimination of pest and disease potential by physical or chemical means'. In effect, this involves the elimination of inoculum sources, and one of the most important – treatment of the soil – has already been discussed. The infected or contaminated remains of the previous crop is a very common source of plant pathogens and often provides a high concentration of contaminating debris. If, at crop termination, the greenhouse is first chemically treated with a disinfectant or fumigant, this helps to reduce the pathogen population on surfaces. As much as possible of the root system and supporting strings and ties should also be taken away. The main sources of pathogens where hygiene is important are:

1. The greenhouse structure, including benches, supporting wires and posts.
2. Water.
3. Dumps.
4. Pots and boxes.
5. Workers.

The greenhouse structure

Pathogens with spores or other propagules which can withstand desiccation, alternate wetting and drying, and considerable variations in air temperature are likely to survive between crops on any surfaces within the greenhouse. Sometimes spores penetrate deeply into cracks and crannies which usually abound in any structure and, although such spores present a potential problem, they must reappear and reach a suitable host before they can induce disease. The chance of such reappearance is unlikely except when they are released during the course of renovation or rebuilding, e.g. when rebuilding a mushroom farm, disease epidemics frequently occur and are often attributed to the release of such spores. Generally, the grower is most likely to treat surfaces where, sooner or later, any surviving inoculum is likely to come into direct contact with the next crop.

The two methods commonly used to clean the structure are to wash down with a disinfectant or fumigate. Washing down can be effective although it is often unpleasant for the operator. It is best done with a powerful jet of water so that plant debris is also removed. A satisfactory result can be obtained with dilute disinfectant, such as 2 per cent formalin or a 2 per cent formulation of a phenolic distillate, with a wetter added – especially if very dry surfaces are to be treated. Alternatively, the structure can be fumigated.

Sulphur was once the main chemical used and rock sulphur was burned at the rate of 450 g/28 m^3 (equivalent to 1 lb/1000 ft^3). The sulphur dioxide produced is a very potent fungicide and is soluble in water, eventually forming sulphuric acid – a powerful corrosive to man, plants and metals. For this reason, fumigation with sulphur must not be done in a house where the fumes may escape into a neighbouring crop nor should it be used in a metal structure. The most commonly used fumigant is formaldehyde, a poisonous chemical which in the vapour phase is an extremely effective biocide. Fumigation can be done very simply by using a powerful oxidising agent such as crystals of potassium permanganate. When these are mixed with formaldehyde, heat is generated and formaldehyde fumes are given off. Various rates of the reactants have been used but 100 g of fine crystals of potassium permanganate to 0.25 litres of commercial formalin (38 per cent formaldehyde) per 28 m^3 (1000 ft^3) has been found to be effective involving the use of a minimum amount of permanganate for an optimum generation of formaldehyde gas. The usual procedure is to place metal containers at intervals along the greenhouse with the formalin in them allowing approximately a 9 litre capacity container for every 1 litre of formalin to be used. If the containers are too small the reactants will overflow and less formaldehyde will be generated. Very large containers and large quantities of the ingredients should not be used and it is advisable not to exceed 10 litres of formalin in any one container which should be of at least 90 litre capacity. It is better to have a number of small containers with smaller quantities of reactants than to have few large ones both for the best distribution of the formaldehyde and also for reasons of safety. The cubic capacity of the greenhouse must be calculated in order to work out the volume of formalin needed. The appropriate amount of potassium permanganate is then dropped into each container. Paper should never be allowed to enter the container because the heat of the reaction may result in a fire. The operators must move quickly along the greenhouse as the reaction is rapid.

For the best results with formalin fumigation, the air temperature of the greenhouse should be at least 10 °C and the relative humidity between 50 and 80 per cent. Puddles and wet surfaces should be avoided as far as possible as the formaldehyde gas dissolves in water and the concentration of gas in the air rapidly decreases. The greenhouse should be kept closed for 24 hours after fumigation and at the end of this period fully ventilated. Replanting can take place within 24 hours of airing.

Similar results can be obtained by fogging formaldehyde using specially designed thermal fogging machine. A formulation of formaldehyde for fogging is available and the recommended rate of use is 1 litre of product per 250 m^3.

If greenhouses are fumigated at crop termination it is important to remove the dead plants within a few days otherwise some pathogens will begin to sporulate from deep seated lesions.

Water

Some pathogens are readily water-borne but it is very unusual for mains water to be contaminated. Water tanks filled from the mains should always be covered to prevent contamination by dust and debris, and also to prevent the growth of algae by excluding light. If pond water must be used it can be sterilised by chlorination before storage. The shorter the storage period, the greater the risk of pathogens surviving the treatment. Water collected from greenhouse roofs and stored in large lagoons is generally disease-free providing the storage area is kept clean. The risk of herbicide contamination of the water in agricultural areas should not be overlooked. Lagoons should be sited in positions where sprays will not drift from nearby cereal crops. However, chemicals may fall on the greenhouse roof and be carried by rain-water to the storage area. Water from dykes has been found to be the source of both Tomato Mosaic Virus and Cucumber Green Mottle Mosaic Virus. Both viruses have been traced to affected crop debris dumped into the dykes. It is vitally important to ensure that crop debris is not dumped anywhere near a water storage area.

Dumps

Disposing of the old crop can present real problems. If the dump is made on the nursery it should be well away from all crops and preferably downwind. The debris should be covered with soil or temporarily covered with plastic sheeting. Spraying the surface of the dump at regular intervals with a disin-fectant can also help. Green debris is extremely difficult to burn and attempts often result in unheated or partially burned pieces left on the surface or, worse still, carried up by convection currents and deposited on a crop or on treated soil. When the dump is visited regularly there is always the possibility that boot-borne inoculum will be reintroduced into sterilised soil. It is important to try to avoid this by using a disinfectant bath at the exit point from the dump, both for boots and for wheels of vehicles. Similarly, a double insur-ance can be obtained by having a disinfectant pad in the doorway of the greenhouse. Almost any disinfectant used to saturate a foam pad will remain effective for some time.

Pots, boxes and other plant containers

Plant debris on containers is likely to initiate disease as soon as the containers are used. Cleaning should begin by washing them in water plus a wetter, to ensure that all the dry soil is removed. Sometimes boxes or pots are dipped in a disinfectant but this process must allow sufficient contact time for patho-gens to be killed. The most effective chemical dip treatment is a 2–5 per cent formalin solution. The pots or boxes should be immersed for up to 1 hour and then covered with a plastic sheet for a further 24 hours after treatment. It takes some while for all the fumes to disperse so treatment should be done several weeks before the containers are required.

Mushroom growers use sodium pentachlorophenate as a box dip and, by having two sets of boxes, it is possible to have one set in use when the other is being aired. This treatment has the additional advantage that it prevents the mushroom mycelium from penetrating the wood and the compost can then be readily tipped out at the end of the cropping. The chemical is also a wood preservative.

Boxes and pots can be steam or methyl bromide treated. Steam treatment without damage, is also possible for some plastics. It is usual to place the pots and boxes in a container which has a grid in the base. They are then covered with a canvas or plastic sheet and steam blown in for 30–60 minutes depending upon the size of the stack. As soon as they are cool they can be used.

Methyl bromide treatment is also effective but is a specialised job and can only be done by a contractor.

Mushroom growers successfully use steam treatment at the end of their crops to kill the pathogens and pests in the compost, to clean the outsides of the boxes and to some extent the inside surfaces, and to surface-clean the structure. This process, which is known as 'cook-out', is effective but regular steam treatment causes considerable damage to the boxes and to the mushroom sheds. For this reason, some mushroom growers prefer to employ a contractor to fumigate with methyl bromide at the end of cropping.

Workers

It is inevitable that workers who are constantly handling infected plants will pick up spores, virus particles, debris and pests on their clothing, tools or hands (Fig. 5.14). If this happens early in the day's work (or even late in the day, if the same contaminated overall is worn the next day) it is likely that the pathogen will be dispersed. Similarly, movement of visitors from nursery

FIG. 5.14 A strategically positioned notice to ensure that all knives are properly cleaned at the end of each day.

to nursery provides a means of dispersal of some pathogens. The movement of various highly infectious pathogens, such as *Verticillium fungicola* and less infectious, but equally important pathogens, such as *Fusarium oxysporum* f.sp. *dianthi*, can be minimised by ensuring that healthy crops are always worked first and that separate overalls are kept for each crop or house. Overalls should also be cleaned very regularly. Washing them in a domestic washing machine with a normal detergent, is generally sufficient to clean contaminated clothing adequately and free it from pathogens.

DISEASE CONTROL BY STATUTORY MEANS

Most countries attempt to regulate the import of plant material and it is usually necessary to have an arrangement for the quarantine of exotic species for an initial period after their import. This enables inspection for alien pests and diseases and also allows time for tests for viruses. Similarly, it is usually necessary to inspect plants that are grown for export because the importing country will require a certificate of health. Unrooted cuttings and young plants of a number of greenhouse crops are regularly imported and are a serious potential source of diseases. In recent years the international distribution of both chrysanthemum and carnation pathogens has created many problems for the industry. To be effective, the inspection of plant material for export must be done very thoroughly. Often diseases are present at extremely low levels or infected plants may be symptomless and in this way some disease escape notice. White rust of chrysanthemums (*Puccinia horiana*) was introduced into Europe from Japan and is now an established disease in much of Europe but not yet in the UK. When a disease of this type is first discovered every effort is made to eradicate it by destroying all affected plant material. The policy of eradication has been evoked in the UK on a number of occasions for White Rust and so far has been successful.

Fusarium Wilt of carnations (*Fusarium oxysporum* f.sp. *dianthi*) is an endemic disease in almost all of the main carnation growing areas of the world but is often first introduced onto a new site in cuttings. This disease has increased in importance since carnation cuttings have been propagated in Mediterranean or subtropical climates and has replaced Phialophora Wilt as the major wilt pathogen of the carnation crop. Symptomless cuttings are imported and it is not until 4–6 weeks after planting that the disease first becomes apparent. The import of such infected material can only be prevented if propagators ensure that all their new stock is initially disease-free and is raised in isolated beds in conditions of extremely high standards of hygiene. The inspection of propagators' premises should be regular, thorough and backed up by a scheme of random tests of cuttings.

Control of diseases by legislatory or statutory means is extremely important and is generally very effective. Its significance only becomes apparent to many growers when there has been a failure in the system and a new disease appears.

BIOLOGICAL CONTROL

The use of the parasitic wasp, *Encarsia formosa*, to control whitefly and the predatory mite, *Phytoseiulus persimilis*, for red spider mite control is commonly practised and used with success by many growers of tomatoes, cucumbers and chrysanthemums (see Fig. 5.15). More recently, *Verticillium lecanii*, a fungal pathogen of aphids, has been used commercially and formulations of this pathogen are available for growers (e.g. Vertalec). When using biological control of pests it is necessary to consider carefully the use of pesticides in the control programme to ensure that the beneficial insects or pathogens are not killed. Some fungicides, for instance, are known to affect adversely one or other of these beneficial organisms (see Table 5.5).

The biological control of fungus diseases of greenhouse plants has not, so

FIG. 5.15 (a) Preparing to distribute predatory mites in a cucumber crop in order to control red spider mite;
(b) the importance one grower attaches to recognising infestation by whitefly at an early stage which will enable control measures, biological or otherwise, to be effective.

(a)

(b)

TABLE 5.5 Suitability of fungicides for use with biological control of pests

Fungicide	Method of application	Phytoseiulus predator		Encarsia parasite	
		Eggs	Adults	Pupae	Adults
benomyl	HV Spray	H	H	—	S
benomyl	Soil Drench	I	I	S	S
bupirimate (wp)	HV Spray	S	S	—	S
bupirimate (ee)	HV Spray	I	S	—	—
captan	HV Spray	S	S	S	S
carbendazim	HV Spray	S	I	S	S
chlorothalonil	HV Spray	S	S	S	S
copper oxychloride	HV Spray	S	S	S	S
copper oxychloride	'Turbair'	S	S	S	S
cupric ammonium carbonate	HV Spray	S	S	S	I
dichlofluanid	HV Spray	—	S	S	S
dicloran	Smoke	—	—	—	—
dinocap	HV Spray	—	S	S	H
dodemorph	HV Spray	—	—	—	—
drazoxolon	HV Spray	—	S	—	—
etridiazole	HV Spray	—	—	—	—
fosetyl aluminium	Soil Drench	—	—	—	—
imazalil	HV Spray	I	S	H	I
iprodione	HV Spray	S	S	—	S
iprodione	'Turbair'	S	S	S	S
mancozeb/zineb	HV Spray	—	S	—	—
maneb	HV Spray	—	S	S	I
nabam	HV Spray	—	—	S	I
nabam	Soil Drench	—	—	—	—
nitrothal-isopropyl/S	HV Spray	—	I	—	S
oxycarboxin	HV Spray	S	S	—	S
pyrazophos	HV Spray	H	I	H	H
quintozene	HV Spray	—	—	—	S
tecnazene	Smoke	—	—	—	—
thiophanate-methyl	HV Spray	H	S	—	S
thiram	HV Spray	I	S	—	S
vinclozolin	HV Spray	—	S	—	S
zineb	HV Spray	—	S	—	S
zineb	'Turbair'	S	S	S	S

H, Harmful; I, Intermediate; S, Safe; –, Not tested.
Reproduced by permission of the Glasshouse Crops Research Institute, Littlehampton, UK.

far, been developed commercially, although various attempts have been made. For instance, the fungus *Ampelomyces quisqualis*, is known to be a pathogen of the Cucumber Powdery Mildew fungus *Sphaerotheca fuliginea*. Some attempts have been made to exploit this parasitism. Similarly a species of *Trichoderma* has been prepared and used in France to control Dry Bubble disease of mushrooms (*Verticillium fungicola*). Some work has been done on the biological control of Black Root Rot of cucumbers but has not reached a commercially exploitable stage. These, and other developments, are in their infancy and there is much scope and a need for research into biological systems of control of diseases of greenhouse crops.

A form of biological control of the virus disease Tomato Mosaic was, until the introduction of resistant cultivars, widely used throughout Europe.

Susceptible tomato cultivars were protected against the severe effects of commonly occurring virulent strains by inoculating them at an early stage with a very mild strain. The mild strain protected the plants from infection by the virulent strains with a resultant increase in yield and quality (see p. 151).

FURTHER READING

Baker, K. F. and Cook R. J. (1974) *Biological Control of Plant Pathogens,* Freeman, San Francisco.

Butter, E. J. and Jones, S. G. (1949) *Plant Pathology*, Macmillan, London.

Horsfall, J. G. and Cowling, E. B. (1977) *Plant Disease: Vol. V How Plants defend themselves.* Academic Press, London.

Roane, C. W. (1973) Trends in breeding for disease resistance in crops, *Annual Review of Phytopathology*, **11**, 463–86.

Russell, G. E. (1978) *Plant Breeding for Pest and Disease Resistance*. Butterworth, London.

Scopes, N. and Ledieu, M. (1979) *Pest and Disease Control Handbook*, The British Crop Protection Council Publications, London.

Wheeler, B. E. J. (1975) *The Control of Plant Disease*, Oxford Biology Readers No. 74, Oxford University Press, Oxford.

CHAPTER 6

FUNGICIDES

Some fungicides are used to protect plants against potential attack; others have curative properties in that they eradicate pathogens that have already become established, although this action is only likely to operate within a short time of infection. No fungicides eradicate disease to the extent of causing a marked decrease in symptoms. Most fungicides have contact activity only, i.e. they only affect the pathogens they directly contact. During the past decade a number of systemic fungicides have been developed. These move to a limited extent within the plant, the movement being particularly in an upward direction in the transpiration stream and they eventually accumulate at the leaf margins. So far, very few fungicides have been shown to move downwards – and these only to a very limited extent.

The ideal fungicide for the greenhouse grower must be:
1. Safe to use, both for the operator and the crop.
2. Have good fungicidal properties, i.e. be able to kill the pathogen rather than inhibit its growth.
3. Have a low mammalian toxicity so that treated crops can be handled and produce marketed within a short time of application.
4. Be sufficiently persistent so that a minimum number of applications are necessary. Fungicides which are too persistent are disadvantageous because of the long-term build-up of the chemical within the environment and because of the longer interval necessary between application and harvest.
5. Have a mode of action which is unlikely to be overcome by development of resistant strains (insensitive or tolerant) of the pathogen.

Having systemic movement within the plant or acting in the vapour phase is sometimes considered to be advantageous, although such properties are often linked with persistent residues and a specific mode of action which may be vulnerable to the development of resistance.

Most of the available fungicides have some of the desirable properties but none of them has them all.

PRINCIPLES OF FUNGICIDE USE

Fungicides are used in two different ways, either as a routine, generally starting at a specified growth stage or time interval after planting, or cropping, or they are used when disease first occurs, or reaches a critical level. Each approach has its merits and disadvantages and it is not possible to generalise and select a best method for all crops and diseases. The routine use of fungicides has the advantage that it is easy to manage and it is not necessary to monitor the crop at regular intervals in order to make spray decisions. It is also likely to give a satisfactory level of disease control because new growth is constantly protected making it more difficult for disease to become established. The major disadvantage is the possible over-use of fungicides because sprays are applied whether or not they are necessary. This can result in considerable expense both in materials and labour which might have been avoidable. Applying fungicides at first disease appearance or at a critical disease level entails regular crop monitoring in order to spot disease and this, depending upon the crop area, can be time consuming but, for success, is absolutely essential. Generally, fewer fungicide applications are made so costs and residue levels are reduced but there is the danger that, unless monitoring is thorough, disease will develop to an extent which makes it difficult to control by conventional means. This system cannot be applied to all diseases because, with some, damage is done as soon as symptoms appear and fungicide application is then too late.

Requirements for the registration of fungicides

Every country has its own requirements for the registration of pesticides although the objective of registration is similar throughout, i.e. to allow the use of pesticides which are known to be safe for the operator, the consumer, the crop and the environment. Also, when the pesticide is used in the way as stated by the manufacturer, it will have the desired biological effect. In the UK registration is voluntary and is a two-stage process which has been agreed by all the major bodies involved in pesticide manufacture and use. The first stage is concerned with the safe use of the pesticide and data on its mammalian toxicity, persistence and effects on the environment, must satisfy the requirements of the Pesticides Safety Precaution Scheme (PSPS). Initially, 'trials clearance' is given for the use of the pesticide on a specified (generally small) area. Often, with edible crops, all treated produce must be destroyed at the end of the experiments or observations. The second stage is 'commercial clearance' either 'limited' or 'full', when a larger area or eventually the whole of the crop can be treated and marketed. Clearance must be obtained for all new products and for new uses of an old product (particularly involving different crops, different methods of application or mixtures with other pesticides).

Much biological data is then accumulated on the performance of the product and the results of experiments are presented to demonstrate its effectiveness for the control of specified diseases. If the claims are substantiated by the data, the fungicide is 'Approved' for a specified use under the Agricultural Chemicals Approvals Scheme (ACAS). Approved products are designated by the 'A' sign on the label, and a list of such products is published every year by the Ministry of Agriculture, Fisheries and Food.

Approval is given for very specific uses and if a product is Approved for the control of a common disease of one crop it will not be Approved for the control of the same disease on a different crop until the necessary data has been submitted.

Methods of application

Sprays.   Fungicidal sprays are the most common means of application and are generally the most effective and labour intensive. Sprays are most commonly formulated as wettable powders, in which the fungicide is suspended in water together with a wetting agent which ensures that all the fine particles of the product are wetted. When the active ingredient is not soluble in water and is formulated as a liquid, often an oil which is not miscible with water, the formulation is known as an emulsifiable concentrate. This formulation, when added to water, spontaneously disperses as fine droplets to form an emulsion. A surfactant is added to aid the process.

Most fungicide sprays are applied in water and the volume used per unit area determines, to a large extent, the efficiency of spraying and the time required to complete the operation. High volume sprays can be as much as 9000 litres/ha (over 800 gal./acre) but are generally around 2000 litres/ha (178 gal./acre). Such sprays are applied with motorised sprayers and have a tank of about 270 litres capacity (60 gal.). For many years, the most widely used machine was the Cheshunt sprayer with a petrol or electric motor which operated the pump and delivered the spray at 2–7 bars pressure (30–100 lb/in^2). The spray is applied with a lance and two or three fan or cone nozzles positioned in such a way to give maximum cover. It has been found that even at the highest volume this method of spraying generally results in no more than 80 per cent plant surface cover and often a lot less. It is labour-intensive and may take up to a day to spray an acre of a crop. Medium volumes (560–1120 litres/ha or 50–100 gal./acre) can be applied with the same equipment and in less time (Fig. 6.1).

Various other spraying machines are available which deliver a much lower volume of spray (see Fig. 6.1d). Low volume rates are generally considered to be in the region of 225–551 litres/ha (20–49 gal./acre) with very low volumes at 56–214 litres/ha (5–19 gal./acre) and ultra-low volume rates at less than 56 litres/ha (less than 5 gal./acre). These all require special equipment and often a different formulation of the fungicide. For very low volumes the fungicides are frequently formulated in a mineral oil and applied without further dilution. By reducing the volume applied, the time taken to make the application is much reduced. For instance, using very low volumes, it is possible to spray an acre in 2 hours, and even less with ultra-low volumes. At these low volumes the droplet size is reduced, often to the extent that much of the fungicide settles out onto the upper surface of the plant. Some of the low volume machines use powerful fans to blow the foliage and fungicide in order to obtain a better cover of both surfaces of the leaves. By electrically charging the droplets as they leave the sprayer, it is possible to improve the cover on the undersides of the leaves. Such electrostatic sprayers, as they are called, are in an early stage of development.

Wetters.   Most fungicides which are formulated for use as sprays contain a wetting agent as well as a chemical to aid retention. The function of the wetter is to ensure efficient distribution of the fungicide on the plant surface, particularly if the leaves are waxy. Wetters are generally soaps or modern surfactants. Because of their surface activity on the active ingredient they are known as either anionic, i.e. they confer a positive charge on the active ingredient, or cationic when a negative charge results. If anionic and cationic materials are mixed, activity of a fungicide suspension may be lost by precipitation of the active ingredient. Most commercially-available wetters have no charge, i.e. they are non-anionic, so can be added to any fungicide without resulting in loss of activity.

Particulate fungicides.   Another approach to fungicide application is one of applying very small particles of the fungicide to the atmosphere and allowing these to settle out. This method is cheap because of its low labour requirement but is best suited for diseases where deposition of the fungicide on the upper surfaces of the plant is required. Special formulations of fungicides are necessary and these include those that can be used as fogs, dusts, smokes and vapours. With all these formulations it is important that the foliage is dry at the time of application because there is an increased risk of phytotoxicity if the particles land in water.

Methods of application of particulate fungicides.   Fogs are generated with thermal fogging machines. Two types are commercially available – one which relies on the heat of the exhaust gases of a petrol engine to generate the fog (exhaust gas fogger) and, the other, where heat is generated by explosions of fuel within a tube (pulsating jet fogger). The latter machines have proved to be much more satisfactory in practice. The best fungicide cover is obtained if the operator carries the machine along a convenient pathway through the crop and directs the fog above the crop. It is best to treat a strip approximately a 10–15 m wide either side of the pathway and not attempt to treat a bigger area from one path.

   Dusts, which usually contain a lower percentage of active ingredient than wettable powders, are applied with machines which vary in size from very small and hand-held to large very powerful tractor-mounted machines. The dust must be directed above the crop to achieve an even distribution.

   Smokes are generated from specially-manufactured smoke generators which usually contain a chemical to generate heat causing the particulate fungicide to be carried upwards in convection currents and deposited on the plant surface. It is usual to state on the product label the cubic capacity that can be treated with each smoke generator and the appropriate number can then be evenly distributed throughout the greenhouse.

   Vaporisers use the same principle except the heat is produced by an electrical heater and the fungicide is placed near to the heating element. Sulphur has been vaporised in this way in rose crops for many years. Vaporisers are placed within the crop and spaced at approximately 9 m (30 ft) intervals. They are operated for up to 6 hours during each night.

Other methods of fungicide application

Drenches.   A drench of a wettable powder formulation is sometimes used for the control of root rot or basal stem rots. The fungicide can be applied with a high volume sprayer using a lance with the nozzle removed. If root treatment is required the fungicide may be applied through the irrigation system using a nutrient diluter to regulate the concentration. Where products are in suspension, there is always the danger that they will settle out within

FIG. 6.1 Equipment used to apply fungicides.
(a) Cheshunt high volume sprayer;
(b) a mechanised means of applying high volume sprays using a spray boom suspended from an overhead rail;
(c) a diluter used for regulating the concentration of the fungicide applied;
(d) a Turbair machine used for applying low volumes of fungicides. Photograph (d) copyright of Turbair Ltd.

(a)

(b)

(c)

(d)

the irrigation system and not reach the plants.

Basal stem applications are made with a modified lance with the two nozzles positioned on the inner ends of a U-shaped piece in order to apply the drenching spray to either side of the stem at the same time.

It is important to apply a precise volume of fungicide when using a product as a drench in order to avoid phytotoxicity. This may require careful calibration of the equipment before applying the fungicide.

Seed and pre-planting soil applications.   Fungicides effective against seed- and soil-borne diseases may be applied to the seed or to the soil before planting. Some seed-borne diseases are controlled by a seed treatment with a fungicide, e.g. some bedding plant diseases with a thiram seed soak or an iprodione dust treatment. Seed treatments have also been used to control soil-borne damping-off pathogens, e.g. captan and thiram for the control of Pythium. Some fungicides may be used as a pre-planting treatment, particularly where the crop is of short duration. Quintozene has been used in this way for many years for the control of *Rhizoctonia solani* and etradiazole for the control of *Pythium* spp.

Paints.   Very occasionally, a fungicidal paint application is justified if lesion treatment will prevent plant death and if this labour-intensive method of application is feasible. Wettable powders and dusts have been used by making them into a slurry which is applied to the lesion. Benomyl mixed with a mineral oil (Actipron) is very effective for the control of lesions of *Didymella lycopersici* on tomato stems and the mixture is Approved for use in the UK.

FUNGICIDE RESISTANCE

The problem of resistance has been known in greenhouse pest populations for many years. Red spider mites and aphids have developed resistance to a range of pesticides and are now no longer controlled by these materials. Resistance in fungal pathogens has only recently been recognised. There are a number of pathogens of greenhouse plants that are known to be resistant to one or more of the commonly used fungicides (Table 6.1). The enclosed environment of the greenhouse or mushroom growing room is often ideal for a rapid increase in the pathogen and can result in the dramatic development of resistance in the pathogen population.

There are various views on the correct terminology for this problem. The term 'insensitive' is sometimes preferred because of the possible confusion between genetical resistance as used in plant breeding and fungicide resistance. Similarly, 'tolerance' can apply to both. Fungi may be said to be sensitive to some fungicides and insensitive to others. They may also develop insensitivity to some previously effective fungicides. Most pathogens show a range of sensitivity to fungicides that are effective for controlling the diseases they produce and the range is within the limits of the concentrations of the fungicide in general use. It would seem logical to retain the terms 'sensitivity' and 'insensitivity' to describe the range of reactions of a pathogen

TABLE 6.1 Pathogens of greenhouse crops where fungicide resistance is known

Crop	Pathogen	Fungicide	Occurrence in crops
Tomato	*Botrytis cinerea*	benzimidazoles	Common
	Fulvia fulva	benzimidazoles	Uncommon
	Verticillium tricorpus	benzimidazoles	Uncommon
	Botrytis cinerea	dicarboximides	Not reported*
Lettuce	*Botrytis cinerea*	benzimidazoles	Common
	Rhizoctonia solani	aromatic hydrocarbons	Not reported*
Cucumber	*Botrytis cinerea*	benzimidazoles	Common
	Sphaerotheca fuliginea	{ dimethirimol benzimidazoles	Common
Chrysanthemum	*Puccinia horiana*	carboxin benodanil	Uncommon Uncommon
Mushroom	*Verticillium fungicola*	benzimidazoles	Common
Carnation	*Fusarium oxysporum* f.sp. *dianthi*	benzimidazoles	Uncommon
Saintpaulia, Reiger begonia, Cyclamen and various ornamentals	Powdery mildew pathogens *Botrytis cinerea*	benzimidazoles benzimidazoles	Uncommon Uncommon

*Not found in crops but known to occur in laboratory studies.

to a fungicide and confine 'resistance' to those situations where the insensitive pathogen is capable of producing disease in the presence of the normal dose of the fungicide. Such resistance has become a problem since the widespread use of fungicides with a very specific mode of action, often affecting one biochemical process of the pathogen (site specific). Other fungicides affect many biochemical processes (multi-site); resistance to these is less common and there are very few records of disease control failure resulting from the use of such fungicides.

The development of resistance

There is only slight evidence that some fungicides induce fungicide-resistant mutants of the pathogen and it seems likely that with most, resistance arises by the selective development of a very small resistant fraction of the population. This is most likely to occur if there is a continuous selection pressure in the form of non-lethal concentrations of the fungicide. Pathogens which produce very large numbers of spores are also more likely to develop resistance merely because of the increased likelihood of a small fraction of the population occurring which is resistant. An effective mode of distribution is then essential for the resistant population to become dominant.

Resistance to some fungicides, or groups of fungicides with a similar or identical mode of action, seems to occur more frequently than with others. For instance, resistance to the benzimidazole fungicides is now widespread in populations of many different pathogens whereas resistance to the carboximides or the ergosterol biosynthesis inhibitors is uncommon. Some pathogens such as *Botrytis cinerea* and the powdery mildew pathogens appear to be more likely to become resistant.

Means of preventing resistance

When planning a programme of fungicide use, care must be taken to minimise the risk of resistance developing. Once established within a pathogen population, resistance may not be rapidly lost. The most successful approach in other biological fields has been the use of materials with different modes of action either alternated or used together in mixtures. Where alternative fungicides are available for the grower, this is a sensible approach and should be adopted as far as possible in spite of some practical difficulties. When planning such a programme, care must be taken to select fungicides which have different modes of action and are in no way related (Table 6.2). If a site specific and a multi-site fungicide can be included within the same programme this is probably the ideal, but the multi-site material must be at least moderately effective against the pathogen in its own right. It is likely that the two fungicides will have different persistence times but this need not be a problem providing they are applied efficiently and are both effective. The chosen fungicides can be applied separately or together as a tank mix. Some fungicides are formulated as mixtures, e.g. Fubol, which is a mixture of metalaxyl and mancozeb. Care must be taken when using tank mixes to ensure that the manufacturers of both fungicides agree that such a mix is safe to use and likely to be effective. The alternative to the mixture is an alternation of the components. This may be just as effective and, providing both

Fungicide group	Common name	Some products	Pathogens or diseases controlled
1. Acylalanine	furalaxyl	–	Downy mildews
	metalaxyl	Fubol*	Phytophthora
	milfuran	Patafol	Pythium
2. Benzimidazoles	benomyl	Benlate	Botrytis
	carbendazim	Bavistin	Verticillium
	thiophanate methyl	Mildothane	Cercospora
	thiabendazole	Hymush*	Fusarium
3. Carboximides	benodanil	Calirus	Rusts, smuts,
	carboxin	Vitavax	Rhizoctonia and some
	oxycarboxin	Plantvax	other basidiomycetes
4. Dicarboximides	iprodione	Rovral	Botrytis
	proxymidione	Sumisclex	Alternaria
	viclozolin	Ronilan	Stemphylium
5. Aromatic hydrocarbons	dicloran	Allisan	Botrytis
	quintozene	PCNB	Rhizoctonia
	tecnazene	Tecnazene	Fusarium (not wilts)
6. Dithiocarbamates	thiram	Thiram	Downy mildews Rhizoctonia Botrytis
	maneb	Maneb	
	mancozeb	Dithane 945	General, but in particular downy
	nabam	Campbell's Soil	mildews, rusts, some pycnidial
	zineb	Fungicide Dithane Wettable	fungi such as Didymella
7. Ergosterol biosynthesis inhibitors	bitertanol	Baycor	
	fenpropimorph†	Mistral	
	imazalil	Fungaflor	
	nuarimol	Triminol	Powdery mildews, but some have
	prochloraz	Sportak	a broader spectrum of activity
	prochloraz manganese	Sporgon	
	propiconazole	Tilt	
	triadimefon	Bayleton	
	triforine	Saprol	
8. Hydroxypyrimidines	bupirimate	Nimrod	Powdery mildews
	dimethirimol	Milcurb	
13. Organic phosphates	pyrazophos	Afugan	Powdery mildew
	tolclofos methyl	Rizolex	Rhizoctonia
14. Anthraquinones	dithianon	Delan-Col	Leaf spots and possibly root rots
15. Izoxazolones	drazoxolon	Mil-Col	Pythium
16. Nitroisophthalates	nitrothal-isopropyl	Kumulan	Powdery mildews
17. Quinoxalines	quinomethionate	Morestan	Powdery mildews
18. Sulphamides	dichlofluanid	Elvaron	Botrytis
	tolyfluanid	Euparen M	Downy mildews
19. Thiocarbamates	propamocarb hydrochloride	Filex Dynone	Phytophthora Pythium
	prothiocarb		
20. Thiadiazoles	etridiazole	Aaterra	Pythium Phytophthora
21. Phthalimides	captan	Captan	Botrytis
	folpet	Phaltan	Leaf spots
22. Phthalonitriles	chlorothalonil	Daconil	Botrytis Downy mildews *Verticillium fungicola*
23. Coppers	Cupric ammonium compound	Fungex	Downy mildews
	copper oxychloride	Cuprokylt	*Phytophthora infestans* Some leaf spots caused by fungi and bacteria. Some powdery mildews

Fungicide group	Common name	Some products	Pathogen or disease controlled
24. Sulphur	sulphur	Thiovit	Powdery mildews
25. Dintro derivatives	dinocap	Karalthane	Powdery mildews
26. Other	fosetyl aluminium	Aliette	Downy mildews and some Phytophthora's

★ Full mode of action not clearly determined and there may be more than one site of activity. †Fungicidal mixture containing a second active ingredient.

TABLE 6.2   Groups of fungicides with differing modes of action, used on protected crops

fungicides are registered for use on the crop, the possible problems of mixtures are avoided. The use of reduced rates of both fungicides in a mixture (half rates) may be satisfactory providing both materials are effective against the pathogen, but as soon as the pathogen becomes less sensitive to one or other of them the half rate mixture is less likely to work well. Half rates of products used on their own can, in some circumstances, aid the development of resistance by allowing a step-wise development of less sensitive strains which eventually become dominant.

Spray programmes

It is important to avoid very regular applications of the same site specific fungicide even though there may be a great temptation to do this when the fungicide is giving good disease control. Dicarboximide resistance in populations of Botrytis cinerea has been found to result in a disease problem when a continuous programme of these fungicides is used, in spite of the resistant fungus being less virulent and not as efficient at spore production as the normal sensitive populations. Only in an environment of continuous fungicide selection pressure can such populations cause disease. Botrytis cinerea is perhaps the most important pathogen of protected crops where there is a problem, or potential problem, of resistance

Botrytis cinerea.   Resistance to the benzimidazole fungicides is now very common and isolates exhibiting resistance may exceed 50 per cent of the pathogen population in greenhouses. Low level dicarboximide resistance is relatively uncommon but develops when these fungicides are frequently used. There is evidence that resistance to the dicarboximides is linked to resistance to the benzimidazoles, so benzimidazole-resistant isolates are more likely to become dicarboximide resistant. Other fungicides suitable for the control of this pathogen include the multi-site fungicides, dichlofluanid, chlorothalonil and thiram. Suitable programmes for some of the main crops are shown in Table 6.3 and these are based on the assumption that benzimidazole resistance is common. The evidence available indicates that, once established, benzimidazole resistance remains in the population almost indefinitely, even if the fungicide is no longer used.

Powdery mildew pathogens.   Cucumber Powdery Mildew (Sphaerotheca fuliginea) developed resistance to dimethirimol (Milcurb) within a very few years of use of the fungicide. Populations of the pathogen in the UK and the Netherlands became totally resistant and growers stopped using this fungicide some years ago. Recent attempts to reintroduce the fungicide in a controlled way resulted in initial success, but within a short time dimethirimol resistance

Tomato		Lettuce	Cucumber	Carnation
Without ghost spot potential	With ghost spot potential			
Alternate dichlofluanid (3) with iprodione (2) or vinclozolin (1) before harvest	Ditto	thiram for the first three weeks after planting and then iprodione (2) with tecnazene smoke (2) used on every third occasion	iprodione (2) alternated with chlorothalonil (0.5)	captan or thiram alternated with iprodione or vinclozolin
iprodione (2) or vinclozolin (1) alternated with chlorothalonil (0.5) during harvest	dichlofluanid (3) two sprays out of every three with iprodione (2) or vinclozolin (1) used as the third during harvest			

Numbers in brackets are harvest intervals in days.

TABLE 6.3 Suggested fungicide spray programmes to control *Botrytis cinerea* and to minimise the risk of a resistance problem arising

became re-established. The related fungicide, bupirimate, has also been used on cucumbers but, not surprisingly, its use has resulted in resistance.

Benzimidazole resistance (in particular Benlate) is also known to occur in the Cucumber Mildew population and the choice of alternative materials for a spray programme is further complicated by the practice of biological control of aphids and red spider mites as many powdery mildew fungicides have insecticidal and acaricidal properties. Possible programmes with or without biological control are suggested (Table 6.4). So far, resistance is not a problem in other powdery mildews (somewhat surprisingly), especially for Rose Powdery Mildew, *Sphaerotheca pannosa*. Rose growers should make sure that they use the wide range of fungicides available to them with care to avoid resistance developing.

Verticillium fungicola. Dry Bubble disease of mushrooms was spectacularly controlled by the use of the benzimidazoles but after a period of about 3 years these fungicides became totally ineffective, with the widespread occurrence of resistance in all the major mushroom growing countries. At low concentrations of the fungicide the pathogen is now stimulated and the use of benomyl does, on some farms, increase the incidence of Dry Bubble. Other

TABLE 6.4 Suggested fungicide spray programme for the control of *Sphaerotheca fuliginea* on cucumbers to minimise the risk of a resistance problem arising

Biological control of pests	
Practised	Not practised
Alternating sprays of bupirimate and dinocap★ with occasional drenches of benomyl	Alternating sprays from any of the following groups 1. Benzimidazole-benomyl, carbendazim or thiophanate methyl (2) 2. Bupirimate (8) 3. Dinocap (7) 4. Imazalil (7) 5. Pyrazophos (13)

★ Does have some effect on the red spider predator.
( ) mode of action groups, see Table 6.2.

benzimidazoles are equally ineffective against the resistant strains, although there is some evidence that some benomyl-resistant strains are somewhat more sensitive to thiabendazole. In addition, benomyl appears to be more likely to be biologically broken down in the casing than thiabendazole and, for these two reasons, thiabendazole has sometimes given a moderate level of disease control even of a benomyl-resistant strain. It is interesting that benomyl resistance has not developed in other mushroom pathogens such as *Mycogone perniciosa* or *Hypomyces rosellus*. Both of these have been subjected to the same selection pressure as *V. fungicola* but neither produces as many spores.

There is not a sufficient choice of alternative fungicides to enable growers to practise an ideal programme of fungicide mixtures or alternations, and until new materials become available mushroom growers must rely on hygiene, prochloraz manganese and the multi-site fungicides, zineb, mancozeb and chlorothalonil.

USE OF FUNGICIDES IN THE NUTRIENT FILM TECHNIQUE (NFT)

The development of nutrient film and other similar systems of crop culture has enabled growers to use fungicides in a new way. Fungicides can be added to the nutrient solution either to protect the roots against root decay or vascular wilt organisms or, if systemic fungicides are used, to protect the plants against foliar and stem diseases. The use of fungicides in NFT is still in its early stages of development and there are only a few products that are known to be safe to use. Because of the contact of the fungicides with the whole root system, there is the increased danger of phytotoxicity and it is essential for experimental work to be done with each fungicide/crop combination in order to establish the correct dose. Etradiazole at 60 p.p.m. has been successfully used in NFT tomato crops to control root decay caused by both Pythium and Phytophthora and the benzimidazoles have been used for the control of foliar pathogens. Generally NFT crops are sprayed in the normal way for the control of diseases which cannot at present be controlled by the addition of a fungicide to the nutrient solution.

FURTHER READING

Anon. (1984) *List of Approved Products and their Uses for Farmers and Growers.* HMSO, London.

Evans, E. (1968) *Plant Diseases and their Chemical Control.* Blackwell Scientific Publications, Oxford.

Marsh, R. W. (1977) *Systemic Fungicides* (Second edition). Longman, London.

Martin, H. (1972) *Insecticide and Fungicide Handbook.* Blackwell Scientific Publications, Oxford.

Worthing, C. R. (1983) *The Pesticide Manual.* The British Crop Protection Council Publications, London.

CHAPTER 7

TOMATO

CULTURE

Pre-planting preparation

Greenhouse soil is sterilised with heat or chemical sterilants such as methyl bromide, dazomet, metham sodium or formaldehyde.

Propagation

The compost is steam sterilised or a sand and peat compost used. Seeds are sown from November until March and germinated at 20 °C, transplanted after approximately 10 days and grown in pots or blocks. Plants may also be raised in 'growing rooms' with artificial light and a day length of 12 hours. The atmosphere is enriched with carbon dioxide to 1000 p.p.m. for the duration of full daylight.

Cropping

Planting takes place when the first truss is visible or at an earlier growth stage for late planted crops. The earliest crops are planted in December, and the latest in May. Generally, 20–30 000 plants are required to plant a hectare (8–12 000 per acre). Systems of culture include growing in border soil, peat bags, rockwool, troughs and NFT. Ring culture is frequently used by amateurs. Training systems vary from layering the stems to archways.

Early planted crops are grown at 21–24 °C by day and at 16–17 °C by night, and enriched with carbon dioxide to a level of 1000 p.p.m. Late planted crops may be grown at lower night temperatures (13 °C).

Early crops are harvested from March until October and maximum yields are in the region of 330 tonne/ha.

DISEASES

Seedlings

Damping-off (*Pythium ultimum, Pythium* spp. *Phytophthora* spp. and *Rhizoctonia solani*) p. 116.

Roots

Brown and Corky Root Rot (*Pyrenochaeta lycopersici*), p. 119
Brown Root Rot (*Phytophthora* spp. as for basal stem rots), p. 116
Calyptella Root Rot (*Calyptella campanula*), p. 121
Other Root Rots (*Rhizoctonia solani, Colletotrichum coccodes, Thielaviopsis basicola, Spongospora subterranea*), p. 122

Stems

Foot Rot (*Phytophthora* spp. including *P. nicotianae* var. *parasitica* (syn. *p. parasitica*), *p. cryptogea, P. megasperma, P. verrucosa* and *P. erythroseptica, Rhizoctonia solani, Didymella, lycopersici* and *Botrytis cinerea*), p. 116.
Didymella Stem Rot or Canker (*Didymella lycopersici*), p. 124
Grey Mould (*Botrytis cinerea*), p. 126
Sclerotinia Disease (*Sclerotinia sclerotiorum*), p. 130
Bacterial Canker (*Corynebacterium michiganense*), p. 132
Pith Nicrosis or Brown Pith Necrosis (*Pseudomonas corrugata*), p. 135
Bacterial Soft Rot (*Erwinia carotovora* var. *caratovora*), p.136
Single Virus Streak (Tomato Mosaic Virus), p. 147
Double or Mixed Virus Streak (Tomato Mosaic Virus and Potato Virus X), p. 151

Leaves

Leaf Mould (*Fulvia fulva* syn. *Cladosporium fulvum*), p. 131
Septoria Leaf Spot (*Septoria lycopersici*), p. 138
Stemphylium Leaf Blight (*Stemphylium vesicarium* and *S. botryosum*), p. 138
Early Blight, Target Spot or Alternaria Blight (*Alternaria solani*), p. 139
Late Blight (*Phytophthora infestans*), p. 139
Grey Mould (*Botrytis cinerea*), p. 126
Bacterial Spot (*Pseudomonas syringae* pv. *tomato*), p. 136
Powdery Mildew (*Leveillula taurica*), p. 137
Verticillium Wilt (*Verticillium albo-atrum* and *V. dahliae*), p. 142
Fusarium Wilt (*Fusarium oxysporum* f.sp *lycopersici*), p. 144
Bacterial Wilt (*Pseudomonas solanacearum*), p. 138
Tomato Mosaic *Tomato Mosaic Virus*, p. 146
Tomato Aspermy *Tomato Aspermy Virus*, p. 153
Tomato Spotted Wilt *Tomato Spotted Wilt Virus*, p. 153
Cucumber Mosaic *Cucumber Mosaic Virus*, p. 154
Other virus diseases, p. 154
Silvering, p. 154
Leaf distortion, p. 154

Fruit

Ghost Spot (*Botrytis cinerea*), p. 127
Buckeye Rot (*Phytophthora nicotianae* var. *parasitica*), p. 140
Didymella Fruit Rot (*Didymella lycopersici*), p. 125
Blight (*Phytophthora infestans*), p. 140

Phoma Rot (*Phoma destructiva*), p. 141
Bacterial Spot (*Pseudomonas syringae* pv. *tomato*), p. 136
Bacterial Canker (*Corynebacterium michiganense*), p. 134
Tomato Mosaic (Tomato Mosaic Virus), p. 148
Tomato Spotted Wilt (Tomato Spotted Wilt Virus), p. 153
Blossom End Rot, p. 155
Blotchy Ripening, p. 156
Herbicide distortion, p. 155

Damping-off diseases

Damping-off is the most common disease of seedlings. Attack of young seedlings by species of *Pythium* and *Phytophthora*, results in typical damping-off symptoms or even pre-emergence decay. Affected seedlings have a lesion on the stem at soil level which is pale brown in colour and usually water-soaked in appearance. Affected seedlings collapse and die. The pathogens spread quickly in wet, cool soils and the disease is especially severe if the seedlings are very close together.

Rhizoctonia solani is also responsible for damping-off although it is frequently more troublesome in drier conditions. It is sometimes a contaminant in peat and is often a cause of disease in peat-based composts. The lesion formed at soil level is brown in colour and often clearly delimited and with a dry appearance.

Control. Of the various sources of these pathogens the compost and containers are by far the most important. Compost containing loam should be sterilised. Peat composts should not be mixed with unsterilised loam and care must be taken to ensure that the compost is not contaminated after sterilisation.

Boxes and pots must be cleaned before use and greenhouse benches treated during the routine cleaning of the structure.

Mains water is generally free from damping-off organisms but may become contaminated on the nursery. When stored in a tank, a lid should be provided to prevent dust and debris blowing in. The tank should be cleaned at regular intervals. Pond or rain water collected into tanks or lagoons may be contaminated and can be cleaned by chlorination, preferably followed by at least a short period of storage, before use.

Soil temperatures should never be below 65 °F (18 °C) during propagation and over-watering always avoided.

By the time damping-off appears it is often too late to use fungicides although they may slow down the spread of the pathogen and retard further disease development. Fungicides are most effective when used as pre-sowing compost treatments; etridiazole is best for Pythium and Phytophthora and quintozene for Rhizoctonia.

Foot Rots or Basal Stem Rots

Symtoms of these diseases become apparent within 6 weeks of planting out. Affected plants often fail to establish, or shortly after establishing, become very dark green, and may wilt, especially under conditions of stress, such as high temperatures or following over- or under-watering. A lesion at or just below soil level may partly or completely girdle the stem.

Greenhouse soils are frequently infested by one or other of the foot rot pathogens. In cold wet soils various species of *Phytophthora* are the most common cause whereas, in well drained soil, *Rhizoctonia solani* is more frequently the pathogen. *Botrytis cinerea* sometimes causes foot rot especially if, during propagation, the plants have been checked and the cotyledon leaves become senescent or the senescence is the result of planting too deeply and partially or totally burying the cotyledons.

Didymella lycopersici causes a serious disease problem on some nurseries and is chiefly soil-borne. First attack takes place at soil level.

It is not easy to distinguish between the symptoms of the various foot rotting diseases. In general the Pytophthoras produce a dark brown to black lesion at soil level, which often extends down into the tap root (Fig. 7.1). When this disease is present, there is invariably some light brown discoloration of the roots. *Rhizoctonia solani* forms a dry lesion on the stem in the region of the soil surface and does not extend down into the main root. The lesion is often light brown and may have strands of light brown mycelium on the surface. This mycelium can be clearly seen with the aid of a hand lens. *Botrytis cinerea* forms a light brown lesion frequently around the scars of the cotyledon leaves. When kept moist, the fungus sporulates freely all around the stem, forming a dense stand of conidiophores and spores (Fig. 7.2). *Didymella lycopersici* is not easy to identify with certainty. The lesion is (see Fig. 7.6b) generally at or about soil level and there is no obvious external indication of the fungus although with a powerful hand lens (× 20) pycnidia can be seen. These may be confused with the heads of glandular hairs which are present on all tomato stems and are approximately the same size as the pycnidia but are generally lighter brown in colour. A check on the stem away from the lesion will help to distinguish glandular hairs and pycnidia.

Plants become more resistant to attack by Phytophthora and Rhizoctonia

FIG. 7.1 Phytophthora Foot Rot – the lesion at the base of the stem extends just above soil level.

FIG. 7.2 *Botrytis cinerea*
sporulating from a tomato
stem lesion after 2 days
incubation in a warm and
damp atmosphere.

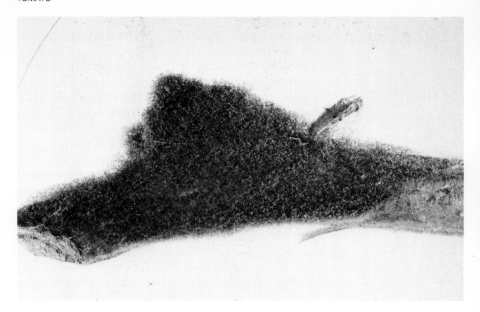

as they age, and 6 weeks after planting are fairly resistant. Often when symptoms are first discovered the disease has developed to its full extent. The unaffected plants at this time are old enough to be relatively resistant.

The sources of the pathogens are similar to those described for damping-off.

Control. Soil used for propagation should be sterilised or a carefully prepared soil-less compost used. Greenhouse soil should also be sterilised. The recovery of plants with basal lesions, whatever the cause, can be aided by encouraging adventitious root growth from the stem above the affected area by mulching with moist peat or sterilised soil.

Etridiazole incorporated into the compost regularly controls Phytophthora Foot Rot or plants may be drenched after planting with a dithiocarbamate, such as zineb.

Quintozene is used for *Rhizoctonia solani* control and is incorporated into the compost or dusted onto the soil surface.

Botrytis cinerea can be prevented by removing senescent cotyledons before planting and by avoiding deep planting. If the disease does occur, a high volume spray treatment around the base of the stem with iprodione or vinclozolin will contain the lesion.

A drench treatment with captan, shortly after planting, followed by a second 3 weeks later controls Didymella Basal Stem Rot.

Root Rots

Root rotting can occur during propagation or at any time in the season after planting out. It usually results in a growth check, the appearance of deficiency symptoms in the leaves, especially interveinal yellowing, and a darker green appearance of the young growth. As the root rot progresses the symptoms become more pronounced and the plants wilt. Usually the youngest leaves

FIG. 7.3 Acute wilting of tomato plants following severe root rot.

are affected first and the growing shoots wilt for short periods during the day, especially when the temperature in the greenhouse is high. Recovery from wilting frequently occurs during the evening and at night but eventually wilting is permanent (see Fig. 7.3). The initial symptoms of wilting caused by the root rot pathogens are similar to those of Verticillium and Fusarium Wilts except with the latter, the lower leaves are often the first to wilt. In both vascular wilt and root rot affected plants, there may be some vascular discoloration, but with root rots it does not extend more than a few centimetres above ground level, whereas with the vascular wilts it is frequently present well up the plant.

Outside rows, ends of the greenhouse, and positions under gutters are often the first areas where plants show symptoms of root rot, generally because these areas are most difficult to sterilise.

The diseases caused by the different fungal pathogens do differ to some extent in the symptoms they produce and also in the control measures that can be applied.

Brown Root Rot and Corky Root (*Pyrenochaeta lycopersici*)

This disease is present on most nurseries where tomatoes are grown. The pathogen also affects a number of other closely related plants and can even survive on the surface of roots of other plants, e.g. lettuce and probably a number of weeds. It is a very slow growing fungus so does not quickly colonise treated soil or root systems. Even where the level of inoculum in the soil is fairly high it takes some weeks for the first symptoms to appear on the roots. The presence of disease is usually not detected in the crop until the first truss is swelling and a number of other trusses are set. Where pre-planting soil treatment has been thorough, symptoms may not become apparent until late in the crop, if at all, but when the roots are dug up some root rot and corky root may be obvious, although a satisfactory commercial yield has been obtained.

The earliest symptoms are light brown areas up to 0.5 cm long on the thin roots. These represent single points of infection and, when numerous early in the crop (16 weeks after planting), they indicate a very high level of inoculum in the soil. Yield loss is proportional to the level of root rot at this time (see Fig. 3.4).

When larger roots are attacked, dark brown, corky areas occur and these are somewhat swollen. The corky lesions are restricted to the thicker roots so that plants grown in a peaty medium, which encourages a mass of fine roots, are unlikely to show corky root symptoms, although the fine roots may be severely affected by root rot (Fig. 7.4).

Microscopic examination of the affected area shows the presence of the mycelium of the fungus packing the cells to form microsclerotia in the outer tissues of the root. These microsclerotia are fairly resistant to adverse conditions and survive in the soil from one crop until the next. The outer tissues of the root are left in the soil when the plants are pulled out and the resting structures of the fungus are released into the soil as further decay occurs.

A corky lesion is often present on the base of the stem of severely affected plants. It is generally restricted to the basal few centimetres and is not in the

FIG. 7.4   Brown Root Rot
and Corky Root.
(a) Root system with
brown rotten areas on the
smaller roots (i) and corky
lesions on the large root
(ii);
(b) corky lesions on large
roots.

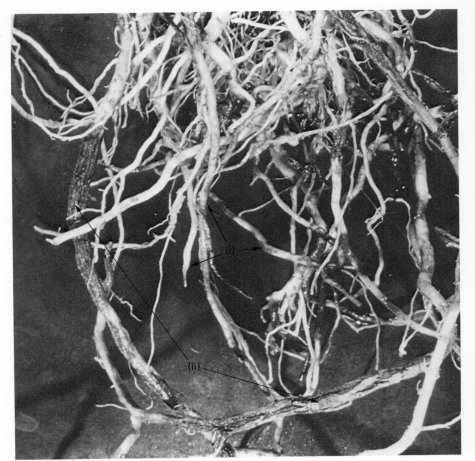

(a)

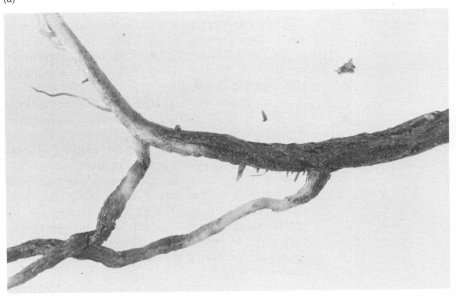

(b)

form of a discrete lesion, so is readily distinguished from the basal rotting diseases.

The slow growth of the pathogen through the soil can be an advantage if a large volume of 'clean' soil is placed around the roots at planting. In this respect a short-term crop planted out from large pots is likely to remain free from serious root rot longer than plants grown in smaller pots.

Phytophthora Root Rot – various *Phytophthora* spp.

Root rots caused by these fungi are common, usually appearing shortly after planting. They occur more frequently early in the life of the crop than other root rots. Light brown, rotten areas are formed on the young roots, often extending from a decay of the main or tap root. Corky lesions are not seen, although the browning of the roots is indistinguishable from that resulting from attack by *Pyrenochaeta lycopersici*. The disease is largely confined to partially heated or unheated crops and is far less frequent in heated early crops.

Colletotrichum coccodes

This fungus is often reported as a cause of root rot but is generally a coloniser of old and already decaying roots. The fungus invades damaged, outer tissues of the root and produces black structures which are responsible for the common name Black Dot. The outer tissues of roots with Black Dot symptoms are readily detached from the central vascular tissue (Fig. 7.5).

Calyptella Root Rot (*Calyptella campanula*)

A root rot caused by the Basidiomycete fungus *Calyptella campanula* has recently been described in England. Affected plants wilt when the first truss of fruit is reaching maturity. The roots of such plants show a nondescript light brown decay without thickening or swelling. The stems near their bases may have a discoloration of the vascular tissue. The most characteristic feature of the disease is the development of the toadstool fruiting bodies of the pathogen. These occur on the soil surface near to the stem and are saucer-shaped, lemon-yellow in colour and 0.5–1.0 cm diameter. Sometimes they may be physically connected to the decaying roots. The fruiting bodies usually appear in early to mid-summer but are generally not seen after August.

So far, this disease has been found affecting crops directly planted into the soil, although there are indications that it may also occur on plants grown in peat. Nothing is known about the epidemiology of the disease although it does appear to be associated with very wet soils.

Control.   There are indications that this pathogen is particularly difficult to control by conventional means of soil treatment. Severe attacks have followed treatment with both steam and methyl bromide. The use of trickle or drip irrigation has been associated with the disease and in one case, control was achieved by moving the trickle irrigation line further away from the plants as soon as the first symptoms were recognised. There is no positive infor-

FIG. 7.5 (a) Black Dot
symptoms on an affected
root system,
(b) Black Dot on larger
roots, the outer cortical
tissue has completely
decayed.

(a)

(b)

mation on the effectiveness of fungicide drench treatments, but there are
indications that captan, as used for the control of Didymella, may at least help
to suppress its development.

Other causes of root rot

Thielaviopsis basicola and various species of *Fusarium*, in particular *F. solani*,
have also been associated with rots. Like *Colletotrichum coccodes*, these fungi

are most frequently secondary invaders of already damaged roots. They occur on root systems damaged by waterlogging, high soil salt concentrations or low soil temperatures at planting.

Spongospora subterranea, the potato powdery scab fungus, has been found on the roots of tomato plants growing in unsterilised soil which has grown potato crops in the recent past. Galls form on the roots which resemble those caused by the root knot nematode although they are usually smaller. It is a relatively rare disease and should be easily controlled by good soil sterilisation.

Control.   The most satisfactory way to control root rotting diseases is by soil sterilisation. Heat sterilisation is the most effective, although control can be obtained with a number of chemical sterilants. Of the materials at present available, methyl bromide and dazomet are the most commonly used.

There are a number of other methods of control that can be useful, particularly where steaming is not possible, and chemicals have been found to be unsatisfactory. There are also a number of cultivars with resistance to Brown Root Rot and Corky Root but not to the other root rots (Table 7.1). In addition, various resistant rootstocks are available onto which susceptible cultivars can be grafted (p. 72). These show a high degree of resistance, not only to Brown Root Rot and Corky Root, but also to vascular wilts such as Verticillium and Fusarium Wilt diseases. They are not resistant to Phytophthora Basal Rot and Root Rot.

Barrier treatments and new growing techniques avoiding the use of soil (p. 87) are often satisfactory. Plants can be grown in pots on the soil surface or on alternative substrates such as peat or straw. These techniques, though satisfactory for disease control, sometimes add to the nutritional and labour requirement problems.

Slightly affected plants are helped by encouraging new root growth from the stem just above soil level. This is often achieved by mulching around the stem with clean soil or peat.

TABLE 7.1 Cultivars and rootstocks resistant to Brown Root Rot and Corky Root

Resistance to other diseases

Cultivars	Leaf Mould	Fusarium Wilt	Verticillium Wilt	TMV resistance factors
Corno	–	–	–	–
Piranto	A,B,C,D,E	Races 1 and 2	–	$Tm-2^2$
Sukro	A,B	–	–	–
Vicores	A,B,C	Race 1	–	$Tm-2^2$
Rootstocks				
KVF	–	Race 1	+	–
KNVF*	–	Race 1	+	–
KNVF2	–	Races 1 and 2	+	–
KNVF/TMV*	–	Race 1	+	$Tm-2^2$
Identistock KVF	–	Race 1	+	–
Hires (Signaal)*	–	Race 1	+	$Tm-2^2$

* Also resistant to Root Knot nematodes
+ Verticillium Wilt resistant

Regular soil drenches with zineb will help to control Brown Root Rot and Corky Root and etridiazole incorporated into the propagation compost inhibits Phytophthora Root Rot.

Stem, leaf and fruit diseases

Didymella Stem Rot or Canker (*Didymella lycopersici*)

This disease varies in incidence from season to season but causes losses on some nurseries every year. Symptoms are produced on the stems, fruit and occasionally the leaves. When a plant is severely affected by one or more stem lesions it frequently wilts and the leaves may show varying degrees of chlorosis and necrosis. Stem lesions are the most common symptom, and generally the first to appear (Fig. 7.6). The pathogen survives between crops in the soil, generally on stem and fruit debris, or is brought into the greenhouse on debris from a previously affected crop. It can also be introduced by air-borne spores, infected seeds, contaminated seed boxes and stakes, although these sources are generally considered to be of less importance than debris in the soil. First infections most frequently occur at soil level when a

FIG. 7.6 (a) Didymella Stem Rot in the axils of leaves; the pycnidia are clearly visible when lesions are examined with a hand lens (b).

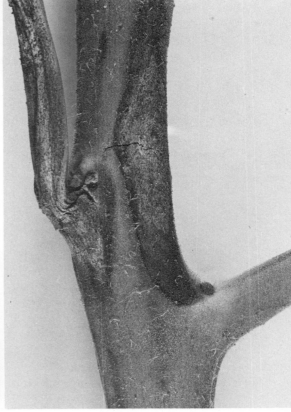

FIG. 7.7 Tomato fruit with Didymella Rot. Affected fruits usually fall onto the soil. The pathogen produces numerous black pycnidia at the calyx end of the fruit.

lesion forms at the base of the plant. The external symptoms are not easy to distinguish from other basal rot diseases. If a Didymella lesion is handled or if, during watering, there is splashing, spores are readily distributed and nearby plants become infected. Subsequent lesions are often around a leaf scar or wound caused by pruning and, with severe attacks, lines of affected plants are found, suggesting that spread is mainly the result of handling lesions. It has been shown that the pathogen can be spread with a contaminated knife for up to 30 cuts after the initial contamination.

Fruit symptoms are not commonly found even where there are many plants with stem lesions in a crop. Infection appears to occur through the calyx end and turns the fruit black and rotten resulting in fruit drop. Pycnidia occur on the blackened area of the fruit (Fig. 7.7). When fruits become infected there is a chance that some seeds will also be infected and in this way the disease may become seed-borne.

Accurate diagnosis of the disease is difficult without the aid of a microscope. If the black lesions are examined carefully the small round black pycnidia of the pathogen can be seen. Pycnidia produce numerous spores which ooze out in tendrils. The small dark brown glandular hairs present on all tomato stems can be confused with pycnidia if the lesion is not examined very carefully. Similar lesions caused by *Botrytis cinerea* generally develop aerial conidiophores giving the Grey Mould symptom, which helps to distinguish the two diseases. It is very important to identify Didymella Stem Rot quickly and take the appropriate control measures as it can be a devastating disease, particularly early in the life of the crop.

Control. It is important to remove the primary infectors before secondary spread has occurred. Plants with lesions at soil level should be carefully dug out without handling the lesion. The diseased plant with the soil around the roots should be put into a polythene sack and removed from the crop, preferably to be burned. Care should be taken when the disease has occurred in the previous crop to prevent its recurrence. The soil should be heat or chemically sterilised and the greenhouse structure washed down with a disinfectant or fumigated before the crop is planted. Any debris from the previously infected crop should be burned or taken away from the nursery. Prunings or dead plants should never be left outside the houses and allowed to decay.

Control can be achieved with an application of captan or a carbendazim fungicide applied within three days of planting out, and repeated 3 weeks later. It is particularly important to make the applications at the correct times.

Secondary spread within the crop is difficult to control. Lesions must not be handled and the practice of cutting out cankers with a knife must always be avoided. Stem lesions can be controlled by painting them with a mixture of benomyl and oil (Actipron). The disease can sometimes be controlled by drenching the roots with carbendazim followed by regular high volume sprays of vinclozolin.

In NFT grown crops carbendazim should be added to the nutrient solution as soon as the disease is found and high volume sprays applied as already described. Dead plants must be removed and burned or taken well away from the nursery. All stakes, boxes, string, etc., associated with the contaminated crop should be removed and burned or, where necessary, soaked in formalin for 24 hours.

Grey Mould (*Botrytis cinerea*)

This is the most common disease of the tomato crop. Leaflets, petioles, whole leaves, stems and fruits may be affected. The disease on the leaves often starts from flower parts and other debris which fall on the leaf surface. Once infection has occurred, a light brown, more or less circular lesion develops, which expands in size eventually covering the whole leaflet. The fungus produces its conidiophores and spores on the affected tissue giving the typical grey mould symptoms. Senescent leaves, often at the base of the plant, are readily colonised and it is probably infection and colonisation of these which results in the development of stem lesions (Fig. 7.8)

Considerable crop losses can occur when this fungus invades the stem, as attacked plants may be killed. Light brown, dry lesions varying in size from a few millimetres up to several centimetres long are characteristic of the

FIG. 7.8 A Botrytis leaf lesion with the pathogen sporulating on the petiole. Copyright May & Baker Ltd.

FIG. 7.9 A stem lesion caused by *Botrytis cinerea*. The pathogen is producing its typical grey mould growth on the lesion surface.

disease, and these may be covered by a brown grey fungal growth (Fig. 7.9). As the fungus mycelium ages, it darkens in colour and the lesions then appear to be black and are very similar in appearance to those caused by *Didymella lycopersici*. When examined closely with a hand lens the dark brown strands of mycelium can be seen distinguishing the lesion from those caused by Didymella.

There are a variety of symptoms on tomato fruits caused by *B. cinerea*. The commonest is ghost spot which consists of a pin-point, and often raised necrotic spot, surrounded by a white halo. Ghost spots arise following infection by a germinating spore but colonisation of the fruit tissue is restricted and rotting does not occur (Fig. 7.10). Occasionally ghost spots cover the whole of the calyx end of the fruit but are generally less numerous at the stylar end. When numerous, the halo symptom does not develop and the pin-

FIG. 7.10 Tomato fruit symptoms caused by *Botrytis cinerea*.
(a) Typical Ghost Spot symptom;
(b) numerous infection points giving the fruit a pimpled appearance as well as ghost spots; note the central necrotic fleck in some of the spots (i);
(c) grey-brown fruit rot at the calyx end – such affected fruits generally fall off (see Fig. 1.12(b) p. 19 for a comparison with aphid damage on tomato fruit; note the irregular blotches and cast skins of aphids).

(a)

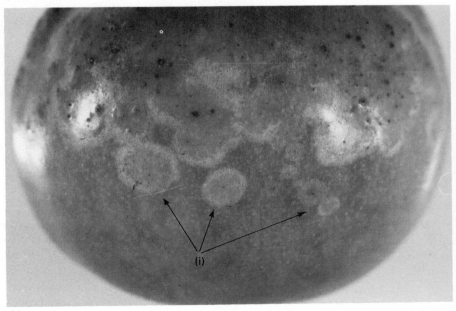

(i)

(b)

(c)

point raised spots or blisters on the fruit give it a rough surface. Tomato fruits are only susceptible to infection by germinating spores of *B. cinerea* during the initial stages of development. As soon as they reach approximately 2–4 cm diameter and their surface becomes shiny they resist infection. Tomato fruits affected by ghost spot are generally downgraded and, where the attack is severe, serious financial losses occur. Fruits can also become infected through flower parts stuck to their surface. This is particularly common at the stylar end. An irregular brown lesion develops on the fruit in the area of the flower parts.

Rotting of mature fruits by *B. cinerea* sometimes occurs and starts from the calyx end. A light brown to grey, water-soaked lesion appears and gradually spreads usually resulting in decay and fruit drop (see Fig. 7.10).

Generally the largest financial losses due to this disease occur when stem lesions kill plants. Why some lesions eventually girdle the stem and cause plant death when the majority remain restricted in size and have little or no effect on growth is not known. The nutrition of the plant does play an important role in the development of this disease and may be involved in the variation in stem lesion development.

Control.   Epidemic development is dependent upon prolonged periods of high humidity and surface wetness. Botrytis incidence can be kept at a low level by ventilating and removing lower leaves to enable a free flow of air through the crop. If heat is used together with ventilation, the relative humidity can be maintained at 70–80 per cent RH and this will prevent epidemic development. All debris from the crop must be removed to prevent the build-up of inoculum.

Control can also be achieved if fungicides are used to protect the crop from invading spores. Only those fungicides which prevent spore germination control ghost spot and, of the materials available, dichlofluanid is the most effective. Stem and leaf lesions are well controlled by sprays of iprodione, and a paint made with this fungicide and oil (Actipron) prevents the extension of stem lesions. The pathogen is commonly resistant to the benzimidazole fungicides which have consequently become less effective for the control of this disease. The continuous use of the dicarboximides, such as iprodione, or vinclozolin may also result in a resistance problem and spray programmes should be carefully planned to avoid this possibility (see Table 6.3).

Methods of fungicide application other than high volume are generally less effective.

Sclerotinia Disease (*Sclerotinia sclerotiorum*)

Although this pathogen is widespread and can infect most parts of the plant, it is only serious when it causes a rot of the stem which leads to the death of affected plants. It is unusual for a large proportion of the plants in a crop to be affected. The disease is most often found in new greenhouses built on sites which have recently been grassland or where new soil, particularly containing turf and weeds, has been used. This pathogen produces large black sclerotia which can be 1 cm or more long. These germinate and form small, cup-shaped apothecia which produce ascospores that are shot into the air. It is the ascospores which infect plants to produce a light brown, wet decay of the stems, leaves and sometimes fruits. Within a short time dense white, fluffy mycelial growth of the fungus is seen in the region of the lesion. Within the mycelial mat new sclerotia are formed which are initially grey-white in colour but eventually turn black. If these sclerotia fall onto the soil surface the pathogen may be carried over into the next crop. Most greenhouse crops are susceptible to this fungus.

Control.   As soon as the disease is recognised the affected plants should be removed and burned. Great care should be taken to avoid dropping debris with sclerotia onto the soil surface. The soil should be steam or chemically sterilised before the next crop, and it is often better to sterilise the soil, even on a new site, to avoid this and other diseases. If a large number of plants are affected and it becomes necessary to apply a fungicide, iprodione, vinclozolin or a benzimidazole fungicide are most likely to be effective.

Leaf Mould (*Fulvia fulva* syn. *Cladosporium fulvum*)

This is a very common disease particularly of unheated crops and may severely affect plant growth and yield. Yields begin to be affected when severe leaf mould has been present in the crop for about 6 weeks. For this reason, there is little point in applying expensive control measures if the disease first makes its appearance near to the end of cropping.

Leaf Mould is generally not seen until the middle of the summer and often increases in intensity as the season progresses. Irregular yellow blotches appear on the upper leaf surface and on the under surface, a grey-brown mould develops. Severely affected leaves are totally chlorotic and necrotic (Fig. 7.11). The uppermost leaves of the plant may only be affected when the attack is very severe. The fungus produces numerous spores which are readily spread. These spores germinate best at very high humidities (95 percent RH and above) and at high temperatures (20 °C and above). In such conditions infection takes place in a few hours. The spores are distributed by air movement, water splash or workers walking through the crop. They are very resistant to drying and may survive for several months in the absence of the crop.

Many pathogenic races of *Fulvia fulva* are known to occur. There are at least 20 genes for resistance, although only a few of them are commonly used

FIG. 7.11 Tomato Leaf Mould.
(a) Upper surface of the leaf with extensive yellowing often sharply delimited at the veins (i); (b) lower leaf surface where the pathogen, *Fulvia fulva* can be seen sporulating (ii).

(a)   (b)

in commercial cultivars. The naming of the races has led to some confusion especially as different systems have been used in various countries. In Canada races have been numbered in chronological order of discovery, whereas in Holland, an attempt has been made to link the nomenclature of the race with that of the corresponding gene for resistance. A complex situation has been somewhat simplified by the grouping of races in five groups A, B, C, D and E. Many of the current cultivars have genes for resistance to one or more of these groups but only a small number of cultivars are resistant to all of them (see Table 7.2).

Control.   Prevention of the disease can be achieved by the use of resistant cultivars and also by the careful control of humidity within the greenhouse. As much ventilation as possible should be given and the lower leaves taken off the plants as soon as possible. To keep the humidity as low as possible, overhead watering and pesticide sprays should be applied early in the day. Greenhouses with drip or trickle systems of irrigation often have lower humidities than those with spray systems. Circulating unheated air through the house often results in the dispersal of the spores and may not achieve a reduction in relative humidity.

There are a number of fungicides, including dichlofluanid and the benzimidazoles, which are effective and these are best used as high volume sprays, although drenches of the benzimidazole fungicides, in particular benomyl, have given a good control. Strains of the pathogen resistant to the benzimidazole fungicides are known to occur although they are not common in Europe.

Bacterial Canker (*Corynebacterium michiganense*)

This is not a common disease in Britain although it has occurred more frequently during the past few years, especially in the Channel Islands and in the south of England. It is common throughout the Continent of Europe

TABLE 7.2 The resistance of some tomato cultivars to Leaf Mould (*Fulvia fulva*)

Cultivar	Race group					Resistance to other diseases*		
	A	*B*	*C*	*D*	*E*	*Wilts*	*Root Rot*	*TMV*
Abunda	+	+	+	+	+	+	−	+
Ailsa Craig	−	−	−	−	−	−	−	−
Alicante	+?	or	more			−	−	−
Amberley Cross	+	+	−	−	−	−	−	−
Angela	+	+	+	−	−	+	−	−
Arasta	+	+	−	−	−	−	−	−
Asixcross	−	−	−	−	−	−	?	−
Bellina †	+	+	+	+	+	+	−	+
Clavito	+	+	−	−	−	−	−	+
Corno	+	+	−	−	−	−	+	−
Cudlow Cross	+	+	−	−	−	+	−	−
Cura	−	−	−	−	−	−	−	+
Curabel	+	+	+	+?	+?	+	−	+
Curato	+	+	−	−	−	+	−	+
Curesto	+	+	−	−	−	+	−	+
Daltona	+	+	+	+	−	+	−	+

Cultivar	Race group					Resistance to other diseases★		
	A	B	C	D	E	Wilts	Root Rot	TMV
Dawn	+	+	+	−	−	+	−	+
Dombito	−	+	−	−	−	+	−	+
Dombo	+	+	−	−	−	+	−	−
Duranto	+	+	+	+	+	+	−	+
Else	+	+	+	+	+	+	−	+
Estrella	+	+	+	+?	+?	+	−	+
Eurobrid	+	+	−	−	−	+	−	−
Eurocross BB	+	+	−	−	−	−	−	−
Eurovite	+	+	+	+	+	+	−	+
Extase	+	+	−	−	−	+	−	−
Flaneur	+	+	+	+	−	+	−	+
Gannet	+	+	−	−	−	+	−	−
Gardeners Delight	−	−	−	−	−	−	−	−
Goldstar†	+	+	+	+	+	+	−	+
Grenadier	+	+	−	−	−	+	−	−
Herald	+	+	−	−	−	−	−	−
Hollandbird	+	+	−	−	−	+	−	−
Kirdford Cross	+	+	−	−	−	−	−	+
Maascross	+	+	−	−	−	−	−	−
Marathon†	+	+	+	+	+	+	−	+
Marcanto	+	+	+	−	−	+	−	+
Martlet	+	+	−	−	−	+	−	−
Milores	+	+	−	−	−	−	−	+
MM Milo	+	+	−	−	−	−	−	−
MM Nova	+	+	−	−	−	−	−	−
Mondial†	+	+	+	+	+	+	−	+
Nemato	+	+	+	+	+	+	−	+
Odine	+	+	−	−	−	−	−	+
Ostona	+	+	+	+	+	+	−	+
Pagham Cross	+	+	−	−	−	−	−	+
Pamela	+	+	+	−	−	+	−	+
Panase	+	+	−	−	−	−	−	+
Piranto	+	+	+	+	+	+	+	+
Primset	+	+	−	−	−	−	−	+
Restino	+	+	+	+	+	+	−	+
Rianto	+	+	+	+	+	+	−	+
Rovato†	+	+	+	+	+	+	−	+
Sarina	+	+	+	−	−	+	−	+
Shirley	+	+	+	+	+	+	−	+
Sobeto	+	−	−	−	−	+	−	+
Solara	+	+	+	+	+	+	−	+
Sonatine	+	+	+	+	+	+	−	+
Sonato	+	+	−	−	−	−	−	+
Supercross	+	+	−	−	−	−	−	+
Surprise C70	+	+	−	−	−	−	−	−
Tamara	+	+	+	−	−	+	−	+
Tarka	+	+	+	−	−	+	−	+
Vicores	+	+	+	−	−	+	−	+
Virosa	+	+	+	+	+	+	−	+
Winterbird	+	+	−	−	−	+	−	−

+ Resistant

+? Precise details uncertain but thought to be resistant.

† Does not show silvering (chimera) symptoms.

★ See Tables 7.1, 7.3 and 7.4 for details of the other disease resistances, e.g. Table 7.3 shows wilt resistance divided into those cultivars resistant to Fusarium Wilt and Verticillium Wilt. A plus in this table indicates resistance to one or other but not necessarily both wilts.

and North America. Generally the first symptom noticed is necrotic spotting. On older plants the margins of the affected leaflets may wilt and curl upwards and inward. Later these leaves become brown and wither but remain attached to the stem. Often, only the leaflets on one side of the leaf are affected, and the plant may show a one-sided development of symptoms. Occasionally, affected plants remain symptomless for some time. Severely affected plants wilt and produce light coloured mealy streaks on the stem. Later some of these streaks rupture to form cankers which give the disease its name. Affected fruits show raised light coloured lesions with a darker centre, referred to as birds-eye spots (Fig. 7.12).

The bacterial pathogen moves in the phloem of affected plants but eventually colonises the pith, cortex and bark of the stem. When the stem is cut longitudinally there is a creamy white, yellow or reddish-brown line just inside the woody tissue. The pith readily separates from the wood along this line. As decay progresses, the pith becomes yellow and mealy in appearance and cavities are formed in the soft tissue. These latter symptoms are also diagnostic of the disease.

Seeds may become contaminated on their surfaces and the pathogen can survive on the seed surface from season to season. The bacteria can also persist in the soil and on debris for up to 2 or 3 years.

Infected or contaminated seed may give rise to infected seedlings, but symptoms usually appear some time after planting. Spread is favoured by high temperatures and wetness, so overhead damping in hot weather can result in epidemic development. Pesticide sprays may even help to spread the disease. Handling diseased plants during cultural operations results in spread along the rows and may also be responsible for the spread of the disease to other nurseries.

Control.   Seed is undoubtedly the most important primary source of this pathogen. Cleaning seeds which are contaminated is no substitute for seed from a clean source because, however efficient the treatment, it is never

FIG. 7.12 Bacterial canker (*Corynebacterium michiganense*), the birds-eye spotting symptom.

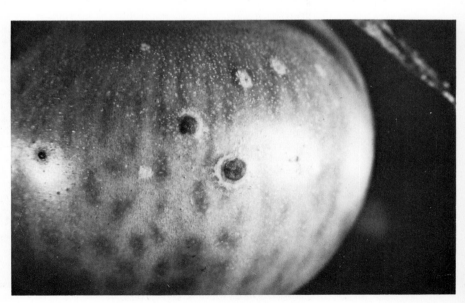

completely effective. If it is essential to use suspect seed, there are a number of treatments which are worth considering. The seed can be extracted by the traditional method of fermentation within the pulp of the fruit for 96 hours, before washing out the seeds. It is important to ferment the seed in its own juice and avoid adding water. Seeds can also be soaked in acetic acid, the concentration depending upon whether they are freshly extracted or dried before treatment.

When affected plants are found they should be removed and destroyed and overhead damping and pesticide applications reduced to a minimum. A copper fungicide applied at 3-day intervals will also help to reduce spread.

Workers should wash their hands thoroughly between visiting green-houses to minimize spread and should also change their overalls when moving from an infected to a healthy crop. If the disease is in the neigh-bourhood, all visitors should wash their hands and wear clean overalls when entering a crop.

Pith Necrosis or Brown Pith Necrosis (*Pseudomonas corrugata*)

This is a disease which varies considerably in its occurrence from season to season although it is found in many different countries in Europe, North America and Australasia. It is most common in crops grown without heat or started with heat but then grown unheated. Affected plants are always very vigorous, with thick fleshy stems and large leaves. Symptoms are seen just before fruit picking begins, often when the first truss has almost completely developed, and they may continue to appear for about 3 or 4 weeks and then stop. Infected plants may first be found when the upper leaves become chlor-otic and the plant wilts. There is some stunting in growth and the stem often shows extensive dry blackened areas which extend from a region about 15 cm above soil level, upwards. The stem in these affected areas may be completely collapsed. Above the black lesions on the stem affected plants are often symp-tomless, but severely affected plants frequently produce bunches of roots on the stem at various heights above soil level. A dark discoloration develops in the pith cavity of the petiole. Similarly, the pith of the main stem is black-ened (Fig. 7.13) or near to the top of the plant, where there is no pith cavity, it is light brown in colour. In older parts of the stem there may be large spaces with cross strands in the blackened pith, giving a ladder-like appearance. Sometimes the pith cavity is completely hollow. A similar dark discoloration is also seen in the large parenchymatous cells outside the vascular tissue. The discoloration of the pith and tissue adjacent to the vascular tissue generally extends down to the base of the stem at soil level, but does not appear to affect the roots. It also does not extend into the fruit, although the pith in the peduncle may be affected.

Diseased plants are not always killed and may continue to crop satisfac-torily. Sometimes the only symptom is the discoloration in the pith, which is only apparent when leaves are removed. The leaf scars do occasionally produce a creamy-white coloured bacterial ooze.

Control. As the type of plant growth is closely linked with the incidence of this disease, attempts should be made to avoid excessively soft or rank growth by manipulating the nutrition of the crop. Generally a high potassium

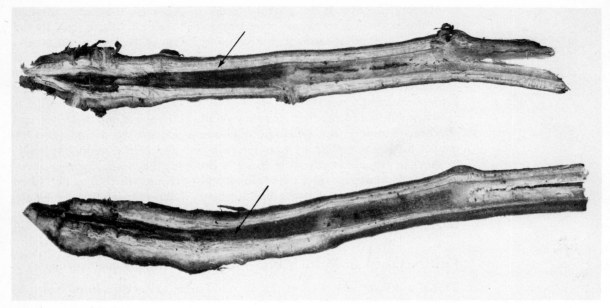

level in the base dressing and a liquid feed with a high potassium content will help to avoid too much vigour. The use of sprays has not proved to be satisfactory.

Bacterial Soft Rot (*Erwinia carotovora* var. *carotovora*)

Soft rotting of tomato stems and fruits occurs occasionally although it is unusual to find very many plants affected in any one crop. Stem symptoms consist of dark brown to black stem lesions, generally on the lower half of the stem, and these are usually soft and wet. If they are near a truss, the peduncle and fruit may also be affected. The rot progresses rapidly and affected plants wilt and die, especially when the crop is very vigorous and temperatures are high. The pathogen is usually present in most greenhouses and enters the plant through wounds. Spread is unusual but may occur through side shoot or deleafing wounds.

Control. This is not often a disease requiring control measures and the general application of techniques aimed at producing balanced growth should ensure that it is not a serious problem. When the disease occurs, affected plants should be removed and careful attention given to hygiene on the nursery.

Bacterial Spot, Speck or Scorch (*Pseudomonas syringae* pv. *tomato*)

Bacterial Spot occurs in the Channel Islands, in countries of Continental Europe and very occasionally in the UK. Very small dark brown spots (2–3 mm diameter) develop on the leaves, often with yellow haloes (Fig. 7.14). These may coalesce to kill the leaf. Similar spots may be present

FIG. 7.14 Small black lesions on tomato leaves caused by *Pseudomonas syringae* pv. *tomato*. Copyright ICI Plant Protection Division.

on the stems and raised black spots are found on the fruit. The pathogen is thought to be seed-borne but, once in the crop, is readily spread by water-splash.

Control.   Affected leaves should be removed, overhead watering avoided and the relative humidity in the greenhouse kept as low as possible. Copper fungicides may give some control of this disease when used as high volume sprays.

Tomato Powdery Mildew (*Leveillula taurica*)

This disease is very common on tomatoes grown in dry climates and occurs in greenhouse-grown crops in southern Europe but has not been found in more northern areas. A yellow spot or blotch appears on the upper leaf surface and on the underside a white to pale brown powdery fungal growth is seen, not unlike Tomato Leaf Mould in appearance. Epidemics develop at low relative humidities and at a temperature varying from 15–25 °C. Crops worst affected are often grown with a low level system of irrigation and those watered by overhead spray lines rarely suffer severe attacks.

This pathogen also infects peppers, eggplants and cucumbers. It is readily spread by the air-borne dissemination of its conidia.

Control.   Where environmental control can be practised Powdery Mildew is controlled to some extent, particularly if an overhead system of irrigation is available. Once established, control by means of fungicides is difficult to achieve, although some success has been reported using the benzimidazoles. Chlorothalonil may also give some suppression of this disease.

Bacterial Wilt (*Pseudomonas solanacearum*)

Although bacterial wilt has not been recorded affecting tomatoes in Europe it is a very serious disease in some warm countries. Other hosts include other plants in the Solanaceae, particularly the potato.

Symptoms of rapid wilting of the entire plant unaccompanied by stunting or yellowing of the leaves are typical. When the stem is cut across near to soil level the pith is darkened and has a water-soaked appearance. A greyish slimy exudate is formed when the stem is pressed. In the latter stages of decay the pith decomposes and a stem cavity results.

The pathogen is soil-borne and infects plants through their roots and stems. Spread from plant to plant is mainly by handling and water splash. The bacteria block the vascular tissue hence the wilt symptom. Resistance to this disease is not known in any commercial tomato cultivar although some sources of tolerance are available for breeders.

Control.   Affected plants should be removed immediately and overhead watering and damping avoided. There are no chemical means of control.

Septoria Leaf Spot or Septoria Blight (*Septoria lycopersici*)

This disease has only occasionally been recorded in the UK although it is very serious in many parts of the world, particularly in North America and Africa. Epidemics of Septoria Leaf Spot are most common in field grown crops in countries where summer temperatures are fairly high and rainfall abundant.

The older leaves near the ground are first affected and develop watersoaked spots. These spots have a grey centre with dark margins and after a time are covered in small black pycnidia. Eventually, the whole of the leaf is colonised and dies. The stems and blossoms are sometimes attacked but the fruits are rarely affected.

The pathogen can grow on a number of weed hosts in the Solanaceae.

Wet weather favours pathogen spread as spores ooze from the pycnidia in moist conditions. Water splash disseminates these spores. The fungus is most active at temperatures in the range of 15–25 °C.

Control.   Good weed control and the removal of all plant debris will help to control this disease. Fungicides such as zineb, maneb and the benzimidazoles are most likely to be effective.

Stemphylium Leaf Blight (*Stemphylium vesicarium* and *S. botryosum*)

This leaf spotting disease of tomatoes is not of great economic significance in Europe but occurs occasionally. A similar disease is known elsewhere and there are records from the UK of *Pleospora herbarum* (perfect stage of *S. botryosum*) causing a foot and fruit rot. Small dark brown to greyish spots up to 1 cm in diameter and irregular in outline are produced on the leaves of affected plants. These may coalesce to produce large dead areas with wilting and death of the older leaves. Petioles, stems and fruits on the plants are not affected.

Control.   Outbreaks have been associated with conditions of high humidity. Some commonly used fungicides, such as benomyl and mancozeb, do not control this disease but iprodione is known to be effective against related fungi.

Early Blight, Target Spot or Alternaria Blight (*Alternaria solani*)

This is not a very common disease in the UK although it has been found on a number of occasions but does cause problems elsewhere, particularly in North America. The fungus produces a stem canker, which is severe on young plants, a fruit rot and a leaf spot. This latter symptom is the only one known in the UK. Small, irregular, brown spots first appear on the older leaves. These enlarge to 1 cm in diameter and are often concentric and ring-like in appearance, hence the name target spot (Fig. 7.15). They are generally surrounded by a chlorotic halo. Spots with raised grey centres may develop on the stem. Lesions around the calyx end of the fruit result in fruit drop. The fungus produces masses of black spores on affected fruits. Disease development is favoured by conditions of high humidity and crop loss is a direct result of death of the foliage and infection of fruit.

Control.   This disease may be seed-borne and seeds should not be saved from an affected crop. Thiram or iprodione seed treatment are effective. Careful attention should be given to hygiene, and high volume sprays of iprodione or vinclozolin should ensure effective control.

Blight or Late Blight (*Phytophthora infestans*)

Blight of tomatoes is caused by the Potato Blight pathogen. It is a serious disease of the field crop in Europe and can also be troublesome in unheated greenhouses. Both leaves and fruits are affected. Large, light to dark brown spots, usually with a paler margin, appear on the leaves. These rapidly

FIG. 7.15   Dark brown spots with a pale centre caused by *Alternaria solani*; the disease is known as Early Blight in some countries. Copyright ICI Plant Protection Division.

increase in size, until the whole of the leaflet and eventually the leaf is affected (Fig. 7.16). On the underside of the leaf the fungus sporulates and a white, downy fungal growth is visible on the affected area. Stems may also be attacked and dark streak symptoms are frequently found. Diseased fruits are completely unmarketable. Large, rusty brown, hard areas appear on the green fruits and these may extend until the whole of the fruit is affected (see Fig. 7.17). Spores are readily air-borne and also spread by water splash.

In unheated greenhouse crops, the first symptoms are often seen in August when the disease is very common in potato crops. Blight frequently develops on plants in the centre of long polythene tunnels where ventilation and air movement is very poor. Consistent high temperatures (25 °C) inhibit this disease completely.

Control.   Potato crops are the major source of the pathogen for the green-house crop. Where unheated tomato crops are near to potato crops, a routine spray application is worthwhile especially in a 'blight year'. Information can usually be obtained locally on the likelihood of occurrence of blight. A minimum temperature of 10 °C with 75 per cent RH maintained for 48 hours constitutes a period of weather favourable for blight development. The dithiocarbamate fungicides, such as zineb and mancozeb, are the most effective but must be used regularly. A mixture of metalaxyl and mancozeb gives a very good control of this disease in potatoes. Any cultural operations which will reduce the humidity within the crop will also be beneficial.

Buckeye Rot (*Phytophthora nicotianae* var. *parasitica*)

This pathogen, which also causes damping-off and a foot rot of the crop. produces symptoms on the fruit. It is a common disease and frequently

FIG. 7.16   Leaf lesions of Potato Blight; initially these are grey-green in colour and the pathogen, *Phytophthora infestans*, may be seen on the lesion surface.

FIG. 7.17 Blight on a tomato fruit, the rot is hard and characterised by the firm brown discoloration of the fruit wall.

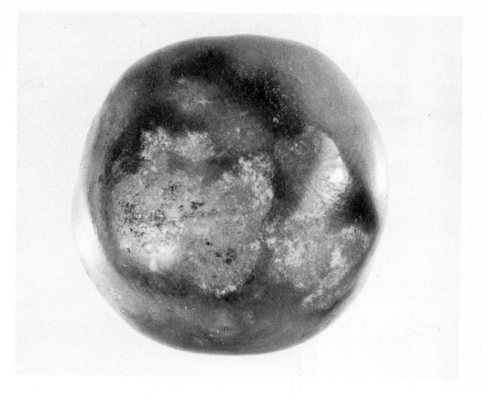

occurs on nurseries where the soil has not been sterilised. Infection usually results when contaminated soil is splashed onto the plants, so is most frequently seen on the lower trusses. Recent developments in cultural systems, involving the layering of plants, results in most trusses developing near to the soil and is likely to increase in the incidence of this disease. The characteristic fruit symptom is the development of brown concentric rings on a grey-brown lesion with a grey centre. Affected fruits often fall onto the soil (Fig. 7.18).

Control.   Soil splashing onto the fruit is the source of the pathogen so this should be avoided. Hose-watering and overhead irrigation systems are most likely to give rise to splash. Sometimes covering the soil surface with straw will prevent soil splashing. By the time symptoms have appeared it is too late to apply control measures.

All affected fruits should be picked up and removed from the house. Greenhouse soil should be sterilised before planting a further crop of tomatoes. Sometimes the use of a copper fungicide will help to control this disease.

Phoma Rot (*Phoma destructiva*)

This disease has been recorded on only a few occasions in the UK, although it is a well known cause of rot in warm countries. Leaves and fruits are affected, although it is the fruit rot stage which causes the most serious loss of crop. Zonate black spots appear on the leaves which increase in size and

FIG. 7.18   Buckeye Rot:
caused by *Phytophthora
nicotianae* var.
parasitica; notice the
concentric rings which
usually occur on a grey-
brown decaying area.

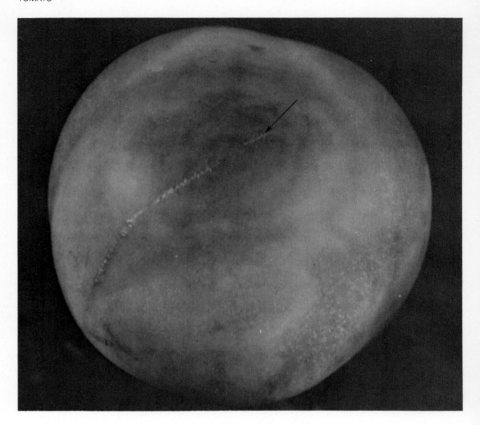

are similar in appearance to those of Alternaria Blight. The stem may also show elongated spots and faint concentric markings. Spotting of the fruit, which often develops during transit, can be a major problem. Slightly depressed spots occur near to the calyx end and these become brown and are covered in pycnidia. The fungus survives on decaying plant debris in the soil which is the primary source of the pathogen.

Control.   Control can be achieved by attention to hygiene and the use of high volume fungicide sprays. The benzimidazole fungicides, zineb and iprodione or vinclozolin are most likely to be effective.

Verticillium Wilt or Sleepy Disease (*Verticillium albo-atrum* and *V. dahliae*)

Verticillium Wilt can be a devastating disease although it is now not very common and usually affects only a few plants. The fungi that cause this disease also attack a number of other greenhouse crops including cucumbers, chrysanthemums and pelargoniums but not carnations. (The wilt disease of carnations often referred to as Verticillium Wilt is caused by a different pathogen – see p. 254). Both species of Verticillium cause very similar symptoms but *V. albo-atrum* is often regarded as the most aggressive. Symptoms of Verticillium Wilt are distinguishable from wilting due to root rot and water shortage by wilting of the older, lower leaves first. During the early stages of attack, wilting may be severe in the day with apparent recovery at night. The interval from first symptoms to death may be 3 or 4 weeks depending upon the weather. Initially the root system appears to be healthy but, as the disease progresses, some secondary rots occur.

If the stem of an affected plant is cut across, a pronounced brown discoloration is seen in the vascular system. This may be traced from soil level to a metre or more above the ground, differentiating it from a similar discoloration associated with root rot which rarely extends more than 10–15 cm above soil level (Fig. 7.19). Infection takes place through the roots and the whole plant is eventually colonised. When the affected plants are removed, any root debris left in the soil is likely to be a source of the pathogen for succeeding crops. As infection at one point of the root system results in the

FIG. 7.19 Discoloration of the vascular tissue caused by *Verticillium albo-atrum*. This discoloration extends well up the plant and is not confined to the basal 20 cm of stem.

complete colonisation and probable death of the plant (unlike root rots where multiple infections are necessary before severe losses occur), it is of utmost importance that the soil should be sterilised to the depth of the root growth. The pathogen survives as resting bodies in the soil and can also multiply to a limited extent in some soils in the absence of host plants.

Spores (conidia) are sometimes produced on affected plants, especially those that have died and been left in the greenhouse. The conidia are readily disseminated by air currents and spread by water splash. There are also a few records of wilt being introduced in propagation soil, resulting in diseased plants at the time of planting. Seed contamination has been reported but is very rare.

A seasonal pattern of appearance of wilt symptoms often occurs. *Verticillium albo-atrum* induces wilt early in the season and again towards the end of the crop. This fungus is not favoured by temperatures of about 25 °C and so may be inhibited in warm conditions. *Verticillium dahliae* is not so temperature dependent and produces wilt symptoms over a wide temperature range. Thus the practice of raising the greenhouse temperature when wilt appears is only of benefit if the disease is caused by *V. albo-atrum*.

Control.   There are a number of ways of controlling Verticillium Wilt. The easiest, and in many ways the most effective, is the use of resistant cultivars or alternatively, grafting susceptible cultivars onto resistant rootstocks (Table 7.3 and Table 7.1). It is essential to sever the scion root system before planting.

If susceptible cultivars are grown, it is necessary to sterilise the soil to a depth of 25 cm. For shorter term crops it may be satisfactory to treat to a shallower depth, but care must be taken with post-treatment cultivations to avoid bringing up untreated soil to the surface and mixing it with the treated.

Once the disease has appeared, there is little that can be done. If *V. albo-atrum* is diagnosed, raising the temperature in the greenhouse will prevent serious crop loss.

Drenching plants in affected crops with a benzimidazole fungicide may help to minimise the effects of the disease. The first application must be made as soon as wilt symptoms appear and further applications given at monthly intervals.

Fusarium Wilt (*F. oxysporum* f.sp. *lycopersici*)

This wilt disease has increased in incidence in recent years and is more commonly found than Verticillium Wilt. Symptoms of Fusarium Wilt are not easily distinguished from those of Verticillium Wilt. There is a tendency for more chlorosis of the leaves and stems of plants affected by Fusarium Wilt, often with one side of the plant severely affected. The first sign of attack is usually chlorosis of the lower leaves and slight wilting of the plant. This symptom increases in intensity until all the plant shows symptoms. During the latter stages of development the stem may develop yellow streaks; a one-sided yellow discoloration of the stem sometimes occurs and the top of the plant may show severe symptoms but new and apparently healthy growth is produced from the base.

When the stem is split longitudinally, a dark brown vascular discoloration is apparent in the vascular tissue extending well up the plant.

TABLE 7.3 The resistance of some tomato cultivars to Verticillium and Fusarium Wilt diseases

Cultivar	Verticillium	Fusarium	
		† Race 0	Race 1
Abunda	+	+	+
Angela	−	+	+
Bellina	−	+	+
Cudlow Cross	−	+	−
Curabel	−	+	−
Curato	−	+	−
Curesto	−	+	−
Daltona	−	+	−
Dawn	−	+	+
Dombito	−	+	+
Dombo	+	+	+
Duranto	−	+	+
Else	−	+	+
Estrella	+	+	−
Eurobrid	+	+	−
Eurovite	−	+	+
Flaneur	−	+	+
Gannet	+	+	−
Goldstar	−	+	+
Grenadier	−	+	−
Hollandbrid	+	+	−
Marathon	+	+	+
Marcanto	−	+	+
Martlet	+	+	−
Mondial	−	+	+
Nemato	+	+	−
Ostona	−	+	−
Pamela	−	+	−
Piranto	+	+	+
Restina	−	+	+
Rianto	−	+	+
Rovato	−	+	+
Sarina	−	+	+
Shirley	−	+	+
Sobeto	−	+	−
Solara	+	+	+
Sonatine	−	+	+
Sonato	−	+	−
Tamara	−	+	+
Tarka	−	+	+
Vicores	−	+	−
Virosa	−	+	−
Winterbrid	+	+	−

† Races 0 and 1 are sometimes referred to as 1 and 2.
+ Resistant

Contaminated seeds are a possible source of this disease. Once established on a nursery, the disease is able to survive in the soil for considerable periods. The fungus is present in root debris but can persist in the soil as chlamydospores.

There are three known races (0, 1 and 2) of *F. oxysporum* f. sp. *lycopersici* and two of them (0 and 1) occur in Europe. Resistance to races 0 and 1 or both has been bred into some commercial cultivars. Some rootstocks are also resistant (see Table 7.1 and 7.3).

Control.   The use of Fusarium Wilt resistant cultivars or rootstocks is the easiest way of controlling this disease. It is essential to sever the scion root system before planting grafted plants.

Treatment of infested soil is most satisfactorily done with steam. It is essential to achieve effective treatment to at least 25 cm for main crop tomatoes, and even with a short-term crop, the depth of treatment must be sufficient to prevent untreated soil being mixed with treated during pre-planting cultivations. Where the disease has been a serious problem, it is often worth using grafted plants in conjunction with steam treatment. Chemical soil sterilants are less effective and should be used in combination with resistant cultivars or grafting.

Drench treatments of the growing crop with benzimidazole fungicides give only partial control.

VIRUS DISEASES

Tomato mosaic

Tomato mosaic is caused by Tomato Mosaic Virus (TMV) and, until the recent development of resistant cultivars, was the most common and important disease of the crop. At present it is relatively uncommon in most countries where the crop is grown in greenhouses. TMV is the most infectious of all known plant viruses and is also very resistant to physical treatments such as high or low temperatures. Because of its durability, it is able to survive in a viable state for many years. The effects of this disease on commercial crops are difficult to establish precisely, but in experimental work up to a 25 per cent reduction in crop yield has been recorded. In addition, the disease also affects fruit quality.

Symptoms.   The symptoms of TMV are very variable and are influenced by a number of factors including the strain of the virus, the environment and the cultivar. Initially, affected plants may wilt in sunshine, especially if the crop is growing quickly. Recovery from wilting follows as soon as the temperature drops. This phase of wilting is temporary and normally lasts for a period of 1 or 2 weeks after infection. The most common symptom of TMV is a mosaic symptom which may vary from an almost inconspicuous pale mottle to bright yellow and green clearly demarcated areas. The clearly defined yellow symptom is frequently referred to as aucuba mosaic (Fig. 7.20).

Another symptom of some strains of TMV is the reduction in leaf width, sometimes to such an extent that individual leaflets are reduced to tendril-like growths known as the shoestrings or fernleaves. Such distortion may be confused with that resulting from growth regulator herbicide injury or Cucumber Mosaic Virus, but differs in the sequence of distortion shown by leaves of various ages (Fig. 7.21). The lowest distorted leaf shows reduced serration, with increasing simplification of shape with successive leaves until the leaves are reduced to a very narrow strap of tissue. These narrow leaves generally have small outgrowths of tissue on their undersides which are known as 'enations' (Fig. 7.22).

FIG. 7.20 Tomato Mosaic Virus – aucuba strain producing distinct bright yellow areas on the green leaves.

FIG. 7.21 Tomato Mosaic Virus – sequence of leaf distortion patterns following infection by a distorting or fern leaf strain. Leaf (a) was developing at the time of infection and shows some distortion of the proximal leaflet; leaf (b) shows total reduction in width of all leaflets; in leaf (c) only the terminal leaflet is severely affected; leaf (d) is pinnate. Subsequent leaves show a reduction in the extent of pinnation until a normal shaped leaf is once more produced although with a marked mosaic. This sequence is consistently shown by plants infected by such strains and to a lesser extent when less severely distorting strains infect plants. Copyright Audio Visual Services Department, University of Guelph.

(a)   (b)   (c)   (d)

Plants recovering from severe leaf distortion initially produce pinnate leaves (vetch-like) and eventually new leaves are normal in shape but usually with a conspicuous mosaic. About six to eight leaves may be affected in this sequence of leaf shape changes. Continuous leaf distortion affecting all the leaves on the plant is not typical of TMV. Some TMV strains do not affect leaf shape as severely, although the leaf serration may be affected (Fig. 7.23).

Mature plants may show stem symptoms varying from pale green to dark green or black stripes, often accompanied by a yellow-brown bronzed colour of the older leaves. This symptom syndrome is known as streak or stripe. A similar symptom results from mixed infection by TMV and Potato Virus X (see p. 151).

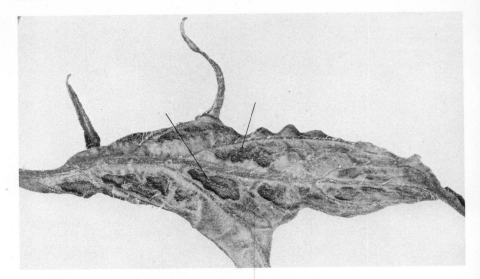

(a)   (b)   (c)   (d)

A wide range of fruit symptoms have been attributed to TMV but by far the most important is bronzing (also known as internal browning) which is distinct from blotchy ripening. Bronzing symptoms are first seen in green fruit, especially at the calyx end where the tissue around the vascular bundles becomes necrotic. This discoloration is clearly seen through the skin. As the fruit ripens, the affected areas often remain green and hard but may eventually turn yellow. Affected fruits are unmarketable. Bronzing is usually confined to one or two trusses on a plant but occasionally affects more.

Non-virus induced bronzing also occurs and has been called physiological bronzing. The main symptom difference between this and virus bronzing is the appearance of black lines, which are clearly visible at the stylar end of fruit (Fig. 7.24)

Sunken areas, sometimes brown or black in colour and known as pits, may be formed at the calyx end of the fruit. Such fruits generally occur in small numbers in crops where bronzing is present. A variety of other fruit symp-

FIG. 7.24 Black lines to the stylar end of the fruit are characteristic of tomato fruits affected by 'physiological bronzing'.

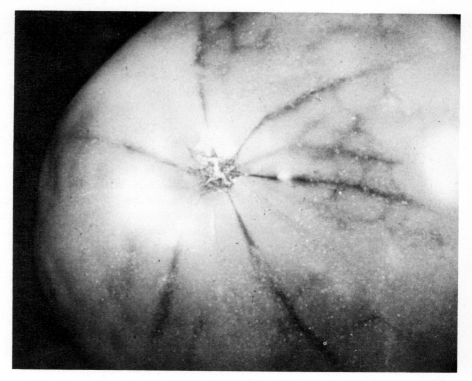

toms have been attributed to TMV but most of them are not as important as bronzing and pitting.

TMV can have serious effects on fruit set and one or more trusses may be lost as a result of flower drop or set failure. Failure to set is confined to the trusses which are developing their flowers at the time of infection. It is usual for one truss to be severely affected and the following two trusses to show some effects. Subsequently, truss set is usually normal.

Strains of TMV.   At present a number of strains of TMV have been recognised and are referred to as strains 0, 1, 2, 1:2 and 2^2. Strain 0 attacks any universally susceptible cultivar and strain 1 all susceptibles, together with any containing the resistance factor (*Tm*-1) (see Fig. 5.1; p. 67).

Most strains of TMV will infect a number of other hosts in addition to tomatoes and this is another way of differentiating strains or forms of TMV. For instance the tobacco form produces a mosaic in both tobacco and tomato, whereas the tomato form does not produce a mosaic in most tobacco cultivars. Symptoms such as aucuba mosaic, fern leaf, green mosaic, etc., have also been used as a means of differentiating strains. There is no obvious relationship between strains defined on the basis of the hosts genes for resistance, host range or symptom production.

Sources of TMV.   The two most important primary sources of TMV are seeds and plant debris. TMV can survive in plant debris in the soil for a considerable period, although the virus concentration decreases with time.

As roots and other debris decompose, the virus is released into the soil where it only survives for a few days.

Seeds can be contaminated externally on the seedcoat or, less frequently, the virus may enter the endosperm. The virus is never found in the embryo. Endosperm infection is most common when fruits are developing at the time the plant becomes infected and even then it is not frequent. Fruits which have formed seeds before infection occurs may eventually produce contaminated seeds.

Other possible primary sources of TMV include contaminated clothing, smoking tobacco, debris on structures and visitors to the crop. The most important agents of spread of the virus are the nursery workers tending the plants, picking fruit or merely walking along the paths and brushing the plants. Initially, a definite pattern of spread can be seen usually following the direction of working in the crop. The outer rows, particularly those which have a path along one side only, are often the last to show symptoms, indicating that movement along the pathways may be the most important means of spread.

Control.   Most of the commonly grown cultivars are resistant to one or more strains of TMV (Table 7.4). This is by far the most effective means of controlling this disease and, since cultivars with the gene Tm-2^2 have been widely used, Tomato Mosaic has become a relatively unimportant disease. Every effort should be made to prevent the entry of TMV onto a nursery. Seed can be freed from TMV by heating them in an oven at 70 °C for 4 days. Providing the seeds are dry during the treatment, germination is unaffected and all TMV on and in the seedcoat is inactivated. Virus in the endosperm may, however, survive this treatment. For growers who save their own seed, the best method of seed extraction to ensure a low virus status is with hydrochloric acid. Ordinary fermentation extraction does not free tomato seeds from TMV. Whenever fruits are saved for seed, it is advisable to take them from the first or second trusses as this minimises the chance of endosperm infection. Infected seedlings which appear during propagation should be carefully removed from the bench and hands washed thoroughly after

TABLE 7.4 The resistance of some tomato cultivars to Tomato Mosaic Virus (TMV)

Cultivar	Gene(s) for resistance
Clavito, Supercross	Tm-1 only
Dombito	Tm-1, Tm-2
Abunda, Angela, Bellina Cura, Curabel, Curato, Daltona, Dawn, Duranto, Else, Estrella, Eurovite, Flaneur, Goldstar, Marathon, Marcanto, Milores, Mondial, Nemato, Odine, Ostona, Pamela, Piranto, Restino Rianto, Rovato, Sarina, Shirley, Sobeta, Solara, Sonatine, Sonato Tamara, Tarka, Vicores, Virosa	Tm-2^2 only
Kirdford Cross, Pagham Cross	Tm-1, Tm-2, Tm-2^2

handling such plants. Great care must be taken to avoid contact between infected plants and their neighbours.

Debris-borne TMV is almost impossible to eliminate from the soil but can be reduced by a 2 year interval between tomato crops or by steam sterilisation. Thick roots (0.5 cm diameter and more) are difficult to heat thoroughly and TMV within them will withstand high soil temperatures. It is important to raise the soil temperature to as near to 100 °C as possible and maintain this temperature for 10 minutes (see pp. 76–82) in order to eliminate such virus. Once the plant debris breaks down in the soil and the virus is released, it does not survive for very long. It is, however, possible for chemical soil sterilants to slow the breakdown of debris by reducing the microflora of the soil and, in this way, their use may prolong the survival of TMV.

Strict hygiene should be practised on the nursery when tending the crop. Visitors from other nurseries should wear a clean overall before entering a tomato crop.

Yield and quality losses are less when plants are grown without excessive vigour. The use of a nitrogen feed when the symptoms first appear may minimise the intensity of the mosaic but generally has no beneficial effect on yield or quality. High temperatures result in an intensification of yellow mosaic and low temperatures may enhance the severity of leaf distortion. It is doubtful whether temperature manipulation helps to reduce the effect of the disease on yield or quality.

Mild and almost symptomless strains of TMV can be used to inoculate susceptible cultivars early in propagation and protect them from infection by more severe strains (Fig. 7.25). In this way yield and quality losses can be considerably reduced. Plants are protected within a few days of infection. The diluted virus is applied at 1.5 atmospheres (approximately 25 lb/in^2) holding the spray gun 10 cm above the plants. Carborundum, 600 mesh, is added at the rate of 1 g per 100 ml of diluted virus. This slightly damages the leaf surface and allows the TMV to enter (Fig. 7.26).

Mixed Virus Streak (Tomato Mosaic Virus and Potato Virus X)

Dark brown and black streaks on the stems accompanied by pitting of the fruits of at least one truss are symptoms of Mixed Virus Streak. The streaks are generally long and narrow, sometimes extending for the greater part of the length of the stem. The youngest growth at the apex of the plant and also the side shoots generally show a conspicuous mosaic symptom. These symptoms can be caused by a strain of TMV, known as the streak strain, but more frequently by mixed infections of any strain of TMV together with Potato Virus X (PVX). It is necessary for PVX to infect the tomato plant first, or for the two viruses to infect the plant simultaneously for the streak symptom to occur. If TMV infects first, the mosaic symptom is intensified by subsequent PVX infection, but streak symptoms do not develop. PVX-infected tomato plants are more or less symptomless or at most there may be slight chlorosis of the older leaves and some pin-point necrotic flecks on other leaves.

All strains of TMV and PVX are very infectious and readily spread so that

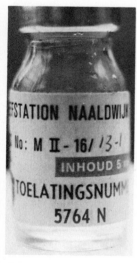

FIG. 7.25 A mild strain of TMV (MII–16) produced in the Netherlands and used to inoculate susceptible tomato cultivars to protect them from the effects of more severe strains.

FIG. 7.26 Tomato seedlings being inoculated with a mild strain of TMV. The virus is applied at high pressure together with a small quantity of abrasive which damages the leaves sufficiently to allow the mild strain of virus to infect the seedlings. Copyright Carborundum Ltd.

streak can spread rapidly through a crop. This disease has become uncommon since TMV resistant cultivars have been widely used.

Control.   Mixed Virus Streak cannot be controlled by the usual methods of TMV control. However, the source of PVX should be traced and further introduction prevented. Potatoes are the most common source of PVX. Occasionally, potato plants are found in tomato houses, particularly on new sites. Clothing may also be a source of PVX, particularly if tomato workers have been working in a potato crop (the home garden can be a source).

When virus streak occurs, affected plants should be carefully pulled out and removed from the crop, making sure that unaffected plants are not brushed with the foliage of the affected plants. This operation should be done at the end of the working week so that the operator is completely freed from contaminating virus before returning to the crop. When the operation is complete, the workers' overalls should be changed and hands washed three times in soap and water using a brush to ensure that microscopic pieces of plant debris are removed from beneath the finger nails.

Other virus diseases

Tomato Aspermy Virus

Aspermy is not common in tomatoes and rarely affects more than a few plants in a crop. This virus also affects chrysanthemums, producing flower distortion symptoms (see p. 274) and, as it is aphid-transmitted, the disease is often seen in tomato crops when aspermy-infected chrysanthemums are nearby. The most conspicuous symptom is the cessation of growth of the apex of the main stem and the development of lateral shoots so that the plants become bushy. The leaves may have a yellow to green mottle with some reddening on their undersides. Fruits are often reduced in size and those formed after infection do not have any seeds (Fig. 7.27). Good aphid control usually prevents this disease from occurring.

Tomato Spotted Wilt Virus

This virus is commonly found in ornamentals but is rarely seen in tomatoes. The young leaves of affected tomatoes show a slight clearing of the veins accompanied by pale rings. Later the foliage becomes bronze in colour and the topmost leaves curl downwards. Fruits may show a pale, irregular mottle, sometimes with distinct concentric rings. This virus is unusual in that it is transmitted by thrips. Where the tomato crop is in close proximity with

FIG. 7.27 Seedless tomato fruits resulting from an attack by Tomato Aspermy Virus.

nursery stock, dahlias and arum lilies, thrip control measures should be regularly applied and a careful watch kept for spotted wilt.

Cucumber Mosaic Virus (CMV)

Although a very common virus disease, it is rarely seen in tomato crops. A leaf mottle is produced in infected plants and leaf distortions occur, similar to those produced by TMV. The narrowing of the leaves develops in all environmental conditions and all leaves are affected. CMV is aphid-borne and has a wide variety of hosts including cucumbers, lettuce and chrysanthemums. Aphid control generally prevents this disease.

Nematode-transmitted virus diseases

Tomato Black Ring Virus, Arabis Mosaic Virus, Strawberry Latent Ringspot Virus and Raspberry Ringspot Virus are all transmitted by dagger nematodes and all can infect tomatoes. Some natural infection has been found, although only rarely. Tomato Black Ring produces a ringspot symptom on the leaves with dark streaks on the petioles and stems. Young plants may be killed but those that survive grow normally producing a mild mosaic.

These diseases are unlikely to be a severe problem on sites where regular soil sterilisation is practised.

NON-PATHOGENIC DISORDERS

Silvering (chimera)

Small and often angular silver coloured spots appear on the leaves of young plants. Older plants show a similar coloration affecting whole leaflets or leaves and sometimes the entire apex of the plant. When plants are severely affected they fail to set fruit. Generally, the longer the crop is grown the greater the incidence of silvering, although during propagation a period of low temperatures may increase the incidence of the silver fleck symptom. The earliest sown crops often show the greatest incidence of silvering.

The silvering symptom is known to be genetically controlled and there are some cultivars which are far less prone to this disease and a few are 'resistant' [see Table 7.2]. Affected plants can sometimes be saved by allowing a side shoot to develop from normal tissue in order to replace the affected apex, which is then removed.

Leaf distortion

Some cultivars produce a leaf distortion, often on one side, somewhat similar to that of the TMV fernleaf or shoestring symptom but affected plants do not recover, although subsequently, normal shoots may grow from the unaffected side of an affected plant. A normal side shoot can be used to replace the distorted part of the plant. This type of distortion is characteristic of some cultivars which do not show the silvering symptom, e.g. Eurocross BB.

Leaf distortion can also result from growth regulator herbicide injury. Chemicals such as 2,4-D, MCPA and 2,3,6-TBA produce gross plant distortion at sub-lethal levels. A characteristic of damage by these herbicides is a change in the vein pattern of the leaflets which become parallel with the tip of the leaflets being drawn into a fine point. Often the youngest leaves have a hood-like appearance. Fruits on affected plants are often elongated becoming plum-shaped with a marked beak at the stylar end. Some herbicides, such as mecoprop, induce prolific adventitious root formation along the stem without distortion of the leaf (Fig. 7.28).

Blossom End Rot

This is a common disorder of plants grown in containers and in polythene bags. The fruit shows a circular brown sunken area at the stylar end and

FIG. 7.28 Herbicide damage caused by sub-lethal doses of growth regulating herbicides.
(a) Typical vein pattern caused by 2,4-D and MCPA; notice the veins tend towards a fan-shaped pattern and the leaf margin shows a marked pointing of the normally blunt-ended lobes;
(b) severe distortion of leaflets caused by 2,3,6-TBA (see Fig. 1.21 (p. 28) for a comparison of the effect of picloram and 2,3,6-TBA on tomato leaves).

(a)

(b)

FIG. 7.29 Black to brown circular areas at the stylar end of the fruit. This condition is commonly known as Blossom End Rot.

affected fruits ripen prematurely (Fig. 7.29). Internally the fruit is blackened. Blossom End Rot is due to calcium deficiency which may be induced by allowing the plants to dry out as the fruit is developing. It can usually be prevented by maintaining an even water supply, although sometimes this is not enough and sprays of calcium nitrate may be necessary. Some cultivars, e.g. Sonatine, are very prone to this problem.

Blotchy ripening

Sometimes diseases such as TMV can result in uneven ripening but occasionally plants produce uneven coloured fruits with large yellow or green areas on their sides or shoulders. Such uneven ripening can result from low levels of potassium in the soil, very high day temperatures giving uneven heating of the fruit and excessive deleafing which exposes the fruits directly to the sun. High temperatures are known to inhibit the formation of the red pigment.

FURTHER READING

Griffin M. J. and Savage, M. J. (1983) *Control of pests and diseases of protected crops – Tomatoes*. Ministry of Agriculture, Fisheries and Food (Publications), Lion House, Willowburn Estate, Alnwick, Northumberland.

Hobson, G. E., Davies, J. N. and Winsor, G. W. (1977) *Ripening Disorders of Tomato Fruit*. Grower Bulletin No. 4. Glasshouse Crops Research Institute, Littlehampton.

McKay, R. (1949) *Tomato Diseases*. At the Sign of the Three Candles, Dublin.

McKeen, C. D. (1972) *Tomato Diseases*. Canada Department of Agriculture Publication 1479. Information Canada, Ottawa.

Kingham, H. G. (1973) *The U.K. Tomato Manual*. Grower Books, London.

Webb, R. E., Good, J. M. and Danielson, L. L. (1967) *Tomato Diseases and Their Control*. Agriculture Handbook Number 203. Agricultural Research Service, United States Department of Agriculture, Washington, DC.

CHAPTER 8

CUCUMBER

CULTURE

Pre-planting preparation

Cucumbers are very susceptible to damping-off and root rot diseases so it is essential to sterilise all propagation media. Steam is used for the treatment of soil; most proprietary brands of sand and peat compost are pathogen free. Greenhouse soil is usually steam treated before planting. It is important to raise the soil temperature to 20 °C before planting.

Propagation

For the earliest crops, seeds are sown in January, and for late planted or second crops, seeds may be sown in May or June. The optimum temperature for germination is 27 °C and emergence occurs in 3–4 days. Seedlings may be raised in blocks or in boxes and transplanted into pots. Supplementary light is used to aid growth early in the year and the atmosphere of the greenhouse is frequently enriched with carbon dioxide (1000 p.p.m.). During propagation, day temperatures are kept at 21 °C falling to 19 °C at night. Within 2 or 3 weeks, plants are ready to plant into their cropping positions. Approximately 7500–12 500 plants are used per hectare (3000–5000 acre).

Cropping

Harvesting begins within 4–5 weeks from planting when the first fruits are taken from the main stems. All the commonly grown commercial cultivars produce only female flowers but some of the older cultivars, mainly used by amateurs, produce both male and female flowers, and care must be taken to avoid pollination by removing the male flowers and by preventing bees entering the greenhouse. Various systems of culture are used including beds made from horse manure and greenhouse soil, straw bales, peat bags, NFT and rockwool. There are various ways of training the plants but most commonly, cordon or archway systems are used. The longest crops are harvested from February until October. They are grown at a temperature of 21 °C during the day, dropping to 19 °C at night. These temperatures may be reduced by 2 or 3 °C towards the end of the crop. Short crops are grown at similar temperatures, although greater temperature fluctuations occur in those that are not heated. Carbon dioxide enrichment to 1000 p.p.m. helps early cropping but is not necessary if a straw substrate is used to make the bed.

Yields vary according to the length of the crop, but a good yield for a main crop is around 50 to 60 cucumbers per plant.

DISEASES

Seedlings

Damping-off (*Pythium ultimum, P. aphanidermatum* and other *Pythium* spp., *Rhizoctonia solani*), p. 160
Topple, p. 184
Uneven Germination, p. 184
Cotyledon Distortion, p. 185
False Damping-off, p. 184

Roots

Black Root Rot (*Phomopsis sclerotioides*), p. 161
Root Rot (*Pythium* spp., *Phytophthora* spp., *Olpidium* spp.), p. 162
Root Mat (*Agrobacterium rhizogenes*), p. 162

Stems

Basal Rots (*Pythium* spp., *Phytophthora* spp., *Rhizoctonia solani* and non-pathogenic rots), p. 163
Grey Mould (*Botrytis cinerea*), p. 166
Black Stem Rot (*Didymella bryoniae* syn. *Mycosphaerella melonis*), p. 166
White Rot (*Sclerotinia sclerotiorum*), p. 170
Fusarium Wilt (*Fusarium oxysporum* f.sp. *cucumerinum*), p. 179
Flowers of Tan or Fairy Butter (*Fuligo septica*), p. 170

Leaves

Powdery Mildew (*Sphaerotheca fuliginea*, and *Leveillula taurica*, p. 173)
Cercospora Leaf Spot (*Cercospora melonis*), p. 175
Colletotrichum Leaf Spot or Anthracnose (*Colletotrichum lagenarium*), p. 175
Alternaria Leaf Spot (*Alternaria cucumerina*), p. 175
Ulocladium Leaf Spot (*Ulocladium atrum*), p. 176
Downy Mildew (*Pseudoperonospora cubensis*), p. 176
Angular Leaf Spot (*Pseudomonas lachrymans*), p. 178
Fusarium Wilt (*Fusarium oxysporum* f.sp. *cucumerinum*), p. 179
Verticillium Wilt (*Verticillium albo-atrum* and *V. dahliae*), p. 179
Cucumber Green Mottle (Cucumber Green Mottle Mosaic Virus), p. 180
Cucumber Mosaic (Cucumber Mosaic Virus), p. 180
Pseudo Yellows, p. 183
Other viruses, p. 183
Cut leaf, p. 185
Leaf distortion, p. 185
Fasciation, p. 188
Burning-out of heads, p. 188

Fruit

Seedling diseases

Damping-off

FIG. 8.1 Damping-off of cucumber seedlings caused by *Pythium ultimum*. Notice the constriction of the stem at soil level.

Damping-off is common when seeds are sown in unsterilised soil or compost. Symptoms usually appear within a few days of germination. The stem of the affected seedling becomes constricted at soil level and eventually the seedling topples over (Fig. 8.1). Initially the roots are healthy but they quickly turn brown and decay. Affected cotyledon leaves are distorted, often with small brown lesions.

Seeds sown in infested soil are sometimes attacked shortly after germination and the seedling decays before it emerges.

A number of species of *Pythium* can cause pre-emergence decay and damping-off. Similar symptoms are occasionally caused by another fungus, *Rhizoctonia solani*. The major source of these pathogens is the soil or debris but they are occasionally water-borne.

Control. Compost used for propagation must be free from damping-off pathogens. Loam based compost should be steam sterilised. Most peat composts are naturally free from these pathogens. Seed trays, pots and benches should be sterilised with steam or chemicals. If chemicals are used, sufficient time must elapse to allow all fumes to escape before the containers are used.

All seedlings should be discarded from boxes in which damping-off has occurred even though some of them may appear to be healthy.

If damping-off is a persistent problem, a thorough investigation should be made of all the possible sources of contamination.

Etridiazole is effective against Pythium when mixed into the compost or it can be used as a post-planting drench. Quintozene is most effective against *Rhizoctonia solani* and should be mixed into the compost allowing 4 days before using it to plant seeds or transplant seedlings.

Root and base of stem diseases

Root and stem base decay is common, occurring during propagation and cropping but usually increasing in incidence as the crop ages. Symptoms vary with the age of the plant and to some extent with the cause of the disease. During propagation, affected plants show a very dark grey-green discoloration of the youngest leaves accompanied by stunting and wilting, especially in sunshine. The roots of such plants are off-white to cream in colour eventually turning brown and withering (Fig. 8.2). Such roots are often described as having a 'cottony' appearance. After planting, root and stem base disease may first become apparent when affected plants show nutrient deficiency symptoms. Often an interveinal mottle, progressing to a marked chlorosis, develops on the older leaves and the plants appear to show magnesium deficiency despite the fact that the soil is not deficient in this nutrient. As the disease progresses the lower leaves may become more chlorotic or even necrotic and at this stage wilting also occurs. Although the vascular tissue may be stained near to soil level, the stain does not extend very far up the plant and this distinguishes wilting resulting from root or basal stem disease from that caused by the vascular wilt pathogens, where the vascular discoloration extends well up the stem.

There are both pathogenic and non-pathogenic causes of root and basal stem rot. The most important pathogens are *Phomopsis sclerotioides* (Black Root Rot), *Pythium* and *Phytophthora* spp. and *Rhizoctonia solani*.

Black Root Rot (*Phomopsis sclerotioides*)

This fungus is the commonest and most important pathogen of cucumber roots. Affected plants initially show a pale brown discoloration of the roots,

FIG. 8.2 A diseased root system (left) and a healthy root system (right). Both plants are otherwise similar in most respects although the youngest leaves of the affected plant may be grey-green in colour.

becoming darker in colour and eventually black as the disease develops. Close examination of the affected roots reveals the presence of numerous, small, black sclerotia-like structures of the fungus, together with dark mycelium growing on the root surface (Fig. 8.3). As the roots decay the leaves show symptoms of chlorosis and necrosis and the plant wilts. The pathogen survives in the soil for considerable periods, generally within affected plant debris. It is able to grow through the soil quickly and in this way colonises the roots of newly-planted crops.

Pythium and Phytophthora Root Rot

The symptoms are initially very similar to those caused by Phomopsis but the affected roots remain brown.

Olpidium sp. can sometimes be found in the discolored roots of young and older plants but it has not been conclusively shown that this fungus is a primary cause of damage.

Root Mat (*Agrobacterium rhizogenes*)

This disease is caused by a bacterium which is thought to be soil-borne. The main symptom is the vertical growth of roots from the surface of the bed up to a height of over 1 cm. Affected plants also grow poorly and the yield is reduced. Little is known about this disease and at present steam treatment of the soil is the only satisfactory means of control.

Non-pathogenic root rots

Affected roots are brown and the cortical tissue often becomes detached to form loose cylinders around the central vascular stele. Factors which cause such root symptoms include adverse soil conditions leading to waterlogging and poor aeration, overheating of the bed due to the use of straw which decomposes rapidly with a resultant rise in temperature, excessive use of fertilisers, toxic levels of chemicals such manganese, ammonium compounds and pesticides, and factors which cause a growth check, such as low temperatures and long periods of very low light intensity. Once damage has been caused, the affected tissue is colonised by soft-rotting bacteria which are present in most soils.

Phytophthora Stem Rot (various *Phytophthora* spp.)

Lesions caused by these fungi have a dark brown to black colour and a wet appearance. The lesions often extend below soil level and the fungus eventually colonises the roots. The disease occurs most commonly during cropping.

Rhizoctonia Stem Rot (*Rhizoctonia solani*)

This disease is characterised by a dry light brown lesion at soil level extending to just below the soil surface. When examined with a lens the brown mycelium of the fungus can be seen on the lesion surface. It occurs most commonly during propagation.

Non-pathogenic Basal Stem Rot

Damage to cucumber stems at soil level is often followed by a wet rot caused by secondary, soft rotting bacteria. Initial damage may result from growth cracks, fertiliser scorch or pest damage.

Control. During propagation and for the initial period after planting out it is important to use soil that is as free from pathogens as possible. Most proprietary composts are satisfactory but greenhouse soil must be sterilised. As cucumbers are so susceptible to root and basal stem rots, it is often difficult to get a good control of pathogens with chemicals and for this reason most cucumber growers steam treat greenhouse soil. Non-pathogenic rots can be prevented by ensuring that the soil is well drained and has the correct nutrient status.

There are no cucumber cultivars resistant to any of these diseases. Once root and basal stem diseases occur it is often difficult to prevent them causing considerable losses. If the cause can be identified and either a fungicide or a cultural remedy applied, affected plants can be saved or the effect of the disease minimised.

Etridiazole is effective for the control of Pythium and Phytophthora, used either incorporated into the propagation compost or applied as a drench.

Quintozene is the most effective fungicide for the control of *Rhizoctonia solani*. If affected plants are removed the area should be treated with this fungicide before replanting. Benzimidazole fungicides have sometimes been

FIG. 8.3 (a) A cucumber root system severely affected by Black Root Rot;
(b) affected roots showing sclerotia-like structures embedded in the rotten root tissue;
(c) plants showing acute wilt symptoms following a severe attack of *Phomopsis sclerotioides*. Copyright Glasshouse Crops Research Institute.

(a)

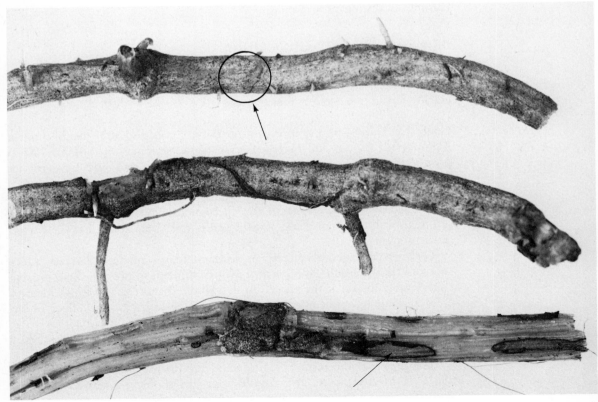

(b)

(c)

successfully used as drenches to arrest the development of Black Root Rot (*Phomopsis sclerotioides*). Pre-planting methyl bromide treatment of the soil does not give a satisfactory control of this disease.

If the cause of the basal stem rot is largely due to secondary soft rotting bacteria, the lesion can be treated with a mixture of lime (10 parts) flowers of sulphur (3 parts) and copper sulphate (1 part). By placing pathogen-free soil, compost or peat around the stem, new roots can be encouraged to grow from the stem above the lesion and in this way the affected plants may recover. It may also be necessary to reduce the stress on the plant by removing the fruit and shading the greenhouse.

Stem, leaf and fruit diseases

Grey Mould (*Botrytis cinerea*)

This fungus frequently affects plants through senescent tissue and wounds. Pruning wounds resulting from the removal of fruit, laterals, tendrils, or leaves are readily colonised. Once established, the fungus is able to parasitise healthy tissue particularly at the nodes on the main and lateral stems, producing lesions often covered with the typical grey mould growth of the pathogen. Leaves are similarly affected. When the main stem is girdled the plant wilts and dies.

Often young fruits are attacked, particularly when the plant produces an excessive number and some of them become senescent.

Mature fruits may also be affected especially if the fungus first becomes established on the withered flowers (Fig. 8.4). A soft rot develops from the distal end which is often covered with the fluffy grey mould growth of the pathogen. *Botrytis cinerea* is common on cucumbers and also affects a very wide range of greenhouse crops. It is most frequently epidemic when the relative humidity is very high or when there are long periods when the leaves or fruits are wet, due to condensation or watering. The spores are readily disseminated in the air and are present in most crops, but the disease only becomes epidemic when the environment is favourable for its development.

Control.   It is important to remove all plant debris from the cropping house and to ensure that the refuse heap is well away from the nursery, as such dead tissue often becomes colonised by Botrytis and provides a source of the pathogen. At the first sign of this disease, measures must be taken to reduce the relative humidity within the crop and prevent surface condensation.

Sprays of a benzimidazole fungicide or iprodione are most likely to give the best control but many isolates of the pathogen are resistant to the benzimidazoles.

Black Stem Rot (*Didymella bryoniae*)

Symptoms of this disease are frequently found and appear on the leaves, fruits and stems. Like *Botrytis cinerea*, it is essentially a wound parasite which attacks an actively growing plant through wounds or senescent tissue. The disease is usually first seen in April or May and by July and August it is often widespread. Symptoms first appear on wounds especially where small stumps remain after the removal of a lateral shoot or leaf. These stumps are colonised by the fungus and about 6 days after infection numerous small, black perithecia or pycnidia are formed.

Stump lesions may increase in size and the healthy stem then becomes attacked. Occasionally, the fungus completely colonises the stem resulting in wilting and eventually, death of the plant (Fig. 8.5).

The disease of the leaves first appears as small, pale green spots which develop a yellow halo. Eventually, the centre of the spot becomes pale brown and dry and at this stage the black fruiting bodies of the fungus are found. The edges of the leaf spots may have a diffuse and water-soaked appearance. Leaf spots are often situated at the edge of the leaf. Young healthy leaves are

FIG. 8.4 (a) A *Botrytis cinerea* lesion on the edge of a cucumber leaf; the grey-mould growth of the fungus can be seen on the lesion surface; (b) a lesion developing at the distal end of the fruit. Note the droplets of liquid; these are a reaction to wounding and occur when fruit is attacked by various pathogens. The Botrytis often establishes first on the remains of the old flower as in this case.

(a)

(b)

only attacked if the inoculum concentration is high and the environment is very favourable for disease development (Fig. 8.6).

Infection of the fruit probably takes place during flowering and a lesion develops at the distal end. At first this is a soft, wet, grey-green rot which becomes black in colour as the pycnidia and perithecia of the pathogen are produced. Sometimes affected fruit show no external symptoms but the distal

FIG. 8.5 (a) Stem
lesions caused by
Didymella bryoniae;
(b) close examination of
the lesions shows the
presence of pycnidia and
perithecia. These are
diagnostic of the disease.

(a)

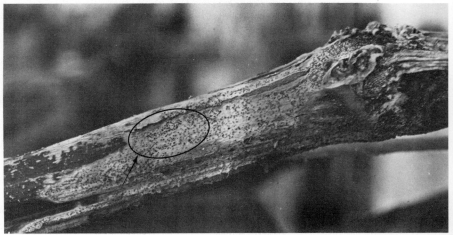

(b)

FIG. 8.6 (a) Leaf lesions of *Didymella bryoniae*; often characterised by their position on the edge of the leaf, by the absence of aerial fungal growth and by the chlorotic halo around the edges of the lesions; (b) a close up examination of the leaf lesion usually reveals perithecia.

(a)

(b)

end is constricted and, if cut longitudinally, shows a brown discoloration in the centre (Fig. 8.7).

Like Botrytis, this disease is epidemic when the relative humidity is extremely high or there is water on the plant surfaces.

Control.   Infected debris may be an overwintering source of the pathogen and should be removed at the end of the crop. Similarly, the haulm of the old crop should be taken well away from the greenhouse before the new crop is sown.

Reducing the relative humidity is the most effective way of controlling this disease and is particularly important from April onwards when, quite commonly, humidities may be very high from late afternoon until late evening.

Fungicides are not particularly effective and of those available for use on cucumbers, the benzimidazole fungicides, iprodione or imazilil, are likely to be the best and give some reduction in disease incidence.

White Rot (*Sclerotinia sclerotiorum*)

This disease is common in greenhouse grown crops but rarely occurs at epidemic levels. Stems, leaves and fruits are affected and the most characteristic symptom of the disease is the development of the white, fluffy mycelial growth of the pathogen. Lesions may girdle the stem and kill the plant (Fig. 8.8). Large black sclerotia up to 1 cm in length develop in the mycelial felt. Affected fruit produce a soft wet rot and, if discarded onto the soil, the white mycelial felt and sclerotia develop very rapidly (Fig. 8.9).

The pathogen is soil-borne and the sclerotia can survive in the soil for long periods. They germinate to produce apothecia and ascospores which are propelled into the air and restart the disease if they land on a suitable host. Many greenhouse-grown plants and some weeds are hosts of this pathogen.

Control.   Sterilisation of the soil is the only effective means of killing the sclerotia. The soil surface can be covered with a barrier, such as polythene, which will prevent the apothecia from discharging ascospores into the air. All the debris of an affected crop should be carefully removed to prevent sclerotia dropping onto the soil surface. If possible, it is best to burn the debris. Fruits should not be left on the soil surface in an affected crop.

The benzimidazole fungicides, iprodione, vinclozolin and chlorothalonil will give some control of this disease when used as high volume sprays. There are no resistant cultivars.

Flowers of Tan or Fairy Butter (*Fuligo septica*)

The presence of this organism (a Myxomycete) is often mistaken for a disease of the stem. The organism forms a slimy mass around the stem or on the supporting stakes, usually just above soil level. The slimy mass changes as it ages becoming more solid and eventually crisp as it dries out completely. It may then be 10–15 cm long and dark red-brown in colour but disintegrates into a powder if the outer surface is broken (Fig. 8.10).

FIG. 8.7 (a) A typical black jelly-like rot of the distal end of a cucumber fruit following infection by *Didymella bryoniae*;
(b) sometimes affected fruit do not rot initially but show a constriction of the distal end;
(c) when cut through, such affected fruit have a decayed area in the centre.

(a)

(b)

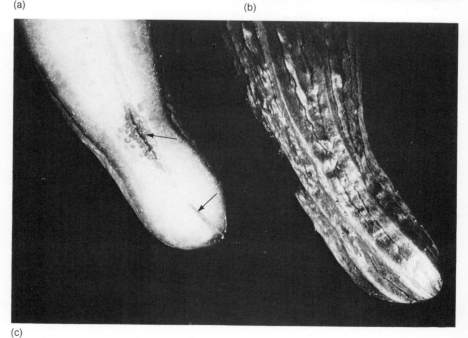

(c)

FIG. 8.8 White Rot stem
lesions caused by
Sclerotinia sclerotiorum;
the sclerotia can
sometimes be found
embedded in the white
mycelium.

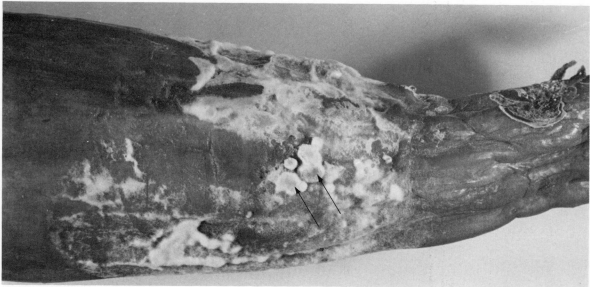

(a)

(b)

FIG. 8.9 (a) Sclerotia of
S. sclerotiorum
developing on an affected
fruit;
(b) numerous sclerotia
formed on a fruit left on
the soil surface; note the
droplets of water on the
developing sclerotia.

The organism does not enter the stem but grows entirely superficially. It is not a pathogen and has no effect on yield.

Powdery Mildew (*Sphaerotheca fuliginea* and *Leveillula taurica*, see p. 237)

In Northern Europe powdery mildew caused by *S. fuliginea* is a very common disease. In warm countries where humidities are commonly low, *L. taurica* may also occur. The disease described here is mildew caused by *S. fuliginea*. Symptoms appear as round, white spots on the upper surface of the older leaves (Fig. 8.11). These spots may enlarge, increase in number and coalesce until eventually both surfaces of the leaf become covered. Severely

FIG. 8.10 Cucumber
stem colonised by the
slime mould *Fuligo
septica*. A second colony
of the mould is growing
on the surface of the
potting compost.

(a)

(b)

FIG. 8.11 Colonies of the
mildew pathogen
Sphaerotheca fuliginea
may be well spaced and
discrete (a) or they may
be very numerous
covering the whole of the
leaf surface (b).
Photograph (b) Copyright
Murphy Chemicals Ltd.

affected leaves turn brown and die. Stems may also be attacked. Normally symptoms are first seen in early summer, but occasionally the disease occurs during propagation.

The vigour of the plant is reduced by an attack of powdery mildew and loss of crop results.

The spores of the fungus are readily air-borne and, unlike many fungal spores, will not germinate in water but require a relative humidity in excess of 90 per cent. Spores can survive in the greenhouse for relatively short periods. It is likely that they are a major source of carry-over of the pathogen particularly on nurseries where the propagation of the new crop rapidly follows the termination of the old one.

Some common weeds, such as the thistles (*Sonchus* spp.) are hosts of this pathogen.

Control. Old crops should be removed as early as possible and the green-house and the propagation area kept free from weed hosts.

If biological control is being used for the control of red spider mite, it is important to use a fungicide which is known to have no acaricidal properties which would reduce the predator population (see Table 5.5).

A large number of fungicides are Approved for the control of cucumber mildew but of those currently available bupirimate and imazilil are likely to give the best results.

The cultivars Bella and Vetomil are resistant to Cucumber Powdery Mildew.

Cercospora Leaf Spot (*Cercospora melonis*)

This disease was serious in the Lea Valley in 1896–1907. In 1903 the resistant cultivar Butcher's Disease Resister was introduced and its adoption by growers practically eliminated Cercospora Leaf Spot.

Symptoms first occur on the upper surface of the leaves as tiny, pale green, water-soaked spots. These rapidly increase in size and coalesce, turning grey at first and afterwards becoming reddish-brown. The spots are definite in outline and irregular in shape. In severe attacks infected leaves may wither and die within 2 days of being infected.

Control. Epidemics only occur at high temperatures and high humidities. The disease can be controlled by maintaining low humidities. By far the most effective and cheapest control is obtained by growing resistant cultivars. Most of the modern cultivars are resistant to this disease.

Colletotrichum Leaf Spot or Anthracnose (*Colletotrichum lagenarium*)

This uncommon disease of greenhouse-grown crops occasionally occurs during propagation but most commonly after planting out. Leaf lesions start as pale green, water-soaked spots becoming dry and reddish-brown in the centre with a yellow, water-soaked surrounding zone. The spots vary in shape from circular to irregular, and under favourable conditions increase in size and coalesce finally giving the leaf a scorched appearance (Fig. 8.12).

In severe attacks petioles and stems may develop sunken lesions and infected fruit show small water-soaked, sunken areas which turn pinkish in colour and eventually develop into black spots. When stems are severely affected all the soft tissues decay exposing the fibrous vascular bundles.

The fungus can live saprophytically on rotten wood and straw manure.

Control. Greenhouses should be thoroughly cleaned and high humidities avoided.

Fungicidal sprays should not be necessary..

Alternaria Leaf Spot (*Alternaria cucumerina*)

This an infrequent disease which only rarely causes economic damage. Leaf spots are confined to the lowest leaves and are usually reddish-brown, circular

FIG. 8.12 Leaf spots caused by *Colletotrichum lagenarium.* Copyright ICI Plant Protection Division.

and occasionally have faint concentric rings around them (Fig. 8.13). Control measures are not usually necessary.

Ulocladium Leaf Spot (*Ulocladium atrum*)

Affected leaves show small pale spots surrounded by a ring of dark necrotic tissue. The margin of the lesion appears slightly water soaked and may be bounded by a chlorotic halo. Large numbers of such spots may occur on affected leaves. (Fig. 8.14).

Generally, the disease is not common and does not reach epidemic proportions. There is no information available on the fungicidal control of this disease but it is likely that it could be contained by one or other of the fungicides used to control *Botrytis*, in particular iprodione.

Downy Mildew (*Pseudoperonospora cubensis*)

Although unusual in Britain, Downy Mildew is very important in the USA and other countries where high summer rainfall, high temperatures and high humidities are prevalent.

The fungus only attacks the leaves. Yellow to red-brown spots appear on the upper leaf surface and the purplish spores of the fungus develop on the lower surface, especially in periods of high humidity. The spores germinate

FIG. 8.13 Pale green leaf
spots caused by
Alternaria cucumerina.
The centres of the spots
are often brown.

FIG. 8.14 Conspicuous
leaf spots caused by
Ulocladium atrum.
Crown Copyright.

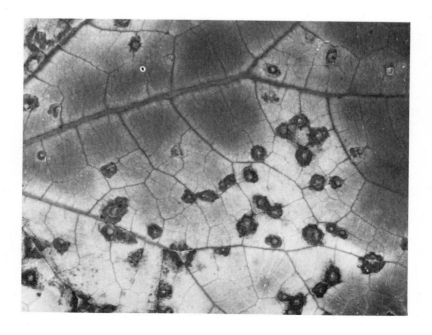

over a wide range of temperatures, 8–30 °C but best at 15–20 °C. Infection takes place at 16–22 °C.

Control.   There are no recommended control measures for Downy Mildew in the UK. Affected leaves should be removed as soon as the disease is seen and the relative humidity reduced.

Angular Leaf Spot (*Pseudomonas lachrymans*)

Angular leaf spot is an uncommon disease in temperate countries. It develops best at high temperatures (24–28 °C) producing symptoms on the leaves and fruit. Spots on the leaves are confined by the veins, starting as water-soaked areas which become grey to tan in colour and an exudate may form on the lower surface. Many of these spots dry up and fall out. Infected fruits show a brown, firm rot and develop an exudate similar to that produced on the leaves. The pathogen is seed-borne and spread by water splash.

Control.   It is reported from the USA that fungicidal seed treatment controls this disease. As the pathogen is spread by water splash, it is important to avoid overhead damping. There are no recommended spray treatments.

Gummosis or Scab (*Cladosporium cucumerinum*)

When this disease is severe a large proportion of the fruit is affected. The fungus produces lesions on the stem and also occasionally leaf spots. Fruit lesions start as small water-soaked spots which rapidly increase in size. A gummy exudate is produced from the lesions and a grey mould growth can often be seen around the exudate (Fig. 8.15).

The fungus is readily spread by spores but only becomes epidemic in cool, moist conditions. As many of the commonly grown cultivars are resistant, this disease is now uncommon.

Control.   The use of resistant cultivars has been largely responsible for the

FIG. 8.15   Gummy exudates from fruit following attack by *Cladosporium cucumerinum*.

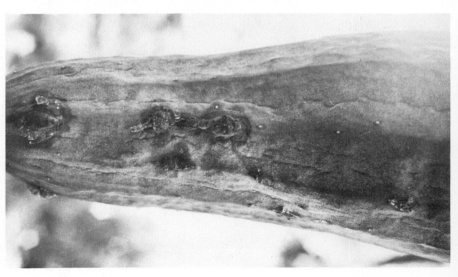

decline in importance of this disease. Of the fungicides available, the benzimidazoles, zineb and chlorothalonil are the most likely to be effective.

Fusarium Wilt (*Fusarium oxysporum* f.sp. *cucumerinum*)

Pre-emergence rot and damping-off can occur during propagation although
the disease is more commonly first noticed 3–4 weeks after planting. The
main symptoms on mature plants are the wilting of one or more of the lower
leaves. Initially, these leaves recover during the evening and at night but
eventually more and more leaves wilt until the plant is totally affected. The
vascular tissues in the stem may become very prominent, especially at soil
level, eventually appearing as silver-white strands. A brown discoloration of
the vascular tissue can readily be seen if the stem is cut across through a node.
If the affected plant is left in the bed, fluffy white mycelium grows out from
the stem. As the plant dies, this mycelial growth may extend along the whole
length of the stem and gradually becomes pale pink to red.

This fungus is soil-borne and will only attack cucumbers and seedling
melons. Some of the commonly grown cultivars show some resistance to this
disease which is now relatively uncommon in the greenhouse grown crop.

Control.   All affected plants should be removed and burned as soon as they
are detected. Heaps of plant debris should not be allowed to accumulate in
the crop. All prunings must be carefully collected and destroyed. If the red
mycelial stage is found, great care must be taken when removing the affected
plants in order to minimise spore dispersal. These spores can set up new
centres of disease in the house or they may contaminate pots or propagating
compost. If the disease is restricted in distribution, it is worth removing the
infested beds at the end of the season.

All affected soil should be thoroughly sterilised, preferably with steam,
and great care taken in the preparations for the new crop, especially of the
propagating compost and in the cleaning of pots and benches. The structure
of a contaminated house must also be cleaned with a fungicidal wash (2 per
cent formalin) or fumigated with formalin. Many of the current cultivars
show some resistance to this disease.

A successful way to control Fusarium Wilt is to graft the desired cultivar
onto a resistant rootstock such as *Cucurbita ficifolia*. Generally the seed of the
cultivar is sown 3 days before the rootstock. The two are grafted using the
'whip and tongue' technique and the union is made just below the cotyledon
leaves of the rootstock. The best growth stage for grafting is when the first
true leaves of the scion and stock are about 5–8 cm in diameter. The graft
union is held together with a strip of metal foil which is easily removed when
the graft has taken. The stem of the cultivar is gradually severed over a period
of about 2 weeks.

The graft union must be as high as possible above soil level in order to
prevent the scion from rooting. When the crop is mulched, care must be
taken to avoid burying the graft union.

Verticillium Wilt (*Verticillium albo-atrum* and *V. dahliae*)

The initial symptoms are very similar to those of Fusarium Wilt. This disease is, however, far less serious and it is unusual for many affected plants to occur in a crop. Symptoms are first seen early in the season and often not after April. Sometimes plants which are affected early in the season appear to recover.

Control.   Sterilisation of the bed and border soil is essential. Benzimidazole fungicides, especially benomyl, used as drenches may minimise spread and treated plants sometimes recover.

VIRUS DISEASES

Cucumber Mosaic Virus

This virus has a very wide host range and symptoms on cucumbers vary according to conditions and the virus strain. It commonly occurs in greenhouse crops, although rarely causes large losses in yield except where root rot diseases are also present.

Commonly, a striking yellow-green mosaic pattern is produced on young and old leaves as well as on the fruit. Sometimes the yellow areas are circular or star-shaped and occasionally a silver pattern is seen.

The symptoms are not always consistent on one plant. The older leaves may show a pronounced yellowing along the veins and the young leaves a mosaic or ring pattern. The symptoms are usually easily distinguished from nutritional disorders by their distribution on the affected leaves. With most nutritional disorders the yellowing is clearly and regularly distributed between the veins. This is not so with Cucumber Mosaic where the yellow blotches and rings are more randomly distributed (Fig. 8.16).

Cucumber Mosaic Virus (CMV) is not seed-borne but is spread by aphids (*Myzus persicae* in particular) and to a much lesser extent on hands and pruning knives. The numerous weed and crop plant hosts are always a potential source and therefore a danger to cucumber crops, especially chickweed (*Stellaria media*) and annual nettle (*Urtica urens*).

Early sown crops do not often become seriously affected by this disease, although the occasional affected plant is often seen near the entrance to the house.

Cold or late planted crops are more seriously affected, sometimes a large proportion of the plants showing symptoms and the fruit is not marketable. If CMV affects plants which have a root rot, they wilt and die within 7–10 days of showing the first symptoms. This suggests that these two pathogens have a synergistic affect.

Control.   Weeds should be controlled in cropping houses and crops known to be affected by CMV kept as far away from cucumbers as possible.

Cucumber Green Mottle Mosaic Virus

This virus is not as common as CMV or as conspicuous, but if it occurs soon after planting, up to 25 per cent loss in crop weight can result (Fig. 8.17a).

The two or three youngest leaves at the end of the growing shoots of an

FIG. 8.16 (a) Yellowing along the veins of an older leaf caused by Cucumber Mosaic Virus; (b) acute yellowing of the young leaves caused by a yellowing strain of Cucumber Mosaic Virus.

(a)

(b)

affected plant show a light-green/dark-green mottle. The light areas are flattened in appearance and the dark areas, in contrast, appear to be raised (see Fig. 8.17b). Although there are slight differences in symptoms on the various cultivars, the symptom pattern is fairly consistent.

The virus is very effectively spread on the hands, knives and clothes of workers. It is not transmitted by insects and there are no known host plants other than cucumbers. It is a seed-borne disease and may be present on the testa (seedcoat) of all the seeds taken from an infected fruit. To a much lesser extent it is also present within the seed but not in the embryo. Infected seed-

FIG. 8.17 (a) The effect
of Cucumber Green
Mottle Mosaic Virus on
growth; the plant on the
left was inoculated
immediately after
germination; the plant on
the right is healthy. Yield
is reduced by about 25
per cent if plants become
infected at this early
stage.
(b) Symptoms on the
youngest leaves; note the
flattened areas (i) and the
bubbled areas (ii) of the
leaf. The older leaves are
symptomless.

(a)

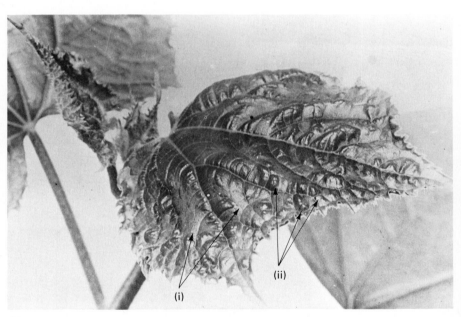

(b)

lings usually result from the transfer of the virus from the testa to the cotyledons during transplanting. Three weeks after this, symptoms appear in the
youngest leaves. Even if affected plants are spotted on the bench, it is almost
impossible to remove them without brushing the leaves against healthy
plants, thereby inoculating them.

Spread from crop to crop takes place on clothes and in particular on hands
and knives. There is little evidence that the disease survives between crops
in the soil but debris left on wires may be a source of inoculum for the new
crop. In the Netherlands contaminated water, taken from dykes, has been

shown to be a source of the pathogen. This occurs when affected plants are dumped into the dykes.

Control. Contaminated seeds can be cleaned by heat treatment for 3 days at 70 °C (158 °F), in a hot-air oven. Accurate temperature control is needed to avoid damaging the seed and also to inactivate the virus. Plants which show symptoms during propagation should be killed 'in situ' taking particular care not to handle them. This is best done by carefully pouring some dilute disinfectant into the pot (e.g. a phenolic sterilant or cresylic acid at 2 per cent concentration). The solution can be applied with a watering can without touching the affected plants.

If a small number of virus-infected plants are seen shortly after planting, it is worth pulling these out together with six plants each side of the affected plants. Care must be taken to wash hands and tools thoroughly after handling the plants. It is advisable to start pulling out plants at the edges of the affected area and work in towards the plants showing symptoms. Soapy water, or preferably 5 per cent trisodium orthophosphate (TSP), should be used to clean hands and tools after handling Green Mottle infected plants.

Separate overalls should be available in each greenhouse block especially if the same workers are used throughout the nursery. This should reduce the risk of transfer from block to block. Pruning knives and hands can easily be cleaned at the beginning of the work session by dipping in TSP.

Cucumber Pale Fruit Viroid

A disease caused by a viroid has been reported in the Netherlands. The main symptom is a loss of colour of the fruits which, on affected plants, are very pale green to yellow. Little is known about this disease, although some other greenhouse crops, such as aubergine and tomato, have been artificially inoculated. Weed hosts include thistle (*Cirsium vulgare*) and groundsel (*Senecio vulgaris*) but neither shows symptoms when infected by this viroid.

Pseudo Yellows

A disease thought to be caused by a virus affecting lettuce and cucumbers has recently been found in the Netherlands. In cucumbers, the main symptom is blotchy, irregular interveinal yellowing of the leaves with the leaf margins of affected leaves often curling downwards. The virus is also known to affect some common weeds such as shepherd's purse (*Capsella bursa-pastoris*), groundsel (*Senecio vulgaris*), sowthistle (*Sonchus oleraceus*) and dandelion (*Taraxacum officinale*).

The causal agent is transmitted by the common greenhouse whitefly (*Trialeurodes vaporariorum*) and, if it is confirmed that the pathogen is a virus, then this is the first record of a whitefly-transmitted virus in Europe.

Other virus diseases

A number of other viruses have been found affecting cucumbers but they are, as yet, of little consequence in the greenhouse crop. These include Tomato Black Ring, Arabis Mosaic and Tobacco Necrosis Viruses.

Non-pathogenic disorders

Topple or False damping-off

The symptoms of topple are almost indistinguishable from damping-off except the constriction of the stem of the seedling may occur well above soil level (Fig. 8.18).

Topple is thought to result from conditions of water stress shortly after germination, possibly due to dryness in the compost or a high soluble salt level, both preventing water uptake.

Uneven germination

Generally, germination is complete by 3 days after sowing, providing conditions are favourable. Sometimes seeds fail to germinate evenly. There are a number of causes, the commonest being:

1. Low temperatures – if the air temperature around the boxes or pots is about 27 °C, germination is even if all other factors are favourable. If the compost temperature is very low, germination is considerably delayed and is uneven. Sometimes the temperature of the compost in an individual tray or between adjacent pots or blocks can vary considerably.
2. Uneven distribution of water in the compost; dryness considerably retards germination.
3. Poor mixing of fertilisers results in small areas with high concentrations which slow down germination.
4. If the soil has been steam sterilised but is left for about 3 weeks toxic concentrates of ammonium or nitrite ions can occur. Boxes affected in this

FIG. 8.18 Topple, a non-pathogenic disease; notice the constriction of the stem well above soil level.

way often show normal germination around the edges but delay occurs in the middle (see pp. 76–77).

5. Pre-emergence damping-off disease, e.g. caused by Pythium.
6. Old seed with very dry and hard seed coats and with reduced viability.

Cotyledon leaf distortion

Occasionally, seedlings occur with distorted and disfigured cotyledon leaves. Sometimes these have saw-toothed edges, are joined together and are cup-shaped, swallow-winged or twisted.

Although some of these symptoms can have a genetical origin and may be characteristic of the cultivar, they are more commonly the result of slow germination or excessively hard seed coats often associated with the use of old seed. It is best to discard all distorted seedlings.

Leaf distortion – cut leaf

Sometimes during propagation and occasionally after planting the youngest leaves become deeply divided into a number of very irregular lobes. Generally, only a few leaves are affected and the plant then resumes normal growth.

The cause of this cut-leaf condition is not known but a period of excessive dryness often occurs shortly before symptom production.

Leaf distortion – weedkillers

Although cucumbers are quite sensitive to the growth regulator type of weedkillers, their growth is not as readily affected as is that of tomatoes. The symptoms which result from damage by 2,4-D, MCPA, 2,3,6-TBA and picloram are very similar. Contamination may result from aerial spray drift or residues in the compost of these materials, particularly 2,3,6-TBA and picloram which are both very persistent.

The first symptom, which occurs within 24 hours of uptake of the herbicides, is downward growth of the leaves (epinasty) giving the plant a wilted appearance although it remains turgid. With sub-lethal doses, epinasty ceases after several days but subsequent leaf development is severely affected. Leaves are greatly reduced in size and as the plant recovers considerable deformation occurs, particularly of the tissue between the veins. A 'bubbly' appearance to the leaf may result and the leaves become inverted and cup-shaped. Soil contamination with 2,3,6-TBA or picloram may persist and cause damage to plants grown in it for several years (Fig. 8.19).

If the bed, peat or soil is contaminated with the more persistent materials it is well worth removing all the contaminated material if at all possible.

Genetical yellowing

Some cultivars sometimes produce occasional fruits with yellow streaks or very rarely completely yellow fruits. Such symptoms result from a genetical change, i.e. they constitute a chimera.

FIG. 8.19 Herbicide injury.
(a) Brilliant chlorosis along the veins resulting from sub-lethal doses of chloroxuron;
(b) epinasty; and
(c) leaf rolling caused by sub-lethal doses of MCPA or 2,4-D;
(d) in-rolling of the leaf margins; and
(e) pitcher-shaped leaves resulting from sub-lethal doses of 2,3,6-TBA;
(f) production of adventitious root initials caused by 2,3,6-TBA; and
(g) nodules on the root caused by MCPA.

(a)

(b)

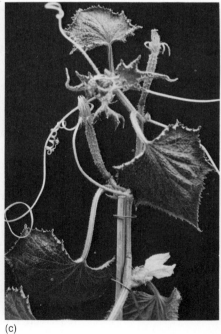

(c)

(d)

(e)

(f)

(g)

Fasciation

When two or more shoots grow fused together the resultant growth is said to be fasciated. This is not uncommon in cucumbers. It probably results from microscopic damage to the growing point which is not sufficient to completely destroy the meristematic tissue.

Burning-out of heads

Usually, early in the life of the crop, the tips of some plants are stunted, grey-green (woolly) and the margins of the leaves may become necrotic. Such plants are said to have 'burnt out' in the heads.

Burning out usually results from an excessive water loss from the leaves. This occurs when root damage has taken place soon after planting and a spell of sunny weather occurs. Wilting of the tops may also occur, although burning-out is not always associated with wilting.

After a check in growth the plants usually recover and grow normally unless the initial root damage was very extensive.

Fruit damping

Early in the life of the crop vegetative growth may become excessive but such a phase may be closely followed by the production of large numbers of fruits at every node of the stem and the lower laterals. Only a few of these flowers eventually develop into mature fruits, the remainder turn brown, shrivel and often become colonised by weak pathogens, e.g. *Botrytis cinerea*. This browning and withering of small female flowers and very young fruit is known as damping.

Damping can occur at any time during the season when too many flowers are present on the plant. Sometimes all the developing fruits damp and in these circumstances a thorough investigation should be made of the plant, especially the root system. Often fruit damping follows root loss.

Fruit cold mark

Cold draught or general low temperatures for short spells during cropping result in 'cold marks' on developing fruits. These show as light brown, corky, superficial streaks. Sometimes they are evenly distributed all round the fruit or they may be on one side only, especially if the marks are the result of a draught (see Fig. 1.17).

Very cold water, and some pesticides, are said to produce similar symptoms.

FURTHER READING

Anon. (1969) *Manual of Cucumber Production*. HMSO, London.
Anon. (1972) *The Biological Control of Cucumber Pests*, Growers' Bulletin No. 1. Glasshouse Crops Research Institute, Littlehampton.
Fletcher, J. T. and Griffin, M. J. (1980) *Control of Diseases of Protected Crops,*

Cucumbers, Lettuce, Minor Vegetables, Mushrooms. Ministry of Agriculture, Fisheries and Food (Publications), Lion House Willowburn Estate, Alnwick, Northumberland.

Morgan, W. M. and Ledieu, M. S. (1979) *Pest and Disease Control in Glasshouse Crops.* British Crop Protection Council Publications, Croydon.

CHAPTER 9

LETTUCE

CULTURE

Pre-planting preparation

The soil is usually treated with methyl bromide immediately before planting and either one or two lettuce crops grown, followed by tomatoes. A peat-based compost is used to make blocks for propagation. This is usually pathogen free but fungicides are sometimes added to control damping-off diseases.

Propagation

Seeds are sown into peat based blocks which are generally approximately 4 cm square. The temperature used depends to a large extent on the growing conditions but varies from 18 °C day and 4 °C night to 23 °C day and 20 °C night when continuous supplementary light is used. Minimum temperatures of 7 °C day and night are more usual. Lettuce seeds can be sown at any time of the year but the interval between sowing and harvesting varies greatly. For instance, whereas seeds sown in May, June and July take about 7 weeks to come to maturity, those sown in November and December can take 20–23 weeks. The greenhouse or growing room atmosphere is commonly enriched with carbon dioxide to give a concentration of 1000 p.p.m. during propagation.

Cropping

Commonly used temperatures are 4 °C at night and 10 °C during the day with carbon dioxide enrichment to 1000 p.p.m. Planting densities vary, but 210×210 mm is common giving 23 plants/m^3. Yields vary according to the time of the year from about 120 g per lettuce in mid-winter to 250 g in March.

DISEASES

Seedlings

Damping-off (*Rhizoctonia solani, Pythium* spp.), p. 191

Stems

Leaves

Damping-off (*Pythium spp.*)

Damping-off of seedlings is not very common. It is caused by various species of *Pythium*, although *Rhizoctonia solani* is a most common cause (*see Bottom Rot, p. 191*). Affected seedlings show typical damping-off symptoms with a constriction of the stem at soil level. Attack by Pythium is favoured by overcrowding of the seedlings and by overwatering. Seed compost or seed-beds should be sterilised or the fungicide etridiazole incorporated into the compost or soil. Once the disease is established it is very difficult to control by the use of fungicides.

Grey Mould (*Botrytis cinerea*)

This disease, which is very common, affects plants at all growth stages although it is often worst early in the life of the lettuce crop and again just before maturity. Seedling attack may start on the stem or on the leaves. Senescent tissue or leaves damaged by downy mildew (*Bremia lactucae*) and *Rhizoctonia solani* damage to the stem, are often colonised by Botrytis. A soft brown rot of the leaves and the stems develops and the pathogen usually sporulates profusely on affected plant parts to produce the typical grey mould symptoms. When stems of mature plants are affected, the leaves turn grey-green and the plant eventually wilts and dies (Fig. 9.1). Sometimes black sclerotia of the fungus are seen on the decaying tissue. These may be up to

FIG. 9.1 (i) Wilting and plant death shortly before crop maturity, a common symptom of *Botrytis cinerea*. This disease is often most severe in the winter months when humidities are high; note the low temperature damage shown by some of the leaves (ii).

3 mm in diameter and are considerably smaller than those of the fungus *Sclerotinia sclerotiorum*.

Because Botrytis is favoured by humid conditions, it is most common in autumn and winter crops. Temperature is less critical for the pathogen which is active over a wide range up to 25 °C. Spores are dispersed by water splash and may also be air-borne. Epidemic attacks are most commonly associated with prolonged periods of high relative humidity or leaf wetness and an abundance of senescent tissue, on which the pathogen becomes established.

Control. Control is best achieved by the avoidance of damage or poor growth which leads to senescent tissue. At planting it is essential to prevent mechanical damage when handling the seedlings or block-raised plants. This is best done by transplanting before the plants are too large. Any check to the growth of the crop often results in wilting or leaf necrosis and 'soft' plants are extremely prone to attack, probably because they are more likely to be damaged. Similarly other cultural conditions, such as waterlogging, drought, very low and very high humidities, can all result in poor growth and be predisposing factors. The elimination of damage caused by other diseases and pests is also essential.

Pre-planting cultivations should be aimed at providing soil conditions suitable for steady and continuous growth. A fine tilth will also prevent damage to the leaves of plants from lumps of soil.

Any techniques which reduce the relative humidity, such as heating the air or increasing the air movement, will minimise the incidence of Botrytis.

It is important with all fungicide programmes to start the treatment early in the life of the crop so that the lower leaves are covered with the fungicide before subsequent growth prevents the fungicidal spray from reaching them. High volume sprays of iprodione or a benzimidazole fungicide give the best control, although resistance to the benzimidazole fungicides is widespread in the Botrytis population (see p. 111 and Table 6.1).

Bottom Rot and Damping-off (*Rhizoctonia solani*)

This fungus is the most frequent cause of damping-off of lettuce seedlings but is also responsible for Bottom Rot at crop maturity. Typical damping-off symptoms are seen in seedlings. A dry, light to chocolate brown, constriction occurs at or just above soil level and the affected seedlings topple over. Botrytis and bacterial rots may develop on the damaged areas.

On the mature plant the main stem and leaf petioles are affected. A dry red-brown rot spreads through the petioles of the bottom leaves and progresses into the heart (Fig. 9.2). A similar rot occurs on the stem. Mycelial webbing may be apparent on the affected tissue. Affected plants may not wilt but secondary organisms, e.g. soft rotting bacteria or Botrytis, may colonise the damaged tissue and the affected plants then collapse and die.

Peat and loam composts may be a source of the pathogen. It is also possible to introduce the pathogen into sterilised soil by using contaminated boxes and in these circumstances, spread is very rapid. Generally, proprietary composts used for propagation and making blocks are free from Rhizoctonia.

The fungus is able to survive in greenhouse soil for long periods. It can grow rapidly through the soil and is often most troublesome after partial soil sterilisation which has eliminated many of the competitor organisms.

Control.   Damping-off occurs most commonly when seedlings are raised in inadequately sterilised soil. Compost used for propagation should be sterilised by heat or with chemicals.

Bottom rot can be controlled by a pre-planting treatment of the soil with quintozene or tolclofos methyl. High volume sprays of iprodione together with the pre-planting treatments of tolclofos methyl are very effective but the sprays must be applied early in the development of the crop in order to protect the stem and leaf bases.

Sclerotinia Disease (*Sclerotinia sclerotiorum*)

This disease develops at high temperatures (22 °C and above) and so is most common in summer grown greenhouse crops particularly affecting plants near to maturity. A soft rot of the stem accompanied by a collapse of the leaves may be the first symptom noticed and this can be mistaken for the disease caused by Botrytis. However, a dense, white fluffy mycelial growth develops on the affected tissue and as the plant decays, large black sclerotia of the fungus occur embedded in the white mycelial growth and also within the rotten plant tissue. These sclerotia may be up to 1 cm in length. They can survive in the soil for considerable periods and germinate to produce mycelium or apothecia and ascospores which are propelled into the atmosphere and will infect any suitable hosts. This fungus has a wide host

FIG. 9.2 (a) A plant
severely affected by
Rhizoctonia solani;
notice some of the leaves
are not wilting but others
are severely affected (cf.
9.1 (i). The weeds in this
crop (i) *Stellaria media*
(chickweed), (ii) *Capsella
bursa-pastoris*
(shepherd's purse) and (iii)
Senecio vulgaris
(groundsel) are all hosts
of lettuce viruses (see
pp. 199).
(b) A lesion at soil level
affecting the stem and
the petioles.
(c) Red-brown
discoloration of the plant
base with flecking on the
petioles, characteristic of
Bottom Rot.

(a)

(b)

(c)

range including tomatoes, cucumbers, chrysanthemums and many other greenhouse crops and herbaceous plants.

Control. All diseased tissue should be removed taking great care to prevent sclerotia dropping onto the soil. As soon as the first symptoms of this disease are recognised, sprays of iprodione or a benzimidazole fungicide should be applied. Once established the disease is not easy to control. Sclerotia are generally killed by heat or chemical soil sterilisation.

Butt Rot (*Pseudomonas marginalis*)

This disease occurs quite commonly in some years, particularly in crops maturing during the early months of the year. Affected plants may not be discovered until they are cut, when a black to green firm rot is found in the stem of the plant (Fig. 9.3). The decay may spread along the veins of the lower leaves and to a small extent down into the roots. The affected plants do not wilt or collapse unless secondary rots occur. Plants growing in conditions of low light and excessive wetness of the foliage are most commonly affected. Most cultivars are susceptible though it is not unusual to find one more seriously affected than an adjacent cultivar, particularly if there is a difference in planting times.

The organism most frequently isolated from plants showing Butt Rot is *Ps. marginalis*, although it has not been established beyond doubt that this bacterium is the primary cause. It seems likely that a combination of the bacterium, the environment and disease-prone plants are all necessary for Butt Rot to become a problem.

Control. The disease can be prevented by avoiding excessive wetness and ensuring that the plants are not unduly soft, especially in the early months of the year. Sometimes soft growth is associated with a high nitrogen status of the soil, particularly in relation to the potash level, and this often occurs if the soil has been sterilised immediately before planting. There are no chemical means of control.

Downy Mildew (*Bremia lactucae*)

Downy mildew is a widespread and important disease of lettuce grown in greenhouses and is often most troublesome in prolonged conditions of high humidity and leaf wetness.

Symptoms are initially inconspicuous and difficult to detect particularly at the seedling stage. Affected seedlings may show slight chlorosis of affected leaves and rolling of the leaf margins. On close examination the pathogen can be seen sporulating on both leaf surfaces. On older plants, the symptoms are easy to see and appear as bright yellow or necrotic patches on the upper leaf surface with a white downy growth of the pathogen (conidiophores and conidia) on the underside of these areas. Often the affected leaf area is demarcated by the veins and may, therefore, have an angular shape (Fig. 9.4). In severe outbreaks, affected leaves become necrotic. Often Botrytis or soft rotting bacteria colonise the damaged leaf tissue.

The optimum temperature for the germination of Bremia conidia is 15 °C

FIG. 9.3 Lettuce Butt
Rot. (a) The first stages of
attack; and (b) acute.
Copyright Glasshouse
Crops Research Institute.

(a)

(b)

and spores germinate in conditions of high humidity or in water. Infection
take place in 2–3 hours over a wide range of temperatures from 2–20 °C.
Above 20 °C, sporulation is greatly reduced, and at 25 °C the disease does
not develop.

Conditions of high relative humidity favour sporulation but periods of low
humidity aid spore release by twisting the conidiophores thereby freeing the
spores. The pathogen is not seed-borne and there is only slight evidence that
the resting spores (oospores), which are sometimes produced in affected
leaves, survive in plant debris or the soil. The conidia are relatively short-

FIG. 9.4 Downy Mildew
(*Bremia lactucae*);
the areas on the
underside of leaf where
the pathogen is
sporulating are clearly
demarcated by the veins.

lived (up to 6 days) and are unlikely to survive for more than a few days. They are readily wind-borne and in this way spread to nearby crops. Downy Mildew is often most serious where lettuce is grown continuously or where outdoor lettuce is grown in the summer and lettuce crops are raised under protection in the winter. Wild *Lactuca* spp. and other composites are suscep-tible to *B. lactucae* but none of these is likely to be an important source of the pathogen for the lettuce crop.

There are a large number of races of the pathogen which have been ident-ified by their ability to infect certain cultivars which have genes for resist-ance. Multivirulent races, i.e. able to overcome the resistance of cultivars with more than one gene for resistance, are common.

Control.   A large number of lettuce cultivars are resistant to some of the races of *B. lactucae*. Eleven different resistance factors have been identified in various lettuce cultivars and *Lactuca* spp. Strains of the pathogen capable of overcoming all but one of these are known to occur. Some lettuce cultivars contain one or more of the resistance factors but control of Downy Mildew by the use of such cultivars has not so far been successful. Most resistant cultivars become susceptible within a very short period following their wide-spread use in commerce.

There are various cultural techniques which can be used to aid Downy Mildew control. New crops should not be planted near existing infected crops. It is important to clear the remains of affected crops thoroughly and as soon as possible. High relative humidities and leaf wetness should be avoided whenever possible.

Dithiocarbamates, such as zineb and thiram, give a satisfactory level of control when disease levels are not high. However, the use of all fungicides containing dithiocarbamate materials, such as mancozeb, maneb, zineb and thiram, is restricted because of the problem of residues which persist on the crop. For protected crops, such fungicides can only be used during propagation and within the first 2 weeks after planting out (or 3 weeks for thiram). The systemic fungicide metalaxyl, with mancozeb (Fubol), used as a high volume spray, is effective in controlling downy mildew. The continuous use of site specific fungicides, such as metalaxyl, on their own is liable to result in fungicide resistance. The mixture with mancozeb may reduce this risk.

Ring Spot (*Marssonina panattoniana*)

Brown circular spots, about 4–5 mm in diameter, occur on the older leaves and also there are sunken brown markings on the veins which may resemble slug damage. The centres of the spots often fall out giving a shot-hole effect. Occasionally, under moist conditions, pink fructifications of the fungus appear around the edges of the brown spots. The pathogen may be seed-borne or more frequently survives on crop debris in the soil. It is, therefore, most commonly found on field crops, especially where cropping is intensive. It is also possible that the pathogen can survive on the common sowthistle (*Sonchus asper*). This disease is not common on green-house grown lettuce but occasionally causes losses particularly where water splash occurs, i.e. under gutters. The spores of the pathogen are readily spread by this means.

Control. It should not be necessary to apply fungicides, but thiram has given good results on field-grown crops when used as a high volume spray, as soon as the disease appears.

Rust (*Puccinia opizii*)

This disease has been found on Dutch lettuce but not so far in the UK. Spots on the leaves consist of a collection of small, cup-shaped aecidia which cluster together to form a large, raised lesion up to 1.5 cm across. The other stages of the life cycle of this rust fungus occur on the sedge *Carex muricata*. Of the fungicides available for use on lettuce, the dithiocarbamates such as zineb and mancozeb are most likely to be effective.

Septoria Leaf Spot (*Septoria lactucae*)

There are only a few records of this disease in the UK although it is widely distributed in other parts of Europe. Cos lettuce are most commonly affected. Irregular, pale yellow areas occur on the leaves. These are about 1 cm across and they enlarge into conspicuous, rounded or irregular olive spots or blotches up to 1.5 cm long, often surrounded by a light yellow halo. Pycnidia occur on these spots. The tissue at the centre of the spot may drop out leaving irregular holes in the leaves. Sometimes the whole of the base of the lettuce may be affected giving a 'bottom-rot like' symptom. The disease is seed-borne and this is probably the primary source of the pathogen. It is possible that fungicidal control could be achieved by the use of one of the benzimidazole fungicides although fungicidal tests have not been done.

Pleospora Leaf Spot (*Pleospora herbarum*)

Small, light brown, more or less circular spots occur on the outer leaves. They may enlarge and coalesce to form large patches. Sometimes the centres of the spots fall out leaving a brown margin to the hole. This disease is not common and it is generally not necessary to apply control measures.

Powdery Mildew (*Erysiphe cichoracearum*)

There have been only a few records of this disease in the UK although it is known to occur in other parts of Europe. The symptoms are typical of most powdery mildew diseases with white powdery fungal growth, mainly confined to the upper surface of the leaf. Of the fungicides available for use on lettuce, only the benzimidazoles and thiram are likely to have effect.

VIRUS DISEASES

Lettuce Mosaic

Lettuce Mosaic Virus (LMV) is the most commonly occurring virus in lettuce both in the greenhouse and in the field-grown crop. In greenhouse crops it affects the size and quality of the plants. Lettuces can become infected at any stage after germination.

Shortly after infection, the youngest leaves show a pale green to dark green mottle with some clearing of the veins which makes them conspicuous. The mosaic symptom may be more pronounced in winter conditions. Generally, the earlier the plant is infected the more severe the effects on the mature lettuce. Sometimes severe leaf crinkling is found and also some necrosis occurs, especially near the leaf margins. Symptoms vary somewhat with the cultivar and the time of the year the crop is growing. Severely affected plants show a pronounced mosaic, are stunted and produce a rosette of leaves, often failing to heart.

The virus is seed-borne and infected seeds are generally the primary source of the virus. Aphids, especially the peach-potato aphid (*Myzus persicae*), transmit this virus but the common lettuce aphid (*Nasonovia ribis-nigri*) does not. LMV is a non-persistent virus; it is rapidly acquired following aphid feeding (about 15 seconds) but is also lost within a short time of further feeding (about 30 minutes). Some weeds, especially sowthistle (*Sonchus asper*) and groundsel (*Senecio vulgaris*), are known to be hosts.

When crops are grown from successive sowings in contiguous greenhouse blocks the disease tends to increase as the season progresses, the virus being transmitted from the older to the younger crops. The increase in disease is often slow at first then becomes more rapid with increasing aphid populations and the late season crops can be severely affected.

Control. Crops grown from seed where less than 0.1 per cent of them are infected, do not suffer significant losses providing they are in isolation from other infected crops and the aphid populations are controlled. The use of such 'mosaic tested' seed is essential, particularly in areas of intensive production and where high aphid populations are common.

Blocks of lettuce should be isolated from each other as far as possible to minimise intercrop spread. It is particularly important that seedbeds and propagation areas are well separated from potential sources of the virus.

Because the virus is transmitted in only short feeding periods, insecticides will not prevent its introduction from outside sources but may reduce its spread within and between crops. The vector may be present in low numbers having no direct effect on the crop but still be sufficient to spread the virus. Aphid control measure should be applied throughout the life of the crop especially in high risk situations, i.e. in successional crops or in the summer.

Infected plants are often unmarketable and, as they are sources of virus, they should be removed as soon as they are discovered.

None of the greenhouse cultivars is resistant to LMV but some of the field cultivars show tolerance.

Cucumber mosaic

Cucumber Mosaic Virus (CMV) is sometimes common in lettuce crops but shows considerable seasonal fluctuations in incidence. Infected plants are stunted with a yellow mottle or necrotic spotting on the leaves. These symptoms cannot be readily distinguished from those of LMV. The symptoms vary with time of infection, time of year, the cultivar and the strain of the virus. CMV does not occur in lettuce seeds but it has been found in the seeds of some common weeds, especially chickweed (*Stellaria media*), red dead nettle (*Lamium purpureum*) and spurrey (*Spergula arvensis*). The virus is transmitted by many aphids, including (*Myzus persicae*). CMV is a non-persistent virus and is acquired and transmitted after a short feeding time (approximately 1 minute). The virus is not retained by the aphids for more than 4 hours. A very wide range of plants including tomatoes, cucumbers, ornamentals, hedgerow plants and weeds are hosts of CMV.

Sometimes CMV and LMV occur together in the same lettuce plant. The symptoms of the combined diseases are more intense than those of either disease separately; there is generally severe stunting, yellowing and necrosis of the affected plants.

Control.   Control measures are similar to those for LMV with the exception of the seed-borne phase. Crops should be grown as far as possible in isolation from other lettuce, and weeds should be controlled, especially those that are known to carry CMV in their seeds. Insecticides should be used from the seedling stage onwards. None of the commercial cultivars is resistant.

Lettuce Big Vein

Lettuce Big Vein is not common in lettuce grown in greenhouses, except where the nutrient film culture technique is used. It is a common disease of field grown crops. Big Vein has many of the characteristics of a virus disease but so far no virus particles or other pathogens have been found in affected plants. Recently, viral RNA has been found in affected plants and it is thought that this is likely to be the cause of the disease.

A light green or colourless vein banding symptom, which is most pronounced towards the base of the leaf, is seen in affected plants (Fig. 9.5). There is a sharp demarcation between the vein banding and the normal green leaf lamina so that the pale-coloured tissue appears to be an extension of the veins, hence the name Big Vein. In addition, the interveinal tissue becomes uneven and bubbled giving affected plants a 'savoyed' appearance. Sometimes hearting is delayed and affected plants reduced in size. The factor which

FIG. 9.5   Lettuce Big Vein.
(a) Butterhead cultivar showing crinkling of the expanded leaves which sometimes gives the plant a 'savoy-like' appearance.
(b) The enlarged veins, typical of the disease and particularly prominent on the crisp cultivars.
Photograph (a) Copyright May & Baker Ltd.

(a)

(b)

causes Big Vein, is known to be transmitted by the soil-borne fungus *Olpidium brassicae*. This same fungus is a known vector of some viruses. *Olpidium brassicae* can be introduced into clean land or compost on implements, within debris, or even in wind-blown dust. The resting spores of the fungus persist, almost indefinitely, as does the cause of Big Vein which they carry. It takes 4–5 weeks from infection by spores carrying Big Vein to symptom production. The disease is most likely to be conspicuous at low soil temperatures and is inhibited at soil and air temperatures of 20 °C and above. Big Vein is not known to occur in weed plants, although its vector has a very wide host range. *Olpidium brassicae*, capable of transmitting Big Vein, has been isolated from leeks, peas, spinach, rhubarb, plantains (*Plantago major*) and speedwell (*Veronica persicae*). Block-raised plants can become infected during propagation if contaminated compost is used or if they are stood on a contaminated surface. As it takes 4 weeks for symptoms to appear, such affected plants are not detected until they have been planted out into their permanent positions. If such plants are used in a nutrient film system, the zoospores of *O. brassicae* spread Big Vein throughout the crop very rapidly.

Control.   No cultivars are resistant although some types show symptoms more prominently than others. The Cos and crisp cultivars are probably the worst affected. Big Vein is most severe on land frequently cropped with lettuce. If land is cropped on a rotational system or the soil is sterilised fairly frequently, Big Vein is not a serious problem. Most of the chemical sterilants will not totally eliminate the fungus vector and therefore complete control is unlikely to be achieved but the disease will be kept at a low level. Methyl bromide treatment of soil has been shown to be very effective although this treatment is very costly. If plants are raised in soil blocks or containers with compost free from *O. brassicae*, the plants will remain Big Vein free for some time, even when planted into infested soil. This delay in disease development may ensure a worthwhile crop. Rotation will not eliminate the infectious vector from land, which will remain infested more or less indefinitely. The incorporation of a carbendazim fungicide (Bavistin) into blocking compost has given some control of the disease. In systems of liquid culture (NFT), the use of a carbendazim fungicide and a wetting agent help to control Big Vein.

Beet Western Yellows Virus

This virus causes bright yellow, inter-veinal chlorosis of the outer leaves of mature lettuce. The virus is transmitted by the peach-potato aphid (*Myzus persicae*). Symptoms do not become apparent for at least 3 weeks after infection. The host range of this virus is known to include sugar beet, radish and some common weeds, such as groundsel (*Senecio vulgaris*) and shepherd's purse (*Capsella bursa-pastoris*). The disease is very common in field-grown crops but rarely occurs in greenhouse crops. Beet Western Yellows Virus is acquired by the aphid vector after a feeding time of 5 minutes; there is an incubation period of 12–24 hours before aphids can transmit the virus but they then remain viruliferous for up to 29 days. The virus distribution in affected plants is somewhat unusual in that it is confined to the phloem.

Control. Control measures are similar to those for LMV except that this virus is not seed-borne. Weeds should be controlled in and around the crop. Insecticides should be used from the seedling stage onwards. No commercial cultivar is resistant to the virus.

Pseudo Yellows

Almost identical symptoms to those of Beet Western Yellows have been reported from the Netherlands in greenhouse-grown lettuce. The disease is thought to be caused by a virus which is transmitted by the common greenhouse whitefly. The exact extent of this disease is not known at present but it has also been identified in cucumbers where similar symptoms are produced (see p. 183). Little is known about this disease but controlling the whitefly vector is the first essential.

Other virus diseases

The following virus diseases are uncommon and generally unimportant in protected lettuce crops although they do occur occasionally.

Dandelion Yellow Mosaic. This virus produces a distinct yellow blotch mosaic on dandelions and is occasionally found in lettuce. Symptoms are similar to those of Lettuce Mosaic but are often more severe. Some cultivars show a fine vein chlorosis or necrosis shortly after infection. Necrotic etching and rings may develop later but these are masked as the leaf ages and necrosis extends over the whole leaf area. Younger leaves formed subsequently are stunted, thickened and blistered with occasional bright yellow blotches.

Lactuca serriola and *L. virosa* are known to be hosts of this virus but dandelions are by far the most common weed source. The virus is not seed-borne. It is transmitted by the potato and shallot aphid (*Myzus ascalonicus*) but not by the peach-potato aphid (*Myzus persicae*). It is acquired after a relatively long feeding time (more than 24 hours for maximum infectivity) but the virus is not retained for longer than 1 hour.

The control of this virus is the same as for CMV but with special attention to the control of dandelions.

Tomato Spotted Wilt Virus. This is found only infrequently on lettuce in Britain although it is fairly common in some other crops. A bronzing occurs on the younger leaves caused by numerous, pin-point sized spots. More prominent general necrosis may develop and the affected area may be confined to tissue on one side of the main vein so that subsequent growth produces a characteristic lateral curvature of the leaf. The virus is transmitted by thrips and is best controlled by preventing the introduction and build-up of this pest.

Tobacco Necrosis Virus. This occurs frequently in the roots of lettuce and many different plant species but is rarely isolated from the leaves. When present in the roots, there are no recognisable foliage symptoms. Like Big Vein, it is transmitted by the fungus *Olpidium brassicae* and as a result can be controlled by soil sterilisation.

Lettuce Necrotic Yellows. This virus is a destructive pathogen of the crop in Australia but has only recently been found in Britain. The symptoms are similar to those described for Spotted Wilt with severe chlorosis when plants are badly affected. It is transmitted by an aphid (*Hyperomyzus lactucae*), which lives mainly on currants (*Ribes* spp.) and sowthistles (*Sonchus oleraceus*).

Tomato Black Ring Virus (Tomato Ringspot Strain). Some lettuce cultivars are symptomless when infected by this virus, but others show a mosaic-like mottle with slight leaf distortion. The virus is transmitted by the nematode *Longidorus attenuatus* and is controlled by soil sterilisation or the use of nematicides applied to the soil.

Arabis Mosaic Virus. This causes stunting and chlorosis with the outer leaves either wholly chlorotic or with a prominent chlorotic mottle and with necrosis ranging from marginal stippling to extensive necrotic areas. The nematodes *Xiphinema diversicaudatum* and *X. index* transmit this virus. This disease is best controlled by controlling the vector in the soil.

Strawberry Latent Ringspot Virus. This produces dwarfing and mottling of the foliage and is transmitted by *X. diversicaudatum*.

Tobacco Rattle Virus. Affected plants are stunted, may fail to heart and show a necrosis of the leaves with distortion. Species of the nematode, *Trichodorus*, transmit this virus.

Aster Yellows. This is caused by a mycoplasma and affects a wide range of plants, including lettuce, which when affected are dwarfed, extremely chlorotic and often fail to heart. Other susceptible crops include carrots, celery, parsnips and tomatoes. So far this lettuce disease, which is transmitted by leaf hoppers, has not been found in Britain, although it is very common in North America.

NON-PATHOGENIC DISORDERS

Tipburn complex

Tipburn is a major cause of crop loss. Brown areas may occur on the leaf margins of the outer leaves or on the heart leaves and sometimes the necrosis also affects the veins. Areas of dead tissue produce ideal entry points for pathogens, especially *Botrytis* and soft rotting bacteria.

Pseudomonas marginalis and *Ps. cichorii* have been isolated from necrotic leaf and vein tissue. These organisms are secondary colonisers of the dead areas although they may cause decay of healthy tissue once they are established.

Various environmental conditions give rise to necrosis on lettuce leaves. In all instances, the occurrence of symptoms is closely connected with the water relations of the plant (Table 9.1).

Excessive water loss will result in water depletion of the leaf tissue, especially at the leaf margins, and this can cause death of the cells at the edges of the leaves. Such water loss is favoured by conditions of low relative

TABLE 9.1 Lettuce
Tipburn, symptoms,
causes and control

| | Water loss from leaves | |
	Excessive	Inadequate
Common names of symptoms	Tipburn Marginal tipburn Dry edge Marginal leaf scorch	Glassiness Veinal tipburn
Symptoms	Necrosis of leaf margins more frequently affecting the older leaves most severely	Necrosis of the leaf margins occasionally between the vein and particularly on the youngest leaves
Cause	An excessive water loss from the leaves over uptake of water by the roots	An excess of water uptake by the roots over loss of water from the leaves
Control	Ensure a. an adequate supply of water in the soil b. a healthy root system c. the soluble salt level in the soil is not excessively high	Ensure a. the relative humidity in the greenhouse is not excessively high for long periods b. there is adequate air movement over the crop to allow water loss from the leaves

humidity and high temperature and if these occur and coincide with a restriction in water uptake, damage is almost certain. A shallow or poorly functioning root system, a dry soil, a low soil temperature and a high salt content are all conditions which limit water uptake. A mature plant is more likely to show symptoms because of the large leaf area for water loss. Generally, maintaining a moist soil and avoiding excessive fluctuations in air temperature will prevent this form of leaf damage.

Similar symptoms may occur when water uptake exceeds water loss. This happens when the root system is functioning well in a moist warm soil, the relative humidity of the air is high and water loss from the leaves greatly reduced. Plants with a large root system are more likely to be affected. Reduction in atmospheric humidity and an increase in air movement over the crop helps to prevent leaf damage. Early stages of damage can sometimes be recognised by the water-soaked and glassy appearance of the leaf margins. If immediate action is taken to reduce humidity, necrosis of the tissue can be prevented.

Weedkiller damage

Contact herbicides result in necrosis and death of lettuce plants but sub-lethal doses of growth regulator herbicides often result in plant deformation. Symptoms caused by many of these latter herbicides are indistinguishable from each other. Within 24 hours of application the plants usually show a down-curling of the leaf-blade. Subsequent new growth is distorted to varying degrees (epinasty) according to the dose of the herbicide. A reduction in the size of the leaf is a frequent symptom which, in extreme cases, results in just the

FIG. 9.6 Typical 'dogs-
tongue' symptom
resulting from sub-lethal
doses of the growth-
regulating herbicide
MCPA.

main vein rounded at the end (dog's tongue symptom) (Fig. 9.6). This symptom occurs with sub-lethal levels of MCPA, 2,4-D, and 2,3,6-TBA. The stem of the plant may elongate and produce adventitious roots, especially just above soil level. With 2,3,6-TBA, the leaf margins fuse to form cup or pitcher-shaped leaves. Sub-lethal levels of CMPP and dichlorprop produce down-rolling of the leaf margin with little disturbance of the interveinal tissue. The stem may elongate and adventitious roots develop at the nodes.

Most of the growth regulatory herbicides applied to the soil will result in the formation of small nodules on the roots.

Acidity

Plants grown in acid soils (usually below pH 6 or pH 5.5 for peat soils) are stunted and may show reddening of the leaves. In extreme conditions the roots are dull grey in colour and often very stunted. Adjustment of the soil pH with lime will correct this, although it is advisable to aim at a pH which is not above 6.5.

Soluble salt injury

Excessive application of chemical fertilisers can result in very high soluble salt levels in the soil which prevents water uptake by plants. Lettuce are fairly sensitive to this condition showing symptoms of slow growth often with an open centre or 'loose heart'. A soil conductivity reading of 2600 million millimhos (Index 3) is considered to be the maximum level for lettuce crops. The salt level of the soil should be checked before planting by having a soil sample tested.

Low temperature injury

Symptoms associated with low temperatures include irregular growth of the leaves which have a bubbled, blistered or crimped appearance (Fig. 9.1ii). Sometimes the outer leaf tissue separates allowing an air space to develop which gives the affected leaves a silvered appearance. The older leaves may be reddened.

FURTHER READING

Fletcher, J. T. and Griffin, M. J. (1980) *Control of Diseases of Protected Crops, Cucumbers, Lettuce, Minor Vegetables and Mushrooms.* Ministry of Agriculture, Fisheries and Food (Publications), Lion House, Willowburn Estate, Alnwick, Northumberland.

Large, J. E. (1972) *Glasshouse Lettuce.* Grower Books, London.

Morgan, W. M. and Ledieu, M. S. (1979) *Pest and Disease Control in Glasshouse Crops.* British Crop Protection Council Publications, Croydon.

CHAPTER 10

MUSHROOM

CULTURE

Preparation of compost

The compost used for most mushroom crops is based on horse manure with nitrogen added either as an organic manure or as other forms of organic material or fertiliser. A commonly used mixture is horse manure (generally with a low solids content) and chicken manure, added at the rate of 8–10 per cent by volume of the horse manure. If necessary, extra nitrogen is added in the form of an organic activator, often based on sewage sludge. The manure is wetted for several days before use and the chicken manure mixed with it when the compost stack is made. The microbial degradation of the compost generates heat and the compost is 'turned' at 2 or 3 day intervals to ensure even fermentation. At the second turn, a small quantity of gypsum is added to give the compost an open texture and to prevent greasiness. After 7 days of fermentation, often referred to as phase I, the compost is boxed or treated in bulk in a specially designed room in which the temperature of the compost can be raised to 60 °C and maintained at or just below this temperature for 4 days. This process is also known as 'peak heat'. At the end of peak heat the compost is cooled down to about 30 °C and spawned, usually with a white or off-white strain but more commonly in North America, with brown strains.

Cropping

After spawning, the compost which is in boxes, beds or very deep trays, is maintained at about 20 °C during the initial spawn-growing period known as 'spawn run'. After 2 to 3 weeks the compost is fully colonised and the casing is applied. The casing is a mixture of peat and limestone, in the form of ground chalk or as small lumps of chalk. The proportion is generally about three of peat to one of chalk, by volume. After casing, the temperature is gradually dropped, and within 2 weeks mushroom initials, known as 'pinheads', are formed. As cropping begins, the temperature should be about 16 °C and is maintained at this level for the 6 weeks of cropping. During the first two flushes, the relative humidity is kept at about 95 per cent. It is usual for the first two flushes to be the heaviest with a decreasing yield from the following three. A good compost will yield about 160 kg/1.02 tonnes (350 lb of mushrooms/ton). Yields are frequently expressed as lb/ft^2 but these depend upon the quantity of compost under each square foot of cropping area. With

20–23 lb of compost for each square foot, a yield of between 4–5 lb is good.

New developments in mushroom culture include the bulk treatment of compost in phase II, the use of beds which can be winched out at emptying, the use of very deep troughs giving a very large volume of compost for a relatively small cropping area and picking machines which, at present, are at an early stage of development.

At the end of the mushroom crop, it is usual to treat all surfaces with a disinfectant and to heat the whole crop and structure to approximately 70 °C for several hours. This process is known as 'cook-out'. Methyl bromide fumigation is sometimes used for cooking out.

Spent compost is usually taken well away from the farm.

DISEASES

Wet Bubble (*Mycogone perniciosa*), p. 210
Dry Bubble (*Verticillium fungicola* syn. *V. malthousei* and *V. psalliotae*), p. 213
Cobweb (*Hypomyces rosellus* stat. conid. *Cladobotryum dendroides* syn. *Dactylium dendroides*) p.216
Shaggy Stipe (*Mortierella bainieri*), p. 217
Gill Mildew (*Cephalosporium* sp.), p. 219
Cap Spotting (*Aphanocladium album*), p. 219
Bacterial Blotch, Bacterial Spot or Brown Blotch (*Pseudomonas tolaasii*) and Ginger Blotch (*Ps. fluorescens*), p. 219
Bacterial Pit, p. 220
Drippy Gill (*Pseudomonas cichorii* and *Ps. agarici*), p. 220
Mummy Disease (*Pseudomonas* sp.), p.221

Mushroom virus diseases

La France, Watery Stipe, Die Back, X disease, Brown Disease, p. 222

Weed moulds

Truffle, False Truffle, Calves Brains (*Diehliomyces microsporus* syn. *Pseudobalsamia microspora*), p. 225
Lipstick Mould, Red Geotrichum (*Sporendonema purpurescens*), p. 226
Olive Green Mould (*Chaetomium olivaceum, C. globosum*), p. 227
Mat Disease (*Chrysosporium luteum*), p. 227
Confetti (*Chrysosporium sulfureum*), p. 227
Vert-de-Gris (*Myceliophthora lutea*), p. 227
Yellow Moulds (*Sepedonium* sp., *Sporotrichum* sp.), p. 227
White Plaster Mould (*Scopulariopsis fimicola*), p. 227
Black Whisker Mould (*Doratomyces stemonitis, D. microsporus*), p. 228
Brown Plaster Mould (*Papulaspora byssina*), p. 228
Green Mould (*Trichoderma viride, T. koningi*), p. 228
Brown Mould (*Peziza ostracoderma, Plicaria fulva* stat. conid. *Ostracoderma terrestre* and *Botrytis gemella*), p. 228
Ink Caps (*Coprinus comatus, C. atramentarius, C. fimetarius*), p. 228

Non-pathogenic disorders

Wet Bubble (*Mycogone perniciosa*)

Symptoms of this common disease vary with the stage of the sporophore development at the time of infection. If the undifferentiated mushroom is infected, a regular and often large mass (10–15 cm diameter) of tissue known as a sclerodermoid mass (Fig. 10.1) results. This is often covered with a white, fluffy, mycelial growth which darkens with time, eventually becoming dark brown. Amber droplets of liquid often exude from the affected tissue (Fig. 10.2). Infection of mushroom initials may occur below the surface of the casing and then a small patch of white mycelium appears on the casing surface (Fig. 10.3). *Mycogone perniciosa* is a pathogen of sporophores only, the mycelium is not affected.

If infection occurs after differentiation of the stalk and cap, a brown streak may form on the stalk and the gills above this streak are colonised in a sector (Fig. 10.4). Affected gills show white mycelial growth which covers a part of the total gill surface.

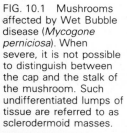

FIG. 10.1 Mushrooms affected by Wet Bubble disease (*Mycogone perniciosa*). When severe, it is not possible to distinguish between the cap and the stalk of the mushroom. Such undifferentiated lumps of tissue are referred to as sclerodermoid masses.

FIG. 10.2 Dark brown or amber droplets of liquid oozing from a sclerodermoid mass caused by *Mycogone perniciosa*.

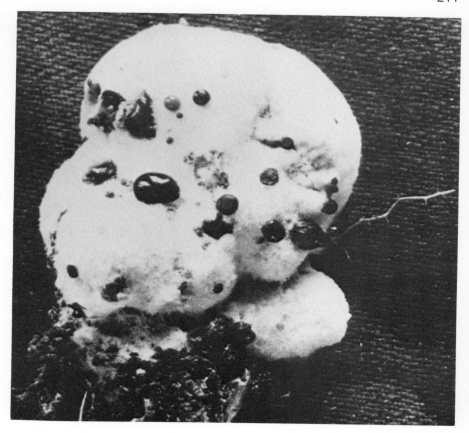

FIG. 10.3 A white and dense felt of mycelium formed on the casing surface resulting from attack by *Mycogone perniciosa* on a mushroom developing below the casing surface.

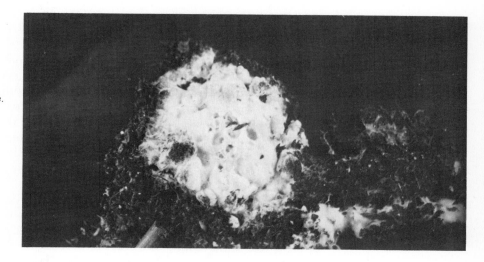

Infection at the base of the stalk when the sporophore is near to maturity causes a light brown discoloration with no obvious growth of the pathogen. When the infected stalk bases are left in the bed they produce a mass of white aerial mycelium which eventually turns brown.

Mycogone perniciosa produces two spore forms, thin-walled conidia and

FIG. 10.4 A sector of affected gill tissue resulting from parasitism and colonisation of the mushroom by *Mycogone perniciosa*, at a late stage in its development. Copyright May & Baker Ltd.

aleuriospores, which are two-celled with a brown, thick-walled terminal cell and a thin-walled basal cell (see Fig. 1.1a). It is believed that these latter spores remain viable for very long periods, perhaps several years.

The interval between infection and the appearance of symptoms is approximately 11 days. The pathogen does not grow through the casing and infection only occurs if spores are near to the developing sporophores which may stimulate their germination. Spores are dispersed from infected mushrooms mainly during watering. Water running off affected beds will carry the pathogen to other beds and also onto the floor of the house. Pickers may distribute spores on their hands, on implements and on boxes. Although conidia can be air-borne, it seems unlikely that this means of dispersal is very important. Flies and other pests are also unimportant as a means of dissemination.

Soil and debris are important sources of *M. perniciosa*. Wild mushrooms and some other soil fungi are also hosts, but their importance as sources of the pathogen for cultivated crops is not known. On farms, contaminated casing is one of the commonest ways of introducing the pathogen. When the disease appears in the first flush, the casing is usually the main source, whereas its appearance during later flushes indicates secondary spread, often by contamination of implements or by pickers.

Control.   None of the spawn strains is resistant to Wet Bubble. Use of excessive water and watersplash should be avoided in order to prevent dissemination of spores. Both spore forms of the fungus are readily killed by heat and disinfectants. However, only exposed spores are killed by disinfectants and the pathogen often survives below the treated surface.

If it is thought that the casing might be contaminated, it can be pasteurised (60 °C for 10 minutes) or chemically treated with formalin using a 1 per cent solution well mixed into the casing at the rate of 27 litres/m³ of casing.

Various fungicides, including benomyl, carbendazim, thiophanate-methyl and thiabendazole, have been successfully used to control this disease, either mixed with the casing or as a spray applied to the bed surface. On some farms, failure to control Wet Bubble disease with benomyl has been associated with the biological breakdown of the fungicide in the casing. Thiabendazole does not appear to be as prone to this form of breakdown. Recently, prochloraz manganese has been shown to give an effective control of this pathogen. Benzimidazole resistance has been found in *M. perniciosa* in Korea but not so far in any other country.

Dry Bubble (*Verticillium fungicola* syn. *V. malthousei*, and *V. psalliotae*)

This desease is probably the most common and damaging fungus disease of the crop and is usually most severe in the summer months, especially when fly populations are high. Epidemics may also occur in the autumn and appear to be favoured by high humidities.

Infection of the developing sporophore before differentiation of the stalk and cap results in an undifferentiated mass of tissue which varies in size from 2–3 mm up to 25 mm in diameter. These are often grey in colour and are similar to the Mycogone sclerodermoid masses but are usually not as white or fluffy and frequently are much smaller and drier in texture. Infection at a later stage causes thickening of the stipe, especially at the base. Affected stipes may be brown and the external tissue peels back (Fig. 10.5). The cap is reduced in size and small wart-like growths occur (Fig. 10.6). Affected mushrooms often dry and crack, producing distortion and tilting of the cap as the mushroom enlarges (Fig. 10.7). Cap infection can occur at a late stage in the development of the mushroom. Circular spots up to 10 mm in diameter, initially pale brown in colour and becoming grey with age, appear within a few days of infection. A yellow-mauve discoloration may also occur around the brown spots (see Fig. 10.8).

Verticillium fungicola is the most common of the two species. Both species produce large numbers of conidia and no other spore forms are known.

Recently, in Holland, two varieties of *Verticillium fungicola* have been recognised. *V. fungicola* var *fungicola* has an optimum growth temperature of 24 °C and produces symptoms an *Agaricus bisporus* as already described. *V. fungicola* var *aleophilum* is morphologically very similar but has an optimum growth temperature of 27 °C. It produces a brown spot symptom on affected mushrooms and has not been associated with growth distortion. Because of its higher optimum temperature it is more likely to be found on crops of *Agaricus bitorquis* (normally grown at 20 °C c.f. 16 °C for *A. bisporus*) or *A. bisporus* when grown in warmer climates.

V. fungicola var *aleophilum* shows an unusual reaction to the fungicide benomyl. Whilst the ED^{50} is less than 1 ppm, the fungus is able to grow even

FIG. 10.5 Tissue of the stipe peeling back following infection by *Verticillium fungicola*, the cause of Dry Bubble disease.

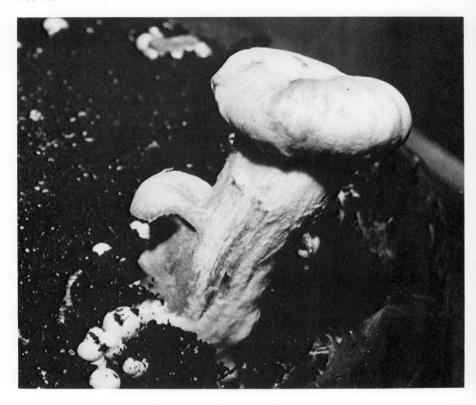

FIG. 10.6 Various distortions of the sporophore associated with *Verticillium fungicola*.
(a) An undifferentiated mass of tissue similar to the sclerodermoid masses caused by *Mycogone perniciosa* (see Fig. 10.1).
(b) Cap and stipe distortion with discoloration of the cap.
(c) Small wart-like outgrowths from an otherwise normal mushroom.

FIG. 10.7   Cap tilting with discoloration of the stipe caused by *Verticillium fungicola*.

FIG. 10.8   Mauve, pale brown or sometimes pale yellow or mauve spots on the cap caused by *Verticillium fungicola*.

at 100 ppm. For this reason it may not be controlled by benzimidazole fungicides. *Verticillium psalliotae* is morphologically distinguishable from *V. fungicola*. It was first found on *A. bisporus* although it occurs infrequently. There have been some recent reports of a brown spot disease of *A. bitorquis* caused by this fungus.

The average time between infection and the production of the distortion symptom is about 14 days. Spores of the pathogen are thought to be stimulated to germinate by the mushroom mycelium or by developing sporophores. Although the vegetative mycelium is not infected, it is thought that the pathogen may grow alongside mycelial strands.

Conidia are dispersed over short distances mainly by watersplash and run-off water. Conidia are produced in sticky clusters and adhere very readily to anything that makes contact with them. In this way, they can be carried by flies and mites or on hands, tools and picking boxes. Conidia may also be dispersed by air currents. Dissemination over longer distances can occur if spores are carried by insects or the wind, or if they adhere to clothing. Both species are common soil fungi, where they parasitise various fungi in addition to species of *Agaricus*.

Control. Scrupulous attention to farm hygiene is essential for the control of Dry Bubble. It is important to control flies and prevent the introduction of debris into cropping houses. Air-borne dust, debris and soil are potential sources of these pathogens.

Benzimidazole fungicides have given good control of Dry Bubble but strains of *V. fungicola* which are resistant, are now widespread. The use of benomyl has been shown to increase the incidence of Dry Bubble disease caused by benomyl resistant strains. Where such strains occur other fungicides, such as chlorothalonil, zineb, mancozeb, or the recently introduced fungicide prochloraz manganese, should be used.

Cobweb (*Hypomyces rosellus* stat. conid. *Cladobotryum dendroides* syn. *Dactylium dendroides*)

Cobweb disease is not uncommon, although it is rarely as damaging as the Bubble diseases. Affected mushrooms are most commonly found in the fourth or fifth flushes. Typically, mushrooms are engulfed by the white mycelium of the pathogen which not only covers the mushrooms but much of the surrounding casing. Frequently, a clump of mushrooms is completely covered by a cotton wool-like mycelial growth, hence the common name of this disease (Fig. 10.9). Mushrooms of any age or developmental stage may be attacked. The cottony, white mycelium turns pink or red with age and the parasitised mushrooms become brown and rot.

The fungus produces large numbers of spores which are readily dispersed by air movement, watersplash and excess water run-off. Contamination of the casing by soil or by spores blown from an affected crop is likely to lead to disease, although symptoms may not appear until the final stages of cropping. The fungus is thought to be an inhabitant of soils.

Control. Strict hygiene will prevent epidemic attacks. The spores are

FIG. 10.9 Cobweb disease caused by *Hypomyces rosellus* (stat. conid. *Dactylium dendroides*). Notice the mycelium of the pathogen growing over the affected mushrooms and also over the casing surface.

readily killed by heat and disinfectants. Benzimidazole fungicides give satisfactory control and resistance to these fungicides has not been recorded. However, if Dry Bubble is also a problem, the use of benomyl to control Cobweb Disease may result in an increase in Dry Bubble. In such situations, thiabendazole or prochloraz manganese may be preferred.

Shaggy Stipe (*Mortierella bainieri*)

This disease has only been recorded recently and is not common. The most characteristic symptom is the peeling of the stalk of the affected mushrooms giving them a shaggy appearance. The stalk and cap are often considerably discoloured, eventually turning dark brown. Coarse, grey mycelium occurs on the stalk and also on the gills of affected mushrooms. It may even spread onto the surrounding casing and then the disease is similar to Cobweb, although the mycelium is more sparse. Some affected mushrooms are stunted and irregular in shape, but others (probably infected late in their development) show only slight discoloration of the stalk with brown blotches on the surface of the cap which may be surrounded by a yellow ring (Fig. 10.10).

Control. The pathogen is a common soil fungus and therefore contamination of casing or compost with soil or debris may result in outbreaks of this disease. Of the fungicides available, zineb is likely to give the most effective control.

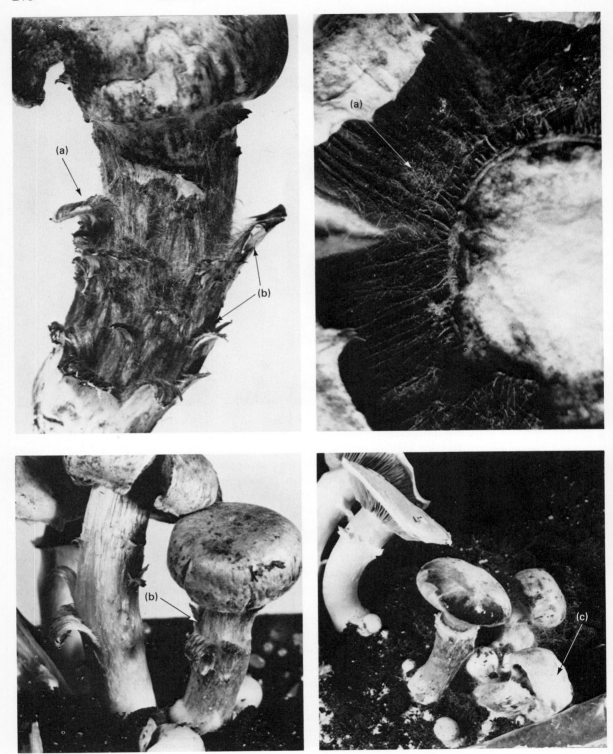

FIG. 10.10 Shaggy Stipe
(*Mortierella bainieri*); the
coarse grey mycelium of
the pathogen (a) grows
over the stipe and gills,
affected stipes peel back
(b) and some small
mushrooms become
engulfed in the coarse
grey mycelium (c). Crown
Copyright.

Gill Mildew (*Cephalosporium* sp.)

Gill Mildew is an uncommon disease. The symptoms may be confused with those of Hardgill (see p. 229). The gills of affected mushrooms are thickened and covered in white fungal growth. There is some doubt about the role of *Cephalosporium* as the true cause of the gill symptoms. Sometimes the apparent mildew is mushroom mycelium growing out of the gills.

Cap Spotting (*Aphanocladium album*)

Aphanocladium album has been isolated from mushrooms showing pale to dark brown circular spots on the caps. These spots vary in number and size but may be up to 10 mm in diameter. Often a piece of organic debris can be found in their centres. This disease is not of economic importance.

Bacterial Blotch, Bacterial Spot or Brown Blotch (*Pseudomonas tolaasii*) and Ginger Blotch (*Ps. fluorescens*)

Bacterial Blotch is one of the most common and damaging diseases of the mushroom crop. Symptoms vary from a yellow or pale ginger-brown discoloration, to dark brown lesions. Part or all of the cap surface may be affected. During the development of the sporophore, asymmetrical caps result when lesions dry and crack (Fig. 10.11). Occasionally, longitudinal lesions develop on the stipes. The gills are rarely affected, although there may be some connection between this disease and Drippy Gill (see p. 220). Generally, the discoloration is superficial, rarely more than 3 mm below the surface. Sometimes blotch symptoms develop after harvesting, especially if the mushrooms are stored at a fluctuating temperature which allows water condensation on their surfaces. *Pseudomonas tolaasii* is the cause of the dark brown blotch symptoms and the ginger coloured spots are caused by *Ps. fluorescens*, a closely related bacterium. Both pathogens have been isolated from the casing, particularly where blotch-infected mushrooms have occurred. However, disease symptoms are most commonly produced when the organism is present in large numbers on mushroom initials. Frequently, lesions occur where water has collected on and between clumps of mushrooms.

Pseudomonas tolaasii is thought to be widespread in nature. It can spread by air-borne means either as bacterial cells or in debris. It has been found in both peat and chalk samples used for casing. It is also spread by flies (particularly sciarids), nematodes, workers and by water splash. The disease develops more rapidly at 18 °C than at 16 °C. The disease is most common when temperature and relative humidity is high. In optimum conditions the bacterium will infect the mushroom and produce blotching in a few hours.

Control.   Surface water on the cap plays an important part in the development of epidemic attacks of this disease. Growing conditions regulated to ensure that water quickly evaporates from the casing and mushroom surfaces, generally result in low disease incidence. Fluctuating temperatures giving periods of high relative humidity are likely to aid blotch. Mushroom caps should be dried as soon after watering as possible. Where the disease is severe,

FIG. 10.11 Bacterial Blotch (*Pseudomonas tolaasii*) causing brown discoloration of the cap (a), often most severe at the margins, and splitting (b).

the watering frequency should be reduced and every effort made to keep the humidity of the house down to 85 per cent RH. Various chemical treatments have been tried, but have given inconsistent results. Chlorine at approximately 150 p.p.m., applied in every watering, may help to keep disease incidence down. Sodium hypochlorite is usually used at the rate of 0.6 litres of a commercial solution (10 per cent available chlorine) added to 360 litres of water. Most preparations of this chemical lose their chlorine very rapidly once the container has been opened so it is advisable to buy small quantities which can be used fairly quickly.

Bacterial Pit

The cause of this disease has not been established although it is thought to be induced by a bacterial pathogen. Pits are produced on the caps of affected mushrooms. They are usually dark brown to black in colour, varying in depth, and often with a shiny inner surface (Fig. 10.12). The pits are usually not numerous but even single pits reduce the quality of the mushrooms. The disease most frequently appears in the latter flushes of a crop, but is rarely severe. There are no specific control measures.

Drippy Gill (*Pseudomonas cichorii* and *Ps. agarici*)

This disease is not uncommon and is frequently associated with outbreaks

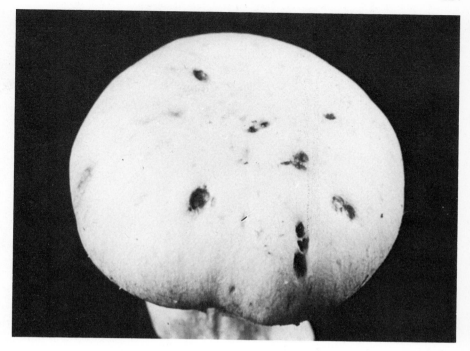

of Bacterial Blotch. There are no obvious external symptoms on the young affected buttons, but if the veil is broken the symptoms can be seen on the gills. Small, creamy droplets of liquid occur on the affected gill tissue which is often discoloured dark brown. On open mushrooms the gills develop brown areas which also have creamy droplets of liquid attached to them. Eventually adjacent gills become colonised until most of the gill tissue has deteriorated into a dark brown, slimy mass. Very little is known about this disease and it does not often occur at epidemic levels. The nature of the pathogen suggests that it is likely to be spread by water and probably insects. Should the creamy bacterial ooze dry, then the pathogen could also become air-borne.

Control. The measures recommended for the control of bacterial blotch may be effective but have not been substantiated by experimental work.

Mummy Disease (*Pseudomonas* sp.)

The main feature of Mummy Disease is its rate of spread and, although it is not common, when it does occur it can cause considerable reductions in yield. Disease symptoms may appear anywhere within a crop and, providing there is a continuous mycelial connection (either along a bed or between trays), the rate of spread is up to 250 mm of bed length per day. It is believed that the pathogen spreads within the mycelium. In the affected areas the mushrooms are malformed, pale brown in colour, with asymmetric tilting of the cap, which is very characteristic (Fig. 10.13). There is often a noticeable development of rhizomorphs from the base of affected stalks and the bases may be slightly swollen. Affected mushrooms do not decay but dry and wither. Stalks and caps of affected mushrooms have brown spots and

FIG. 10.13 Mummy Disease, thought to be caused by a bacterium. Affected mushrooms show tilting of the cap (a) and when cut longitudinally, brown spots can be seen in the stalk and cap (b).

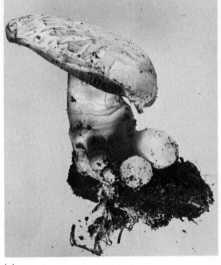 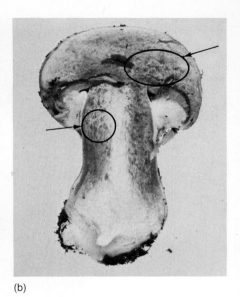

(a)   (b)

streaks within them which are apparent when the mushrooms are cut. The gritty feel of the stalk at cutting is also a feature of this disease.

Spread from tray to tray or along a bed will only occur by mycelial contact and for this reason it is common to have an affected bed adjacent to a healthy one. This situation persists for the duration of the crop providing mycelial contact between the adjacent beds is prevented.

It is thought that there is a close association between a species of *Pseudomonas* and Mummy Disease. The organism has been used in an infection experiment, and when introduced with spawn has resulted in Mummy Disease symptoms appearing 2–3 weeks later in a small proportion of the inoculated plots. Other attempts to reproduce the disease with similar organisms have failed.

Control. Spread of the disease can be limited by isolating affected areas of bed or by preventing mycelial contact between trays. Where long lengths of bed are used, the routine use of polythene barriers at intervals can limit the extent of spread. There are no known chemical treatments. It has been claimed that some mushroom strains are more susceptible than others, but there is no experimental evidence to support this.

Mushroom virus diseases

Diseases of mushrooms thought to be caused by viruses have been called La France Watery Stipe, Die Back, X Disease and Brown Disease. The most consistent affect of these diseases is a decline in yield which may be only slight or, in extreme cases, can result in total crop failure. Various more specific symptoms have been described, including elongation of the stalk with a small cap (drumstick), tilted caps (German helmets), water-soaked sporophore tissues, progressive deterioration of the mycelium resulting in bare patches in the crop (die-back) and small brown mushrooms which open prematurely. There is little direct evidence that any of these symptoms are the result of virus infection, but virus-like particles (VLPs) can often be found in such affected mushrooms. However, VLPs, usually in low concentrations, can also be found in mushrooms from crops which show no symptoms and are cropping satisfactorily. For these reasons it is difficult to assess the importance of VLPs although their presence in mushrooms is common.

The VLPs found in mushrooms are differentiated according to their size and shape. Five different types of particles have been found in Britain, and particles of slightly different dimensions have been described elsewhere. It is not clear whether these are the same or different particles. The major shapes and sizes of particles found in Britain include spherical particles 25 nm diameter (Virus 1), spherical particles 29 nm diameter (Virus 2), bacilliform particles 50 × 90 nm (Virus 3), spherical particles 35 nm diameter (Virus 4) and spherical particles 50 nm diameter (Virus 5). A club-shaped VLP has been described from mushrooms in France. These particles may occur alone or in any combination.

The only accurate way to diagnose the presence of VLPs in mushrooms is by electron microscopy, although when their concentrations are low, they are not easy to detect by any method. Some workers have reported that VLPs occur in all mushroom crops and in all mushroom spawns, whilst others claim that their distribution is much more limited. When they are found in large concentrations, crop yields are invariably severely affected. The growth rate of cultures made from sporophores with high concentrations of particles, is generally considerably reduced. For this reason, comparisons of growth rates have been used as an indication of the presence of these diseases.

The frequency of occurrence of the particles of different dimensions has varied with time; for instance, in the early 1960s 29 nm spherical particles were most commonly found, but these are now rare and 35 nm spherical particles are the most common. With the exception of the 50 nm spherical particles, all of the others have been found in mushroom spores and it seems likely that this is one of the main means of their dissemination.

Mushroom VLPs cannot exist for any length of time outside mushroom tissue and mycelium, spores and crop debris containing VLPs are the main sources for the crop. Mycelium can survive on wooden boxes and in small fragments of compost. It can be blown or carried around the farm and is often widely disseminated during the emptying of the old crop. Mushroom spores, which are between 5 and 8 μm diameter, occur in very large numbers in cropping houses especially when the mushrooms are picked after they open (Fig. 10.14). They can be air-borne and travel considerable distances but the highest concentrations are usually within and near to cropping houses. Wild mushrooms are also potential sources, although there is no evidence to suggest that they are a major source of virus on most farms.

Mushroom spore germination is stimulated by actively growing mushroom mycelium. If spores are introduced during the spawn run they will germinate and hyphal fusion between mycelium, originating from an infected spore and the healthy spawn, will result in the transfer of the VLPs. Infection early in the development of the crop has the greatest effect on yield. Infection at or after the first flush stage may have an insignificant effect on yield. Some mushroom spawns may contain VLPs although such spawns do not necessarily give poor yields. The significance of low concentrations of VLPs in spawn or during cropping is not yet understood. The mechanism of the

FIG. 10.14 A scanning electron microscope picture of mushroom spores on the surface of a mushroom sporophore. Notice, at this very high magnification, the sporophore is seen to be a collection of mycelial strands with large spaces between. Reproduced by kind permission of Dr W. C. Wong.

change from low to high concentrations has not been explained. Although VLPs are common in mushrooms, more work needs to be done to determine their exact role.

Control. The control of these diseases depends upon rigid adherence to hygienic measures. The same measures would generally control many other diseases. The main aim of the hygiene programme is to prevent the contamination of the new crop with mushroom spores or debris from the old ones. Contamination during spawn running must be avoided as this is likely to have the maximum effect on yield. Air-borne spores can be filtered out of the air taken into the peak heat rooms, the spawn running area, spawn running rooms and holding rooms. Ideally, a 1 μm air filter should be used and every effort made to ensure that the exhaust air from cropping houses is taken away from the farm and not recirculated. Farms with a central corridor from which air is taken for the cropping houses, are particularly vulnerable as such corridors are likely to have a high mushroom spore concentration. Filtration of the exhaust air from cropping houses will help to reduce risk of the VLPs spreading.

All wooden parts of growing units should be thoroughly cleaned to kill any mushroom mycelium and spores remaining from the old crop. Where virus disease is causing severe crop loss, it may be advantageous to reduce the length of picking to 4 weeks and pick all mushrooms before they open. Some spawns are more tolerant to virus disease than others and, although VLPs can be found in them the effects of these on yield is usually less. Spawns, often off-white and related to the types used in cave culture, show this tolerance. They also withstand higher levels of carbon dioxide than normal white strains but show severe flaking of the cap when exposed to low levels of air movement. Brown or cream spawns also show virus tolerance.

Agaricus bitorquis has recently been used by some growers in place of *A. bisporus*. This species does not appear to be susceptible to the VLPs found in

A. bisporus and is therefore a useful alternative if the disease is severe. It is possible that *A. bitorquis* might be susceptible to a range of virus diseases of its own which may not affect *A. bisporus*. The alternation of the two host species on a farm could keep virus diseases at a low level.

Weed moulds – competitors and antagonists

Weed moulds may affect the growth of mushroom mycelium by direct antagonism or by competing for nutrients. In either case, the amount of compost available to the mushroom is decreased and the yield is proportionally reduced. Sometimes, weed moulds are indicators of an unsuitable medium for mushroom growth and may help to pin-point errors in compost preparation.

Truffle, False Truffle, Calves Brains (*Diehliomyces microsporus* syn. *Pseudobalsamia microspora*)

False Truffle is common and is frequently responsible for crop loss. Initially, it is difficult to diagnose, as well developed False Truffle mycelium is an orange-cream colour, sometimes matted into a felt, not unlike mushroom stroma. The orange colour is the distinguishing feature as mushroom mycelium is dull-grey to white. The Truffle fruiting bodies are found in the compost or casing and are frequently most abundant at the edges of the compost, particularly at the casing/compost junction. They vary in size from 3–40 mm in diameter, are initially a bright cream colour, but turn red-brown and dark brown as they mature (see Fig. 10.15). They are irregular in shape

FIG. 10.15 Ascocarps of the False Truffle fungus (*Diehliomyces microsporus*) in mushroom compost.

and the surface is folded and corrugated and looks like a brain, hence the common name 'calves brains'. The truffles are the ascocarps of the fungus and contain large numbers of ascospores. As they disintegrate, these spores are released.

Where the compost is colonised by *Diehliomyces* mycelium, there is no mushroom mycelium and the compost appears dark brown in colour and is often wet. Affected beds usually show a patchy distribution of the crop, and may eventually cease to produce mushrooms altogether. When the Truffle fungus is established in the first flush, the mushroom crop may be reduced by over 50 per cent. Severely affected crops give off a chlorine-like odour which is said to be diagnostic of the problem.

The fungus is thought to occur in soil and some of the worst attacks on mushroom farms have followed soil disturbance during building operations. The spores have long been thought to be difficult to kill, but recent research work suggests that they do not withstand temperatures much above those achieved during the peak heat (60 °C) and it is probably their large numbers which accounts for their survival as some, particularly on boxes and in growing houses, do not always reach this temperature. The ascospores are stimulated to germinate in the presence of mushroom mycelium, particularly at high temperatures (30 °C), although they will germinate at a much lower temperature (16 °C). Spores may persist on boxes, tools and other equipment and are frequently introduced into crops in casing or compost.

Control. Care must be taken to avoid contaminating compost or casing with soil as this may lead to outbreaks of False Truffle. The ascospores are difficult to eliminate from a farm, but as they require a temperature of 16 °C or above for germination, it is possible to minimise the problem by ensuring that bed temperatures during spawn run and cropping are kept down. Boxes should be regularly treated between crops with a disinfectant and cropping houses as well as concrete surfaces should be washed with a disinfectant. All affected crops should be cooked-out, i.e. heated up to at least 70 °C for 1 hour, wherever possible. By regular box and house cleaning, cooking-out and filtration (especially during spawn running), it is possible to eliminate False Truffle from a farm (see p. 230).

Benomyl added to compost at the rate of 160 g of product (Benlate) per tonne of compost also helps to control this fungus.

Lipstick Mould, Red Geotrichum (*Sporendonema purpurescens*)

This competitor is common, although infrequently responsible for large reductions in yield. It grows in the compost and casing, producing a fine, white mycelial growth which turns bright pink and finally buff as it ages. Frequently, the first colonies appear in cracks or crevices in the casing. Vast numbers of wind-borne spores of the fungus are produced as the colonies become red and powdery. Lipstick Mould is thought to be antagonistic to mushroom mycelium.

Cracks in concrete, particularly where casing is stored, can be a source of this fungus. Good farm hygiene should prevent Lipstick Mould becoming a problem (see p. 230).

Olive Green Mould (*Chaetomium olivaceum, C. glososum*)

The mycelium of *Chaetomium* spp. is initially grey, becoming whiter with age, and it may be cottony. When prolific, it is often referred to as White Chaetomium (but this may be a different species). Shortly after the appearance of the mycelial growth, the perithecia of the fungus are formed and these are olive green to brown in colour and about the size of a pin-head. They often occur in large numbers on pieces of straw in the compost.

Where Chaetomium grows the spawn does not. Chaetomium is often associated with composts which have been overheated (in excess of 61 °C) during peak heating. Such composts frequently have a high ammonia content at spawning and it is likely that Chaetomium is able to withstand the high ammonia levels.

An insufficient flow of air over the bed surface during peak-heat, or over-wetness, or compaction, or undercomposting during the first stages of compost preparation result in an accumulation of ammonia in the compost, and if this is not all removed before spawning, Chaetomium is likely to develop.

The fungus is thought to have an antagonistic effect on mushroom mycelial growth and crop yield is reduced in proportion to the extent to which Chaetomium colonises the compost.

It is essential to control the peak heat conditions to remove all the ammonia. The peak heat should be ventilated to give an air exchange capacity of about 28 air changes per hour in the room, based on its empty volume. A compost can sometimes be made suitable for use by lengthening the peak heat for several days at a safe temperature (below 60 °C) giving plenty of fresh air during the extended treatment period.

Yellow Moulds and Vert-de-Gris

Various yellow or yellow-green moulds occur occasionally in mushroom compost irrespective of the presence of mushroom mycelium. Once established, they compete with mushroom mycelium, either reducing the food supply or even killing the mycelium by the production of toxins.

Yellow moulds may develop in a layer below the casing (Mat Disease, *Chrysosporium luteum*) or form circular colonies in the compost (Confetti, *C. sulfureum*), or they may be generally distributed throughout the compost (Vert-de-Gris, *Myceliophthora lutea, Sepedonium* sp. and *Sporotrichum* sp.).

Large numbers of spores are produced by these fungi and they are readily disseminated through the air. They have the greatest effect on yield when introduced at spawning. Good farm hygiene will reduce the spore population although, when there is a persistent problem, filtration of the air during spawning and in the spawn-running areas may be necessary. When well established on a farm they are often very difficult to eradicate.

White Plaster Mould (*Scopulariopsis fimicola*)

White Plaster Mould has decreased in incidence in recent years. Where it occurs it produces dense white patches of mycelial growth so that the casing surface or the compost appears to have a dense covering of flour. Spawn growth may be retarded. White Plaster Mould generally dies out after the early flushes and mushroom mycelium grows into the affected areas. The large numbers of spores produced by the fungus result in very efficient dissemination. White plaster mould is usually thought to be a good indicator of undercomposting and excessively high compost pH (pH 8.2 or above).

Black Whisker Mould (*Doratomyces stemonitis, D. microsporus*)

Black Whisker Mould is named after the dark grey to black whisker-like bristles produced in the compost. These spore-bearing structures (synnemata) may be up to 2 mm long. Spawn growth is not affected but workers may be allergic to the spores. The fungus is often abundant in wet composts.

Brown Plaster Mould (*Papulaspora byssina*)

Colonies of this fungus are initially white but turn brown and powdery in appearance at maturity. Large dense patches cover the surface of the compost or casing but remain for a relatively short time, eventually disappearing. The brown coloration is due to the production of large numbers of spores which are readily disseminated.

Papulaspora byssina appears to prefer wet composts and may therefore be a problem of overcomposting but may also occur when the compost is wet but undercomposted.

Green Mould (*Trichoderma viride, T. koningi*)

These moulds are generally considered to be weed moulds but they may also be pathogenic on *Agaricus bisporus*. *Trichoderma viride* grows on undecomposed organic matter in the casing or compost, such as the remains of the grain spawn, young mushroom sporophores which have died and the wood of trays, especially when it is 'green' and untreated. *Trichoderma koningi* grows in a cottony web of mycelium over the casing surface engulfing mushrooms in a soft, wet rot. Sometimes it causes a superficial purple-brown spot with a dry cracked surface. Both moulds can be controlled by attention to hygiene (see p. 230).

Brown Mould (*Peziza ostracoderma, Plicaria fulva* stat. conid. *Ostracoderma terrestre* and *Botrytis gemella*)

These fungi grow on the casing surface producing colonies which are white at first but turn grey or yellowish and finally cinnamon brown. Brown apothecia may also be formed. They are thought to be somewhat antagonistic to mycelial growth although rarely affect yield. The mycelial growth generally disappears fairly quickly.

Ink Caps (*Coprinus* spp., including *C. comatus, C. atramentarius, C. fimetarius*)

The sporophores of ink cap fungi often appear before the first flush of mushrooms. As they mature, their caps disintegrate into a black slimy mess. They are sometimes said to be an indication of a good compost, but more often are a sign of undercomposting. Spores of ink caps are readily air disseminated and will not cause crop loss providing they can be kept out of the compost from the end of peak heating until the casing is applied. Ink caps can be prevented by the preparation of good compost and by attention to hygiene (see p. 230).

NON-PATHOGENIC DISORDERS

Hardgill or Open Veil

Affected mushrooms have poor or incomplete gill formation. The cause of the symptom is unknown. None of the white spawns appears to be immune, although some show a greater incidence than others. Various environmental factors have been associated with Hardgill, particularly fluctuations in temperature and consequential changes in relative humidity.

Rose or Cock's Comb

Upturning of the edges of the cap and gill formation on the upper surface of the cap, sometimes in the form of a vertical column of pink gill tissue, is characteristic of this common condition. The distortion on the top of the cap is sometimes reminiscent of a cock's comb, hence the alternative name (see Fig. 1.23, p. 29). The earliest flushes are usually affected. Various chemical contaminants are known to induce this symptom, the commonest being mineral oils, creosote, phenolic materials and diesel fumes.

Stroma or Overlay

Commonly, in conditions of very high humidity, often induced by poor air circulation, mushroom mycelium grows onto the surface of the casing sometimes forming a dense mat which is impervious to water. As soon as the first signs of surface mycelium appears, the surface of the casing should be gently ruffled and additional casing applied. If the ventilation across the bed surface is not increased, the stroma will recur. If only slight, it can be kept in check by frequent light watering.

Mass Pin-heads

Crops in the autumn often produce very large numbers of sporophore initials so densely packed together that a mat of tissue forms which prevents water entering the compost. A large number of the mushroom initials die, turning brown and remaining on the bed often throughout the crop. Crops affected in this way often give very poor yields. By the time the problem occurs, there is little that can be done to prevent yield loss.

Dirty mushrooms

Drying of the casing results in sporophore initiation deep in the casing layer, and the mushrooms emerge covered in casing. This can be prevented by keeping the casing moist, especially during the early flushes.

Carbon dioxide damage

A carbon dioxide concentration of the air of between 340–1000 p.p.m. favours mushroom initiation. If ventilation is not adequate, or if the compost does not fill the beds so that there is a shielding effect of the sides of the beds preventing air movement over the bed surface, the carbon dioxide concentration on the bed surface can be well above this level. The first sign in the crop is the elongation of the stalk, and at extremely high levels of carbon dioxide (in excess of 3000 p.p.m.) the cap remains small and the stalk elongated, giving the mushroom a drumstick appearance. Manipulation of the carbon dioxide level, to give slight elongation of the stipe, may help with mechanical picking.

Distortions and deformations

Mushroom distortion is sometimes common, particularly in the autumn and early winter months. Affected mushrooms may be irregular in shape, or at the extreme, an undifferentiated mass of tissue is produced. Fused or Siamese twin mushrooms are not uncommon in affected crops. Mushrooms are most commonly distorted in the first flush, especially after a vigorous spawn run, but the seasonal effect on incidence is probably the major predisposing factor. The cause of the distortion is unknown but, as it occurs most commonly in the autumn, it is often assumed that it is associated with conditions of high relative humidity.

THE ROLE OF HYGIENE IN THE CONTROL OF MUSHROOM DISEASES AND WEED MOULDS

Disease control on every mushroom farm is dependent upon good hygiene which, when done efficiently, can be very effective in keeping pathogen populations to a minimum. Farm hygiene can only be satisfactory if a series of requirements are meticulously and consistently satisfied. Some of them are apparently unimportant when considered individually.

Farm design and cleanliness

The farm layout should be such that areas to be kept as clean as possible, for instance the casing material store, spawning area, spawn running and holding rooms, are the maximum distance from the cook-out rooms and on the windward side of the growing sheds. Cropping houses should be positioned so that ventilation air is not contaminated by exhaust air from nearby cropping houses. Central corridors should be avoided if at all possible, but where they exist, they should receive particular attention and be regularly disinfected.

Wherever possible, all roadways and working surfaces should be concreted so that they can be regularly cleaned by hosing down and spraying with a disinfectant. This should be done immediately before an operation such as composting, mixing casing, etc., or at minimum intervals of at least once a week.

Personnel

The whole work-force on a farm is an important factor in the dissemination, either directly or indirectly, of pests and diseases, particularly by carrying contaminated debris on their feet and clothing. By ensuring that there is only one entrance to each clean area, e.g. peat store, peak heat room, spawning area, spawn running room, holding room and cropping houses, and that there is a foot-bath of disinfectant at the entrance, it is possible to minimise the introduction of debris. Work should be organised so that staff do not pass from old crops to newer ones. Overalls should be cleaned and changed frequently. The use of overalls of various colours will help management to check the regularity of changing.

Equipment

Equipment should be washed down with a disinfectant before use, particularly after emptying old crops and before spawning and casing. Tools used by workers should be regularly sprayed or dipped in a disinfectant. Contamination of clean areas can be minimised by keeping a separate set of tools in these areas.

Crop preparation

Trays, boxes or shelf boards, can be cleaned before filling by dipping or spraying with a wood-preserving disinfectant plus wetter. The use of a disinfectant on the wood, has the additional benefit of preventing the mycelium growing into it, which makes emptying easier. Compost yards that are concreted can be easily cleaned down between batches. The use of a high pressure hose will remove much of the debris. After filling the clean boxes or beds, it is important to keep the compost free from contamination during pasteurisation. Ventilation air should be filtered (preferably using a 1 μm filter) especially during the period when the compost is cooling down. Generally, the maximum temperature reached during peak heat (60 °C) is not sufficiently high to kill all pathogens although many are killed, as well as insect pests and nematodes.

   After peak heat, the compost is spawned using disinfected equipment. It is particularly important to prevent contamination from this stage until the casing has been applied.

   Air should be filtered into spawn running rooms and doors should be tight fitting.

   Contaminated casing is one of the most common sources of pathogens. Casing materials should be stored in a covered area well away from sources of contamination. If casing becomes contaminated, it can be pasteurised (60–70 °C for 30 minutes) or treated with 1 per cent formalin (27 litres/m^3 casing). Fumigation of the casing with methyl bromide is also effective.

Cropping

Good lighting is essential so that crops can be thoroughly and regularly inspected for disease. Outbreaks of disease should be treated as soon as possible, either by removing the diseased sporophores or by covering them with a plastic cup or common salt. If plastic cups are used for the control of bubble diseases, they must be pressed well into the casing otherwise there is still some risk of spread.

A special team of workers should be used to remove diseased mushrooms, suitably equipped with protective clothing so that disinfectants can be liberally used. Special gloves covered with sponge, impregnated with a disinfectant, have been found by some growers to be very effective for this purpose.

Run-off water often disseminates spores of pathogens, many of them reaching the floor of cropping houses. If the floor dries out and is swept, these spores become air-borne. It is therefore important to keep the floor moist.

Post-cropping

Sterilisation at the end of cropping, which is often referred to as cook-out, is one way of reducing the pathogen population and preventing spread. It is usually done with steam, by raising the temperature of the coldest part of the compost to 70 °C. Methyl bromide treatment is an alternative. If heat or methyl bromide are not used, the crop can be sprayed or fumigated with formaldehyde – especially before it is moved. Formalin (2–5 per cent plus wetter) can be effectively used as a spray or applied either as a fumigant, using a fogging machine, or by vaporising the formaldehyde with heat (see p. 95).

Disinfectants or sterilants

A large number of proprietary disinfectants, many of them poisonous, are used and the manufacturers' recommendations should be strictly followed.

TABLE 10.1 Some disinfectants commonly used on mushroom farms

Chemical	Trade name	Use
Formaldehye	Various including Formasan, Steriform and Dynaform (a fogging formulation)	Disinfecting surfaces and fumigating buildings
Phenolic mixture	Environ, Vesphene D39	Disinfecting surfaces, boxes and beds
Phenolic distillates	Various including Sterizal	Disinfecting surfaces
Sodium pentachlorophenate	Crytogil	Disinfecting boxes and other woodwork
Dichlorofen	Panocide M	Disinfecting surfaces and boxes or other woodwork
Sodium and calcium hypochlorite	Various including Chloros and Deosan	Disinfecting surfaces
Chlorinated and brominated trisodium orthophosphate	Diversol BX	Disinfecting structures, surfaces and woodwork especially after virus disease
Fatlyamine with lactic and salicylic acids	Nuodex 87	Disinfecting surfaces

The choice of a disinfectant for a particular purpose depends to a large extent on the organism to be killed. No single material is equally effective for all purposes. Where concrete, brick or wooden surfaces are to be treated, the effectiveness of the chemical can often be improved by the addition of a wetting agent (e.g. any detergent). Some commonly used materials and their uses are shown in Table 10.1.

FURTHER READING

Atkins, F. C. (1974) *Guide to Mushroom Growing*. Faber and Faber, London.

Kligman, A. M. (1950) *Handbook of Mushroom Culture*. J. B. Swayne, Kennett Square, P.A.

Vedder, P. J. C. (1978) *Modern Mushroom Growing*. Educaboek BV, Industrieweg 1, Culemborg, The Netherlands.

Wuest, P. J. (1982) *Penn State Handbook for Commercial Mushroom Growers*, The Pennsylvania State University, University Park Pennsylvania.

CHAPTER 11

PEPPER AND AUBERGINE

CULTURE

PEPPER

Pre-planting preparation

The crop often follows lettuce, celery or early tomatoes and is grown in peat bags or in the soil. Soil sterilisation is not commonly done specifically for this crop but is included in the cropping cycle, often following the pepper crop.

Propagation

Peppers are raised from seeds sown in soil-based or peat-based compost. Sowing is done from December until April depending upon the proposed planting-out time. The optimum temperature for seed germination is 24 °C and seedlings are ready for transplanting 12–14 days after sowing. After transplanting into pots, the temperature is maintained at 18–23 °C and the relative humidity kept as high as possible. Carbon dioxide enrichment to 1000 p.p.m. is commonly used during propagation and cropping.

Cropping

Planting is done when the first flower buds are visible and the plants are spaced at 35 × 45 cm. Planting density varies from 20 000 to 25 000 plants per hectare (8000–10 000 per acre). Temperatures during cropping are 15 °C at night and 21 °C during the day. Sometimes, somewhat higher temperatures are used during the initial period of establishment. The relative humidity is maintained at 75 per cent and carbon dioxide is used to enrich the atmosphere to 1000 p.p.m. For late planted crops, the night temperature may be allowed to drop to 10 °C, but at this temperature very little vegetative growth is made. Yields depend upon the time of sowing but long-term crops may produce 150–200 tonne/ha (60–80 ton/acre).

AUBERGINE

Pre-planting preparation and propagation

Aubergines are grown in much the same way as peppers with similar pre-cropping preparation and propagation. Seeds are germinated at 20 °C and sometimes plants are grafted onto tomato rootstocks resistant to Verticillium Wilt. It is necessary to sow aubergine seeds 2 weeks before the rootstock seed. After transplanting, a temperature of 16–19 °C night and 19–22 °C day is used. Carbon dioxide enrichment to 1000 p.p.m. is used during propagation and cropping. Supplementary light during propagation greatly assists the growth of aubergines.

Cropping

Plant spacing and density is similar to that of peppers and the crop is initially grown at 18–20 °C night temperature and 21–22 °C day temperature but dropping to 17 °C at night when the flowers appear. Night temperatures may be dropped still further when picking begins (15 °C) to encourage vegetative growth.

DISEASES OF PEPPER AND AUBERGINE

Seedlings and Roots

Damping-off (*Pythium* spp., *Phytophthora* spp. and *Rhizoctonia solani*), p. 235

Stems

Grey Mould (*Botrytis cinerea*), p. 236
Basal Stem Rots (*Pythium* spp. and *Phytophthora* spp.), p. 235
Tobacco Mosaic (Tobacco Mosaic Virus), p. 238

Leaves

Verticillium Wilt (*Verticillium dahliae* and *V. albo-atrum*), p. 239
Grey Mould (*Botrytis cinerea*), p. 236
Powdery Mildew (*Leveillula taurica*), p. 237

Fruit

Tobacco Mosaic (Tobacco Mosaic Virus), p. 238
Blossom End Rot, p. 239

DISEASES OF PEPPER

Damping-off of seedlings, basal stem and root rots (*Pythium* and *Phytophthora* spp.)

Damping-off occurs shortly after germination, the seedlings showing the typical constriction of the stem just above soil level. At a later stage in the life of the plant the same pathogens can cause browning of the roots and also a wet, brown decay, at the base of the stem (Fig. 11.1). Pythium and Phytophthora are commonly soil-borne although water, especially from

(a)

FIG. 11.1 Phytophthora
Stem and Root Rot of
peppers.
(a) Young plants showing
acute symptoms; those
labelled 1–7 have been
inoculated with various
isolates of *Phytophthora
cryptogea*, isolates 1 and
2 are less virulent than
the others.
(b) Older plants showing
acute symptoms.
Photograph (a) Copyright
Glasshouse Crops
Research Institute and (b)
Copyright Murphy
Chemicals Ltd.

(b)

ponds, can also be a source. The most severe attacks usually occur when drainage is poor and the soil is excessively wet for long periods.

Control.   Propagation should be done in sterilised soil or in a proprietary compost. If a soil-based compost is used then etridiazole should be incorporated before sowing. Drenches of zineb and etridiazole to the growing crop may help to minimise root decay.

Grey Mould (*Botrytis cinerea*)

Grey mould is the most common disease of greenhouse-grown peppers and can cause considerable losses. Leaves and stems may be affected. Often the symptom first noticed is wilting of one branch of a mature plant resulting from a lesion which girdles the stem. The fungus often gains entry through wounds or via senescent tissue. Flower parts which fall onto the leaves, damaged leaves and stems, especially where cracking occurs in the angles of branches, are all good starting entry points for this pathogen.

The fungus is favoured by conditions of high relative humidity and, as the foliage of the crop increases in density, the conditions under the canopy become ideal for disease development. At high humidities, *Botrytis* sporulates prolifically on affected plant parts, and spores are dispersed when affected plants are handled and the spores shaken free.

Control.   It is possible to keep this disease in check by assuring good air movement through the crop and by keeping the relative humidity at or below 85 per cent. Humidity control may not be possible in an unheated crop, but by the removal of the lower foliage and by ventilation, air movement throughout the crop can be maintained. If necessary, control can be aided by the use of high volume fungicide sprays. Benzimidazoles, thiram and iprodione are most likely to be effective. It is important to get as good a cover on the foliage and stems as possible, particularly within the crop, as these fungicides are mainly protective in their action.

Powdery Mildew (*Leveillula taurica*)

This disease is confined to the countries of southern Europe where it affects not only peppers but also cucumbers and tomatoes. Symptoms consist of a chlorosis of the upper leaf surface, generally confined to well defined spots or blotches. On the lower surface the pathogen produces brown conidiophores and conidia which give the spots a felt-like appearance (Fig. 11.2). The

FIG. 11.2   Dense patches of brown conidiophores and conidia of the Powdery Mildew fungus *Leveillula taurica* on the underside of a pepper leaf. Copyright ICI Plant Protection Division.

conidia are able to germinate at low humidities. Disease development is discouraged by leaf wetness.

Control.   There is little evidence available on the effectiveness of fungicides. Thiophanate methyl has been reported to be satisfactory and it is likely that many of the fungicides which are used for the control of Cucumber Powdery Mildew would also be effective against this disease (see p. 112).

Overhead systems of irrigation, which keep the leaf surface wet, are likely to prevent the development of this disease.

Tobacco Mosaic Virus (TMV)

Various strains of this virus are capable of attacking peppers. Many cultivars such as Bellboy are resistant to the tomato form of TMV but recently a pepper form has been found which is capable of attacking most cultivars. The tomato form has a dramatic effect on susceptible cultivars, such as Sweet Spanish Yellow and Sweet Spanish Red. The first noticeable symptom is necrosis along the main veins, followed by wilting and eventual defoliation (Fig. 11.3). The plant is not killed and subsequent growth from lateral buds shows a slight mosaic symptom. The pepper form of TMV does not induce necrosis or leaf loss, but the leaves on affected plants have a mild mosaic and the fruits may also be similarly affected. In addition, fruits may be distorted, being rugose in shape with occasional necrotic patches.

FIG. 11.3 Tobacco Mosaic Virus affecting the pepper cultivar Sweet Spanish Red. Symptoms include necrosis of the main veins and petioles which results in wilting and eventually defoliation. Axillary shoots develop later but show mosaic symptoms. Crown Copyright.

Both forms of the virus may be soil-borne and can survive in infected root debris for a very long time. The pepper form may also be seed-borne. Neighbouring tomato crops can be a source of the tomato form, although most commercial tomato cultivars are now TMV-resistant and the disease is not common. Only the cultivar Novi is resistant to both tomato and pepper strains of TMV.

Control.   TMV is the most infectious plant virus known and, once plants are infected, spread in the crop is extremely rapid. Even walking through the crop and brushing affected plants, or working in the crop and handling affected plants, is all that is necessary to result in considerable spread of the pathogen. It is important to isolate affected plants as soon as they are recognised and always work towards them. Removal of affected plants is generally not worthwhile as it is likely that spread has already occurred and there will be infected but symptomless plants within the crop.

Seeds can be treated to free them of TMV by using heat or acid extraction or a soak in trisodium orthophosphate (see Tomato Mosaic control, p. 150). Sprays of dried milk powder have been shown to slow down the rate of spread of the pepper strain.

Blossom End Rot

This is a disorder very similar to Blossom End Rot of tomatoes (see p. 155). Affected fruits show a dry, black area at the blossom end and, when cut through, the fruit wall and some seeds show necrosis. Sometimes there may be no external symptoms, with the necrosis confined to a small part of the fruit wall or some seeds.

Plants most commonly affected are those which have grown well and produced a lot of foliage. If, during fruit ripening, there is a restriction in water uptake, or if water loss exceeds water uptake, Blossom End Rot symptoms develop. The most common cause is a shortage of water, especially when accompanied by periods of high transpiration. Calcium deficiency has also been associated with this symptom, and in extreme conditions, sprays of calcium nitrate may help to minimise the disorder.

DISEASES OF AUBERGINE

Aubergines are susceptible to almost all the diseases that affect peppers. Botrytis, Pythium and Phytophthora cause similar symptoms to those already described for peppers. In addition, aubergines are especially susceptible to Verticillium Wilt.

Verticillium Wilt (*Verticillium dahliae* or *V. albo-atrum*)

Although the disease can occur at any stage in the life of the crop, it is most likely to appear within 6–8 weeks of planting. The first symptom is the yellowing of the older leaves accompanied by a grey-green colour of the younger growth. As the disease develops, necrotic areas occur on the older leaves and the plant wilts, eventually to a point where it does not recover.

A brown discoloration develops in the vascular tissue of affected plants and can be traced for some distance up the stem. The fungus is soil-borne and can survive in the soil for many years.

Control.   Once established in the soil it is very difficult to eradicate this pathogen. Soil treatment with heat or chemicals is essential before another crop is planted. With some other crops, a benzimidazole drench treatment at 3–4 weekly intervals has given some control of Verticillium Wilt, but the treatment must be started very early in the development of the disease.

FURTHER READING

Smith, D. (1979) *Peppers and Aubergines*. Grower Guide No. 3. Grower
    Books, London.

CHAPTER 12

CARNATION

CULTURE

Pre-planting preparation

Pre-planting preparation is dependent upon the system of culture used. Few crops are grown in soil beds but, where used, it is essential to steam treat them thoroughly before every crop. Most frequently, plants are grown in a peat medium either contained in polythene bags, within polythene-lined troughs or in isolated beds. Peat bags are placed sideways to make 1.2 m (4 ft) wide beds. The bags are discarded at the end of each crop. Peat in troughs can be reused by sterilising with steam which is passed through the central tile drain. The peat is pushed from the sides and formed into a heap over the drain. Occasionally, methyl bromide is used but the crop is very sensitive to bromide residues and, in order to reduce these to a safe level (5 mg/kg or less), it is necessary to apply 30 cm (12 in) of water to the beds after treatment and before planting. This can only be done if drainage is excellent.

Propagation

Rooted carnation cuttings are produced by a small number of specialist propagators and only a small proportion of cuttings are sold unrooted. Rooting is done in various media but commonly in peat/Perlite mixes. The optimum temperature for rooting is 20 °C and takes 2 weeks.

Cropping

The plant spacing varies from 12.7 × 12.7 cm (5 × 5 in) to 15.2 × 12.7 cm (6 × 5 in) depending upon the time of the year the crop is planted. 300 000 plants are required to plant a hectare (120 000/acre). The main planting times are October–early November, flowering in May or June, and February–March for flowering in October. For winter planting, the temperature is maintained at 12.5 °C (55 °F) for the first 2 weeks, during which time the plants establish, followed by 7.5 °C (45 °F) or lower. From February onwards the temperature is raised to 10–12.5 °C (50–55 °F). Carbon dioxide enrichment is not used for carnations. During the winter months in particular, but during the period mid-August to mid-March, crops may be given a 2–3 week period of continuous light of low intensity which results in earlier flower production.

    The crop is supported by wires and string and generally disbudded to give single blooms, although some multiflowered or spray cultivars are grown. Cropping continues for about 18 months but occasionally crops of 12 or 24 months are grown. A good yield from a productive cultivar is 36 blooms/m²/year (33/yd²/year).

DISEASES

Cuttings

Black Mould (*Alternaria dianthi*), p. 243
Rhizoctonia Stem Rot (*Rhizoctonia solani*), p. 243
Fusarium Basal Rot (*Fusarium culmorum*), p. 244
Basal Rots (*Phytophthora* spp., *Pythium* spp.), p. 245
Bacterial Stem Crack (*Pseudomonas caryophyllii*), p. 245

Stems

Fusarium Stub Rot (*Fusarium culmorum*), p. 245
Botrytis Stem Rot (*Botrytis cinerea*), p. 246
Alternaria Branch Rot (*Alternaria dianthi*), p. 246
Bacterial Stem Crack (*Pseudomonas caryophyllii*), p. 255
Fusarium Wilt (*Fusarium oxysporum* f.sp. *dianthi*), p. 251
Etched Ring (Etched Ring Virus), p. 257
Grassiness, p. 258
Boron deficiency, p. 259

Leaves

Rust (*Uromyces dianthi*), p. 246
Alternaria Leaf Spot or Blight (*Alternaria dianthi*), p. 247
Septoria Leaf Spot (*Septoria dianthi*), p. 248
Leaf Rot (*Heteropatella valtellinensis*), p. 248
Fairy Ring Spot or Ring Spot (*Cladosporium echinulatum* syn. *Didymellina dianthii, Mycosphaerella dianthi, Heterosporium echinulatum*), p. 249
Greasy Blotch (*Zygophiala jamaicensis*), p. 249
Powdery Mildew (*Oidium* sp.), p. 250
Fusarium Wilt (*Fusarium oxysporum* f.sp. *dianthi*), p. 251
Phialophora or Verticillium Wilt, Fan Mould (*Phialophora cinerescens* syn. *Verticillium cinerescens*), p. 254
Bacterial Wilt or Stem Crack (*Pseudomonas caryophyllii*), p. 255
Slow Wilt or Bacterial Stunt (*Erwinia chrysanthemi*), p. 255
Leafy Gall (*Corynebacterium fascians*), p. 256
Virus diseases, p. 256
Low temperature injury, p. 258
Herbicide injury, p. 259
Curly tip, p. 259

Flowers

Botrytis Flower Rot (*Botrytis cinerea*), p. 249

Diseases of cuttings

Black Mould (*Alternaria dianthi*)

Attack by this fungus is not uncommon and may result in a rot at the base of the cutting shortly after planting out. The rot is characterised by a very dark brown or black discoloration of the affected stem base. Leaf spots usually accompany the stem rot (see p. 247). Severe attacks are often associated with prolonged periods of cold storage of the cuttings. The pathogen produces large numbers of spores on affected stems and leaves and spread of these spores is by water splash. The disease is not commonly epidemic.

Control.   Affected cuttings should be discarded before planting. Recovery may be helped by high volume sprays of thiram or iprodione, although the disease rarely spreads to any extent after planting-out. Fungicide applications to stock plants should prevent serious disease development, even if it is necessary to cold-store cuttings before rooting them.

Rhizoctonia Stem Rot (*Rhizoctonia solani*)

Symptoms occur from 1–6 weeks after planting, usually first showing as the complete and sudden wilting of the attacked plant. A lesion develops on the stem at or just below soil level but the roots are not often affected. The lesion is initially dry and pale brown in colour with brown strands of the pathogen on its surface but, if the damaged tissue becomes colonised by secondary organisms, a darker wet rot may develop. Rhizoctonia Stem Rot may be difficult to distinguish from Basal Rot caused by *Fusarium culmorum*, especially as this latter often colonises Rhizoctonia lesions. One characteristic symptom of Rhizoctonia Stem Rot is the weakness of the stem at or just above soil level in the area of the lesion which often causes the stem to break.

The pathogen is a common soil-borne fungus and may be present in peat. Disease incidence varies in its severity and, although seen frequently, it is rarely epidemic.

Control.   Cuttings appear to be more susceptible than established plants and most plant losses occur during the first 6 weeks after planting. Peat or other materials should be added to the soil before steam treatment. Quintozene dust applied to the soil before planting, or high volume sprays of thiram or iprodione may reduce the incidence of this disease. Often, by the time the disease is recognised, it is not worth applying a fungicide because unaffected plants have reached the stage when they have become resistant.

Fusarium Basal Rot (*Fusarium culmorum*)

This fungus is a very common cause of poor establishment and the disease is present in most carnation crops. *Fusarium culmorum* often enters the plant through wounds and also attacks plants that are growing poorly. Cuttings can be severely affected during rooting, when the fungus enters the cutting through the stem base (Fig. 12.1). Spores may be air-borne or water-splash spread. Lesions on stock plants provide inoculum which infects cuttings. During the rooting period, a rot may develop from the cutting base which can extend one or two nodes up the stem. The lesion is usually chocolate brown in colour, and orange-to-pink spore pustules of the pathogen are often present. Secondary spread by water splash and by the fungus growing through the rooting medium can occur from these early affected cuttings and lesions may develop on the stems of neighbouring cuttings, usually at the surface of the rooting medium. Entry into cuttings may also be through senescent leaf tissue. At planting, some cuttings show only a very slight brown discoloration in the root zone, which later develops into a larger area of decay.

FIG. 12.1 A basal rot of carnation cuttings caused by *Fusarium culmorum* preventing normal rooting; a healthy well rooted cutting on the right.

After planting out, affected cuttings show a sudden wilt symptom caused by the development of the lesion at soil level. The presence of the orange-pink fungal pustules distinguishes these lesions from those caused by *Rhizoctonia solani* and the stems are also less likely to break at soil level.

Control.   During propagation stock plants should be sprayed with captan or benomyl at 7–10 day intervals. When cuttings are taken, they should be inserted into the rooting medium with a minimum delay. If a delay is unavoidable the cuttings should be retrimmed, removing approximately 0.5 cm from the base of each cutting immediately before rooting.

The propagation medium should be sterilised between each batch of cuttings. Weekly applications of captan or benomyl will minimise disease development during rooting.

Any factors which check growth at planting will encourage attack. Very often a high soluble salt concentration in the soil or very deep planting are major contributory factors. Two or three days after planting, the cuttings should be sprayed with captan or benomyl, with two or three further applications at 14 day intervals.

Other basal rots (*Phytophthora* spp. and *Pythium* spp.)

Various species of *Pythium* and *Phytophthora* have been isolated from newly planted carnations which have shown symptoms similar to those described for Fusarium and Rhizoctonia Stem Rot. Generally, these fungi are pathogenic in wet, undrained, unsterilised soils. Control can be achieved by avoiding soil wetness and by soil sterilisation. If the soil is not sterilised, etridiazole should be incorporated before planting or used as a post-planting drench.

Bacterial Stem Crack (*Pseudomonas caryophyllii*)

Cuttings taken from infected stock plants or infected during propagation show symptoms and these are described on p. 255. This disease is uncommon in Europe.

The pathogen is readily spread on hands and knives and by water splash. It can survive in the soil although is unlikely to persist for a long time.

Diseases of established plants

Fusarium Stub Rot (*Fusarium culmorum*)

This disease is invariably present in all crops and can cause considerable loss. It often starts on stem wounds caused by growth cracks or where side shoots have been removed. Stubs left after flowers have been cut are also potential sites for the establishment of the pathogen. Lesions may eventually girdle the stem, resulting in wilting. The leaves on affected stems turn from grey-green to a straw colour in a short time. In humid conditions the pathogen sporulates profusely on the lesions and spores are readily spread by water splash. Some cultivars seem to be more susceptible than others, particularly those with a habit which results in stem cracking at the base of the plant. Generally, the disease is most severe in the autumn, winter and spring when conditions of high relative humidity are common.

Control.   Fusarium Stub Rot can be very effectively controlled by preventing conditions of high relative humidity in the crop, particularly during the winter and early spring. High volume sprays of captan or benomyl will help to control this disease, particularly in poorly-heated crops where it is advisable to continue with this spray programme throughout the winter months. In the summer months the interval between sprays can be extended from 2 weeks to 4–6 weeks according to the weather.

Botrytis Stem Rot (*Botrytis cinerea*)

Symptoms of Botrytis Stem Rot are very similar to those described for Fusarium Stem Rot. Botrytis readily attacks poorly growing plants, especially through wounds or damaged tissue. The affected plants wilt and become straw coloured. Characteristic grey mould growth of the pathogen can usually be seen on the lesions, especially if conditions are humid. Small black sclerotia are also formed on the diseased tissue. Spores are air-borne and are likely to be dispersed when affected plants are disturbed. The disease only becomes a problem in crops where there are long periods of excessive moisture. These conditions are usually associated with insufficient heat to reduce the relative humidity.

Control. The disease is well controlled by maintaining a low relative humidity, but if this is not possible high volume sprays of iprodione, captan or thiram will help to keep it in check. Many populations of *B. cinerea* are resistant to benzimidazole fungicides (see p. 111).

Alternaria Branch Rot (*Alternaria dianthi*)

As well as causing a basal rot of cuttings this fungus also affects stems, usually at the nodes where it enters through wounds or growth cracks producing black lesions. Control measures are as described for the basal stem rot of cuttings (see p. 243).

Rust (*Uromyces dianthi*)

This is a common disease of carnations. Rusty brown pustules occur on the stems and leaves and even on the calyx, if the disease becomes epidemic (Fig. 12.2). Often severely affected plants may be growing alongside relatively unaffected ones, although spread does occur in the crop and air-borne spores or spore dispersal by water splash are the main means by which the pathogen spreads. Spread is greatest in the autumn and winter months. Rust is often introduced on the cuttings which may appear healthy at planting because the time between infection and symptom production can be as long as 3 or 4 weeks. Drops of water or very high humidity ensure spore germination and infection. The disease does not develop at high temperatures (21 °C).

Control. Any cuttings showing symptoms should be discarded. The environment should be controlled to prevent long periods of wetness and high relative humidity. Leaks in roofs and gutters often provide ideal conditions of wetness in the crop for epidemic development. Fungicide sprays

FIG. 12.2 Carnation Rust
(*Uromyces dianthi*)
producing concentric rings
of pustules on the leaves.

of benodanil, bitertanol, zineb or drenches of oxycarboxin to crops grown
in peat bags help to control this disease.

Alternaria Leaf Spot or Blight (*Alternaria dianthi*)

This disease is rarely a severe problem in flowering crops. Small purple-
coloured spots appear on the leaves. Under moist conditions these enlarge
to form leaf spots up to 1 cm in diameter. The margin of the spot is usually
purple in colour, the centre grey-brown and black spores may also be present
in this area giving the spot a sooty appearance (Fig. 12.3). Several spots may
merge, resulting in the death of the leaf. The fungus is spread mainly by
water splash.

FIG. 12.3 Alternaria Leaf
Spot (*Alternaria dianthi*);
the centre of the spot is
grey-brown (a) and the
surrounding halo usually
purple in colour (b).

Control. By maintaining a low relative humidity this disease can be avoided, but if sprays are necessary then thiram or iprodione are most likely to give good control.

Septoria Leaf Spot (*Septoria dianthi*)

This disease is not common and the symptoms are similar to those of Alternaria Leaf Spot, except that the purple margins of the spots are usually less pronounced and the grey centre does not have the black, sooty mould growth although small, black pycnidia may be present. Generally, symptoms are confined to the older leaves. The spores of the fungus are readily disseminated by water splash. Infected cuttings are the most common source of the pathogen.

Control. Affected cuttings should be discarded and the crop sprayed with zineb if the disease appears.

Leaf Rot (*Heteropatella valtellinensis*)

Under very unfavourable growing conditions (high moisture, low temperature) this fungus can attack the lower leaf bases producing dark, water-soaked lesions which turn grey and papery when conditions become drier.

It is usually possible to achieve control by the manipulation of the environment.

Fairy Ring Spot or Ring Spot (*Cladosporium echinulatum* syn. *Didymellina dianthi*, *Mycosphaerella dianthi* and *Heterosporium echinulatum*)

Tan-coloured spots occur on the leaves and stems covered by dark, powdery spores. The spores are often formed in concentric rings, hence the common name. Like most of the other leaf spot diseases, this pathogen is encouraged by conditions of high moisture and can be controlled by reducing the relative humidity, or by using high volume sprays of benomyl, benzimidazole dithio-carbamate mixtures, daconil or dichlofluanid.

Greasy Blotch (*Zygophiala jamaicensis*)

This fungus is quite common but of very little economic importance. The first symptoms occur on the lower leaves and consist of a spider web-like pattern on the leaf surface which results from the fungus breaking down the wax bloom on the cuticle of the leaf. If the entire leaf is affected, all the wax is removed and the leaf appears to have been washed with soapy water or a wetter. The fungus only grows on the leaf surface if the relative humidity at the leaf surface is extremely high.

Control.   It is usually not necessary to apply fungicides to control this pathogen. This disease generally has no effect on yield but affects quality if the upper leaves are attacked. However, its presence is an indication of very humid conditions within the crop and if these persist more important diseases, such as Fusarium Stem and Stub Rot may occur.

Botrytis Flower Rot (*Botrytis cinerea*)

Occasionally, this fungus causes a flower rot which starts on the tips of the petals and under very moist conditions a dense mat of fungal growth is produced (Fig. 12.4). The disease is readily controlled by reducing the relative humidity. Fungicidal sprays, as mentioned for the control of Botrytis Stem Rot (see p. 246) will control the flower disease.

Anther Smut (*Ustilago violacea*)

This is an uncommon disease of modern cultivars, partly because very few of them produce anthers. The pathogen is systemic and affected plants are stunted often producing excessive numbers of side shoots. Purplish-black spores of the fungus replace the pollen in the anthers giving the flower a dirty, sooty appearance. The disease is quite common in other members of the Caryophyllaceae, such as the white campion (*Melandrium dioicum*).

Fusarium Bud Rot (*Fusarium tricinctum* f. *poae*)

Attack by this pathogen results in the decay of the inner floral parts leaving

FIG. 12.4 A flower rot of
carnation caused by
Botrytis cinerea.
Copyright Murphy
Chemicals Ltd.

the rest of the flower unaffected. A mass of white mycelium is produced on the decayed petals. A mite, *Siteroptes graminum*, is associated with this disease and is probably the vector of the fungus as well as being responsible for the initial damage which allows its entry. White cultivars are thought to be the most susceptible. The disease can be controlled by removing all affected flowers and by controlling the mites which spread the pathogen.

Powdery Mildew (*Oidium* sp.)

The most conspicuous symptom of this disease is the white powdery growth of the pathogen which develops on the calyx of the flower (Fig. 12.5). Often,

FIG. 12.5 Symptoms of
Powdery Mildew (*Oidium*
sp.) often first appear on
the calyx. The lower
leaves may also be
affected.

the upper leaves of the flowering shoot are free from the disease although the
basal leaves may be severely affected. Attacks are severe in the autumn and
winter months when relative humidity is very high which allows spore
germination and infection. Spores of the pathogen are air-borne. This fungus
is confined to carnation and closely related species and is not very common.

Control.   As much diseased tissue as possible should be removed by cutting
flowers very regularly. High volume sprays of dinocap, oxythioquinox or
chlorothalonil will aid control. Where possible, sprays should not be applied
to buds showing colour because of the risk of damage to, and fungicide
deposit on, the petals.

Fusarium Wilt (*Fusarium oxysporum* f.sp. *dianthi*)

Fusarium wilt is now the most serious disease of the carnation crop. It can
cause considerable economic losses and on some nurseries is probably the
major single factor which prevents the continuous cultivation of carnations.

The first symptom is a slight chlorosis of the lower leaves, sometimes
affecting the leaves on one side of the plant only, and occasionally only half

of an individual leaf. Gradually, more leaves become affected and the chlorosis spreads up the plant. A purple-red mottle, not unlike that shown by Phialophora-affected plants, may also occur. Chlorotic leaves with a red mottle are diagnostic of Fusarium Wilt as distinct from a grey-green leaf with a red mottle which is diagnostic of Phialophora. A dark brown discoloration occurs in the vascular tissue of affected plants and can usually be traced up the stem to a considerable distance above soil level. The length of time between symptom occurrence and plant death varies with the time of the year. Generally, it is most rapid at high temperatures in the spring and summer months when the disease appears to spread very rapidly. There is evidence to show that the pathogen spreads as rapidly in the winter as in spring and summer, but because of the lower temperatures, symptom expression is suppressed and the affected plants remain symptomless until the temperature increases in the spring. In a standard density carnation crop the rate of spread can be as much as 50 cm of bed length a month.

The pathogen is soil-borne where it can survive for considerable periods of time as chlamydospores. There is some evidence that these spores are very resistant to both heat and chemicals and may even withstand temperatures near to boiling point for short periods of time. Conidia are produced in large numbers in pink conidial cushions on the stems of plants recently killed by the pathogen. These spores can be air-borne or spread by water splash.

The pathogen is most frequently first introduced onto the nursery in cuttings or in the rooting medium attached to the roots. A random distribution of affected plants within 6–8 weeks of planting is a good indication that the cuttings were infected. If, when symptoms are first seen, the affected plants are grouped together, it is likely that the pathogen has originated from the soil. Once established in a crop, spread takes place by root contact between affected and healthy plants and by spores of the pathogen, both chlamydospores and conidia, which can be moved throughout the crop either by air or water. Excessive water on the surface of the bed is frequently one of the main means of spore dispersal.

The pathogen is known to exist in at least two forms and some cultivars are resistant to one or other of these forms but none is resistant to both.

Control.   In order to control this disease it is necessary to try and eliminate the sources of the pathogen, to minimise its spread should it occur and to use fungicides when necessary to help contain it.

Elimination of sources: Cuttings are the most important primary source of the pathogen but this source is often the most difficult to eliminate, and is out of the control of most growers. When received from the propagator, the cuttings are symptomless and the disease will only develop some weeks after planting out. Even then, it is often difficult to be sure that the pathogen has originated from the cuttings or the rooting medium received with them because the greenhouse soil is also a possible source. Most cutting producers have strict systems of hygiene to minimise disease incidence and this has contributed considerably to the maintenance of wilt-free cuttings. However, the recent trend to propagate carnations in Mediterranean and subtropical countries has made the task of control of Fusarium Wilt more difficult as the temperatures in these countries are very favourable for its development and spread.

The greenhouse soil is the other important source of the pathogen. If carnation crops have been grown on the same site for some years, the grower knows which areas are wilt-infested from his previous crops and, by paying particular attention to these during the course of soil sterilisation, it is sometimes possible to keep the succeeding crops wilt-free for 14–16 months. Complete sterilisation of the soil is often not possible and roots reach inoculum in the lower regions of the soil within the second year of cropping. Soil treatment to depth can be improved if metham-sodium is injected into the subsoil of the affected areas before the whole greenhouse is steam-treated. The effectiveness of steam treatment is improved, where isolated beds are used, although the cost of building concrete troughs which are isolated from the greenhouse soil, is now considerable and it is doubtful whether this is an economic system. The use of other isolated systems of crop culture, such as peat bags, peat beds and rock wool have been successfully used on nurseries where the disease has become endemic. The advantage of peat beds is that the peat can be reused. The peat is generally steam sterilised by piling it into the centre of the bed over a tile drain through which steam is blown.

Carnations are very sensitive to bromide residues and, for this reason, methyl bromide is infrequently used to sterilise soil or peat. When used, it is essential to leach the bromide residues, reducing the bromide to at least 5 mg/kg of soil. To obtain this level it may be necessary to apply about 30 cm of water.

Prevention of spread: If the disease is recognised early in the life of a crop, and is confined to a small area, it is sometimes worth removing all the affected plants together with some healthy ones from around them and treating the soil with a sterilant, such as metham-sodium or dazomet. These small patches are then covered with polythene and left.

Spread from crop to crop or within a crop can occur by the movement of contaminated debris and by spores, particularly in surface water. It is important to prevent the spread of debris on boots by using a disinfectant bath or mat at the entrance of the greenhouse and by preventing foot contact with the bed surface. (This is particularly relevant when flowers are being cut.) The dispersal of spores in soil water can be minimised by using a drip form of irrigation which prevents surface flooding.

Fungicides: These are generally not very effective for the control of this wilt, although there are some reports of success with the benzimidazoles and more recently with prochloraz manganese if they are applied at the correct time. Plants should be drench-treated shortly after planting out and this treatment must be repeated at regular intervals during cropping.

Resistant cultivars: There are no cultivars resistant to Fusarium Wilt, but recently plant breeders in various parts of the world have produced some very promising lines. Some of the hybrids which are based on the cultivar Orchid Beauty, and a breeding line from California known as Carrier 929, together with other sources of resistance, have been hybridised and the resultant range of plants is being selected for flower quality and plant vigour. So far, most of these cultivars are resistant to only one of the two known strains of the pathogen, but as these strains have a somewhat restricted world-wide distribution it is possible that such resistant cultivars may be of considerable use.

Phialophora Wilt, Verticillium Wilt or Fan Mould (*Phialophora cinerescens* syn. *Verticillium cinerescens*)

Phialophora Wilt was the most important disease of the carnation in Europe until the early 1970s but is now relatively uncommon. The symptoms are not unlike those of Fusarium Wilt with the exception that the affected plants are not chlorotic but show a dull grey-green colour together with the production of a red pigment on the affected leaves. Symptoms are most conspicuous in the spring when the crop is making maximum growth. The vascular tissue shows a brown discoloration which is not as dark as in plants affected by Fusarium Wilt. When some of the yellow, tangerine and light-coloured cultivars are affected a bronze discoloration of the leaves, and not the purple-red colour, accompanies the grey-green leaf symptom. If plants become infected in the autumn, symptoms may develop over a period of several months before they die. During the early stages of attack the root system remains intact and affected plants are then often difficult to pull out.

The pathogen is soil-borne where it exists in the form of spores and mycelium, either in the soil or within carnation debris. Large numbers of conidia are produced on affected plants, particularly during advanced stages of the disease. These may be air-borne or spread in irrigation water. The pathogen enters the plant through the roots and spreads from plant to plant by root contact or by the dispersal of spores and debris (Fig. 12.6). Generally, spread radiates from centres, particularly if the disease is soil-borne. If introduced in cuttings, an initial random distribution of affected plants is seen, but each develops into a patch which increases in size at the rate of approximately 20–50 cm diameter per month. Spread occurs equally effectively in the winter as well as in the summer months. It has been shown experimentally that by

FIG. 12.6 A patch of Phialophora Wilt (*Phialophora cinerescens*) starting from an end of a bed and spreading along the side.

confining the spread of water in the bed, especially on the surface, by using a drip form of irrigation, the rate of spread of the disease can be considerably reduced.

Control. The same measures of control as described for Fusarium Wilt apply with the exception that fungicidal treatments with the benzimidazoles are very much more effective for the control of Phialophora. A drench treatment with benomyl shortly after planting out, followed by regular drench treatments throughout the life of the crop, gives a very effective control of this disease. On some soils, benomyl may be broken down by bacterial action and then will not be effective.

There are no known sources of resistance to Phialophora Wilt.

Bacterial Wilt or Stem Crack (*Pseudomonas caryophyllii*)

This bacterial disease is fairly common in the United States but uncommon in most European countries. Affected plants show progressive wilting, which over a period of time, sometimes many months, affects the whole plant. Eventually the root system decays. Some affected plants show longitudinal stem cracks between a number of the lower nodes with the epidermis peeling back from these to reveal a wide and deep split in the stem, which sometimes becomes colonised by various black moulds particularly, *Cladosporium* spp. (Fig. 12.7). Another characteristic of attack by *Ps. caryophyllii* is the arching of the tops of young shoots.

Affected plants may show an extensive vascular discoloration which is present even in infected cuttings. A root decay of infected cuttings is also caused by this pathogen and can be distinguished from other root decay diseases by the presence of the extensive vascular discoloration. The pathogen is spread by handling affected plants and water splash. It can survive in the soil although is unlikely to persist for long periods of time.

Control. Affected plants should be removed as soon as they are recognised and watering done with a system which avoids splashing. There are no effective chemicals which can be used as sprays. At the end of the crop, the plant remains should be carefully removed and the soil sterilised.

Slow Wilt, Bacterial Stunt (*Erwinia chrysanthemi*)

Affected plants grow very slowly and gradually show wilt symptoms which start as a grey coloration of the leaves. Over a period of 6–8 months the wilt becomes more severe until the plant dies. During the whole of this time affected plants make little or no growth so they are conspicuously stunted in comparison with healthy plants. Infected plants show a vascular discoloration but this disease is probably best distinguished from Bacterial Wilt or Stem Crack by the absence of extensive stem splitting. The disease is not common in Europe.

Control. Where the disease occurs the same control measures as described for Bacterial Wilt should be applied.

FIG. 12.7 Cracks on the stem resulting from an attack of Bacterial Wilt or Stem Crack caused by *Pseudomonas caryophyllii*. Affected plants are also stunted.

Leafy Gall (*Corynebacterium fascians*)

The most characteristic symptom of this disease is the proliferation of leafy outgrowths from the base of the stem or from the nodes. This disease does not have a marked effect on growth unless it is very severe. It is most likely to be damaging on young plants. Affected plants, especially those used for cutting production, should be removed and preferably burned. The soil or rooting medium can be a source of this pathogen.

Virus diseases

Although there are a number of virus diseases of carnations, most have been eliminated from commercial cultivars by the use of the meristem culture and heat treatment techniques (see pp. 65). Virus-free clones are available from Nuclear Stock Associations in several countries and these have contributed greatly to the increase in yield and quality which has occurred during the recent past. The reintroduction of viruses into commercial crops would see a return to lower yields and poorer quality. The main symptoms of a number of the previously common virus diseases are described.

Carnation Mottle.   Symptoms of this disease vary from a mottle in the young growth, which is best seen by looking at a leaf held up to the light, to a very slight mottle which may be difficult to discern. Affected plants may be slightly stunted although frequently there are no obvious growth symptoms. The virus is spread by handling infected plants.

Carnation Vein Mottle or Mosaic.   This virus, which is also common in sweet william (*Dianthus barbatus*), produces a green mottle on the calyx and colour breaking of the flowers. It is normally spread by aphids, in particular *Myzus persicae*.

Carnation Ring Spot.   Carnation Ring Spot Virus produces more severe and conspicuous symptoms than those of Mottle or Vein Mottle. Necrotic rings or flecks are produced in a number of cultivars, particularly 'Joker'. The virus is very readily spread by handling. Because symptoms are so conspicuous, this disease can be easily rogued from stocks.

Carnation Etched Ring.   Like Carnation Ring Spot Virus, Carnation Etched Ring Virus produces necrotic flecks on leaves of many of the Sim cultivars and necrotic rings on the flowering stems, hence the name 'etched ring'. Joker and other crimson cultivars may show severe leaf necrosis along the leaf margin, somewhat resembling a physical scorch, or sometimes, because of a purple margin, Alternaria Leaf Spot. Symptoms are produced more commonly on the middle leaves than on the young or older leaves. Affected plants may be symptomless for part of the year. The virus can be transmitted by grafting and by aphids (*M. persicae*), but only to a limited extent by handling.

Carnation Latent.   This virus produces no symptoms but when in combination with any of the other viruses causes symptom intensification. It is sap transmissible and also spread by *M. persicae*.

Carnation Streak.   Streak symptoms appear on the leaves and are caused by a combination of two viruses, Carnation Mottle Virus and Carnation Necrotic Fleck Virus. Carnation Mottle Virus is readily sap transmissible but Carnation Necrotic Fleck Virus can only be transmitted by aphids (*M. persicae*).

Carnation Italian Ring Spot.   Affected plants show chlorotic spots and oval rings similar to those produced by Carnation Mottle Virus.

Carnation Necrotic Fleck.   Affected leaves show greyish-white to purple-red flecks, streaks or spots. This virus is transmitted by the aphid, *M. persicae*.

NON-PATHOGENIC DISORDERS

There are a number of non-pathogenic disorders of carnations which result in conspicuous symptoms. These are most commonly caused by environmental or genetical factors.

Grassiness or excessive lateral growth

Affected plants develop shoots from almost every node, have few or no flowers and make prolific vegetative growth, sometimes overgrowing nearby normal plants (Fig. 12.8). The condition appears to be genetically determined; affected plants do not recover and are best removed from the bed. If such affected plants occur in carnation stock plants they produce large numbers of useless cuttings.

Low temperature injury

Carnations withstand temperatures as low as 0 °C for short periods but plants may suffer some damage. A few hours of a temperature around freezing results in the development of silvery white flecks on the undersides of the leaves and on the stem. These are usually more or less circular and completely cover the leaf surface. Flowers are also affected, red or pink cultivars show circular white blotches on their petals whilst white cultivars produce similarly shaped red blotches.

Calyx splitting

Many factors induce calyx splitting although temperature fluctuations have

FIG. 12.8 A genetical abnormality which results in the prolific growth of side shoots. Such affected plants are said to be 'grassy'.

long been recognised to be one of the most important. Short periods of low temperatures (4 or 5 °C below normal) are favourable for petal initiation, and if such conditions occur 3–5 weeks before flower maturity, the calyx may then be too small to accommodate the extra petals that are formed and splitting occurs.

High day temperatures near to flower opening (10 °C above normal) may also result in bud splitting. Some clones are more prone to calyx splitting than others.

Herbicide injury

Carnations are not very sensitive to growth regulator herbicides but some non-selective herbicides, such as sodium chlorate, produce conspicuous symptoms. If levels of sodium chlorate are present in the soil in quantities not sufficient to kill the plant, symptoms are produced which resemble one or other of the vascular wilts, particularly those caused by the bacterial pathogens. Generally, the lower leaves become chlorotic with some reddening, the young growth shows a systemic mottle or yellow vein banding and the plants may be very stunted. Cuttings taken from such plants develop similar or, occasionally, more intensive symptoms. These symptoms are often followed by necrosis of the affected plants and eventually death.

Curly tip

When young leaves fail to separate in the terminal bud the shoot tip becomes bent and distorted, especially as internode lengthening continues. High incidence of curly tip is usually associated with low light intensities and/or low nitrate levels.

Petal curling or sleepiness

The outer petals of some flowers sometimes curl before or shortly after cutting. This symptom can result from the toxic effects of minute quantities of ethylene but may also be due to some cultural factors, possibly high soluble salt concentrations in the soil.

Boron deficiency

Carnations do not often show marked symptoms of mineral deficiencies but boron deficiency does occasionally occur, producing very characteristic symptoms. The terminal bud of an affected shoot aborts and the laterals continue to grow but are very thin and have purple-coloured leaves. The deficiency is easily corrected with an application of sodium borate (see Fig. 1.16 page 23).

FURTHER READING

Anon (1967) *A Manual of Carnation Production*. Bulletin 151, HMSO, London.
Forsberg, J. L. (1975) *Diseases of Ornamental Plants*. University of Illinois

Press, Urbana, IL.

Griffin, M. J. and Fletcher, J. T. (1981) *Control of Diseases of Protected Crops: Cut Flowers*. Booklet 2364, Ministry of Agriculture Fisheries and Food (Publications), Lion House, Willowburn Estate, Alnwick, Northumberland.

Holley, W. D. and Baker, R. (1963) *Carnation Production*. William C. Brown and Co., Dubuque, Iowa.

CHAPTER 13

CHRYSANTHEMUM

CULTURE

There are three major ways in which chrysanthemums are grown in green-houses:

1. High density planting and intensive cropping to produce cut flowers all the year round (AYR).
2. High density production of flowering plants in pots (Pot mums).
3. Disbudded plants producing single flowers, planted in late summer and flowering at Christmas (Natural season).

ALL-YEAR-ROUND

Pre-planting preparation

This crop is generally grown in 1.5 m (5 ft) wide soil beds with 11 or 12 rows of plants across the width. There are a few crops grown in NFT. The soil is steam sterilised before planting using the sheet steaming method and each bed is treated for 1–1.5 hours. Pre-planting steaming is general but sometimes it is omitted for summer crops.

Propagation

Cuttings are usually rooted in a peat/Perlite mixture or in peat blocks by the grower who buys unrooted cuttings from specialist propagators. The cuttings are rooted at 21 °C soil temperature with an air temperature of 15 °C and rooting takes 10 days.

Cropping

Plants are spaced 12.7 × 12.7 cm (5 ×5 in) to give a population of about 450 000 plants/ha (180 000/acre). Generally, 3.5 crops are produced in each greenhouse in each year. Carbon dioxide enrichment to 1000 p.p.m. for about 7 hours a day is used in the winter months (November–March). Night temperatures vary with the time of the year, from 13 °C maximum in March to October, 16 °C in November, 17 °C in December and January, 16 °C in February, all with a day temperature of 16 °C and ventilation at 21 °C. From late April onwards, crops are frequently grown without heat.

From August to March the day length is artificially increased with low intensity lights, to give a satisfactory stem length before the plants are allowed to initiate flowers. In summer, the day length is reduced, by covering the crop with black shading material, in order to induce flower formation.

A good yield is 99 000 bunches (wraps)/ha with 16 stems to a wrap (40 000/acre).

POT CHRYSANTHEMUMS

Propagation

Five cuttings are rooted in a 14 cm (5.5 in) pot using a peat-based compost. A growth-dwarfing chemical may be mixed into the compost to regulate plant height.

Cropping

When a growth-dwarfing compound has not been used in the compost, sprays of such chemicals are applied as soon as the cuttings have rooted, again after the terminal bud has been removed and the laterals are 2–3 cm long and finally 2 weeks later.

The normal cropping temperature is 15 °C for the initial establishment period of about 4 weeks, subsequently dropping to 13 °C. Carbon dioxide enrichment is not used.

The number of pots per unit area is dependent upon the bench system used. With mobile benches 494 000 pots/ha (200 000/acre) per annum is usual, with 370 000–395 000/ha (150 000–160 000/acre) for a fixed bench system.

NATURAL SEASON

Pre-planting preparation and propagation

This crop is grown in soil beds with no special pre-planting treatment. Unrooted cuttings, produced by specialist propagators, are rooted as described for AYR crops and planted into the greenhouse bed in July to mid-August.

Cropping

All stems are disbudded to produce single blooms. The earliest planted crops produce three flowers per plant, the latest one flower. Plant spacing is 20 × 23 cm (8 × 9 in) for the early planted three flower crops, 18 × 18 cm (7 × 7 in) for two flowers and 13 × 15 cm (5 × 7 in) for the single flower crops. A night temperature of 14–15 °C is used from planting until the end of September, 13–14 °C in October, 11–13 °C in November and 10–12 °C in December. Sometimes, only sufficient heat to give frost protection is used in the winter. The yield obtained from a good crop is 12 350 boxes/ha (5000/acre) with 17 blooms per box.

DISEASES

Roots

Phoma Root Rot (*Phoma chrysanthemicola*), p. 263

Stems

Rhizoctonia Stem Rot (*Rhizoctonia solani*), p. 264
Pythium Stem Rot (*Pythium* spp.), p. 265
Ray Blight (*Didymella chrysanthemi* syn. *Mycosphaerella ligulicola*), p. 265
Botrytis Stem Rot (*Botrytis cinerea*), p. 267
Sclerotinia Rot (*Sclerotinia sclerotiorum*), p. 267
Crown Gall (*Agrobacterium tumefaciens*), p. 270

Leaves

Powdery Mildew (*Oidium chrysanthemi*), p. 268
Brown Rust (*Puccinia chrysanthemi*), p. 269
White Rust (*Puccinia horiana*), p. 269
Blotch or Leaf Spot (*Septoria chrysanthemella*), p. 270
Ray Blight (*Didymella chrysanthemi*), p. 265
Leafy Gall (*Corynebacterium fascians*), p. 270
Verticillium Wilt (*Verticillium dahliae, V. albo-atrum*), p. 270
Stunt (Chrysanthemum Stunt Viroid), p. 271
Chrysanthemum Chlorotic Mottle (Chrysanthemum Chlorotic Mottle Viroid), p. 273

Flowers

Petal Blight or Flower Scorch (*Itersonilia perplexans*), p. 273
Flower Damping (*Botrytis cinerea*), p. 274
Ray Blight (*Didymella chrysanthemi*), p. 265
Flower Distortion or Aspermy (Tomato Aspermy Virus), p. 274
Chrysanthemum Stunt (Chrysanthemum Stunt viroid), p. 271
Chrysanthemum Chlorotic Mottle (Chrysanthemum Chlorotic Mottle Viroid), p. 273
Alternaria Flower Spot (*Alternaria* sp.), p. 276
Downy Mildew (*Peronospora radii*), p. 276
Flower Shatter (*Pseudomonas* sp.), p. 276
Crumpled Petal, p. 277

Phoma Root Rot (*Phoma chrysanthemicola*)

This disease occurs commonly on nurseries where chrysanthemums are grown frequently and soil sterilisation is not practised. Symptoms include yellowing and necrosis of the lower leaves accompanied by stunting. In the early stages, red areas of varying length appear on the roots but these quickly become brown as the pathogen progresses, until the whole root system is decayed (Fig. 13.1). In severe attacks, stem bases may show corkiness which

FIG. 13.1 Chrysanthemum root systems showing symptoms of Phoma Root Rot (*Phoma chrysanthemicola*). The plant on the left is unaffected, the centre plant severely affected, and the plant on the right partially affected.

adversely affects cutting production if stools are saved. An affected crop often produces poor quality blooms.

The pathogen persists for long periods in the soil, usually within chrysanthemum root debris. Spread is mainly by root contact and the growth of the pathogen through the soil. Contaminated debris may be water distributed on the bed surface.

Cultivars vary in their susceptibility; the most susceptible include the Shoesmith sports, Portrait, Valentine, Chip sports, Loveliness, Parade, Dorothy Wilson and Delight, whereas the Princess Anne sports, Heyday, Supertop and Snowcap appear to be more resistant.

Control.   The soil should be sterilised by steam or chemicals before each chrysanthemum crop, but if this is not possible, plants can be watered with nabam at every watering. Results with this fungicide have been good, particularly where the soil is well drained and of good structure. The addition of materials such as peat or grit to the soil will help to increase the effectiveness of the fungicide. The most susceptible cultivars should not be grown on sites where the pathogen is known to be present.

Satisfactory crops may also be grown using an isolated cultural system such as peat bags or NFT.

Rhizoctonia Stem Rot (*Rhizoctonia solani*)

This disease is common and can be serious, particularly in AYR crops. It is most frequently found in warm conditions when the soil is moist but not wet. The disease often occurs in newly planted crops affecting individual plants or small patches. A stem lesion develops just above soil level and extends up to 10 cm above the soil. This lesion is brown and dry and, if examined closely, the brown mycelium of the fungus can be seen. Affected plants eventually wilt and die within a short time. *Rhizoctonia solani* is a common soil-borne fungus and may also occur in peat, probably as a contaminant. The pathogen grows through the soil quickly and is a rapid coloniser of pasteurised soil. It is occasionally introduced on cuttings.

Control. Regular soil treatment with heat or chemical sterilants keeps this disease at a low level. It is important to add peat or other materials to the beds before soil treatment. Quintozene, or tolclofos methyl mixed into the soil, before planting is also effective. High volume sprays of iprodione may help to minimise the spread of the disease if applied as soon as affected plants are found.

Pythium Stem Rot (*Pythium* spp.)

This disease severely affects some cultivars and was once very common on the cultivar Iceberg. It is sometimes known as 'Iceberg disease'. Other susceptible cultivars include Shoesmith sports, Lightning, Hurricane, Delightful and Indianapolis sports. Affected plants wilt suddenly and are soon killed. A sunken black lesion occurs at soil level and extends 20–25 cm up the stem. Lesions may first appear well above soil level with no apparent connection with the base of the plant. Affected roots show some browning and decay, particularly around the basal part of the stem. There is some evidence that the disease may be carried on cuttings and this risk is increased if cuttings are taken from near to soil level. Pythium Stem Rot is frequently epidemic following a period of excessive soil wetness. Oospores of the pathogen can persist in the soil for very long periods, and in wet soils the fungus spreads either by the production of zoospores or by the growth of vegetative mycelium.

Control. Beds should never be excessively watered and must be well drained to prevent waterlogging. Steam or chemical treatment should be used regularly and, as an alternative or for every other crop, the soil can be treated before planting or the plants drenched with etridiazole or propamocarb hydrochloride. Care must be taken to ensure that the drenches are not phytotoxic on the cultivars being treated.

Ray Blight (*Didymella chrysanthemi*)

The symptoms on the stem are very similar to those described for Pythium Stem Rot. A wet black lesion develops at soil level or above, and often extends for 10–15 cm (Fig. 13.2). Examination of the stem lesions with a hand lens may show the presence of small pin-head sized pycnidia of the fungus and the presence of these is the diagnostic feature of this disease.

The disease is common and frequently occurs on cuttings, causing a black stem lesion and death of the growing points, or less frequently, black spots on the leaves. Leaf lesions rarely occur in mature plants, but may be present on the lower leaves, where they are black and more or less circular, sometimes 10–15 mm in diameter. Pycnidia are also present on leaf lesions. The pathogen may also affect the roots, producing symptoms similar to those

(a)

(b)

FIG. 13.2 (a) A stem lesion caused by the fungal pathogen *Didymella chrysanthemi* which causes the disease known as Ray Blight. (b) Affected flower buds result in flower decay and shattering of the flowers.

described for Phoma Root Rot. This symptom is not common. Sometimes affected plants show distortion of the growing tip with no obvious sign of other symptoms. It is believed that when *D. chrysanthemi* attacks the base of the stem, it produces a toxin which is responsible for this distortion. Symptoms on the flowers are relatively uncommon. The pathogen sometimes affects the apex of the flower stem or the capitulum, resulting in a black decay and shattering of the flowers. The disease may not be apparent at the time that the flowers are cut but develops during transit so that the flowers shatter when they are taken from the boxes.

The pathogen is most commonly introduced into a greenhouse on infected cuttings, although it can be soil-borne and contaminated debris is also a possible source. When pycnidia are produced, the spores are readily spread by water splash and by handling lesions. Conditions of wetness and high humidity are necessary for infection to occur.

Cultivars vary in their susceptibility, although no extensive studies have been made of this aspect and lists of susceptible and resistant cultivars are not available. The Shoesmith and Princess Anne sports are very susceptible.

Control. The propagator has a major role to play in the control of this disease. By producing disease-free cuttings, Ray Blight can be kept at a very low level. The grower should try to avoid conditions conducive to disease development. High volume sprays of fungicides such as zineb, mancozeb iprodione or vinclozolin give a good control. Spread of the disease is particularly rapid under conditions of very high humidities and at temperatures around 15 °C. Propagators should discard all affected stock plants and obtain fresh, clean stock.

Botrytis Stem Rot (*Botrytis cinerea*)

This disease is rarely the primary cause of stem disease but invades damaged tissue. It produces light brown stem lesions of varying lengths on which masses of dark grey-brown conidiophores of the fungus develop (Fig. 13.3). The means of controlling this pathogen are described under flower damping (see p. 274).

Sclerotinia Rot (*Sclerotinia sclerotiorum*)

Sclerotinia Rot occurs occasionally, but rarely causes serious losses. Wilting of affected plants is often the first conspicuous symptom. Light brown lesions may develop anywhere on the stem but are frequently found about midway between soil level and the flower. Eventually these lesions become covered with a dense, white, fluffy fungal growth in which sclerotia, up to 10 mm in diameter, are embedded. Similar sclerotia can be found in the pith cavity of the affected area, although these are sometimes longer and narrower, being somewhat cylindrical in shape. The sclerotia enable the fungus to survive between crops and, under suitable conditions, they produce mycelium or apothecia and ascospores which restart the disease cycle. This disease develops over a range of temperatures (10–24 °C), although conditions of high humidity or leaf wetness are required for the ascospores to infect.

Control. It is important to remove diseased plants carefully so that the sclerotia are not dropped onto the soil surface. Steam and chemical treatment of the soil is likely to kill most, if not all of the sclerotia, although if they are buried they may survive for a considerable time and will germinate when conditions are favourable. High volume sprays of iprodione, or benomyl,

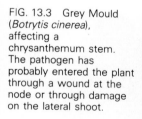

FIG. 13.3 Grey Mould (*Botrytis cinerea*), affecting a chrysanthemum stem. The pathogen has probably entered the plant through a wound at the node or through damage on the lateral shoot.

may help to prevent the spread of this disease. There are some reports of effective biological control of Sclerotinia with the fungus *Coniothyrium minitans* but so far no commercial preparation of the fungus is available.

Powdery Mildew (*Oidium chrysanthemi*)

The white powdery growth on the upper surfaces of the leaves is characteristic of this common disease and the pathogen may also attack the stems and flower buds (Fig. 13.4). The spores, which are produced in large numbers, are readily air-disseminated and will develop at high humidities but not in free water. There are no other common hosts of the pathogen. The perfect state of the fungus is not known and survival of the pathogen is dependent upon the presence of chrysanthemums. The conidia are unlikely to survive for long periods in the absence of the host. The disease is severe when little heat is used, a condition which often occurs when blooms reach maturity too quickly and are held for a specific market, e.g. Christmas or Easter.

Control.   Although a low relative humidity will check powdery mildew, it is usually necessary to use a high volume fungicidal spray once the disease has become established. There are a large number of fungicides on the market which will control powdery mildew diseases but chrysanthemum cultivars vary in their sensitivity to fungicides, so if there is doubt about the phytotoxicity of a product it is advisable to try a fungicide spray on a few plants before the whole crop is treated. Fungicides which have been successfully used include dinocap, oxythioquinox, imazalil and pyrazophos. A mixture containing thiram, permethrin and white spraying oil is frequently used and is particularly successful if the incidence of the disease is low. This mixture has the additional benefit in that it can be used shortly before marketing without leaving an unsightly spray deposit on the foliage.

FIG. 13.4   White powdery pustules of the Powdery Mildew fungus *Oidium chrysanthemi*.

Brown Rust (*Puccinia chrysanthemi*)

This rust disease is now uncommon and occurs less frequently than White Rust. Small red-brown pustules, about the size of a pin-head, occur on the undersides of the leaves and may be scattered or in concentric circles. Each pustule produces many uredospores which are readily air-borne and are also spread by water splash. The spores germinate in conditions of high humidity or in water. In the absence of chrysanthemums, the only known host plant, they remain viable for only a few weeks. Cultivars are known to vary in their susceptibility to rust although the differences have not been documented.

Control. By avoiding very high relative humidity, leaf wetness and water splash, epidemic development can be prevented. Affected cuttings are a most likely source of the pathogen and stock plants should be regularly checked for the presence of rust. Hot water treatment of the stools to control eelworm may aid rust control. High volume fungicidal sprays of benodanil, oxycarboxin, triforine, triadimefon, zineb or mancozeb are also effective.

White Rust (*Puccinia horiana*)

This disease can be recognised by the presence of yellow spots on the upper surface of the leaves. The centres of these spots later turn brown. White, buff or pinkish teleuto-pustules are present on the undersides of the affected leaves. These pustules become white as they age and increase in size up to 4 mm in diameter. This rust produces only teleutospores and basidiospores. It is favoured by conditions of high relative humidity and leaf wetness in very much the same way as Brown Rust. There are no known hosts of the fungus outside of the genus *Chrysanthemum*.

White Rust is common in Japan but was first found in Britain in 1963 and since then has become established in most other European countries. It has been repeatedly reintroduced into UK on cuttings and cut flowers. A policy of eradication has been followed since its first introduction and despite several multi-site outbreaks the disease is still not endemic. Because it is restricted in its host range to chrysanthemums, it is unlikely to survive outside the greenhouse except on garden-grown plants in exceptionally mild winters. Spores do not survive in the greenhouse for very long and are unlikely to be the source of the pathogen for succeeding crops unless an intensive cycle of cropping is practised. However, once established in an area, air-borne basidiospores are a very effective means of pathogen dissemination.

Control. At present in the UK suspected attacks of White Rust should be reported to the Ministry of Agriculture, Fisheries and Food. Routine preventative high volume sprays can be applied as a precautionary measure particularly in areas near to outbreaks of the disease. The most effective fungicides are benodanil, bitertanol and oxycarboxin, but triforine, triadimefon, chlorothalonil, zineb and mancozeb are known to have some effect. Chrysanthemum cultivars vary in their sensitivity to these fungicides, and it is advisable to spray a few plants first to check for possible phytotoxicity, before spraying the whole batch.

Blotch or Leaf Spot (*Septoria chrysanthemella*)

Septoria Leaf Spot occurs most commonly in stock beds and in outdoor crops where foliage is dense and conditions are wet. Round, brown or black spots or blotches up to 2 cm diameter appear on the lower leaves. When the attack is severe the blotches coalesce and the plant is defoliated. Small, black or brown pycnidia of the pathogen occur on the spots. Spread is mainly by water splash of the pycniospores. Infected cuttings are probably the major primary source.

Control.   It is important to control this disease during propagation and this can be done by using high volume sprays of benomyl, zineb or mancozeb. All obviously affected plants should be removed.

Crown Gall (*Agrobacterium tumefaciens*)

This disease occasionally affects stock plants and cuttings. Small, fleshy galls develop on the stem often at the base of the cutting. The bacterium is soil-borne and readily spread on hands and knives. It is usually necessary for a high inoculum level to develop before the disease becomes serious.

Control.   All diseased plants should be removed and burned, rooting media and benches sterilised and strict attention paid to hygiene. There are no chemical treatments.

Leafy Gall (*Corynebacterium fascians*)

This bacterial disease is not often severe although it is not uncommon. Affected plants produce a mass of short thickened or distorted buds and shoots at the base of the stem. The bacteria are readily spread on hands and knives and by water splash. Infected cuttings are a major source of the pathogen.

Control.   Remove and burn all diseased plants and discard any stock plants showing slight symptoms. Steam or chemical treatment of the soil before planting will eliminate the pathogen enabling a clean crop to follow an affected one.

Verticillium Wilt (*Verticillium dahliae* and *V. albo-atrum*)

Wilt is common and one of the most serious diseases of the crop. The leaves of affected plants are yellow and limp and often the yellowing is initially confined to one or more of the lower leaves. Eventually more leaves become affected and the older ones turn brown and die (Fig. 13.5). Infection takes place through the roots and the fungus invades the vascular tissue of the plant. Brown staining of the vascular tissue occurs infrequently and is not a reliable diagnostic symptom. Both species of *Verticillium* are soil-borne and can survive in the soil or in plant debris for many years. Infected cuttings are also a common source of the pathogen. Spread is by root contact, by the vegetative growth of the pathogen through the soil, and by the dispersal of

FIG. 13.5 Verticillium Wilt (*Verticillium dahliae*) affecting a plant in a pot of the cultivar Golden Princess Anne; healthy plant (a) and a severely wilted plant (b). Symptoms often first become conspicuous as the plant develops flower buds.

conidia, which are sometimes produced on the surface of an affected stem.

Cultivars vary in their susceptibility, although there are no up-to-date lists of resistant and susceptible cultivars.

Control.   It is important to propagate cuttings from healthy stock and national Nuclear Stock Associations have helped to minimise wilt by ensuring health standards. Regular heat or chemical treatment of the soil will minimise the incidence of this disease. Isolated methods of culture offer an alternative to soil sterilisation as a means of producing a wilt-free crop. The use of fungicides is generally not effective, although some success has been achieved with benomyl drenches when the treatment is started early in the life of the crop.

Stunt (Chrysanthemum Stunt Viroid)

This disease is caused by a viroid and has been known to occur in chrysan-themums for many years especially in AYR crops. Its incidence varies according to the amount of stunt in propagators' stock plants. Many different cultivars can be affected and show symptoms of smaller leaves and flowers, earlier flowering and stunting of growth. Flowers may be distorted and show a loss of colour (Fig. 13.6). Affected leaves are of normal colour and shape

FIG. 13.6 Chrysanthemum Stunt; this disease is caused by a viroid. The affected plants are stunted and flower early, the flowers are often paler in colour.

in the majority of cultivars. The disease is very infectious and can be spread on hands and knives. There are no known vectors (except man) or other natural hosts of this disease. The disease can only be positively identified by graft transmission to the indicator chrysanthemum cultivar Mistletoe which shows marked chlorotic spotting 3–4 months after grafting or in the laboratory using a technique known as PAGE (polyacrylamide gel electrophoresis).

Control. It is important to ensure that all stock plants are free from stunt. This can only be done by a careful programme of selection and testing, gradually building up disease-free stock. Some strains (English Stunt) can be cleaned by heat treatment and meristem culturing, but the majority cannot. Crops showing symptoms should be carefully removed and discarded. If the disease is suspected in a crop, none of the stools should be saved for cutting production.

Chrysanthemum Chlorotic Mottle (Chrysanthemum Chlorotic Mottle Viroid)

This viroid produces symptoms very similar to those of stunt with the exception that leaf symptoms in some cultivars are very marked. Marked chlorotic or bright yellow mottled or blotched areas are produced on the leaves; the cultivar Blue Ridge shows these symptoms very clearly. A viroid disease of the Princess Anne sports, which may be Chlorotic Mottle or perhaps a strain of Stunt, also results in the production of marked leaf symptoms. The leaves at the base of the stem, initially show pin-point brown spots which may be quite numerous and, as the plant matures and the flowers open, these leaves often become chlorotic. Affected plants are smaller, the flowers open earlier showing a distinct loss in flower colour, sometimes with some streaking of the petals.

Control. Chrysanthemum Chlorotic Mottle Viroid can only be controlled by the use of clean stock. If the disease is found in stock plants they must be scrapped.

Petal Blight or Flower Scorch (*Itersonilia perplexans*)

The disease is often common in the autumn and winter months and starts as pinpoint pinkish-brown spots on the outer florets which increase in size becoming oval and brown in colour. The petal lesions are frequently covered by a dull white bloom, and it is the presence of this bloom which is characteristic of the disease (Fig. 13.7). The petal lesions extend and the fungus spreads quickly from floret to floret until the whole flower is affected. At this, or earlier stages, Botrytis may also invade the decayed petals.

Petal Blight is most serious on outdoor crops and those grown in poorly or unheated structures. High humidities and foggy weather, which lead to the development of free moisture on the flowers, favour the disease. The fungus is a fairly common leaf surface organism and can be found on the

FIG. 13.7 A petal lesion of Petal Blight caused by *Itersonilia perplexans*. Notice the well defined lesion with a white bloom on the affected area. Copyright Glasshouse Crops Research Institute.

leaves of many different crops. It is particularly abundant in the autumn and early winter months. Large numbers of basidiospores are produced on the leaf surface and on petals, and it is these which produce the bloom on the petal lesions. The basidiospores are shot into the air and the fungus is thus readily disseminated by air currents.

Control.   Petal Blight is never a problem if the relative humidity is maintained at a low level and surface condensation prevented. Crops which are held during autumn or early winter for the Christmas market, are often most severely affected because of the use of low temperatures to prevent rapid flower development. High volume fungicide sprays are only moderately effective and must be started before the disease appears. Zineb used regularly gives some control, but regular use may result in unsightly fungicidal deposit on the leaves.

Flower Damping (*Botrytis cinerea*)

Damping is a very common disease. Botrytis colonises flowers, often those that have previously been damaged or attacked by other diseases or pests. Under conditions of low temperatures and high humidity it can be a primary pathogen, attacking healthy flowers. The early symptoms of the disease are similar to those of Petal Blight but the spots become watersoaked and the brown areas are not covered by a bloom. Usually the outer florets are the first to be attacked and eventually the characteristic fluffy grey mould, characteristic of Botrytis, develops on these (Fig. 13.8). This fungus affects a wide range of crops and weeds and spores are present in most greenhouses. When conditions are suitable for infection symptoms of the disease appear within a few days and as soon as the pathogen sporulates spread by air-borne spores can be very rapid.

Control.   A small amount of heat and ventilation is sufficient to cause air circulation and reduce the relative humidity so that conditions are unfavourable for attack. High volume fungicidal sprays of iprodione, vinclozolin, or one of the benzimidazole fungicides will give effective control, providing the pathogen is not resistant to these fungicides (see p. 111).

Flower Distortion or Aspermy (Tomato Aspermy Virus)

Infection by this virus is recognised by the irregular shape of the flowers, often accompanied by flower breaking, petal rolling or quilling, and a general loss of colour and size (Fig. 13.9). There are no leaf symptoms. Plants affected near to maturity may show only mild symptoms or none at all. Tomato Aspermy Virus also affects tomatoes (see p. 153).

The virus is spread entirely by aphids (*Myzus persicae*) and is of the non-persistent type, i.e. acquired following a short feeding period and transmitted equally quickly after acquisition. It is not readily sap transmissible and is unlikely to be spread by handling affected plants. Infected cuttings are the most important primary source.

Control.   Plants can be freed from Aspermy Virus by heat treatment and

(a)

FIG. 13.8   (a) A flower
affected by Damping
(*Botrytis cinerea*). The
lesions are not as well
defined as those of Petal
Blight particularly when
examined closely (b).
Photograph (b) Copyright
Glasshouse Crops
Research Institute.

(b)

FIG· 13.9 Chrysanthemum Aspermy Virus causing Flower Distortion. The healthy normal flower is on the left and the flower on the right shows typical distortion; an irregular outline, quilling of some petals and a reduction in size.

FIG· 13.9 Chrysanthemum Aspermy Virus causing Flower Distortion. The healthy normal flower is on the left and the flower on the right shows typical distortion; an irregular outline, quilling of some petals and a reduction in size.

meristem culture (see p. 65) although these techniques are generally only carried out by specialist propagators. The production of disease-free cuttings from stock originating from the national Nuclear Stock Associations has virtually eliminated this virus from the majority of chrysanthemum cultivars. The regular use of insecticides will minimise the risk of spread by aphids.

Other Flower Disease

Three, less common, flower diseases have been recorded in the UK each producing characteristic symptoms. An unidentified species of the fungus *Alternaria* is known to produce small necrotic spots on petals and these are usually surrounded by a pink border. The spots enlarge to form dark areas which may affect most of the floret. This disease is likely to be controlled by using the same cultural and fungicidal treatments as recommended for flower damping (p. 274).

Downy mildew (*Peronospora radii*) has occasionally been found in Britain. Affected flowers appear to have been lightly dusted with black powder. This disease sometimes develops after cutting when the flowers are in the packing shed. Control of the relative humidity and the use of high volume sprays of zineb are likely to be effective.

A flower shattering disease caused by a bacterium in the genus *Pseudomonas* has been found in both greenhouse and field-grown crops. The pathogen becomes established in the capitulum just as the buds are opening, causing a black rot. There are no known control measures for this disease.

NON-PATHOGENIC DISORDERS

A distortion of the flowers of the cultivar Balcombe Perfection and its sports occurs frequently. Symptoms include a delay in opening of the flower buds, which are unusually flat in shape, and the affected florets have a characteristic twisted appearance remaining incurved and somewhat crooked as the flower opens. The whole flower has a crumpled appearance and the disorder is known as Crumpled Petal for this reason. No pathogen has been identified and it is thought that the condition is initiated by various adverse environmental factors.

FURTHER READING

Forsberg, J. L. (1975) *Diseases of Ornamental Plants.* University of Illinois Press, Urbana, IL.

Griffin, M. J. and Fletcher, J. T. (1981) *Control of Diseases of Protected Crops: Cut Flowers. Booklet 2364.* Ministry of Agriculture Fisheries and Food (Publications), Lion House, Willowburn Estate, Alnwick, Northumberland.

Machin, B. J. and Scopes, N. E. A. (1978) *Chrysanthemums, Year-Round Growing.* Blandford Press, London.

Scopes, N. E. A. (1975) *Pest, Diseases and Nutritional Disorders of Chrysanthemums.* National Chrysanthemum Society, London.

CHAPTER 14

FREESIA

CULTURE

Pre-planting preparation

Freesias are usually grown in beds in the greenhouse. The soil is either steam or methyl bromide treated before planting.

Propagation and cropping

Crops are raised from seeds, corms or cormels and the system of crop production varies according to the planting material. Seed-raised crops are in the greenhouse for 10–12 months, whereas corm-raised crops take 7–10 months. Seeds of a range of cultivars of various colours are available and most are tetraploids. There is some variation in flower colour within a cultivar. Before sowing, the seeds are scarified to break the testa and allow the free uptake of water. Following scarification, the seeds are soaked for 24 hours in water at room temperature, blotted dry and sown into the greenhouse soil at 5 mm deep and spaced 8 × 8 cm to give 125–150 seeds/m². The optimum temperature for germination is 18–22 °C reducing to 10 °C when the seedlings have established, or 12–15 °C if quick growth is required. The plants are supported by wire mesh.

Flower buds are initiated when the fifth leaf is visible and continue to be formed for about 6 weeks. Temperature has a marked effect on bud initiation, and soil temperatures of 13–17 °C are known to result in the best yields. At lower temperatures, stems are short and at higher temperatures, flowering is delayed. Eight to twelve weeks after bud initiation flowers are ready for harvest. During this time, optimum temperatures are 15 °C night and 19 °C day reducing to 13 °C night and 16 °C day for summer produced crops, and 14 °C night and 17 °C day reducing to 12 °C night and 15 °C day for winter crops.

Following harvest, the corms are left in the soil to ripen, particularly if cormel production is required. Cormels are very small corms which are produced around the base of the parent corm in addition to one main corm.

The interval between seed sowing and harvesting is 18–35 weeks, depending upon the planting date, being shorter in winter and longer in summer.

Crops grown from corms have the advantage that named cultivars of high quality can be grown. The disadvantage is the greater disease risk with such vegetatively propagated plants. Corms are stored at 13–15 °C immediately before planting but should be planted within 4 weeks of the pre-planting treatment which consists of 13 weeks storage at 30 °C. This treatment breaks dormancy. Planting density varies from 65–100/m² for high quality cultivars, to 125–150/m² for corms raised from seed and 190/m² for cormels. Corms are usually planted so that they are just covered by soil. The optimum temperature for culture is similar to that of the seed-raised crop. Flower buds are initiated about 6 weeks after corm treatment which is usually between 2 to 6 weeks after planting.

Crops can be raised from seeds, corms or cormels at any time of the year and the yield varies accordingly and also with the cultivar. The variation is from 1.5 to 4 flowering stems per plant, irrespective of the planting material.

DISEASES

Corm Rot (*Fusarium oxysporum* and *F. moniliforme*), p. 279
Grey Mould and Flower Spotting (*Botrytis cinerea*), p. 280
Virus diseases, p. 280
Leaf scorch, p. 281

Corm Rot (*Fusarium oxysporum* and *F. moniliforme*)

This disease is sporadic in its occurrence. Symptoms may appear shortly after emergence or develop later at any time during the growth of the crop. Affected plants are stunted and the leaves senesce prematurely, first turning yellow, then red and eventually dying (Fig. 14.1). An area of decay may be present on the base of the shoot and the corms are also affected, showing a rusty brown discoloration of the vascular tissue which may lead to corm decay (Fig. 14.2). Affected corms which appear normal at lifting may rot in storage, especially if they are not stored in a cool environment. The pathogen can be seed-borne, soil-borne or corm-borne. None of the commercially-grown cultivars is resistant.

Control.   The soil should be heat or chemically treated following a disease

FIG. 14.1   Severe effects of *Fusarium moniliforme* on freesia seedlings. Copyright Glasshouse Crops Research Institute.

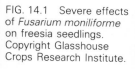

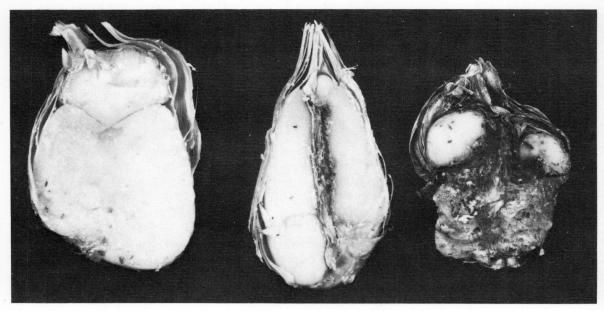

FIG. 14.2   Corm rot caused by *Fusarium oxysporum*. The corm on the left is healthy, the one in the centre shows the early stages of rot, and on the right the parent corm is severely decayed with the cormlets also beginning to decay. Copyright Glasshouse Crops Research Institute.

outbreak, although it is advisable to treat routinely, as low levels of disease may go unnoticed and a build-up to epidemic proportions can occur within a short time. Corms should be carefully examined at planting in order to eliminate any with rot symptoms. The disease can be checked by drenching shortly after planting with a fungicide, such as captan or benomyl. It is also advisable to dip corms in benomyl immediately after lifting and again before planting.

Grey Mould and Flower Spotting (*Botrytis cinerea*)

This common disease results in red spots, up to 4 mm in diameter, on the petals. The flowers are likely to be attacked at any stage, including after cutting. The fungus also colonises damaged leaf lesions and occasionally causes the death of plants, by girdling the stem just above soil level. On affected leaves and stems the disease is easily recognised by the prolific growth of the grey mould fungus. Epidemics develop when there is a lot of senescent tissue in the crop and the relative humidity is maintained at high levels for long periods.

Control.   The humidity within the crop should be kept as low as possible by careful watering and by ventilating as frequently as possible. The removal of dead plants and senescent leaves will help to prevent the pathogen building up within the crop. Control of the relative humidity is particularly important during flowering to prevent flower spotting. The most effective fungicidal control is achieved using high volume sprays of iprodione, vinclozolin or iprodione fog.

Virus diseases

Bean Yellow Mosaic Virus.   Leaves of some cultivars may be symptomless but others show a chlorotic mottle which eventually becomes necrotic. Severely affected plants are considerably stunted. Flowers of red and blue cultivars develop spots and streaks, and are small and distorted, usually with shortened petals, which allow the stamens and style to protrude. The virus is aphid-borne in a non-persistent manner. Spread during the growth of the crop may not result in symptom production but the corms will be affected and the virus will then have a maximum effect on subsequent plant growth.

Freesia Mosaic Virus. Although the leaves may be symptomless, the flowers of affected plants may be mottled but not distorted. The virus is aphid-borne and is of the non-persistent type.

Leaf Necrosis and Severe Leaf Necrosis. The first symptoms of Leaf Necrosis often appear on the fourth leaf of plants grown from corms or on the second leaf when the plants are grown from cormels. Chlorotic spots and stripes start at the leaf tip and eventually spread over the whole leaf. These later turn grey-brown to become necrotic. Flowers and corms show no symptoms.

Severe Leaf Necrosis may start to appear on the first leaf and progress rapidly, producing similar but more severe symptoms than with Leaf Necrosis. The plants may die before flower formation, but if flowers are formed, petals are severely discoloured. Necrotic spots occur on the corms and these spread until the whole corm is affected. Freesia Mosaic Virus has been associated with severe necrotic symptoms, but such symptoms only occur when a plant with Leaf Necrosis disease becomes infected with Freesia Mosaic Virus. Freesia Mosaic Virus on its own does not produce the same symptom severity. The exact cause of the Leaf Necrosis disease is not known, neither has it been experimentally transmitted to healthy freesias.

Control. There are no freesia cultivars resistant to the virus diseases and the only way that these pathogens can be satisfactorily controlled is either by producing the crop from seeds (freesia viruses are not seed-borne) or by careful selection of corms. The aphid vectors should be controlled at all times.

Leaf scorch

Necrosis occurs on the apices of the older leaves and the leaf margins. Such symptoms are associated with any form of damage to the roots, or the application of toxic chemicals. The use of water containing high levels of fluoride has been associated with the production of this symptom. Some cultivars are more affected than others although none is known to be resistant. The cultivar Tosca is particularly susceptible.

Control. Crops grown from seeds are often more severely affected. High light intensity or any other cultural factor which affects the plant's water relations may increase symptom expression.

FURTHER READING

Griffin, M. J. and Fletcher, J. T. (1981) *Control of Diseases of Protected Crops: Cut Flowers*. Booklet 2364. Ministry of Agriculture Fisheries and Food (Publications) Lion House, Willowburn Estate, Alnwick, Northumberland.

Smith, D. (1979) *Freesias*. Grower Guide No. 1. Grower Books, London.

CHAPTER 15

ROSE

CULTURE

Pre-planting preparation

The soil is sheet steamed before planting to give 25–30 cm depth of pathogen-free soil.

Propagation

Bushes are propagated by budding or grafting. Budding is done in the field and 12–18 month old bushes are transplanted into the greenhouse. Dormant eyes are used for grafting and the grafted plants are subsequently raised in heated frames until the grafts have taken. Most greenhouse rose crops are propagated on *Rosa canina* or *R. canina inermis* rootstocks. These are hardier than *R. manettii* or *R. indica major*, although the latter are more commonly used for the production of 12–18-month old bushes.

Cropping

The planting density is 7–8 plants/m^2 or 69 000–79 000 plants/ha (28 000–32 000/acre) generally in 1.2 m (4 ft) wide beds. The plants are spaced 25–30 × 25 cm (9–12 × 9 in) or 25–30 × 12.5 cm (9–12 × 4.5 in) apart according to whether the planting pattern is in double or single rows respectively.

Traditionally, roses are given a winter rest, generally in December to January, and this lasts for 6–8 weeks during which the crop is pruned. Some crops are grown with no rest period but cropped all the year and pruned, to reduce height, either in the winter or in the summer. Temperatures in winter when growth is slow are 8 °C night and 10 °C day, rising to 16 °C night and 18 °C day in summer. Carbon dioxide enrichment to 1000 p.p.m. is used for 6–7 months of the year, generally from October to April. The crop is supported by poles and wires. Yields vary according to the cultivar from 12–14 flowers per bush per year for Baccara to 25 flowers per bush for Sonia. Most crops are grown for 6 years.

DISEASES

Roots

Crown Gall (*Agrobacterium tumefaciens*), p. 292
Armillaria Root Rot (*Armillaria mellea*), p. 291

Stems

Grey Mould (*Botrytis cinerea*), p. 288
Brand Canker or Canker (*Leptosphaeria coniothyrium* syn. *Coniothyrium fuckelii*), p. 291

Leaves

Powdery Mildew (*Sphaerotheca pannosa*), p. 284
Downy or Black Mildew (*Peronospora sparsa*), p. 286
Blackspot (*Diplocarpon rosae*), p. 268
Rust (*Phragmidium mucronatum*), p. 288
Verticillium Wilt (*Verticillium dahliae*), p. 291
Rose Mosaic (various viruses), p. 292
Other viruses, p. 292
Leaf drop, p. 293
Chlorosis, p. 293

Flowers

Flower Spot (*Botrytis cinerea*), p. 288
Bull heads and blind shoots, p. 293
Virus diseases, p. 292

Powdery Mildew (*Sphaerotheca pannosa*)

This disease occurs on most greenhouse-grown crops and frequently reaches epidemic proportions. Small, white powdery pustules of the pathogen appear on the leaves, stems and occasionally the flowers. First symptoms often appear on the youngest leaves where a reddish-purple blotch develops which may cause the affected leaves to twist and curl. Often both leaf surfaces are equally severely affected. When the disease is epidemic, the whole plant becomes white and the flowers are unmarketable (Fig. 15.1).

Sphaerotheca pannosa is confined in its host range to *Rosa* species. Very large numbers of conidia are produced on affected plants and these are readily airborne but can also be spread by workers on their clothing. Perithecia also occur, although ascospores may not be important in the epidemiology of this pathogen in the greenhouse. The pathogen overwinters as dormant pustules on the stems or as mycelium in dormant buds. The disease develops rapidly as soon as temperatures increase in the spring, particularly in conditions of high relative humidity.

None of the commonly grown cultivars is resistant to this disease although

FIG. 15.1 Severe Powdery Mildew (*Sphaerotheca pannosa*) affecting the old and young leaves. Notice the flower, calyx and petals are also affected. Copyright Murphy Chemicals Ltd.

there are marked differences in susceptibility. The type of rootstock is also said to affect the susceptibility of cultivars. It is likely that rootstocks that produce a vigorous extensive root system, confer greater resistance than one with less vigorous root growth.

Control.   Environmental control to maintain a low relative humidity will help to minimise disease development although, as the crop is usually grown at a low temperature, it is often not possible to reduce the relative humidity whilst maintaining the required temperature. Crops that are rested in the winter should be pruned to remove as much affected tissue as possible and debris must not accumulate on the bed surface. During dormancy, it is possible to use a fungicidal winter wash, not only to clean the surfaces of plants but also the greenhouse structure. Generally, Powdery Mildew can only be controlled by the regular use of fungicides. Traditionally, sulphur has been used to fumigate the crop, often daily. Rock sulphur is vaporised in electrically operated heaters which are spaced about 10 m apart along the length of the house. It is vitally important to ensure that the sulphur does not ignite and produce sulphur dioxide as this gas is extremely damaging, not only to the plants but also to the greenhouse and the operator. When conditions are favourable for mildew development the vaporisers may be operated for 6 hours every night. The use of sulphur vapour also helps to minimise the incidence of other fungal diseases. In wet conditions, vaporised sulphur may partially bleach some dark coloured cultivars, especially reds.

High volume fungicidal sprays are now more frequently used than vaporised sulphur. Fungicide such as dinocap, dodemorph, bupirimate, imazalil, chlorothalonil, drazoxolon and nitrothal-isopropyl and sulphur are all effective and, by alternating them, the risk of pathogen resistance should be minimised.

Downy or Black Mildew (*Peronospora sparsa*)

This disease is sporadic in its occurrence but can be very damaging. The first symptoms may be confused with those of Powdery Mildew. Small reddish, purple areas appear on the youngest leaves resulting in leaf distortion. Symptoms on the older leaves are very distinctive. A paler-coloured and somewhat indistinct area appears on the upper surface, which gradually lightens in colour eventually becoming grey or brown (Fig. 15.2). Leaf drop occurs at this stage and this is often the first symptom seen by the grower. Leaflets with very slight symptoms drop as soon as the affected plant is touched. Symptoms on older leaves may be mistaken for a chemical or physical scorch and accurate diagnosis is often difficult because the pathogen is not easily seen (Fig. 15.3). Sporangiophores may occur on the underside of affected leaves but are generally not visible without the aid of a hand lens (Fig. 15.4).

The sporangia are readily detached from the sporangiophores especially in conditions of decreasing humidity when the sporangiophores twist and shake the sporangia free. Air-borne sporangia will germinate in water and, following infection, produce a new generation of spores in 10–14 days at temperatures of about 15 °C. Oospores also occur in the leaf tissue although their significance is not known.

Perorospora sparsa only infects members of the rose family. None of the commercial cultivars is resistant but some are extremely susceptible. The disease becomes epidemic when there are prolonged conditions of high relative humidity and surface wetness. It occurs most commonly in the autumn and spring.

FIG. 15.2 Downy or Black Mildew (*Peronospora sparsa*) symptoms on the upper surface of the leaf. The affected areas are initially pale green in colour and often clearly delimited by the veins.

FIG. 15.3 At a later stage Downy Mildew (*Peronospora sparsa*) causes scorched areas on the leaves often accompanied by some distortion.

FIG. 15.4 *Peronospora sparsa* does not sporulate prolifically on lesions but the pathogen can sometimes be seen if the leaf is curled over the finger and the underside viewed against the light, preferably using a hand lens.

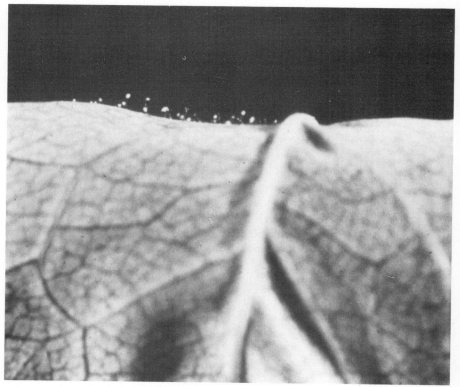

Control.   The disease can be prevented by avoiding conditions of high humidity and surface wetness. For the rose crop it is especially important to consider environmental factors when using thermal screens for heat conservation or enriching the atmosphere with carbon dioxide; both techniques reduce the amount of ventilation and may increase the relative humidity. Fungicides applied as high volume sprays may help to minimise disease spread and prevent epidemic development. The fungicides most likely to give control are those based on copper (e.g. cuprous ammonium carbonate) or zineb, mancozeb, fosetyl-*tris*-al, and metalaxyl/mancozeb mixtures. Regular applications may be necessary until environmental conditions no longer favour downy mildew development.

Grey Mould (*Botrytis cinerea*)

Grey mould is not often serious although it is frequently present in rose crops. Sometimes, young plants are severely affected during propagation or soon after they are planted out. The pathogen attacks the young growth producing a brown lesion on the stem which, if the stem is girdled, causes wilting and death. In humid conditions typical grey mould symptoms develop as the fungus sporulates on affected tissue. Occasionally in conditions of high relative humidity, the flowers are affected and small purple-red spots occur, especially on light coloured flowers. The pathogen grows equally well on dead rose tissue and on any other debris on the soil surface.

Control.   Grey Mould should not be a problem providing the environmental conditions are controlled to avoid prolonged periods of high humidity. Fungicide sprays of iprodione or vinclozolin applied at high volume will also help to control this disease.

Blackspot (*Diplocarpon rosae*)

This disease was once uncommon in greenhouse-grown rose crops, probably because of the widespread use of vaporised sulphur. Now it occasionally occurs particularly in newly planted crops, where typical black circular spots up to 1.5 cm in diameter appear on the young leaves (Fig. 15.5). Affected leaves absciss after the development of Blackspot symptoms. It is most likely that plants are infected during propagation in the field and before they are planted in the greenhouse. Large numbers of conidia are produced by the pathogen on the leaf lesions and these are readily spread by water splash to nearby plants where they infect leaves and stems.

Control.   All affected tissue should be removed from the plants and from the soil surface. Pathogen spread can be prevented by avoiding water splash. High volume fungicide sprays with a benzimidazole fungicide, chlorothalonil, captan or maneb, applied regularly from shortly after planting, give an effective control.

Rust (*Phragmidium mucronatum*)

This disease is not common on greenhouse roses although when it does occur

FIG. 15.5   Black Spot
caused by *Diplocarpon
rosae*. Affected leaves
often absciss.

it can cause severe damage. The leaves are most frequently affected, but the pathogen may also attack the stems and flowers. On the leaves, pustules up to 5 mm in diameter are produced on the lower surface and these are very conspicuous because of their bright orange colour. On the upper surface, circular yellow spots occur (Fig. 15.6). Similar, but larger, pustules may develop on the stem causing growth distortions and occasionally shoot death. This is the aecidial stage of the pathogen and infection by aecidiospores results in the production of uredopustules which are small and not so bright in colour, but usually more numerous. Towards the end of the summer, the uredopustules may be replaced by the teleutopustules which are similar in size but black in colour (Fig. 15.7). Teleutospores can withstand adverse environmental conditions and germinate to produce basidiospores which are propelled into the air. If they land on suitable rose tissue they germinate and infect the plant to restart the cycle by producing the aecidial stage. The teleutospores are able to withstand adverse conditions and are capable of survival between crops. Although there are no other hosts of this rust outside of the genus *Rosa*, the wild dog rose (*R. canina*) is often affected and is an important source of infection.

As with other rusts, the spores are mainly air-borne or water-splash spread. Germination occurs at high relative humidity or in water.

Control.   If environmental conditions which favour the disease are avoided, rust should never be a serious problem. Diseased tissue should be removed and high volume fungicidal sprays of benodanil, oxycarboxin or mancozeb applied regularly, starting as soon as the disease occurs.

FIG. 15.6 Rose Rust
(*Phragmidium
mucronatum*) is
conspicuous on both leaf
surfaces. On the upper
surface, circular yellow
spots mark the areas
where the orange aecidia
of the fungus are present
on the underside.

FIG. 15.7 Later in the
year uredo- and
teleutcpustules of Rust
(*Phragmidium
mucronatum*) occur on
the undersides of the
affected leaves. The
uredopustules (a) are red-
brown and the
teleutopustules (b) black
in colour. Copyright
Murphy Chemicals Ltd.

Brand Canker or Canker (*Leptosphaeria coniothyrium* syn. *Coniothyrium fuckelii*)

This pathogen occurs occasionally, especially on poorly-growing plants or where it is able to gain entry into healthy tissues by first colonising dead tissue. Affected stems are light brown in colour often with a grey centre. When the lesion girdles the stem, wilt symptoms occur. Pycnidia are produced on the dead tissue and spores are spread by water splash.

Control. All dead tissue should be removed to prevent the establishment of the pathogen. Affected tissues should be cut out wherever possible. Sprays of mancozeb may help to control this disease. If the outbreak is extensive, it is likely that the culture of the crop is at fault and the system of crop production should be carefully examined in order to determine the likely cause of the poor growth and disease outbreak.

Verticillium Wilt (*Verticillium dahliae*)

Although relatively uncommon, Verticillium Wilt does occasionally occur in greenhouse-grown roses. Affected plants are usually stunted, with chlorosis of the older leaves, and eventually defoliation results. There is often no obvious vascular discoloration, a symptom typical of many wilt diseases. Affected plants may not be killed and may show some signs of recovery during the late summer and early autumn.

The pathogen is soil-borne but may also be introduced in affected plants, rootstocks or graft wood. It has a wide host range and may affect a number of other greenhouse crops including tomatoes, cucumbers, peppers and chrysanthemums.

Control. Affected plants should be removed and the soil sterilised before planting another crop. There are no effective fungicidal control measures, although drenches with benzimidazole fungicides have given good control of this disease in herbaceous crops.

Armillaria Root Rot (*Armillaria mellea*)

This disease occasionally occurs when roses are planted in a greenhouse which has been built on a site of an old hedgerow or area where trees once grew. Affected plants grow slowly showing no distinctive symptoms other than poor growth. They sometimes develop canker diseases. The disease is best diagnosed by the examination of the roots of affected plants. By carefully paring away the bark, the tissue immediately underneath can be examined and, if Armillaria is the cause, the white fan-like mycelial growth of the fungus is visible. Affected tissue smells strongly of mushrooms. Armillaria produces rhizomorphs which grow along the roots or even near to the soil surface, and in this way the pathogen spreads to surrounding plants. It is capable of surviving in the soil for very long periods providing there is a food base present, such as a decaying tree stump or root debris from dead trees.

Control. Affected plants should be pulled out and the area excavated to remove stumps or roots which may be acting as a food base for the pathogen. This may involve excavation to a depth of a metre or more. Soil should be sterilised before replanting.

Crown Gall (*Agrobacterium tumefaciens*)

Although not uncommon, this disease is only serious when the crop is grown for many years when the accumulated losses can be considerable. The bacterial pathogen induces secondary growth of the rootstock or cultivar tissue at or just below soil level (Fig. 15.8). The galls that are produced may reach 10–20 cm diameter. Affected plants usually grow slowly. The pathogen may be soil-borne but can be spread on hands and knives, especially if the latter are used to cut away affected tissue.

Control.   Affected plants should be removed and the soil sterilised before replanting. There are no effective sprays.

Virus Diseases

A number of virus diseases affect the greenhouse-grown rose crop, although there are only a few records of serious crop loss. Strawberry Latent Ring Spot

FIG. 15.8 Crown Gall (*Agrobacterium tumefaciens*), a bacterial disease which causes the formation of galls which often occur near to soil level at the graft union.

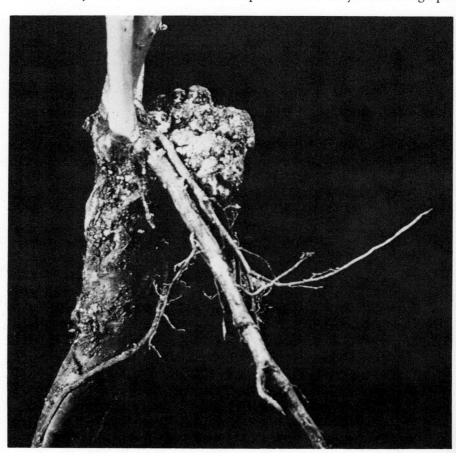

Virus is known to affect the cropping of the cultivars Baccara, Carol, Super-star and Pink Sensation. Affected plants grow more slowly, young leaves are somewhat crinkled and grey-green in colour with a faint yellow fleck, and some loss of colour is noticeable especially in Pink Sensation. This virus, like Arabis Mosaic Virus which has also been found in rose crops, is transmitted by nematodes. Elimination of the affected plants and the nematode population is the only effective means of control. Complete nematode control is often difficult, with the result that the disease may recur in the second or third year after planting.

Rose Mosaic is perhaps the most common virus disease. It is likely that the mosaic symptom is caused by one or more of a number of different viruses including Prunus Necrotic Ring Spot Virus, Arabis Mosaic Virus and Tobacco Streak Virus. Symptoms include a bright yellow mosaic pattern, streaks and conspicuous lines or chevrons (Fig. 15.9). The cultivar New Yorker shows chevrons on the leaves in the spring, accompanied by necrosis of the flower stem and some abortion of buds. In the summer, affected plants may flower normally although a mild mosaic symptom occurs on the leaves. Affected plants should be discarded. Care should be taken to avoid plants with virus symptoms when selecting material for propagation.

NON-PATHOGENIC DISORDERS

Leaf Drop

Acute leaf drop symptoms occur in the spring and sometimes in the autumn particularly affecting some cultivars, e.g. Baccara. The symptoms on the older leaves are almost indistinguishable from those of downy mildew. The cause of the problem is not known but it is often most severe when greenhouse temperatures are raised rapidly. Excessive stem growth is made before the soil temperature is raised sufficiently to ensure enough root growth and water uptake to balance water loss from the leaves.

Bull Heads and Blind Shoots

Shoots which fail to produce flowers or buds or where the stem immediately below the bud thickens and prevents the formation of a straight flower stem giving a 'crook' or 'bull head', frequently occur in the first spring flush. Although the cause of these symptoms is not fully understood, it is thought that the growth rate in relation to light intensity is important. Symptoms occur most commonly when crops are grown at high temperature in very poor light conditions.

Chlorosis

Roses often suffer from iron deficiency if grown in alkaline soil. The younger leaves show a very marked interveinal chlorosis which may extend to cover the whole of the leaf surface. Generally, the symptoms can be prevented by incorporating peat or sulphur into the soil or by applying a chelated form of iron.

ROSE

(a)

(b)

(c)

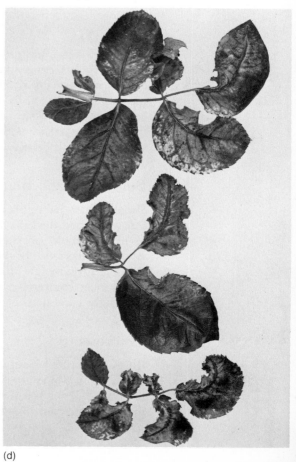

(d)

(e)

FIG. 15.9 Symptoms of rose virus diseases.
(a) Chlorotic line patterns often forming chevrons or oak leaf patterns caused by Prunus Necrotic Ring-spot Virus; cv. New Yorker
(b) small angular pale green areas, particularly conspicuous on recently fully expanded leaves caused by Strawberry Latent Ringspot Virus; cv. Baccara (c) a reduction in the leaflet width to produce strap-like leaves; a result of infection by Strawberry Latent Ringspot Virus in some cultivars; cv. City of Leeds
(d) a yellow mosaic and extensive chlorosis of affected leaves caused by Arabis Mosaic Virus on the rootstock *Rosa rugosa*;
(e) a distinctive yellow vein pattern resulting from the effects of two viruses, Arabis Mosaic Virus and Prunus Necrotic Ringspot Virus, in *Rosa multiflora*. Photographs (a) Crown Copyright; (b), (c), (d) and (e) Copyright Glasshouse Crops Research Institute.

FURTHER READING

Anon. (1980) *Roses under Glass*. Grower Guide No. 9. Grower Books, London.

Forsberg, J. L. (1975) *Diseases of Ornamental Plants*. University of Illinois Press, Urbana, IL.

Griffin, M. J. and Fletcher J. T. (1981) *Control of Diseases of Protected crops: Cut Flowers*. Booklet 2364. Ministry of Agriculture Fisheries and Food (Publications), Lion House, Willowburn Estate, Alnwick, Northumberland.

Mastalerz, J. W. and Langhans, R. W. (1969) *Roses*. Pennsylvania Flower Growers Association; New York Flower Growers Association Inc.

CHAPTER 16

BEDDING PLANTS

CULTURE

A large number of different plant species are grown for planting out into gardens but in the UK the most popular are alyssum, antirrhinum, begonia, dahlia, geranium, lobelia, marigold, nemesia, petunia and salvia. These are raised from seeds with the exception of the geraniums, which may also be vegetatively propagated. There are some differences in the cultural requirements of the different species, although these are generally not great, for any unusual requirement would make any species unsuitable for use as a bedding plant.

It is usual to use a peat-based compost both for seed sowing and transplanting, although soil is still used to a limited extent. It is important to start with a pathogen-free medium and, if soil is used, it should be steam sterilised and care taken to avoid toxic levels of ammonium or manganese ions. Seeds are usually sown in a compost (50: 50 peat and sand) of very low nutritional status and the seedlings transplanted into a compost (75: 25 peat/sand) with enough fertiliser to enable the plants to establish and then grown to saleable size with regular liquid feeding according to the species. The feeding requirement varies with the species grown and its speed of growth. The slower growing species, such as begonia, antirrhinum, salvia and lobelia, may require feeding over a longer period than the quicker species, such as alyssum, marigold, aster and mesembryanthemum.

Wood or plastic boxes, measuring approximately 36 × 22 × 5 cm, are usually used for seed sowing. Germination temperature varies over the range 13–21 °C depending on the species but is most commonly 18–21 °C. After transplanting (pricking-out) the plants are grown at 10–13 °C for 2 weeks and then at as low a temperature as possible but avoiding frost damage. It is usual to transplant 48–54 seedlings into each box to get the highest quality plants, but sometimes up to 70 plants are sown. There is an increasing tendency to grow bedding plants in plastic containers specifically for garden centre sales and these are frequently in units of twelves.

Bedding plants are produced for the spring market and sowing begins in January, the slower growing species being sown first. Some hardy species, such as violas, pansies, aubrietia and bellis, are sown in the autumn and overwintered outside or with a minimum of protection.

A modern trend in bedding plant production is the production of seedlings by specialists. This enables growers to buy expensive F_1 cultivars which often require special germination treatment, in order to get the best value from expensive seeds.

Production varies tremendously with the grower and the system used, but a good output is 200 000–250 000 boxes, or their equivalent, per hectare.

DISEASES

Seedlings

Damping-off and Foot Rots (*Pythium* spp., *Phytophthora* spp., *Rhizoctonia solani*, *Alternaria* spp., *Pseudomonas* spp.), p. 297

Roots

Root Rots (*Pythium* spp., *Phytophthora* spp., *Rhizoctonia solani*, *Thielaviopsis basicola*, *Fusarium* spp., *Nectria radicicola* syn. *Cylindrocarpon destructans*, p. 300

Stems

Stem Rots (*Botrytis cinerea*, *Sclerotinia sclerotiorum*, *Alternaria* spp.), p. 301

Leaves

Alternaria Leaf Spots (*Alternaria alternata* and other species), p. 302
Antirrhinum Leaf Spots (*Pseudomonas syringae* pv. *antirrhini* and *Phyllosticta antirrhini*), p. 302
Phlox Leaf Spot (*Septoria drummondii*), p. 303
Downy Mildew (*Peronospora parasitica*), p. 303
Powdery Mildews, various, p. 304
Distortions, *Corynebacterium fascians* and environmental/chemical factors, p. 304

Flowers

Flower disorders, p. 304

Damping-off and foot rots of seedlings (*Pythium* spp., *Phytophthora* spp., *Rhizoctonia solani*, *Alternaria* spp., *Pseudomonas* spp.)

Damping-off is probably the most important single disease problem of bedding plants affecting almost all species. *Pythium* spp. are the most common organisms causing damping-off. The seedlings can be attacked shortly after germination; the developing stems and roots rot before the cotyledon leaves have emerged through the soil. This disease is known as pre-emergence damping-off. Attack after emergence results in the characteristic damping-off symptoms caused by a lesion in the hypocotyl cortex, at or just below the soil surface, which weakens the stem causing the seedling to topple over (Fig. 16.1). Circular patches of affected seedlings frequently occur within a seed tray and a patch may spread rapidly, especially if the seedlings

FIG. 16.1 Damping-off of
asters (*Callistephus
chinensis*) caused by
Pythium ultimum;
healthy seedlings on the
left, severely affected
seedlings on the right.
Both were grown in the
same compost but those
on the left were sown
after compost treatment.
Copyright ICI Plant
Protection Division.

are densely packed together. Damping-off may occur after transplanting (pricking-out) resulting in similar symptoms or slow and stunted growth, caused by root and basal stem decay. Generally, as plants age, they become more resistant to attack by Pythium, although even plants ready to be planted out into the garden can suffer root loss if conditions favour disease development. There are no easy ways of distinguishing damping-off caused by Pythium from damping-off caused by other pathogens.

Phytophthora spp. are less commonly the cause of damping-off although some plants such as petunias appear to be especially susceptible to these pathogens.

Rhizoctonia solani most commonly causes damping-off of stocks, aubrietia and salvias. It is sometimes possible to distinguish damping-off caused by Rhizoctonia because of the dryness or withering of the stem lesion which is frequently pale brown in colour. This symptom is often referred to as wire stem. The brown hyphae of the pathogen can sometimes be seen on the affected stem tissue and occasionally mycelial webbing occurs around the stem bases of the affected plants and also on the compost surface.

Damping-off caused by *Alternaria* spp. is often associated with leaf decay as well as stem rot (see p. 302, Alternaria Leaf Spot of lobelia). Circular patches of affected seedlings frequently occur. Similarly, bacterial pathogens (*Pseudomonas* spp.) affect leaves and stems and not just the stem base.

Pythium spp., *Phytophthora* spp. and *R. solani* are all common soil-borne fungi and the first two are frequently found in pond water. Peat is sometimes contaminated and is a source of these pathogens. Conditions which favour damping-off vary according to the pathogen involved as do the most appropriate control measures so it is essential to identify the cause of the damping-off in order to achieve the best control.

Pythium spp. and *Phytophthora* spp. (the water moulds) are favoured by wet conditions and are also more likely to cause losses when germination and growth of the seedlings is slow. Both pathogens survive through adverse conditions as oospores, which germinate to produce motile zoospores. These spores infect seedlings and in wet soils sporangiophores and sporangia are formed in large numbers on the decaying plant parts. *Rhizoctonia solani* is most frequently a problem where the soil is in an ideal condition for seedling growth, i.e. moist and warm. It generally does not produce spores but the mycelium aggregates to form small sclerotia which can survive adverse conditions. Greenhouse soil is likely to be a source of all these pathogens and, if containers of bedding plants become contaminated by standing them on a dirty surface, or by splashing soil into the boxes during watering, or by using boxes for a second time without cleaning them, damping-off is likely to occur. Water is another possible source of the water moulds especially if it has not come directly from the mains.

Control.   Hygiene is of paramount importance and if care is taken to ensure that the compost is pathogen free, containers are clean, mains water is used, and the greenhouse kept clean, damping-off is unlikely to occur (Fig. 16.2). Some plants, e.g. antirrhinums, lobelia and salvias, which are particularly prone, may require special attention including the routine use of fungicides. Generally, proprietary compost is free from the damping-off pathogens, although this cannot be guaranteed. To be absolutely certain that compost is pathogen free, it is necessary to treat it with steam. This treatment is very effective but may result in the generation of toxic levels of ammonium or manganese ions (see p. 76–77). Antirrhinums are particularly sensitive to ammonium ion toxicity and may be as severely affected by this problem as

FIG. 16.2 A test of compost or soil for damping-off fungi using bait plants, in this case cucumbers and cress. In lines (a) and (b), heat treated soil is used and in (c) and (d) the same soil untreated. Such tests will detect damping-off pathogens providing the soil is kept moist and warm (12–15 °C). It is important to use test plants that are very susceptible to all the organisms which cause damping-off. The test takes about 2 weeks to complete and will readily distinguish between heavily contaminated and clean soil but may not detect low levels of inoculum.

(a)　　　(b)　　　(c)　　　(d)

by damping-off. Steam-air mixtures, which do not result in these toxicities, have been successfully used for soil and compost treatment in some countries (see p. 81). Chemical sterilants, such as dazomet, are generally effective. Cultural conditions favourable for damping-off are likely to result in epidemic development of the disease but no matter how favourable the conditions, damping-off will not occur if the pathogens are not present.

Factors which favour damping-off include the overcrowding of seedlings, adverse conditions which slow down germination and growth rate, such as low temperatures, excessive wetness or even excessive dryness, followed by the flooding of the soil, and root damage resulting from a high soluble salt level in the compost, or the presence of toxic chemicals.

Fungicide treatments can be applied to the compost before sowing or used as a drench to the seedlings after germination. It is often unwise to use apparently healthy seedlings from affected trays because of the risk of transferring the pathogens in the compost at transplanting and also because of the difficulty of recognising the very early stages of disease development.

Only by knowing the precise cause of the diseases is it possible to select the best fungicide treatment. Pythium and Phytophthora are best controlled by etridiazole or propamocorb hydrochloride used either before sowing mixed into the compost or applied after sowing. Copper-containing fungicides, such as Cheshunt compound, are moderately effective but can be phytotoxic causing seedlings and young plants to grow more slowly. *Rhizoctonia solani* is not controlled by etridiazole, but quintozene tolclofos methyl and iprodione are effective. Quintozene or tolclofos methyl is best incorporated into the compost before sowing. It is important to use the recommended rates in order to avoid phytotoxicity especially with quintozene which vaporises when the compost is warmed up quickly and may then harden the plant growth. Iprodione is best used as a drenching spray.

Some fungicidal mixtures are available (e.g. etridiazole and chlorthalonil) which will control damping-off caused by Pythium, Phytophthora and Rhizoctonia. The control of Alternaria and Pseudomonas diseases is described on p. 302.

Root Rots (*Pythium* spp., *Phytophthora* spp., *Rhizoctonia solani*, *Thielaviopsis basicola*, *Fusarium* spp., *Nectria radicicola* syn. *Cylindrocarpon destructans*)

Root rot symptoms usually occur after seedlings have been transplanted and have grown almost to the stage when they are ready to be planted out. Earlier attacks are usually associated with damping-off symptoms. Symptoms vary from a general discoloration of the roots which may be cream or light brown in colour, to a dark brown or black discoloration. The first indication of root rot is generally stunting of affected plants, often resulting in unevenness of the growth of the plants within a box. It is not easy to identify the cause of root rot but a knowledge of the history of the seedlings may help in the identification, especially if damping-off has occurred at the seedling stage. Black discoloration is often an indication of the presence of *Thielaviopsis basicola*, which produces black chlamydospores on the affected root tissue. This pathogen is favoured by low temperatures. Initially, affected plants may show white mycelial growth on their roots. Violas, sweet peas and delphiniums are most commonly affected.

Nectria radicicola, a weak pathogen, is most likely to occur on plants which are growing poorly.

The damping-off organisms, especially the water moulds, are often responsible for a progressive rot resulting in wilting and collapse of the affected plant.

All these fungi are soil-borne and by producing resting spores they can remain viable in a soil or compost for long periods.

Most bedding plant species are susceptible to one or more of these root rotting pathogens.

Control. The method described for the control of damping-off diseases applies equally well for the control of root rotting organisms. Hygiene, soil sterilisation and careful watering with a clean water source, are all important. The use of specific fungicides will control the water moulds and *R. solani* (see p. 300). *Thielaviopsis basicola* and *Nectria radicicola* may be successfully controlled by drenching the compost and plants with one of the benzimidazole fungicides, or zineb, or captan.

Stem Rots (*Botrytis cinerea*, *Sclerotinia sclerotiorum*, *Alternaria* spp.)

Stem decay can occur at soil level at the seedling stage causing damping-off (p. 297), or on older plants resulting in wilting of the affected plant parts. The commonest cause of stem rots is *Botrytis cinerea*. Lesions often start from wounds or senescent tissue, first appearing light brown in colour but rapidly becoming covered by the grey-brown mycelial and spore-producing growth of the fungus, especially if conditions are consistently humid. In such conditions the spores germinate within 2 hours.

Sclerotinia sclerotiorum causes white rot symptoms on the stems of fleshy plants, e.g. dahlias, antirrhinums and marigolds, but many other species are also susceptible. The prolific white, cottonwool-like mycelial growth on the affected stem, is diagnostic of this disease. After a short while, black sclerotia are formed within this mycelial mat. It is these sclerotia which survive adverse conditions, germinating to produce apothecia and ascospores which restart the disease cycle. Spread within an affected box by mycelial growth can be very rapid.

Various species of *Alternaria*, but most often *A. alternata*, cause stem lesions distinguishable from those caused by other pathogens by the growth of a black mould, the conidia of the pathogen, on the lesion surface.

Control. The appropriate control measures depend upon the pathogen involved. *Botrytis cinerea* is best controlled by avoiding prolonged conditions of leaf wetness and high relative humidity, ensuring that senescent tissue does not develop or wounds occur. Fungicidal sprays may be necessary, especially if it is not possible to control the environment. The most effective fungicides are iprodione, vinclozolin, thiram or one of the benzimidazoles, applied high volume at 10–14 day intervals.

Sclerotia of *S. sclerotiorum* are the primary source of this pathogen and must be eliminated in order to control the disease. Steam or chemical sterilisation in the soil is generally effective. Covering the soil with polythene or any other suitable barrier, e.g. peat or gravel, will help to prevent germinating sclerotia from forming apothecia. Once this disease has occurred, high volume sprays of vinclozolin or iprodione will help to minimise spread.

For the control of Alternaria, see below.

Alternaria Leaf Spots (*Alternaria alternata* and other *Alternaria* spp.)

The most commonly affected plants are lobelia, zinnia, alyssum, antirrhinum, callistephus, dianthus, nemesia, pelargonium, tagetes and viola. Various species of *Alternaria* are involved. Most of these pathogens produce circular brown spots on affected leaves. These spots darken with age as the fungus sporulates on the lesion surface. Damping-off symptoms and stem lesions may also be present in the affected crop. Many of these pathogens are known to be seed-borne. The disease establishes on seedlings from infected seed and spreads to neighbouring plants in water by splash. Alternaria diseases are encouraged by conditions of high humidity and surface wetness.

Control.   Control of the seed-borne sources of Alternaria diseases often results in complete control. Seed treatment is frequently done as a routine or offered as a service by seed merchants. One seed treatment depends upon the differential thermal death point of the pathogen and the seeds. A mixture of steam and air, to produce a temperature of 60 °C, is used and a short exposure at this temperature kills the pathogen leaving the seeds unaffected. Other treatments involve the use of fungicides, either with or without an accompanying heat treatment. A seed soak in 0.2 per cent a.i. thiram at 30 °C for 24 hours is effective, not only in reducing the level of seed-borne Alternaria but also in giving a stimulus to germination and growth of some plant species. Lobelia are somewhat sensitive to this treatment but can be successfully treated by reducing the treatment time to 12 hours.

For some Alternaria diseases a seed treatment with iprodione dust gives a good control. Spraying affected plants with iprodione may help to contain the disease.

Antirrhinum Leaf Spots (*Pseudomonas syringae* pv. *antirrhini* and *Phyllosticta antirrhini*)

Both pathogens produce brown, circular spots up to 0.5 cm diameter, on the leaves, generally starting on the older leaves and progressing up the plant. It is not easy to distinguish between the symptoms of the two diseases, although the bacterial disease (*Ps. syringae*) is more common and the spots of this disease may be surrounded by a water-soaked area or a chlorotic halo. The fungus leaf spot (*Phyllosticta antirrhini*) has marked purple margins to the spots and black pycnidia can sometimes be found in the centre. The purple margin is not diagnostic and may be present around bacterial spots, especially around the older lesions.

Both pathogens are seed-borne and spread from the initial lesions on the lower leaves by water splash. Epidemics often develop when affected boxes are stood out in open frames in conditions of frequent heavy rain showers. Some cultivars appear to be more susceptible to bacterial leaf spot than others, although there are no published lists of their relative susceptibilities.

Control.   Bacterial leaf spot is best controlled by using seed which is free from the pathogen. It is possible to treat seeds with heat (dry heat for 8 hours at 49 °C), although this may adversely affect germination. When the first symptoms of the disease occur, sprays with a copper fungicide may help to limit spread. It is very important to avoid water splash and only apply water in conditions when the leaf surface will dry quickly.

There is little information on the control of the Phyllosticta Leaf Spot but seed treatment with iprodione, sprays of zineb, mancozeb and possibly a benzimidazole fungicide are likely to prevent spread.

Phlox Leaf Spot (*Septoria drummondii*)

This disease is quite commonly found on *Phlox drummondii*, usually first appearing when the plants are some weeks old and sometimes becoming epidemic before planting out. Grey-coloured spots up to 0.5 cm in diameter, often with a red or purple margin, occur on the affected leaves. On close examination, black pycnidia of the pathogen can be seen on the central area. Spores are produced in large numbers from the pycnidia and are readily spread from plant to plant by water splash. Infected seeds are the only important source of the pathogen.

Control.   As the seeds are the source of the pathogen, it is important to treat seed as described for the control of Alternaria Leaf Spot of lobelia. Avoiding water splash and discarding boxes with affected plants in them, will also minimise incidence.

Downy Mildew diseases

These are generally not a serious problem during propagation, although they frequently occur after planting out. Bedding plants in the family Cruciferae are most likely to be affected, in particular stocks, alyssum and wallflowers. Downy mildew diseases are generally recognised by the sporulation of the fungus on the underside of the leaves accompanied by chlorosis of the same area on the upper surface. Sometimes the stems are also affected and the whole plant may be distorted. The spores are readily wind-borne or water-splash spread and germinate in water or at a high humidity. The downy mildew pathogen affecting the Cruciferae is *Peronospora parasitica*. It affects brassicas and such common weeds such as shepherd's purse (*Capsella bursa-pastoris*). These hosts are likely to be sources of the pathogen for bedding plants.

Control.   Control of the environment to avoid wetness and high relative humidity is one of the most effective means of controlling downy mildew. There are few fungicides that are very effective. Regular high volume sprays of dithiocarbamates, such as zineb or mancozeb, or mixtures of these fungicides with an acylalanine fungicide, will give a worthwhile control.

Powdery Mildews

Powdery mildew diseases are relatively uncommon on bedding plants during propagation but do sometimes occur on susceptible species such as myosotis, salvias and begonias. Typical grey-white, powdery growth of the fungus occurs on the upper leaves and, when attacks are severe, the whole leaf surface is affected. The spores are readily air-borne and germinate quickly at high temperatures and at high relative humidities, but not in free water. Air-borne spores are the most likely sources of these pathogens.

Control. As soon as the symptoms appear, a high volume spray of a powdery mildew fungicide should be used (see p. 110 for a list of possible fungicides).

Leaf distortions

Some species, petunias and nemesias in particular, show leaf distortions. Leaves of young seedlings become thickened and twisted and may fuse together to form pitcher-shaped structures. Often whole boxes are affected even though previous and subsequent batches from the same seed source may be free from the trouble.

There are a number of possible factors which may induce this type of distortion. The bacterium *Corynebacterium fascians* is sometimes responsible. It is probably introduced on the seeds but can also be debris-borne. When young shoots are affected, a leafy gall may develop, particularly at the nodes of the lower leaves.

Some fungicides, especially thiram, have been associated with the distortion symptom although it is more frequently used with no symptoms resulting. It is possible that a period of low temperature and fungicide at a critical stage in the development of the seedlings, may be necessary to induce the symptom.

A somewhat similar distortion of bedding plant seedlings can be caused by an infestation of the stem and leaf eelworm.

Control. By the time symptoms appear, there is little that can be done. All affected plants should be well separated from those that are unaffected. It is often worth continuing to grow affected plants as recovery can occur if damage is not too severe.

Flower disorders

There are very few flower disorders of bedding plants mainly because few species reach this stage of development before they leave the protected environment. Species that are in flower when sold, e.g. tagetes and marigolds, may sometimes show flower rot, generally caused by Botrytis. This disease may be encouraged by the presence of pollen on the petals. Pollen is known to stimulate the germination of the spores of *B. cinerea*. The disease can be easily controlled by applying the control measures described on p. 301.

FURTHER READING

Forsberg, J. L. (1975) *Diseases of Ornamental Plants*. University of Illinois Press, Urbana, IL.

Shurtleff, M. C. (1966) *How to Control Plant Diseases in Home and Garden*. Iowa State University Press, Ames, Iowa.

CHAPTER 17

POT PLANTS

CULTURE

Pot plants are a very diverse group of plant species varying from those requiring tropical conditions, to those that are winter hardy in a temperate climate (Table 17.1). Some are grown for their flowers, others for their decorative foliage and some for both. Most are raised vegetatively by taking cuttings, but some are produced from seeds and others from corms or tubers. Some are annuals, others are perennials.

Pre-planting preparation

In general, a greenhouse temperature of 21 °C is satisfactory for the propagation of many species. Ideal conditions for seed germination and the transplanting of seedlings are very similar to those described for the production of bedding plants. A 50:50 peat and sand mix is commonly used, although loam is still used by some growers. It is usually not necessary to sterilise loamless composts but very important to steam treat loam thoroughly before use. Cuttings are rooted in a peat, sand and peat, or Perlite mix, and root formation is quicker if the cuttings are turgid, rooted in a mist unit and the rooting medium heated to 20 °C. It is usually unnecessary to use a rooting hormone if rooting conditions are near optimal. The type of cutting taken varies with the species, for instance nodal stem cuttings are used for geraniums, internodal stem cuttings for fuchsias and hydrangeas, leaf bud cuttings for cissus and hedera, leaf petiole cuttings for peperomias and saintpaulias and leaf blade cuttings for begonia rex.

Young plants are potted into small pots (7 cm) generally using a loam-less compost consisting of a 75:25 mix of peat and sand. Depending upon the species, the plants may or may not be repotted into larger pots. Some plant species respond to artificial light either by growing faster, or by inducing or preventing flower bud formulation. For example, the flowering of calceolarias can be advanced by 6–8 weeks for marketing in April by low level supplementary light, *Campanula isophylla* produces many cuttings in long days or with a 2 hour night break and also flowers earlier, poinsettias produce flowers and bracts when the day length is 13 hours or less and to delay flowering for Christmas it is necessary to extend the day length.

Various systems of automatic or semi-automatic watering are used for pot plants including various drip-watering systems, water-absorbent matting, trough benches which can be flooded, and capillary benching. Environmental conditions for pot plants vary with the species. Many of the commonly

TABLE 17.1 Pot plants: Latin names, common names and reference names used in this book

Latin name	Common name	Reference name
Adiantum sp.	Maiden-hair fern	Fern, p. 323
Agave sp.	Aloe	Aloe, p. 309
Aphelandra squarrosa	Saffron spike	Aphelandra, p. 315
Asplenium bulbiferum	Mother spleenwort	Fern, p. 323
Begonia dregei × *B. sacotrana*		Begonia, p. 316
Begonia × *hiemalis*	Rieger elatior begonias	Begonia, p. 316
Begonia rex	Fan plant	Begonia, p. 316
Begonia semperflorens		Begonia, p. 316
Beloperone, guttata	Shrimp plant	Beloperone, p. 317
Calceolaria × *herbeohybrida*	Calceolaria	Calceolaria, p. 318
Calceolaria × *hybrida multiflora*	Calceolaria	Calceolaria, p. 318
Campanula isophylla and *C. isophylla* var. *alba*	Campanula	Campanula, p. 318
Celosia cristata var. *pyramidalis*	Cockscomb	Celosia, p. 319
Chlorophytum comosum var. *variegatum, C. capense* var. *variegatum*	St. Bernards lily	Chlorophytum, p. 318
Cissus antarctica	Kangaroo vine	Cissus, p. 319
Coleus blumei	Coleus	Coleus, p. 319
Collinia elegans syn. *Neanthe elegans*	Parlour pine	Collinia, p. 319
Cordyline terminalis		Cordyline, p. 319
Cyclamen persicum	Cyclamen	Cyclamen, p. 319
Crytomium falcatum	House holly fern	Fern, p. 323
Dieffenbachia exotica and *D. amoena*	Dumb cane	Dieffenbachia, p. 321
Dracaena sanderi and *D. terminalis*	Dragon tree	Dracaena, p. 322
Euphorbia pulcherrima	Poinsettia	Poinsettia, p. 332
Fatshedera lizei (*Fatsia japonica* × *Hedera helix*)	Ivy tree	Fatshedera, p. 322
Fatsia japonica		Fatsia, p. 322
Ficus benjamina	Weeping fig	Ficus, p. 323
Ficus elastica var. *decora*	Rubber plant	Ficus, p. 323
Ficus lyrata	Fiddle leaved fig	Ficus, p. 323
Ficus pumila		Ficus, p. 323
Ficus radicans var. *variegata*		Ficus, p. 323
Fittonia verschaffeltii var. *rubra*		Fittonia, p. 311
Fuchsia corymbiflora, F. boliviana and other species	Fuchsia	Fuchsia, p. 323
Gynura scandens		Gynura, p. 324
Hedera helix, H. canariensis, H. maculata	Ivy	Ivy, p. 324
Hoya carnosa		Hoya, p. 311
Hydrangea hortensis		Hydrangea, p. 328
Kalanchoe blossfeldiana	Kalanchoe	Kalanchoe, p. 326
Nephrolepis exultata	Ladder fern	Fern, p. 323

Latin name	Common name	Reference name
Pelargonium domesticum	Regal pelargonium	Pelargonium, p. 326
Pelargonium peltatum	Ivy-leaved geranium	Pelargonium, p. 326
Pelargonium zonale	Geranium	Pelargonium, p. 326
Pellionia daveauana		Pellionia, p. 311
Peperomia caperata		Peperomia, p. 330
Peperomia hederaefolia	Crinkled metal plant	Peperomia, p. 330
Peperomia magnoliaefolia	Desert privet	Peperomia, p. 330
Pilea cadierei var. nana	Aluminium plant	Pilea, p. 331
Primula acaulis,	Primulas	Primula, p. 332
P. kewensis,		
P. malacoides,		
P. obconica,		
P. polyantha,		
P. sinensis		
Pteris cretica	Brake	Fern, p. 323
Rhododendron simsii	Azalea	Azalea, p. 316
Rhoicissus rhomboidea	Grape ivy	Rhoicissus, p. 332
Saintpaulia ionantha	African violet	Saintpaulia, p. 332
Sansevieria trifasciata	Bowstring hemp	Sansevieria, p. 333
and S. trifasciata var. laurentii	Mother-in-law's tongue	Sansevieria, p. 333
Schizanthus pinnatus		Schizanthus, p. 334
Scandapsus aureus	Devil's ivy	Scindapsus, p. 333
Senecio cruentus	Cineraria	Cineraria, p. 318
Sinningia speciosa	Gloxinia	Gloxinia, p. 324
Sonerila margaritacea		Sonerila, p. 334
Solanum capsicastrum and S. pseudocapsicum	Christmas cherry	Solanum, p. 334
Streptocarpus × hybridus	Streptocarpus	Streptocarpus, p. 334
Synogonium podophyllum		Synogonium, p. 334
Tradescantia fluviatilis,		
T. blossfeldiana	Wandering Jew	Tradescantia, p. 334
Zantadeschia aethiopica		
and Z. elliottiana	Arum lily	Zantadeschia, p. 334
Zebrina pendula	Wandering Jew	Zebrinia, p. 334
Zygocactus truncatus	Crab cactus	Zygocactus, p. 335

grown pot plants withstand low temperatures and frost protection is all that is necessary.

The output of pot plants varies according to the age of the plants and therefore the plant size at the time of sale but is in the range of 300–600 000 plants/ha.

DISEASES

The diseases described in this section are those that occur during propagation and plant production. After the finished product is sold it may be subjected to a whole new range of pathogens and problems. These are not described, although some of the propagation problems occur at any stage in the plant's life. There are some symptoms that are common to a large number of plants, such as root rots, and where symptoms are similar and the disease caused by the same or a related pathogen, all such diseases are combined and a list of hosts given. The absence of any one particular species of plant from this list does not necessarily mean that it is resistant but more likely that although the particular disease may occur, it has not been recorded. Because many pot plants are from tropical or subtropical habitats, they are susceptible to diseases which are not common in the temperate countries in which they are grown. This, and also the fact that pot plants are frequently propagated in one country and grown on in another, often results in the occurrence of diseases that are new to a particular country. Often, new diseases of pot plants are recorded once only, although conversely, some pathogens become established and are then common problems. Disease control with fungicides sometimes presents problems because there is little or no information on their use on many of the species, especially those that are less commonly grown. If information is not available it is wise to try a fungicide on a few plants before treating the whole batch. Treated plants need to be left for at least a week to be sure there are no obvious adverse effects and even then longer term effects, such as growth distortions, may not have had time to appear.

It is very important during propagation to practise strict hygiene to ensure that the propagation medium is free from pathogens. Water is also a common source of infective propagules. Details of hygiene measures which are applicable to pot plant production have been described in Ch. 5.

Root Rots and Basal Stem Rots

Pythium and Phytophthora Rots (*Pythium* spp. and *Phytophthora* spp.), p. 309
Rhizoctonia Stem and Root Rot (*Rhizoctonia solani*), p. 311
Black Root Rot (*Thielaviopsis basicola*), p. 311
Brown Root Rot (*Nectria radicicola* syn. *Cylindrocarpon destructans*), p. 312
Grey Mould (*Botrytis cinerea*), p. 312

Leaves

Powdery Mildews – various, p. 314
Oedema, p. 315

Diseases of the main pot plant species are described in alphabetical order of the host, by common name, which is also often the generic name (see Table 17.1).

Diseases affecting many species

Root Rots and Basal Stem Rots (*Pythium* spp. and *Phytophthora* spp.)

Almost all pot plants are susceptible to diseases caused by these fungi. Symptoms include damping-off of seedlings, a rot of corms, root rot usually of a nondescript nature, a basal stem decay of cuttings and a stem rot of rooted plants which may be almost ready for sale.

Hosts.   Aloe, Azalea, Begonia, Calceolaria, Campanula, Chlorophytum, Celosia, Coleus, Cineraria, Cyclamen, Dracaena, Fatshedera, Fuchsia, Gloxinia, Hedera, Hydrangea, Kalanchoe, Peperomia, Philodendron, Poinsettia, Primula, Saintpaulia, Scindapsus, Zygocactus.

Often the first obvious symptom of root, basal stem or corm decay is reduced growth which is followed by chlorosis of the leaves and sometimes wilting, especially in sunny conditions. Because of the wilting, there is always a tendency to over water affected plants and this generally accentuates the symptom. When the affected plant is examined, the basal lesion (usually black and wet) or root decay (usually with the cortex sloughing-off) or corm rot are immediately apparent (Fig. 17.1).

The pathogens are common soil and water-borne organisms. They are most likely to be introduced with unsterilised loam but may be present on dirty pots, boxes or on propagation benches. Mains water is unlikely to be a source but tank or pond water is frequently contaminated. Cuttings can sometimes be a source of these pathogens if they are contaminated with soil.

Epidemic development is usually associated with a high inoculum level, a wet soil and a soil temperature in the range of 10–20 °C. The optimum temperature varies with the pathogen. Sometimes a compost which has given a severe problem early in the season will grow healthy plants when growing conditions are ideal. Symptom production is often dependent upon the rate of plant growth and if new roots are produced quickly the plant will remain healthy in appearance. As soon as root growth slows down, acute symptoms are seen.

FIG. 17.1 Root Rot and Basal Stem Rot of cineraria seedlings caused by *Phytophthora cryptogea*. The plant in the top left position is healthy, all the others are showing the effects of the disease to a greater or lesser extent. Copyright Glasshouse Crops Research Institute.

Control. It is important to practise good hygiene, to use healthy stock plants, and ensure that propagation is done in clean containers in a pathogen-free compost. Where large numbers of plants are propagated in a small area it is advisable to discard all plants showing even the slightest symptoms and also some apparently healthy plants from around the affected area. Some help in the control of Pythium and Phytophthora diseases can be obtained by using

fungicides such as etridiazole or propamocarb hydrochloride incorporated into the compost or as a drench after rooting. Captan, zineb and thiram drenches have also been used successfully on some species, but it is unlikely that an effective control will be obtained with fungicides if treatment is started after symptoms have appeared.

Rhizoctonia Stem and Root Rot (*Rhizoctonia solani*)

Symptoms produced by this pathogen are often indistinguishable from those caused by Phytophthora and Pythium. Roots, corms, stems and sometimes leaves are affected.

Hosts   Azalea, Begonia, Calceolaria, Cineraria, Cissus, Coleus, Cyclamen, Fittonia, Fuchsia, Gloxinia, Gynura, Hoya, Hydrangea, Kalanchoe, Pellionia, Peperomia, Poinsettia, Primula, Schizanthus, Sonerila, Tradescantia.

Close examination of affected tissue may sometimes reveal some diagnostic features. The pathogen produces coarse, brown mycelium which may form a web over affected parts, especially stems and leaves, and this web may extend onto the surface of the rooting medium or potting compost. The mycelium often binds the affected plant parts to the medium so that compost or soil adheres to the diseased plants when they are lifted. Stem lesions, corm rots, bud rots and leaf rots caused by this pathogen are usually pale brown in colour and generally dry in appearance.

The pathogen is a common soil-borne fungus and grows through the compost quickly especially at temperatures of around 20 °C. It is often most aggressive when the medium is moist and warm; it does not thrive in very dry or waterlogged conditions. Spore production is sporadic, and spread is by growth or by the movement of diseased plants or contaminated materials.

Control.   The same hygiene and control measures as described for Pythium and Phytophthora diseases apply equally for the control of *R. solani*. Once the disease appears, it is essential to discard affected plants and also those adjacent to them, particularly when there are many plants close together. Fungicides which are effective against this pathogen include iprodione, quintozene tolclofos methyl and, to some extent, benomyl. Quintozene is best used incorporated into the compost, although some plants are very sensitive to this fungicide and so it is advisable to test a few plants first. Both iprodione and benomyl can be used as a spray or drench, either as a precautionary measure or to contain the disease once it has been found.

Black Root Rot (*Thielaviopsis basicola*)

Symptoms resulting from root damage caused by this pathogen are very similar to those described for Pythium and Phytophthora Root Rot. Affected plants are generally unthrifty, show chlorosis of the older leaves and often wilt in conditions of environmental stress.

Hosts.   Begonia, Cineraria, Cyclamen, Gloxinia, Kalanchoe, Pelargonium, Poinsettia, Primula.

It is not easy to distinguish this disease from other root rots without the aid of a microscope. Affected roots generally show a rot of the cortex which is frequently light brown in colour but in some instances may be black. Sometimes the stem base is similarly affected. The pathogen produces large numbers of chlamydospores which are capable of survival for long periods in the soil. These spores, and the asexual conidia, can be distributed on debris, by water splash or via drainage water. Compost or contaminated containers are likely to be the main source of the pathogen. Epidemic attacks usually occur when the compost is wet and is maintained at a temperature of 15–20 °C.

Control.   Routine hygiene and attention to cultural details should prevent this disease from becoming epidemic. Experience has shown that some fungicides used as drenches protect root systems and prevent or slow down Black Root Rot. The benzimidazoles are most likely to be effective, although propamocarb hydrochloride, zineb and captan may also give some control.

Brown Root Rot (*Nectria radicicola* syn. *Cylindrocarpon destructans*)

This pathogen causes a brown rot of the roots of many pot plants and produces symptoms indistinguishable from those of other root rot diseases.

Hosts.   Azalea, Begonia, Cyclamen, Gloxinia, Pelargonium.
Affected roots usually show considerable damage to the cortex resulting in loose sheaths of cortical tissue around the central vascular core. The decay may progress along the root and into the base of the stem. Sometimes the root tips are affected and lateral roots develop which are also attacked, giving the root system a branched appearance (see Fig. 17.2). In moist conditions the pathogen produces numerous spores on the affected tissue and these are dispersed in drainage water. Spores are generally not air-borne. Compost and soil are the main sources of the pathogen.

Control.   Hygiene and the use of pathogen-free compost is likely to result in low disease incidence. Unusual compost mixes often result in severe attacks of Brown Root Rot largely because some of the ingredients, such as leaf mould, have not been sterilised.
Fungicide drench treatments with zineb, captan or benomyl, applied before symptoms appear, are most likely to be successful. Treatment of affected plants repeated at regular intervals (2 or 3 weeks) may prevent further root loss and aid plant recovery.

Grey Mould (*Botrytis cinerea*)

This ubiquitous pathogen affects the leaves, stems and flowers of a great many plants. Those where damage is often severe include the following.

Hosts.   Begonia, Cineraria, Cyclamen, Fuchsia, Pelargonium, Poinsettia, Saintpaulia, Tradescantia.
Affected leaves and stems show a characteristic light brown decay, which in conditions of high humidity is covered by the grey mould of the pathogen.

FIG. 17.2 Root Rot of cyclamen caused by *Nectria radicicola*. Note the brown to black discoloration of many of the fine roots (a), the 'rat-tail' effect at the ends of some rotten roots (b), and the production of lateral roots when the main root is rotten (c).

Flowers may have small dark colour spots (often purple) and these sometimes spread until the whole flower is decayed. The fungus is able to grow sapro-phytically on any organic material producing large numbers of spores which are readily air-disseminated. Black sclerotia are sometimes formed on affected tissues and these are capable of survival through periods of drought or high or low temperature conditions. High relative humidity and temperatures ranging from 15–25 °C favour disease development.

Control.   The most effective way of controlling Grey Mould is to restrict the relative humidity in the greenhouse so that conditions never favour epidemic development. The removal of senescent leaves and the avoidance of wounds, both ideal entry points for the pathogen, will also minimise the incidence of this disease.

The use of fungicidal sprays and environmental control will invariably keep Botrytis at a very low level. The most effective fungicides are iprodione, vinclozolin, and the benzimidazoles (providing the pathogen is not resistant to these fungicides, (see p. 111). Captan and thiram are also effective. Care must be taken when controlling flower spotting as the danger of phytotoxicity and the spray deposit, on the flowers and leaves, can be worse than the disease.

Powdery Mildews (mainly *Oidium* spp.)

Powdery mildews occur on a wide range of pot plants generally producing white powdery symptoms on the upper surfaces of the leaves but also occasionally on the stems, petioles and flowers.

Hosts.   Begonia (*Oidium begoniae*), Cissus (*Oidium* sp.), Gloxinia (*Oidium* sp.), Hydrangea (*Microsphaera polonica*), Cineraria (*Sphaerotheca fuliginea*), Kalanchoe (*Erysiphe polyphaga*), Saintpaulia (*Oidium* sp.).

Powdery mildews are common on some hosts such as hydrangeas, saint-paulias, *Cissus antarctica* and Begonia Rex. Mildew pustules are usually circular, varying in colour from dull, grey-brown to white, with or without obvious aerial growth. On saintpaulias, the pedicel and calyx is often first affected. Most powdery mildews require conditions of high relative humidity and temperatures generally between 15–20 °C, for epidemic development. Plants which are short of water and are on the point of wilting, are thought by many growers to be more prone to Powdery Mildew attack. Spread is almost entirely by air-borne spores which are able to travel long distances, although they do not survive during adverse conditions, such as excessive dryness or extreme fluctuations in temperature. The pathogens are generally host specific or have a very limited host range so the most likely source of the pathogen is another crop of the same host.

Control.   It is important to keep stock plants clean. Once the disease is established in the crop, it is very difficult to eliminate completely, usually becoming apparent as soon as environmental conditions are suitable. By controlling the environment to avoid long periods of high relative humidity, epidemic development can be prevented but this is generally not enough to do more than keep the disease at a fairly low level. Routine high volume fungicidal sprays are necessary for most crops. There are a large number of effective fungicides against Powdery Mildew on the market but, because of the large number of different species of pot plants and cultivars, it is important to use fungicides of unknown performance on a few plants first before spraying a large batch. Also, most materials leave a deposit on the leaves and are likely to affect the market quality adversely if used just before marketing. Some Powdery Mildew fungicides may cause physical damage to flowers resulting in flower spotting. Bupirimate, dinocap, imazalil, pyrazophos, and the benzimidazoles are generally effective. The combination of thiram, spraying oil and permethrin (Combinex) is used by many growers especially at flowering or near to marketing, because this material does not leave an unsightly deposit on the leaves although generally it only controls mildew when it is at low levels.

Oedema (non-pathogenic)

This disorder occurs quite commonly on some pot plants especially ivy-leaved pelargoniums and kalanchoes (see Fig. 17.12, p. 331).

Hosts.   Ficus, Hedera, Hydrangea, Kalanchoe, Pelargonium (zonals and ivy-leaved), Pilea, Solanum.

The most conspicuous symptoms are on the undersides of the leaves where raised pin-head sized blisters or corky pimples appear. Sometimes the whole of the underside of the leaf may be affected. Growth is otherwise normal and the problem may only affect market quality. Oedema usually occurs when water uptake exceeds water loss so that water-filled areas occur in and around the stomata, especially on the underside of the leaves. This condition most frequently develops when the relative humidity and the soil temperature are high. The larger and more vigorous the root system, the greater the water uptake and the more severe the problem. Sometimes oedema can be caused by sprays or deposits on the leaves which effectively seal the stomata and other pores of the leaf surface. Oil-based sprays or those which contain spraying oil are known to have this effect. Sometimes the damaged leaf tissue becomes colonised by secondary pathogens such as *Alternaria* sp., *Botrytis cinerea* and soft rotting bacteria.

Control.   This disorder can be prevented by avoiding the environmental conditions conducive to oedema development, i.e. high relative humidity and high soil temperature, especially when the plants are growing very vigorously. Oil-based sprays should always be used carefully avoiding frequent applications.

Affected plants should be well spaced to allow air circulation, watered sparingly and observed regularly to detect the development of secondary rots.

Diseases of individual species

In addition to the diseases occurring on many pot plant species, there are other diseases which produce specific symptoms on one host. These are described under each host but, for completion, mention is also made of the common diseases of each host which have already been described in the initial section.

Aphelandra

Leaf Spot (*Corynespora cassicola*)

Circular spots, black to brown in colour and 10–20 mm in diameter, occur on the leaves. The fungus is probably largely a secondary invader of wounds. The disease can be avoided by not creating wounds or, when necessary, by applying sprays of benomyl.

Azalea

Basal stem rots occur most frequently during propagation when the rooting medium is likely to be the main source of the pathogens. Phytophthora root rots are most common. *Botrytis cinerea* starts on damaged tissue, on both leaves and stems. The control measures vary according to the pathogen involved.

Leaf Gall (*Exobasidium vaccinii*)

This disease is not common on azaleas forced in greenhouses for sale at Christmas, but does occur on plants that are grown under protection for planting outside. The fungus produces a conspicuous distortion of the leaves which are thickened and red in colour. Sometimes stems and flowers are also affected. The discoloured area becomes covered with a white bloom of spores of the pathogen (Fig. 17.3). These spores (basidiospores) are propelled from the leaf surface and dispersed by air currents. The pathogen has a restricted host range and is confined to members of the Ericaceae.

It is unlikely that wild members of the Ericaceae are an important source of the pathogen for the cultivated crop. Affected stock plants are the most likely source.

Control.   Affected parts should be removed as soon as they are seen and the plants sprayed. There is little information on the relative effectiveness of fungicides but the dithiocarbamates (zineb) and copper fungicides are thought to give some control. Of the systemic fungicides, it is possible that benodanil, which is effective against related pathogens, could be effective.

Begonia

The three types of begonia which are regularly grown as pot plants are

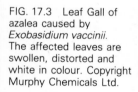

FIG. 17.3 Leaf Gall of azalea caused by *Exobasidium vaccinii*. The affected leaves are swollen, distorted and white in colour. Copyright Murphy Chemicals Ltd.

Begonia Rex, the foliage plant, the flowering Reiger begonias, and the large flowering begonias, grown from tubers. Root rots and tuber rots caused by Pythium and Phytophthora, corm and stem rot caused by *Rhizoctonia solani*, Brown Root Rot (*Nectria radiciola*), Black Root Rot (*Thielaviopsis basicola*) and Grey Mould (*Botrytis cinerea*) can affect all types. Powdery Mildew is most troublesome on the Rex and Reiger begonias. Other important diseases include Bacterial Leaf Spot and Verticillium Wilt.

Bacterial Leaf Spot or Blight (*Xanthomonas campestris* p.v. *begoniae*)

This disease is most serious on Reigers and the corm-grown begonias. Symptoms are first seen on the older leaves where small brown spots occur. As the disease progresses these spots enlarge until eventually large sectors of the leaf may be affected. Severely diseased leaves are often initially pale yellow-green in colour often with some necrosis at the leaf margin and a conspicuous V-shaped area of affected tissue. Chlorotic zones may be present around the necrotic spots. The bacterial pathogen is readily spread by water splash and infection is favoured by warm and wet conditions. Spread can also occur if affected plants are handled so that hands and knives become contaminated.

Control. It is important to propagate from disease-free stock plants. Spread can be minimised by preventing water splash, by avoiding unnecessary pesticide sprays, and by using a watering system which avoids the overhead application of water. There are no known resistant cultivars or effective means of chemical control.

Verticillium Wilt (*Verticillium dahliae*)

This disease can devastate Reiger begonias. First symptoms of the disease include slow and stunted growth with sections of the leaf appearing paler in colour. Affected plants gradually show increasingly severe leaf symptoms and eventually die. The pathogen can be cutting-borne and soil-borne although, where epidemic attacks occur, it is invariably because cuttings have been taken from affected stock plants.

Control. The use of stock plants that are known to be free from wilt and pathogen-free propagation compost will prevent this disease from becoming a problem. If wilt occurs, it is advisable to discard all affected plants.

Beloperone

This plant is particularly susceptible to Leafy Gall (*Corynebacterium fascians*). Green and somewhat leafy galls develop at the nodes and may be 1–2 cm in diameter. The whole plant becomes distorted and unmarketable. The pathogen is spread by handling affected plants and by taking cuttings from affected stock plants. There is little that can be done to control this disease once it is established. It is essential to ensure that all stock plants are free from the disease.

Calceolaria

Diseases of this flowering pot plant include root rots caused by Pythium
and Phytophthora and stem rot caused by *Rhizoctonia solani*. Grey Mould can
cause decay of the stems, leaves and flowers.

Campanula

Root rots and basal stem rots of this flowering pot plant caused by
Pythium and *Rhizoctonia solani* can cause wilting and death, or in less severe
cases poor, or slow growth. *Verticillium dahliae* is also thought to be a cause
of poor growth. All these diseases can be controlled by using clean stock
plants and pathogen-free compost.

Chlorophytum

A species of *Pythium* is responsible for a root rot and Grey Mould (*Botrytis
cinerea*) is sometimes found colonising damaged areas of the leaves and stems.

Cineraria

This very commonly grown flowering pot plant is subject to quite a
number of diseases. It is particularly prone to root problems and non–pathogenic wilting resulting from its large leaf area in relation to its root size.
Wilting may result from under or overwatering and the plant is best grown
in an environment where transpiration is not excessive but where there is a
constant water loss. Such conditions rarely occur in homes and, for this
reason, it is not the easiest of houseplants to grow successfully.

Root rots and foot rots caused by *Pythium* and *Phytophthora*, *Rhizoctonia
solani*, *Thielaviopsis basicola*, Grey Mould (*Botrytis cinerea*) commonly affect
this host. Powdery Mildew (*Sphaerotheca fuliginea*) is also common. This same
pathogen affects cucumbers but it is not certain whether cross infection
between the two hosts occurs. Leafy Gall (*Corynebacterium fascians*) is not
serious but causes distortions at the stem base and in the axils of the leaves.

Rusts (*Coleosporium tussilaginis* and *Puccinia lagenophorae*) affect this plant.
Orange pustules of these pathogens occur on the undersides of the leaves.
Coltsfoot (*Tussilago farfara*) and groundsel (*Senecio vulgaris*), are also hosts of
these two rusts. The spores are air-borne and germinate best in a film of
water or at a very high relative humidity. Regular sprays with fungicides such
as zineb, mancozeb, benodanil or oxycarboxin should give effective control.

Downy mildew (*Bremia lactucae*) occasionally occurs on cinerarias causing
a blotchy and yellow discoloration of the upper leaf surface with the characteristic white, fluffy growth of the sporangiophores on the under surface. The
pathogen is readily air-disseminated and the spores germinate in water or at
high humidity, especially at temperatures of about 15 °C. It is not clear
whether the fungus, which also affects lettuce, will readily cross infect
between both hosts. The pathogen from cinerarias is most likely to be the
greatest threat to the cineraria crop. The means of control of this pathogen
are fully described in Ch. 9 on lettuce diseases (see p. 195).

Leaf spot, caused by *Alternaria senecionis*, causes brown spots of varying
size, most frequently on older leaves. The pathogen is favoured by humid

conditions but can be controlled by high volume sprays of iprodione or captan.

Cissus

A root rot caused by *Rhizoctonia solani* and Powdery Mildew (*Oidium* sp.) are common diseases of this plant. A leaf spot caused by the fungus *Pestalotiopsis sydowiana* is also common and often starts on previously damaged tissue. There is no known fungicidal control.

Celosia

Pythium causes a root rot. Stem lesions with well defined, but irregular margins are caused by the fungus *Giberella baccata*. Older lesions show a zonation pattern associated with the sporodochia of the pathogen. It is likely that this fungus is both soil and air-borne. There is no information available on fungicidal control but the benzimidazole fungicides are effective against related species.

Coleus

This decorative pot plant is generally disease free. Occasionally, root rots caused by Pythium or Rhizoctonia occur but rarely cause major crop loss. Verticillium Wilt also occurs but only rarely. All these diseases can be controlled by using pathogen-free compost and disease-free stock plants.

Collinia

A stem rot of this palm plant, caused by a species of *Nectria*, results in extensive damage. The whole of the stem base becomes affected and covered by numerous pink fungal cushions about the size of pin-heads. Eventually the stem decay is total and the plant dies. Spores are readily air-borne and water-splash spread. There is no information on the use of fungicides to control this disease.

Cordyline

Pythium causes a root decay which is generally first noticed because of the very slow growth of affected plants. It often takes a long time for plants to show the usual chronic symptoms associated with root loss.

A leaf spot disease caused by a species of *Cercospora* causes rust-coloured rectangular areas 5–20 mm in size and parallel with the veins. Symptoms are generally most pronounced on the old leaves. Spores of the pathogen are readily air-borne and water-splash spread. By keeping the relative humidity low and by using fungicides such as the benzimidazoles, this disease can be controlled.

Cyclamen

Various root rots of this crop occur and are commonly caused by *Pythium* sp. *Nectria radicicola* and *Thielaviopsis basicola*. A characteristic symptom of root attack is the branching of the affected roots (see Fig. 17.1, p.313). A severely affected root system often shows a series of dichotomous branches. Such affected plants are stunted and in extreme cases the older leaves become prematurely senescent.

A corm rot of cyclamen caused by *Rhizoctonia solani* usually occurs together with root decay. The corm decay starts at soil level as a firm, dry rot. Grey Mould (*Botrytis cinerea*) is one of the most important diseases of the crop causing a decay of the bases of petioles, particularly of the leaves in the centre of the plant (see Fig. 17.4). The uniformly green leaf cultivars appear to be more susceptible than the more decorative silver leaf types. It is essential to remove all the senescent tissue at regular intervals as well as to apply regular fungicide sprays. The same pathogen can cause serious damage at flowering by inducing a flower-spotting symptom. An alternation of the available fungicides (see p. 111) may be essential to prevent the build-up of fungicide resistance.

Fusarium Wilt (*Fusarium* spp.) is a serious disease of the crop affecting the roots and corms and resulting in wilting and death of the whole plant. It is likely that the pathogen is soil-borne and it is essential to grow the crop in a pathogen-free compost. Drenching affected plants with a benzimidazole fungicide may help to arrest the symptoms but is unlikely to result in complete control.

A somewhat similar symptom results when the corm is attacked by soft rotting bacteria such as *Erwinia carotovora* var. *carotovora*. This organism usually enters the corm through damaged tissue but, once established, is able

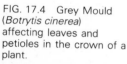

FIG. 17.4　Grey Mould (*Botrytis cinerea*) affecting leaves and petioles in the crown of a plant.

to induce a soft rot of the corm, especially if the temperature is 20 °C or above. Control is best achieved by avoiding damage to the corms (caused by pests and other pathogens) and by ensuring that conditions are not continuously warm and moist.

Dieffenbachia

FIG. 17.5 A stem rot of Dieffenbachia caused by a bacterium, *Erwinia carotovora* var. *carotovora*.

Various species of *Dieffenbachia* are grown as foliage pot plants and are subject to a number of important diseases.

Bacterial Leaf Spot (*Xanthomonas dieffenbachia*) is characterised by the initial production of small translucent spots which enlarge to form circular to elongated, yellow to orange-yellow areas, which reach several millimetres in diameter. The centre of the spots is a dull, watery green colour with an orange-yellow border. When leaves become severely affected they wilt and die. The bacterial pathogen is spread by water splash and epidemic development is favoured by high temperatures (25 °C). The disease can be controlled by preventing water splash and by lowering the greenhouse temperature. Chemical control is generally not effective.

Bacterial Stem Rot (*Erwinia chrysanthemi* pv. *dieffenbachiae* and *Erwinia carotovora* var. *carotovora*) affects stems above and below soil level and also leaves (Fig. 17.5). The stem lesions are water-soaked, initially grey becoming tan-coloured with a clear area of demarcation between diseased and healthy tissue. Leaf spots are small, water-soaked and pale brown with a diffuse yellow margin.

The pathogen generally originates from affected stock plants. Diseased plants should be discarded and knives used for taking and trimming cuttings regularly disinfected. Chemical sprays are unlikely to be effective but control of the environment to avoid wet and warm conditions will help to minimise this disease.

Fungal leaf spots are caused by various fungi including a species of *Leptosphaeria*, *Glomerella* and *Cephalosporium*. Leptosphaeria Brown Leaf Spot is characterised by circular spots from 1–10 mm in diameter, usually with a brown centre and an outer halo which is orange-yellow in colour. Cephalosporium Leaf Spot occurs on the young convolute leaves as small, yellow to red-brown spots, circular in shape. All spots may show a concentric ring pattern. This pathogen becomes more progressive at higher temperatures and at high relative humidities. *Glomerella cingulata* often colonises damaged tissue producing a rot which is characterised by the ring pattern arrangement of the acervuli (Fig. 17.6).

These pathogens are spread by water splash and encouraged by high temperatures. Fungicidal sprays of a dithiocarbamate, such as mancozeb, will help to minimise the incidence of these diseases.

Dasheen Mosaic Virus is present in many stocks of the various species of *Dieffenbachia*. The main effect of the virus is to reduce growth but a mosaic symptom and distortion of the symmetry of the leaves can also occur. Virus is restricted to members of the Araceae including some other commonly grown pot plants such as Anthurium, Philodendron and Zantedeschia. The particles are flexuous rods 700–800 mm in length and are transmitted by aphids. The only effective control is to ensure that stock plants are free from this virus and that the routine control of aphids is practised.

FIG. 17.6 Glomerella Leaf Rot (*Glomerella cingulata*) of Dieffenbachia. The acervuli have a more or less concentric arrangement.

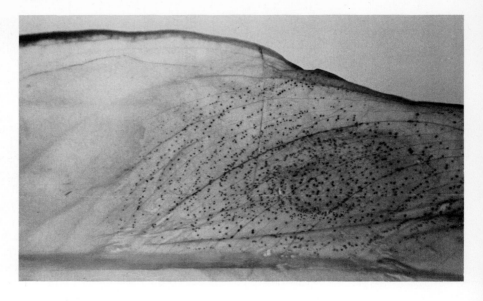

Dracaena

A root rot caused by Pythium affects species in this genus. *Fusarium oxysporum* is also known to cause a root decay. In addition, there are a number of leaf spotting organisms. Leaf spot caused by *Phyllosticta dracaenae* causes circular to irregular spots 1–5 mm in diameter. Spots commonly have a brown centre and are surrounded by a yellow halo. In extreme conditions, all the foliage may be affected resulting in a complete decay of the leaves. Similar symptoms are caused by *Macrophoma draconis*. Spores of both pathogens are produced in pycnidia and spread by water splash. Fungicidal sprays of mancozeb and the avoidance of surface wetness will help to control these diseases. A leaf spot caused by a bacterium, *Pseudomonas* sp., causes circular water-soaked spots with red-brown margins and with a surrounding chlorotic halo. These spots enlarge to affect the whole leaf, leaving the affected tissue brown and papery. The bacterium is spread by water splash and the disease encouraged by high temperature and wetness. By avoiding such conditions, this disease and the fungal leaf spots can be controlled. *Dracaena* species are very sensitive to fluoride in water and produce oblong, brown leaf spots in the white band along the leaf margin when this chemical is present at low concentrations. Eventually, as the spots enlarge, the whole of the leaf edge becomes necrotic. Water containing fluorides should be avoided, especially during propagation.

Fatshedera

Pythium causes a root decay which can be controlled using chemical and cultural means.

Fatsia

Root rot caused by *Armillaria mellea* has been found on this host. The white, fan-shaped mycelium of the pathogen can be seen under the cortical tissue of the affected roots which also smell strongly of mushrooms. The disease is unlikely to occur unless wood bark is used as an ingredient in the compost. There is no control.

Ferns

Ferns are generally disease free although adverse environmental conditions, especially periods of low humidity, may result in leaf necrosis. Grey Mould (*Botrytis cinerea*) sometimes colonises damaged tissue causing stem and leaf rot symptoms but can be controlled with fungicides. A leaf spot caused by the fungus *Ascochyta necans* causes red-brown spots on the fronds of some ferns. The centres of the spots become light brown in colour as they age. The lesions are usually elongated in shape and orientated longitudinally. Spores are produced in pycnidia and are spread by water splash. Similar symptoms are caused by another fungus, a species of *Cylindrocladium*. A dithiocarbamate or chlorothalonil fungicidal spray will help to control both of these pathogens.

Ficus

Various leaf spot diseases occur on rubber plants and necrotic areas of tissue often develop in the centres of leaves. These start as chlorotic, diffuse patches which gradually become necrotic but rarely spread to affect the whole leaf. Various fungi have been associated with these symptoms including *Glœosporium elasticae*. It is not clear whether this, or related fungi, are primary pathogens or whether they merely colonise damaged tissue.

A *Cercospora* sp. causes minute pimples on the undersides of leaves. These are initially yellow-green in colour but later become brown as they enlarge. Severely affected leaves absciss. Cercospora Leaf Spot is favoured by high relative humidity and high temperatures and can be controlled by modifications of the growing conditions and, when necessary, by sprays of benomyl.

Large (1–2 cm) angular necrotic areas, red-brown in colour, mainly apparent on the lower leaf surface, are said to result from potassium deficiency. Severe necrosis of the yellow tissues at the leaf edges of the variegated cultivars may also be related to crop nutrition especially potash levels. This symptom invariably develops as variegated plants age and it is often difficult to produce a large variegated plant without necrotic leaf margins. Symptoms of oedema appear on the undersides of the leaves.

Fuchsia

There are a large number of cultivars of fuchsia which are grown either as greenhouse plants or for planting outside in the flower border. Root rot and basal stem decay caused by *Rhizoctonia solani* and Pythium cause losses during the rooting of cuttings. Grey Mould (*Botrytis cinerea*) decays stems, leaves and flowers after establishing on wounded tissue or where flower parts have fallen.

With the rust disease (*Pucciniastrum epilobii*) large numbers of rusty coloured pustules occur on the undersides of the leaves resulting in leaf chlorosis and defoliation. Spores are readily air-borne and germinate in warm and wet conditions. Sprays of a dithiocarbamate, benodanil or oxycarboxin should control this disease but, as there are many different cultivars, it is advisable to try these fungicides on a few plants before spraying the whole batch.

Gloxinia

Brown Root Rot (*Nectria radicicola*), a root rot caused by Pythium or Phytophthora, and Black Root Rot (*Thielaviopsis basicola*) all result in stunted growth, wilting, premature senescence and plant death. A species of Pythium (probably *P. echinulatum*) is known to cause a rot of the corm which results in a wet decay and a rapid collapse of affected plants. A leaf and bud rotting disease of gloxinias caused by *Rhizoctonia solani* has been recorded although it does not appear to be very common. Grey Mould (*Botrytis cinerea*) causes a rot of leaves and petioles and is generally a coloniser of damaged tissue (Fig. 17.7). Powdery Mildew (*Oidium* sp.) occurs occasionally on this crop.

Gynura

This plant is very susceptible to a stem rot of cuttings caused by a species of *Phytophthora*. Root rot has also been associated with Pythium.

Hedera

Root rots of ivy have been associated with both Phytophthora and Pythium. Bacterial Leaf Spot (*Xanthomonas hederae*) is one of the most troublesome diseases. The leaf spots are first small, round and dark in colour with a water-soaked halo (Fig. 17.8). They increase in size up to 4–5 mm in diameter and become black and sometimes angular in shape. A brown deposit (probably

FIG. 17.7 Grey Mould (*Botrytis cinerea*) attack of gloxinia at soil level causing stem decay and plant collapse.

FIG. 17.8 Bacterial leaf spot (*Xanthomonas hederae*) of hedera.

dried bacterial ooze) appears around some spots. Leaves generally do not absciss or senesce but the plant quality is reduced by the black spotting.

The pathogen is readily spread by water splash and epidemics develop in warm and wet conditions. The avoidance of these conditions will help to minimise spread. It is important to propagate from disease-free plants. Once the disease has occurred, there is no effective chemical means of control although copper-containing sprays are thought to slow down the rate of spread. Unfortunately, these materials also leave a conspicuous deposit on the foliage.

A fungal leaf spot caused by *Phyllosticta hedericola* produce very similar symptoms. Pycnidia can be seen on the spots which are not quite so dark in colour as those of Bacterial Leaf Spot. Spores are spread by water splash. A high volume spray of a benzimidazole fungicide will help to control this disease, although such sprays may spread the bacterial pathogen so it is important to diagnose the disease correctly. A leaf and petiole rot of ivy has been associated with the fungus *Colletotrichum trichellum*. This disease differs from the other two in the extent of the leaf rotting, and the decay of the petioles. Benzimidazole fungicides may also be effective against this pathogen.

Ivy commonly shows symptoms of oedema especially on the undersides of the leaves. The small, pimply spots become corky as they age.

Hydrangea

A basal stem and root rot caused by *Rhizoctonia solani* or Phytophthora can result in stunted growth, wilting and death. Powdery Mildew (*Microsphaera polonica*) is common and Grey Mould (*Botrytis cinerea*) affects the leaves and flowers.

A leaf spot caused by an *Aschochyta* sp. is known to be a cause of damage on cuttings and mature plants. The leaf spots are more than a centimetre in diameter with dark brown centres, a concentric ring pattern and numerous pycnidia. They occur on both the upper and lower surfaces. There is no information on the control of this disease, although it is likely that a dithio-carbamate fungicide, such as mancozeb, will help to stop spread of spores by water splash.

Many stocks of hydrangeas are uniformly affected by Hydrangea Ring Spot Virus. Yellow spots and rings up to several centimetres in diameter occur on the older leaves. The growth of the affected plants is not markedly affected although, when symptom expression is severe, plant quality is reduced. Symptoms often disappear after mid-summer but will reappear again in the following year.

A green petal symptom occasionally occurs in hydrangeas especially if they have been stood outside for a time. This disease is caused by a mycoplasma, transmitted by leaf hoppers. Affected plants should be discarded.

Hydrangeas sometimes show symptoms of oedema on the undersides of the leaves and the stems.

Kalanchoe

Root and basal stem diseases have been associated with *Pythium*, *Thielaviopsis basicola* and *Rhizoctonia solani*. A Powdery Mildew (*Erysiphe polyphaga*) can cause severe damage and *Botrytis cinerea* sometimes causes stem and petiole rots. *Verticillium dahliae* occurs occasionally causing stunting of affected plants and premature senescence. *Sclerotinia sclerotiorum* is responsible for a stem rot with the typical white, cotton wool-like, mycelial symptoms and large black sclerotia. A leaf spot caused by *Ascochyta* sp. has also been recorded. Little is known about the control of these diseases.

Pelargonium

Zonal, regal, ivy leaved cultivars and pelargoniums raised from seeds, are amongst the most commonly grown pot plants, although many are used for planting out in the flower borders. There are a number of important and potentially very damaging diseases of this crop.

Black Stem Rot (*Pythium splendens*)

The characteristic symptom of this disease is the production of a soft, wet stem rot at the base of the cutting or of the stem base and roots at latter stages (Fig. 17.9). At rooting, affected plants are detected by the grey-green colour of the young leaves and eventually by wilting and collapse. Mature plants generally show stunted growth and premature senescence before the stem lesion becomes apparent above soil level.

This pathogen is soil-borne and the control of this and other Pythium diseases is described on p. 309. Phytophthora, *Thielaviopsis basicola* and *Nectria radicicola* have also been associated with root rot symptoms.

Bacterial Wilt and Leaf Spot (*Xanthomonas pelargonii*)

This is the most serious disease of the crop affecting particularly the zonal cultivars. It sometimes only becomes apparent some months after infection

has occurred but, once established within a stock, it is very difficult to eliminate. Symptoms include a black stem rot very similar to that caused by
Pythium splendens, although frequently rather drier. Lesions may extend some
distance above soil level, particularly in old woody plants. Leaf spot symptoms also occur although these are less common. The small, brown circular
spots on the leaves are often surrounded by a water-soaked halo. They may
increase in size and result in leaf abscission. Chlorotic sectors of leaf tissue
may also follow infection by this pathogen.

The bacterium is spread by water splash but more important, on the hands
and knives of workers. Once a knife becomes contaminated, it is likely that
many cuttings taken subsequently will be infected and the pathogen may also
be spread to other stock plants.

Control.   Bacterial wilt can only be controlled by the use of clean stock
plants. Once a stock is affected it should be discarded and a fresh start made
from clean stock. It is sometimes possible to save valuable clones by using
a clonal system of propagation. All cuttings taken from a parent plant must
be identifiable for a period of 6 months and if, during this period, the disease
occurs in any of the plants, the whole of the clone is discarded. Obtaining

disease-free plants from stock plant producing associations, is an easier way for the grower to ensure the supply of clean plants. There are no chemical means of control and high volume sprays of a fungicide for the control of other diseases can aid the spread of this pathogen.

Verticillium Wilt (*Verticillium alboatrum* and *V. dahliae*)

Wilt is a particularly severe disease of Regal types although it also affects zonals to a lesser extent. Ivy-leaved cultivars appear to be resistant. Affected plants show symptoms of stunting and slow growth with chlorosis of the lower leaves and a dull green coloration of the youngest (Fig. 17.10). A sector

FIG. 17.10 Verticillium Wilt (*Verticillium dahliae*) of
(a) a zonal cultivar Paul Crampel, and
(b) a regal cultivar Grand Slam. On the left is a healthy plant; the affected plant on the right is stunted and with a tendency for the older leaves to wilt although this disease rarely kills these plants. Photograph (b) Crown Copyright.

(a)

(b)

of leaf tissue may become chlorotic. There is no pronounced vascular staining. Symptom expression is most acute at flowering, and in the late summer infected plants may start to grow normally.

The pathogen can be soil-borne but is most likely to be introduced in infected cuttings. Once stock plants become infected it is advisable to discard them and not save any plants as a source of cuttings. Similarly, it is unwise to save plants for use as stock plants that have not been sold, because these are more likely to have been affected by wilt but to have subsequently become symptomless.

Control. Symptom expression can be masked by drenching plants with benomyl. There is the danger that, if this treatment is done as a routine, some infected plants may be chosen for stock. Drenching should be done only as an emergency treatment until clean stock can be obtained.

Rust (*Puccinia pelargonii-zonalis*)

This disease has spread rapidly throughout Europe since it was first identified in 1962. It affects the zonal cultivars producing typical rust pustules on the undersides of the leaves (Fig. 17.11) and small chlorotic spots on the upper surface. If the attack is severe the affected leaves senesce and die. The uredo-spores are readily disseminated by air currents and by water splash and epidemic development occurs in moist and warm conditions.

Control. Clean stock production is the most effective way to control rust.

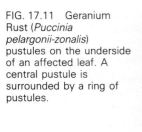

FIG. 17.11 Geranium Rust (*Puccinia pelargonii-zonalis*) pustules on the underside of an affected leaf. A central pustule is surrounded by a ring of pustules.

Once the disease has occurred, the relative humidity must be kept at 80–85% or less and surface wetness avoided in order to minimise spread. Once established, it is difficult to eliminate. Affected leaves should be removed as often as possible. Applications of a dithiocarbamate fungicide, such as zineb or maneb, or possibly one of the rust-specific materials such as benodanil will keep this rust at a very low level if not eliminate it completely.

Leaf Spot (*Alternaria alternata*)

Zonals are most commonly affected by this pathogen. Symptoms start as water-soaked spots on the undersides of the leaves, often with a brown fleck in the centre of the spot. The spots may enlarge and coalesce to form large lesions. Regal cultivars are also affected although mainly on the older leaves. The symptoms are not unlike those of oedema. Spores of the fungus are airborne and spread by water splash.

Control.   High volume sprays of zineb applied regularly will control this disease.

Other diseases of pelargoniums

There are a number of other diseases of pelargonium, mainly of lesser importance. Now that clean stocks are available, virus diseases are no longer a major problem. Pelargonium Leaf Curl Virus was once very common causing distortion of the youngest leaves, especially in the spring and early summer, often accompanied by numerous yellow spots. It is likely that, in the past, many stocks had a complex of virus diseases and the symptoms of distortion, mosaic, ring spots and yellow blotches resulted from mixed infections by several viruses.

The bacterial diseases Crown-Gall (*Agrobacterium tumefaciens*) and Leafy Gall (*Corynebacterium fascians*) sometimes occur. Crown Gall results in the formation of woody galls on the stem, often near to or at soil level. With Leafy Gall, the gall-like distortions with the leaf-like outgrowth are generally at the stem base. Affected plants should be destroyed. Grey Mould (*Botrytis cinerea*) is very common on all types of pelargonium, affecting leaves, stems and causing flower spotting especially on Regals. This disease is generally easily controlled by environmental manipulation and the use of fungicides, but care must be taken to avoid the build-up of fungicide resistant populations of the pathogen (see p. 111).

Oedema is common on pelargoniums, especially ivy-leafed cultivars, in the winter months. Although unsightly, it does not cause undue damage (Fig. 17.12).

Peperomia

A number of different species of *Peperomia* are grown as foliage plants and are subject to various diseases. A Phytophthora rot of the leaves and stems occurs during propagation and subsequently in mature plants. This disease is characterised by a soft, wet, black-coloured rot, which may spread very

FIG. 17.12 Oedema of pelargonium. This symptom is caused by lack of water loss from the leaves, which produce blister-like outgrowths on their undersides. Such damaged leaves may become colonised by weak pathogens.

rapidly especially in warm, wet conditions. A Rhizoctonia rot of cuttings and a leaf spot caused by the same fungus have also been found.

Various leaf spot diseases occur, some of these resulting from the colonisation of senescent or damaged tissue. Myrothecium Leaf Spot (*Myrothecium roridum*) is one such disease. The spores are readily spread by water splash and the disease can usually be satisfactorily controlled by growing the plants in drier conditions. Leaves of *Peperomia magnolifolia* commonly show a clearing symptom of the outer tissues which become translucent. Eventually, affected leaves show faint, black lines and streaks and become dull and dirty in appearance. The problem has been associated with iron deficiency although the exact cause of this disease is not known.

In the USA, there are other diseases of Peperomias including a Cercospora Leaf Spot, causing oedema-like symptoms on the undersides of the leaves or a yellow spotting symptom, a Bacterial Leaf Spot (*Xanthomonas campestris* pv. *dieffenbachiae*) which causes water-soaked spots and blotches of the leaf margins and leaf-blade; a bacterial soft rot of the leaves (*Erwinia chrysanthemi*) and a leaf spot caused by *Dactylaria humicola*, where the leaf spots are tan to yellowish-green and watersoaked. A ring spot virus disease is also known to cause chlorotic or necrotic ring markings on the leaves together with leaf distortion. Young leaves are particularly severely distorted showing a cupping and twisting symptom. Little is known about the control of these diseases.

Pilea

Root rot caused by Pythium results in defoliation of this plant. Oedema symptoms occur on the undersides of the leaves if conditions favour their development.

Poinsettia

This popular pot plant is relatively free from disease problems. Root rots are among the most common diseases although these often follow attack of the roots by pests. Phytophthora, Pythium, *Thielaviopsis basicola* and *Rhizoctonia solani* are known to cause root decay and can be controlled with fungicidal drenches (see pp. 309–311). *Botrytis cinerea* is a common coloniser of senescent and damaged tissue and occasionally a stem rot caused by *Erwinia carotovora* var. *carotovora* generally follows some primary cause of stem damage.

A non-parasitic problem known as crud is common on young plants. A light brown, gritty deposit occurs at the nodes and sometimes on the petioles. This material is thought to be a plant exudate and is largely calcium sulphate. Sometimes the tissue under the crud is damaged and secondary organisms colonise the damaged area. Little is known about the conditions that lead to crud formation.

Primula

Various species are grown as flowering pot plants and some are subsequently planted out into flower borders. Pythium, Phytophthora and *Thielaviopsis basicola* are all known to cause root rots. Brown Core disease of primulas, caused by *Phytophthora primulae*, results in wilting and plant death. The most characteristic symptom of this disease is the brown coloration of the vascular stele of the roots. Brown Core can be controlled by soil sterilisation and by the use of fungicidal drench treatments (see p. 310).

A leaf spot caused by the fungus *Ramularia primulae* is quite common. Spots are up to 5 mm in diameter, light brown in colour and irregular or round in shape, often surrounded by a chlorotic halo (Fig. 17.13). The fungus produces conidia which are spread by water splash. There is little information available on the control of this disease.

Rhoicissus

A black leaf spot, up to 1 cm in diameter and caused by *Pestalotiopsis sydowina*, occurs on this host and can cause considerable damage. The pathogen sporulates freely on the leaf lesions. It is most likely to colonise senescent or damaged tissues. The disease can be minimised by reducing the relative humidity and by using a fungicidal spray of a dithiocarbamate, such as zineb.

Saintpaulia

A progressive rot of the petioles and leaves is caused by *Phytophthora nicotianae* var,. *parasitica*. Decay is firm and brown to black in colour. It spreads along the leaf in a characteristic wave-shaped front and quickly results in leaf decay and plant death. The compost is the most likely source of the pathogen, and the disease can be controlled by using pathogen-free compost or by fungicidal treatment (see p. 310).

Powdery Mildew (*Oidium* sp.) is generally first seen on the pedicels and calyces of the flowers and is rarely very damaging to the leaves. It is essential to control this disease as soon as it is seen in order to minimise fungicidal

FIG. 17.13
Ramularia Leaf Spot
(*Ramularia primulae*) of
primula. Each brown spot
is surrounded by a yellow
halo.

deposits. Leafy Gall (*Corynebacterium fascians*) occurs on saintpaulias although it rarely causes much damage. A black rot of the leaves during propagation caused by *Pseudomonas marginalis* can cause large losses of plants and is generally an indication that the rooting medium needs sterilising or replacing and the propagation area must be thoroughly cleaned.

A yellow ring and line pattern on the leaves, which is very much like a virus symptom in appearance, is known to be caused by low temperatures, especially if cold water lies on the leaf surface.

Sansevieria

Leaf blotches, usually grey in colour, sometimes develop on the middle of mature leaves and extend across the leaf blade causing the distal portion to sag. Blotches do not generally extend after the initial phase. A fungus, *Fusarium moniliforme*, has been associated with this symptom, although it is not clear whether it follows the intial damage or is its cause.

Scindapsus

Bacterial Soft Rot, caused by *Erwinia carotovora* var. *carotovora*, causes a decay of the stems and leaves and is thought to follow primary attack by *Pythium splendens*. Measures to control Pythium will control this disease (see p. 309).

Schizanthus

Root and stem rots caused by Phytophthora, Pythium and *Rhizoctonia solani* have been recorded.

Solanum

A Phytophthora basal stem and root rot is probably the most serious disease of this pot plant. Oedema is common. Flower drop is a major problem and most frequently results from failures in pollination. Poor growth and chlorosis of the leaves frequently follows excessive wetness of the compost.

Sonerila

A basal stem lesion and root rot, caused by *Rhizoctonia solani*, occurs on this plant. The first symptoms include stunted and slow growth, leaf senescence and wilting.

Streptocarpus

Rhizoctonia solani causes a crown rot of this plant.

Synogonium

A rot of this plant, caused by *Sclerotium rolfsii*, has recently been described in the UK. The disease is characterised by brown sclerotia of the pathogen, about the size of radish seeds, and produced on the decaying stem and leaf tissue. It is important to eliminate totally this disease from countries where it does not normally occur, like the UK, because it is potentially very damaging to a large number of plant species.

Tradescantia

Although very commonly grown, species of *Tradescantia* are generally disease free. *Rhizoctonia solani* and *Botrytis cinerea* are known to cause stem and root rots and leaf rot respectively.

Zantedeschia

These plants are sometimes grown in pots for cut flower production but they are also grown in the border soil. A bacterial rot of the rhizomatous roots, caused by *Erwinia carotovora* var. *carotovora*, is one of the most troublesome diseases. Affected plants show a soft, wet rot of the roots together with senescence of the foliage. The disease can only be controlled by selecting young healthy rhizomes and propagating in a pathogen-free medium. Similar symptoms can be caused by *Phytophthora richardiae* but this disease can be controlled by fungicide drenches (see p. 309). Tomato Spotted Wilt Virus is said to be common and causes a mild mosaic symptom on the leaves. Affected plants should be discarded.

Zygocactus

A rot of the stem and collapse of the whole plant is caused by the fungus *Fusarium oxysporum*. It is likely that the pathogen is introduced in the soil and the disease is best controlled by using clean propagation material, a pathogen-free compost and, when disease risk is high, drench with a benzimidazole fungicide. A root and basal stem rot can also be caused by Pythium.

FURTHER READING

Anon. (1969) *Pot Plants*. Bulletin 112. HMSO, London.

Forsberg, J. L. (1975) *Diseases of Ornamental Plants*. University of Illinois Press, Urbana, IL.

Horst, R. K. (1979) *Westcott's Plant Disease Handbook*. 4th edition. Van Nostrand Reinhold Company, New York.

Mastalerz, J. W. (1971) *Geraniums*. Pennsylvania Flower Growers Association.

Pirone, P. P. (1978) *Diseases and Pests of Ornamental Plants*. John Wiley and Sons, New York.

Shurtleff, M. C. (1966) *How to Control Plant Disease in Home and Garden*. Iowa State University Press, Ames Iowa.

INDEX